Private Water Rights

002725

STUDIES IN SCOTS LAW

Series Editor
Kenneth G C Reid

Editorial Board

Alan R Barr
Sandra M Eden
George L Gretton

Volumes in the series

1. Ross Gilbert Anderson, *Assignation* (2008)
2. Andrew J M Steven, *Pledge and Lien* (2008)
3. Craig Anderson, *Possession of Corporeal Moveables* (2015)
4. Jill Robbie, *Private Water Rights* (2015)

STUDIES IN SCOTS LAW
VOLUME 4

Private
Water Rights

Jill Robbie

Lecturer in Private Law,
University of Glasgow

EDINBURGH LEGAL EDUCATION TRUST

2015

Published by
Edinburgh Legal Education Trust
School of Law
University of Edinburgh
Old College
South Bridge
Edinburgh
EH8 9YL

http://www.centreforprivatelaw.ed.ac.uk/monograph_series

First published 2015

ISBN   978-0-9556332-8-7

British Library Cataloguing in Publication Data
A catalogue record for this book is available from the British Library.

Typeset by Etica Press Ltd, Malvern
Printed and bound by Martins the Printers, Berwick-upon-Tweed

Contents

Preface

This book is a revised version of my thesis entitled 'Private Water Rights in Scots Law' submitted for the degree of Doctor of Philosophy in August 2012. I have attempted to state the law as at 1 October 2014 but it has been possible to take account of some later developments, notably the coming into force of the Land Registration etc (Scotland) Act 2012 on 8 December 2014, the publication of the Smith Commission Report in November 2014, the response of the UK Government to that report in January 2015 and the Scotland Bill.

I wish to acknowledge several people who have helped me over the years. I am incredibly grateful for the excellent supervision of my PhD provided by Professor Kenneth Reid as well as his assistance and encouragement in the production of this book. I have benefited greatly from the time and effort he has spent as well as the intellectual rigour he has consistently shown. My second supervisor, Scott Wortley, also made valuable comments at various stages of my progress.

I also wish to thank: Professor George Gretton and Dr Andrew Steven for their help with various issues of property law; Dr Paul du Plessis for assistance with Latin and Roman law sources; Professor Elspeth Reid and Dr Eric Descheemaeker for guiding me through delictual difficulties; as well as Professor Roderick Paisley and the late Professor William Gordon for aiding investigation into historical matters. Professors Gretton and Paisley were also my examiners and allowed my viva to be an extremely enjoyable experience. Their corrections and comments undoubtedly enriched this book. To Professor Niall Whitty I owe a particular debt both for his chapter 'Water Law Regimes' in K G C Reid and R Zimmermann (eds), *A History of Private Law in Scotland* (2000) and for the inspiration which he provided at the early stages of my PhD when he handed me, with extraordinary foresight, a copy of the index of the session papers on water rights cases in the Signet Library and his volume of E Chadwick, *Report on the Sanitary Conditions of the Labouring Population of Great Britain* (1842).

Several academics beyond the foreshore of Scotland are worthy of mention. I made many memorable trips as part of the *Ius Commune* training programme in the first year of my PhD. Through this programme I met, among many others, Dr Bram Akkermans, Dr Koen Swinnen and Dr Eveline Ramaekers who have remained faithful property law companions. Professor Reinhard Zimmermann facilitated a research trip to the Max-Planck-Institut für ausländisches und internationales Privatrecht in Hamburg in the second year of my PhD. Residence at the South African Research Chair in Property Law in Stellenbosch in my third year reminded me of the significance of my subject and stimulated my intellectual imagination at a crucial time. My thanks go to Professor Andre van der Walt for the kind invitation to South Africa and to Dr Ernst Marais for his friendship and infectious enthusiasm. Lastly, Professor John Lovett of Loyola University, New Orleans caught me at an important moment and ensured I stayed on the right academic path.

The Edinburgh Legal Education Trust provided generous funding without which my PhD would have been impossible. Recognition should also go to the Max-Planck-Institut, Clark Foundation for Legal Education, Cross Trust and South African Research Chair in Property Law for monetary assistance regarding my foreign travels.

Libraries are essential to research and the librarians of the Law Library of the University of Edinburgh, Signet Library, National Library of Scotland and Advocates Library have all helped me enormously. In particular, Andrea Longson, Senior Librarian of the Advocates Library, and Felicity Cross, Information Manager of the Signet Library, put up with my relentless requests for session papers. Nick Dyson of the University of Edinburgh also provided much technical advice.

I am indebted to my friends Dr Thomas Horsley, Dr Findlay Stark, Dr Karen Baston, Katarzyna Chalaczkiewicz, Stephen Bogle and Christopher George. Each has been important throughout the research and writing of this book in different ways that have all been meaningful to me.

I hugely appreciate the encouragement that my Mum has provided to me at every stage of my academic development. Finally, I am truly thankful to Marius Røe Nåvik for sacrificing our evenings and weekends for 'Project Book' as well as the infinite kindness and patience he has shown towards me during the past two years.

This book is dedicated to Henry Home, Lord Kames, whose worth as a great scholar of Scots law deserves to be better appreciated.

Jill Robbie
Glasgow
October 2015

Table of Cases

References are to paragraph numbers

Table of Statutes

References are to paragraph numbers

Table of Statutory Instruments

References are to paragraph numbers

Abbreviations

AJIL	American Journal of International Law
Badenhorst et al	P J Badenhorst, J M Pienaar and H Mostert, *Silberberg and Schoeman's The Law of Property* (5th edn, 2006)
Balfour, *Practicks*	Sir James Balfour of Pittendreich, *The Practicks of Sir James Balfour of Pittendreich* (1754; reprinted P G B McNeill (ed), Stair Society, Vols 21–22, 1962–63)
Bankton, *Institute*	Andrew McDouall, Lord Bankton, *An Institute of the Law of Scotland in Civil Rights* (1751–53; reprinted Stair Society, Vols 41–43, 1993–95)
Bell, *Principles*	George Joseph Bell, *Principles of the Law of Scotland* (4th edn, 1839; reprinted Old Studies in Scots Law, Vol 1, 2010)
CLJ	Cambridge Law Journal
Cal L Rev	Californian Law Review
Craig, *Jus Feudale*	Thomas Craig of Riccarton, *Jus Feudale* (1655; J A Clyde, Lord Clyde (trans), 1934)
Cusine & Paisley	D J Cusine and R R M Paisley, *Servitudes and Rights of Way* (1998)
Edin LR	Edinburgh Law Review
EJCL	Electronic Journal of Comparative Law
Erskine, *Institute*	John Erskine of Carnock, *An Institute of the Law of Scotland* (8th edn, J B Nicholson (ed) 1871; reprinted 1989)
Ferguson	J Ferguson, *The Law of Water and Water Rights in Scotland* (1907)
Forbes, *Great Body*	William Forbes, *A Great Body of the Law of Scotland* Vols 1–3 (available at http://www.forbes.gla.ac.uk/contents/)
Ga L Rev	Georgia Law Review
Getzler	J Getzler, *A History of Water Rights at Common Law* (2004)
Gordon, *Land Law*	W M Gordon, *Scottish Land Law* (2nd edn, 1999)
Gordon & Wortley, *Land Law*	W M Gordon and S Wortley, *Scottish Land Law*, Vol 1 (3rd edn, 2009)

Harv L Rev	Harvard Law Review
Hope, *Practicks*	Sir Thomas Hope, *Hope's Major Practicks* (1608–33; reprinted J A Clyde, Lord Clyde (ed), Stair Society, Vols 3–4, 1937–38)
Hume, *Lectures*	Baron David Hume, *Lectures 1786–1822*, Vols I–VI (G C H Paton (ed), Stair Society, Vols 5 (1939), 13 (1949), 15 (1952), 17 (1955), 18 (1957) and 19 (1958))
JLSS	Journal of the Law Society of Scotland
Johnston, *Prescription*	D Johnston, *Prescription and Limitation* (2nd edn, 2012)
Jur Rev	Juridical Review
Justinian, *Institutes*	P Birks and G McLeod (trans), *Justinian's Institutes* (1987)
Kames, *Principles*	Henry Home, Lord Kames, *Principles of Equity* (3rd edn, 1778; reprinted Old Studies in Scots Law, Vol 4, 2013)
La L Rev	Louisiana Law Review
Mackenzie, *Institutions*	Sir George Mackenzie of Rosehaugh, *The Institutions of the Law of Scotland* (2nd edn, 1688)
Murray et al, 'Water'	C D Murray, J Keith and J F Gordon, 'Water and Water Rights' in J L Wark (ed), *Encyclopaedia of the Laws of Scotland* (Vol 15, 1933)
Neb L Rev	Nebraska Law Review
Perruso, 'Res Communes'	R Perruso, 'The Development of the Doctrine of *Res Communes* in Medieval and Early Modern Europe' (2002) 70 Tijdschrift voor Rechtsgeschiedenis 69
Rankine, *Landownership*	J Rankine, *A Treatise on the Rights and Burdens Incident to the Ownership of Lands and Other Heritages in Scotland* (4th edn, 1909)
Reid, *Property*	K G C Reid et al, *The Law of Property in Scotland* (1996)
SALJ	South Africa Law Journal
Shaw, *Water Power*	J P Shaw, *Water Power in Scotland 1550–1870* (1984)
SLPQ	Scottish Law and Practice Quarterly
Stair, *Institutions*	James Dalrymple, Viscount Stair, *The Institutions of the Law of Scotland* (6th edn, D M Walker (ed), 1981)
SME	T B Smith et al (eds), *The Laws of Scotland: Stair Memorial Encyclopaedia* (25 Vols, 1987–96) with cumulative supplements and reissues

TvR	Tijdschrift voor Rechtsgeschiedenis
Van der Merwe, 'Things'	C G van der Merwe, 'Things' in W A Joubert (ed), The Law of South Africa Vol 27 (Reissue 1, 2002)
Van der Vyver, 'Étatisation'	J D van der Vyver, 'The Étatisation of Public Property' in D P Visser (ed), *Essays on the History of Law* (1989)
Whitty, 'Nuisance'	N R Whitty, 'Nuisance' in *The Laws of Scotland: Stair Memorial Encyclopaedia* (Reissue, 2001)
Whitty, 'Water'	N R Whitty, 'Water Law Regimes' in K G C Reid and R Zimmermann (eds), *A History of Private Law in Scotland* Vol 1 (2000)
ZEuP	Zeitschrift für Europäisches Privatrecht

1 Introduction

A. OVERVIEW

1-01.   Water is vital for all forms of life as well as being necessary for social and economic progress. Due to various environmental and societal developments, the law of water and water rights is destined to become an ever more controversial and contested subject. Climate change threatens to result both in the absence of water in certain areas through climbing temperatures and its unwanted presence in others due to rising sea levels as well as other ecological developments which can as yet hardly be foreseen. Furthermore, the desire to tackle the causes of climate change and cease dependency on fossil fuels has resulted in a greater interest in renewable energy and harnessing the power of water. Couple these factors with increasing world population and rapid industrial growth in developing countries and it is not surprising that water is predicted to become the oil of the 21st century.[1]

1-02.   This book is about how property law regulates water in Scotland. Water is an awkward thing for the law to deal with. As a physical substance, it is different from the typical subjects of property law. Its liquid state means that it is perpetually moving and difficult to contain whether collected in the vast mass of an ocean, flowing through the course of a river, or slowly percolating through soil. As a natural phenomenon and one of the elemental forces which comprises the environment, its distribution and movement are continually subject to change and remain inherently unpredictable. The effects of these changes can range on a spectrum from beneficial to devastating.

---

[1] H Ingram, J M Whiteley and R W Perry, 'The Importance of Equity and the Limits of Efficiency in Water Resources' in J M Whiteley, H Ingram and R W Perry (eds), *Water, Place & Equity* (2008) 1.

1-03.   Due to the significance of water, the determination of who has the right to it, and the extent of that right, are of fundamental importance. Yet due to the unusual characteristics of water, these questions are difficult to answer. Further, as with many other areas of property law in Scotland, the law of water rights is under-researched. The only monograph dedicated to the subject – James Ferguson, *The Law of Water and Water Rights in Scotland* (1907) – was published over one hundred years ago. Moreover, being largely a collection of cases and materials, it fails to address water rights from a critical stand-point. The topic has been examined in general works on property law[2] and, in one case, from a historical perspective,[3] but the scope of academic scrutiny in these chapters is limited by the context in which they were written. This book aims to remedy this analytical gap by providing a comprehensive study of a distinct sub-category of water rights in Scots law.

1-04.   This book examines the rights of landowners with respect to the water flowing through their land. The specialised and heavily regulated topic of fishing is not considered. The equally important issue of landowners' rights regarding underground water is not investigated in detail. Public rights over water are not explored in depth but will be referred to at various stages; instead, private water rights are our concern. In a sense, 'private water rights' is a somewhat unsatisfactory phrase for reasons which will become clear but it is one which most immediately conveys the subject of study.

1-05.   This book is in three, unequal, parts. The first part consists solely of Chapter 2, on the Division of Things. This is primarily concerned with the extent to which water is capable of ownership, but answering that question involves a general analysis of the Roman categories of *res communes* and *res publicae* and how these interact with the classification of things as either *res in commercio* or *res extra commercium*. Although these classifications were received into Scots law, they are seldom mentioned in modern scholarship. Yet, as this book shows, they have had a pivotal role in shaping our understanding of both the ownership of land beneath water and the right to water itself. This chapter establishes that water is a communal thing which, due to its inherent characteristics, cannot be subject to private ownership or other real rights in its natural state. Instead, the only right which anyone can have, and which everyone indeed does have, is the right to obtain ownership through appropriation. This is not a private but a public right. Thus, landowners do not have any right to the water flowing through their land which is superior to any member of the public. However, due to their ownership of the beds of water bodies such as rivers and lochs, they do have the best opportunity in practice to use water and acquire its ownership.

1-06.   The second part of the book comprises Chapter 3 on the Ownership of Land Beneath Water and Chapter 4 on Alluvion and Avulsion. Ownership of land is significant for the ability to use water because, if one does not own the land under water, any attempt to access water without a sufficient public

---

[2] For example, Rankine, *Landownership* Ch 29; Reid, *Property* Ch 6; Gordon & Wortley, *Land Law* Ch 6.

[3] Whitty, 'Water'.

or private right will be trespass. Yet for an extended period the ownership of land under water was unclear. Determining the ownership of the sea-bed, foreshore and *alveus* of public rivers and lochs required ascertaining the meaning of the Roman category of *res publicae*, investigated in Chapter 2, and its relationship to the concept of the Crown's regalian rights. The law regarding ownership of the *alveus* of private rivers and lochs was confused for a time due to the developing rights and obligations imposed by the doctrine of common interest – which is the subject of the third part of this book. Chapter 3 aims to clarify who owns the land under water and present a full account of the modern law as a logical precursor to discussions about what landowners can do with the water running through their lands.

1-07.   Due to the nature of water, those areas of land which are dry and those which are under water are constantly changing. While it is desirable for the law to reflect these changes to some extent, the law must also ensure the stability and security of landownership. Chapter 4 investigates the effect that water can have on the boundaries of land by studying the doctrines of alluvion and avulsion.

1-08.   The final and most substantial part of the book comprises Chapters 5, 6 and 7 on the doctrine of common interest. Common interest defines the limits within which landowners can exercise their ownership rights of land in relation to water and their public right to appropriate water. The doctrine comprises a set of (generally) reciprocal rights and obligations attached to the ownership of the *alveus* and banks of rivers and lochs. The primary right provided by common interest is the right to the natural flow of water, and each proprietor along the course of a body of water is under a corresponding obligation not to interfere materially with natural flow, except to appropriate water for domestic purposes. The rights provided by common interest are those which can most accurately be referred to as private water rights. Yet, the rights burden the land rather than the water; they are rights *regarding* water rather than *to* water.

1-09.   The evolution of the doctrine of common interest became a necessity due to the burgeoning use of water power particularly in the period 1730 to 1830. In view of the limited material available from Roman law and the institutional writers, advocates and judges had to experiment with different types of argument to resolve the water rights disputes with which they were confronted. In considering the development of the law it has proved fruitful to consult the session papers of cases within this period to unpack the various theories which were before the courts. One figure stands out in particular: Henry Home, or Lord Kames as he was to become known on the bench. Through his work as an advocate, judge and scholar, Lord Kames established the doctrinal foundation for common interest using as inspiration the Roman categories of the Division of Things. This early history is the subject of Chapter 5, Common Interest: The Search for a Doctrine. This foundation enabled the future rapid development of the doctrine. Flesh was put on the bones of common interest between the late-18th and mid-19th centuries when the content of the rights and obligations of landowners with respect to water on their land was expounded and the right to natural flow, in particular, was introduced. Chapter 6, Common Interest: The Establishment of a Special Regime, analyses the doctrine in this time period. Finally, Chapter 7, Common Interest: Modern Law, provides a comprehensive restatement of the current law of common interest in light of the preceding explanation of its historical background.

1-10. There is a general principle which is, and should be, ever-present in the law of water and water rights and which underlies this entire book. This is that water is a communal thing which is, and should be, incapable of ownership in its natural state. Due to water being generally outwith ownership, everyone in principle has the right to use it. As Kevin Gray states: 'In the end the "property" notion, in all its conceptual fragility, is but a shadow of the individual and collective human response to a world of limited resources and attenuated altruism.'[4] The collective response to the limited resource of water should be that is it available for the use of all.

B. METHODOLOGY

(1) Doctrine

1-11. This book adopts a historical approach. Reid and Zimmermann have given a number of justifications for the use of such a method with respect to legal doctrine.[5] Firstly, 'a study of history gives context and texture to contemporary law.'[6] Knowledge of the origin and progression of rules aids understanding of the modern law. Secondly, 'an uncodified system makes no break with history, so that ancient history remains part of the living law'.[7] Not only does history help to understand the law, it often *is* the law. However, as the authors acknowledge, using historical sources can be problematic due to lack of knowledge of the context in which they were written. To tackle this problem, this book has attempted to be sensitive to the legal, social and economic background behind the materials which have been accessed. This was particularly important in Chapters 5 and 6 on common interest as well as with regard to the Crown's ownership of land beneath water examined in Chapter 3. A further challenge is presented by awareness of the modern law which inevitably tends to colour interpretation of older sources. To limit as far as possible the effect of hindsight, the research for each chapter began with the earliest relevant material – which in each case was Roman law – and worked forward in time. Primary sources were read before secondary sources to ensure that the analyses of academic writers did not interfere with the tracing of historical development. Yet, despite these precautions, it is accepted that complete objectivity will never be achieved as each 'historian is trapped, not only by his knowledge of the present, but also by his hopes for the future'.[8]

[4] K Gray, 'Property Law in Thin Air' (1991) 50 *CLJ* 252 at 307.
[5] K G C Reid and R Zimmermann, 'Legal Doctrine in a Mixed Legal System' in K G C Reid and R Zimmermann (eds), *A History of Private Law in Scotland* (2000) 10–12.
[6] Reid and Zimmermann (n 5) 11.
[7] Reid and Zimmermann (n 5) 11.
[8] Reid and Zimmermann (n 5) 10.

1-12.   This book has had recourse to three, generally underused, historical sources. The first, already mentioned, is the session papers.[9] Boswell commented: 'Ours is a court of *papers*. We are never seriously engaged but when we write.'[10] Unlike today, pleadings in the 18th century were mainly written. 'Contested cases might generate an apparently bewildering variety of pleading papers: summonses, bills, libels, petitions and additional petitions, petitions and complaints, condescendences and memorials, answers and additional answers, replies, duplies, triplies, even quaduplies, observes, informations, minutes, lists of authorities, etc.'[11] These comprise the session papers. In contrast, decisions of the court were made through majority vote and any opinions by individual judges were given orally. It was seen as contempt of court to record the opinions *verbatim*.[12] By the beginning of the 19th century, it was thought that written pleadings were 'voluminous, bloated and unfocused'[13] as they would 'try to contain something for all: rhetorical devices would be employed; appeals *ad populum* and *ad hominem* would be included; and most commonly apologies would preface the pleadings – apologising for having so to detain their Lordships but with the explanation that it was due to the unreasonableness or recalcitrance of an adversary.'[14] Forbes commented that reading the papers 'visibly shortens their [the judges] days'.[15] The session papers certainly contrast with modern legal arguments but their volume means that they are a mine of information about early cases. Where a decision reported in *Morison's Dictionary* may consist of a few lines, the session papers often run to many pages, outlining previous procedure, detailing essential facts, containing plans of the disputed property, and most importantly showing the arguments – with authorities and sources – of the advocates. Although session papers are not available for cases before 1666, and even then are handwritten and thus difficult to decipher until around 1705, printed papers exist from many cases of the 18th and early 19th centuries. The session papers turned out to be invaluable with regard to common interest and have enabled a new history of the doctrine to be presented.[16] My days may have been shortened but this book has been correspondingly enriched.

1-13.   The second source is the original manuscript from which the Stair Society published Hume's *Lectures 1786–1822*, as well as students' notes of these lectures delivered at the University of Edinburgh between 1789 and

---

[9] In this book I will cite session papers from the Advocates Library by name of the collection with volume and paper number and from the Signet Library with the initials 'WS' and the index number. I will also give the date and the name of the advocate who wrote the pleading.

[10] Quoted in H M Milne (ed), *Boswell's Edinburgh Journals* (2001) 238 (2 Feb 1776).

[11] A Stewart, 'The Session Papers in the Advocates Library' in *Miscellany IV* (H MacQueen (ed), Stair Society, Vol 49, 2002) 201.

[12] Stewart, *Miscellany IV* (n 11) 200.

[13] D Parratt, *The Development and Use of Written Pleadings in Scots Civil Procedure* (Stair Society, Vol 48, 2006) 24.

[14] Parratt, *Written Pleadings* (n 13) 28.

[15] W Forbes, *Journal of the Session* (1714) x.

[16] See below, Chs 5 and 6.

1820. Use of these notes has shown how the content of Hume's lectures on common interest changed during this crucial period. Although Hume updated his lecture notes to take account of case law, he failed to change his initial conception of the doctrine. This did violence to the coherence of his explanation of the law and indicates that caution is to be exercised when making reference to common interest as described in the printed version of the *Lectures*. Further research on these notes could reveal much about the mind of this scholar and his role within Scots law.

1-14.   The third source is William Forbes' *A Great Body of the Law of Scotland*. Forbes held the Regius Chair in Civil Law at the University of Glasgow between 1714 and 1739. This work was written during that period but was never published. On 29 March 2011, the manuscript of the *Great Body*, held by the University of Glasgow, was made accessible online.[17] Use has been made of this treatise in every section of this book. Where Stair and Bankton's discussion of the law is often brief and cryptic, Forbes is positively prolix. Such research as was undertaken for this book, however, does not suggest that Forbes was an outstanding scholar. For example, his account of private water rights seems to consist largely of a replication of William Strahan's translation[18] of Jean Domat's *Les Lois Civiles Dans Leur Ordre Naturel* (1689).[19] Nevertheless, the *Great Body* is of considerable interest and it is certain that this enormous work still holds many secrets waiting to be uncovered.

1-15.   Of course, even after this exhumation of rarely consulted authority, a significant number of matters remain uncertain. There are conflicting statements in works of the institutional writers and in case law to be reconciled, gaps in lines of authority to be explained, and questions of doctrine to be answered if a full account of the modern law is to be given. In making arguments with respect to undecided matters, my primary aim was to ensure coherence in the law.[20] Through studying private water rights, the general principles of this area of law can be deduced and made to fit in with the principles of property law as a whole. Within this framework, particular rules can be located and answers to unclear points of law can be sought. It is hoped that, through this method, the values of certainty and predictability in the law are upheld.

(2) Comparison

1-16.   This book is about Scots law, but reference is made to the Common Law jurisdiction of England and the Civilian jurisdictions of Germany, France and the Netherlands as well as the fellow Mixed Legal Systems of Louisiana, Sri Lanka, South Africa and Quebec. Lawyers in Mixed Systems are often

---

[17] Available at: http://www.forbes.gla.ac.uk/contents/.

[18] J Domat, *The Civil Law in its Natural Order* (W Strahan (trans), 1722).

[19] See below, para 5-34.

[20] On the role of coherence and principles in legal reasoning see N MacCormick, *Rhetoric and the Rule of Law* (2005) Ch 10.

required to look to the laws of other countries due to the heritage of their legal system and the generally small scale of their jurisdiction. Scotland is no exception. In particular, comparative law is used in this book both to explain Scots law and as a bank of ideas. As such, the utility of comparative law has been dependent on the specific area of study. Where Scotland may have been subjected to outside influence, such as by English law on the doctrine of common interest, this has been explored and tested.[21] Where Scotland may have been one of many jurisdictions influenced by Roman law, this has been investigated.[22] Inspiration has been drawn from the approach of other jurisdictions to the difficult doctrines of alluvion and avulsion.[23] It is hoped that this sideways glance at the laws of other nations has enhanced this book. Much more comparative law could have been undertaken and can be in the future. Yet there are limitations of time and space, and in this book the study of Scots law has always been made the priority.

C. PUBLIC AND PRIVATE, RIGHTS AND RIVERS

1-17.   The use of the words 'public' and 'private' in the context of water rights is a matter of some difficulty. It is argued in this book that the primary and predominant private water rights in relation to running water, supplemented by servitudes and leases, are those provided by common interest and all of these are rights only in relation to water rather than directly to the water itself. The only right that anyone has to water is a public right – the right of appropriation.

1-18.   A further problem is caused when the terms 'public' and 'private' are used, especially regarding rivers. Reid avoids the classification altogether,[24] citing Lord President McNeill's statement in *Montgomerie v Buchanan's Trs*[25] that 'a public river is capable of various meanings, and the dexterous use of the term "public" is apt to mislead'. In this book, it has been deemed impossible to omit use of the terms due to their historical importance but a prefatory explanation is required. In Roman law, a distinction was made between rivers which were *res publicae* – defined as perennial rivers – and those which were *res privatae* – the torrential or occasional rivers.[26] It is argued in Chapter 2 that this classification as 'public' is primarily concerned with public rights of use rather than ownership. This focus on public rights may have also once been the position of Scots law as Craig and Stair's analyses indicate. Due to climatic differences from Italy, public rivers in Scotland were those which were navigable (rather than perennial) and private rivers those which were non-navigable.[27] However, the category of

---

[21] See below, paras 5-72–5-77 and 7-14–7-17.
[22] See below, Ch 2.
[23] See below, Ch 4.
[24] Reid, *Property* para 277.
[25] (1853) 15 D 853 at 858.
[26] See below, Ch 2.
[27] See below, para 2-24.

public things became intermingled with the concept of the *regalia* and there began to be more emphasis on Crown ownership or control of navigable rivers. This can be noted in Bankton and Erskine. By the time of Hume and Bell, the concept of public things is almost completely submerged within that of the *regalia*. The Crown then sought to assert its regalian rights and it became established through case law that the Crown owned the *alveus* of public (navigable) rivers. Public rights over such rivers were held by the Crown in trust.[28] The classification 'public' therefore became associated with those rivers where the *alveus* was owned by the Crown.

1-19.   These difficulties of the shift from 'public' meaning subject to public rights to meaning Crown ownership of the *alveus* were further compounded by the case of *Colquhoun's Trs v Orr Ewing*[29] in 1877 where it was decided that Crown ownership was restricted to the *alveus* of tidal (and not as previously, navigable) rivers. With the limitation of Crown ownership came the corresponding restriction of common law public rights. There can still be public rights with respect to non-tidal, navigable rivers, but they are not tacit and have to be acquired.[30] Thus, when discussing the modern law in this book, 'public rivers' are those which are tidal, the *alveus* of which is owned by the Crown as *inter regalia*, and over which the public have common law tacit rights. 'Private rivers' are those which are non-tidal, the *alveus* of which is generally owned by the adjacent landowners. The terms 'public' and 'private' are also used in this way when considering lochs in the modern law although the history of the classifications with regard to lochs is slightly different.[31]

---

[28] See below, paras 3-45–3-49.
[29] (1877) 4 R 344 (reversed on a different point in (1877) 4 R (HL) 116).
[30] See Reid, *Property* para 516.
[31] See below, paras 3-72–3-86.

2 The Division of Things

A. INTRODUCTION

2-01. The title of this chapter may have little meaning to the modern Scottish lawyer. To a jurist who studies Roman law or who has been educated in another Mixed Legal System, however, it may sound more familiar. The Division of Things is concerned with the classification of certain objects with regard to their inherent nature and characteristics, the law by which such objects are governed[1] or the uses to which they can be put. Things can be classified as moveable or immoveable, corporeal or incorporeal. These specific categories are well known to the Scots lawyer, as they are to lawyers in other jurisdictions. However, this chapter is principally concerned with the part of the Division devoted to the categories of communal things and public things and how this interacts with the classification of things as within or outwith commerce. The latter classification is primarily concerned with whether a thing is exempt from private ownership. Water is central to these classifications. These aspects of the Division of Things can be traced back to Roman law, are discussed by many Scottish institutional writers and have been significant in the development of the law of water rights. Yet, towards the end of the institutional period, discussion of the categories begins to wither away. In modern textbooks on Scots property law, if the categories of the Division are mentioned at all, they are often also misinterpreted or questioned.[2]

2-02. Whether a thing is subject to private ownership is a fundamental issue of property law. Gray states that:

> 'the refusal to propertise a given resource is absolutely critical – because logically anterior – to the formulation of the current regime of property law. The decision to leave a resource outside the regime is, pretty clearly, a fundamental precursor to all property discourse. Yet the factors weighing on this decision – even the fact that there is a decision to be made – remain largely unrecognised and unanalysed in legal discussions of property.'[3]

This lack of discussion makes this topic a challenging one to analyse. This chapter aims to promote debate on the issue by tracing the historical development of the Division of Things in Scots law, considering why the categories have been abandoned, and evaluating their meaning and worth in the modern law.

B. ROMAN LAW

2-03. The idea of classifying things according to their characteristics or use was an important achievement of Roman law. However, the Roman

---

[1] For example, things may be governed by human law or divine law. See further below.

[2] See, for example, Gordon's doubts in Gordon & Wortley, *Land Law* para 6-17; Ferguson's conflation of communal things and common interest in Ferguson 169, and discussion below, paras 2-70–2-72.

[3] K Gray, 'Property Law in Thin Air' (1991) 50 *CLJ* 252 at 256.

classification is capable of many interpretations and the 'true' Division of Things in Roman law is a matter of dispute.[4] This section will give an overview of the relevant categories of Roman law which will serve as a background to the discussion of the Division of Things in Scotland.

2-04. Justinian's *Institutes* begins the discussion of property with the statement that some things are *res in nostro patrimonio*, meaning capable of being subject to property, and other things are *res extra nostrum patrimonium*, meaning incapable of being subject to property.[5] There is a similar categorisation of things which are *res extra commercium*, meaning exempted from commerce, and *res in commercio*, meaning included in commerce.[6] Some scholars think that there was no difference between these divisions.[7] Yiannopoulos, however, argues that the *res extra nostrum patrimonium* were those things which were incapable of ownership as a practical matter while there was the possibility that the *res extra commercium* were capable of being owned but they were exempted from private law relations on the basis of public utility or some other community concern.[8] A different division is between things which are *res divini juris*, meaning governed by divine law, and *res humani juris*, meaning governed by human law. Finally, but crucially, Roman law distinguishes between things which are *res communes* meaning communal, *res publicae* meaning public, *res universitatis* meaning things belonging to corporations, and *res nullius* meaning ownerless. However, most things belong to individuals.[9]

2-05. How these categorisations interact is unclear and it may be that it was not intended for the various divisions to fit together. Van der Vyver argues that *res communes* and *res publicae* were not owned by anyone[10] while some scholars claim that *res publicae* were owned by the state.[11] Another view is that both *res communes* and *res publicae* were *extra commercium* and exempted from private ownership but both may have been owned by the state.[12] However, it is possible that some *res publicae* were privately owned.[13] If the categorisation of *res publicae* in Roman law was based on public rights of use, as explored below, the state of ownership is relatively unimportant because the public rights will exist regardless of ownership.

2-06. In the *Digest* it is stated that the air, the sea, and running water are *res communes*.[14] It is not clear whether reference to the sea means the sea-bed,

---

[4] See Perruso, 'Res Communes'; Van der Vyver, 'Étatisation'.

[5] Justinian, *Institutes* 2.1.pr. Some of these categories were already to be found in Gaius' *Institutes*. See W M Gordon and O F Robinson (trans), *The Institutes of Gaius* (1988) 2.1–11.

[6] D.20.3.1.2 (Marcian).

[7] For example, A M Prichard, *Leage's Roman Private Law* (3rd edn, 1964) 154.

[8] A N Yiannopoulos, 'Introduction to the Law of Things: Louisiana and Comparative Law' (1961–1962) 22 *La L Rev* 757 at 765.

[9] Justinian, *Institutes* 2.1.pr.

[10] Van der Vyver, 'Étatisation' 264–265.

[11] P Birks and G MacLeod (trans), *Justinian's Institutes* (2001) 2.1.2 translates *res publicae* as state property, as does J A C Thomas, *The Institutes of Justinian* (1975).

[12] See, for example, Yiannopoulos, 'Introduction to the Law of Things: Louisiana and Comparative Law' (n 8) at 766.

[13] See further below with regard to river-beds.

[14] D.1.8.2.1 (Marcian).

the waters of the sea or both. Perennial rivers,[15] harbours or ports,[16] lakes[17] and highways[18] are *res publicae*. A perennial river was one with a continuous flow even though it sometimes dried up in the summer.[19] The public were also entitled to use the river banks but ownership was vested in the adjacent landowners.[20] The position of the shore, defined as extending as far as the highest winter tides,[21] is unclear as it is described as both *res publicae* and, in a different passage, as *res communes*.[22]

2-07. It may be asked how running water and perennial rivers or lakes could be subject to different classifications because both inevitably consist of running water.[23] Some possible explanations are outlined by Buckland.[24] One is that the bed of the body of water was public. However, the rules regarding the ownership of islands suggest that river-beds were owned by the adjacent landowners.[25] Another is that the body of water, as a separate object from the water, was the object which was public. A third is that classification only concerned public rights of use.

2-08. The possibility of analysing a river or loch as a separate object is a recurring idea throughout this book. A distinction is made between the body of water as a permanent entity and the constantly moving individual particles of water which comprise it. The result is the body of water is treated in a similar way to a separate tenement.

2-09. In addition to questions concerning the subjects of classification, there is uncertainty about who is entitled to use *res publicae* and *res communes*. If *res publicae* is translated as state property, then it can be inferred that only Roman citizens could use these things.[26] Another view is that there is no difference between the people entitled to use *res communes* and *res publicae*.[27]

2-10. The difference in substance between the two categories of *res communes* and *res publicae* is also a contested issue. One possible distinguishing feature is that *res communes* are governed by the law of nature, this being the body of

---

[15] D.1.8.5.pr. (Gaius).

[16] D.1.8.4 (Marcian). *Portus* is translated as harbours by Birks (n 11) in Justinian's *Institutes* 2.1.1 and as ports by Thomas (n 11)

[17] D.43.14.1.pr-3 (Ulpian).

[18] D.43.8.2.22 (Ulpian).

[19] D.43.12.1.2–3 (Ulpian). A private river was therefore one which was torrential (D.43.12.1.2–3 (Ulpian)) but the *res privatae* are not enumerated.

[20] D.1.8.5.pr. (Gaius); D.43.12.3.pr. (Paul).

[21] Justinian's *Institutes* 2.1.3; D.50.16.112 (Javolenus).

[22] *Res communes* – D.1.8.2.1 (Marcian); *res publicae* – D.39.2.24.pr. (Ulpian).

[23] It is perhaps not conventional to think of lochs as containing 'running' water but by definition lochs require a perennial outflow and therefore the water will always be moving, see below, para 7-27.

[24] W W Buckland, *Textbook of Roman Law from Augustus to Justinian* (3rd edn, P Stein (ed), 1963) 185. See also Whitty, 'Water' 439.

[25] See below, para 4-07.

[26] J A C Thomas, *The Institutes of Justinian* (1975) 75.

[27] Perruso, 'Res Communes' 73; P T Fenn, 'Justinian and the Freedom of the Sea' (1925) 19 *AJIL* 716 at 725.

principles determined by reason.[28] It is impossible to possess *res communes* in their entirety due to their natural state. The air, the waters of the sea (if that is indeed the subject of the classification) and running water are constantly moving and have no definite bounds. Of course, a portion of water can be captured and taken into possession, but it then ceases to be running or in its natural state. As a result, the law of nature classifies the sea, air and running water as *res communes* and outwith ownership. This is the logical result of the inherent characteristics of these things. In addition, to the extent that no one can own these things so no one can be prevented from using them. The use of *res communes* is therefore open to all.

2-11. In contrast, *res publicae* are governed by the law of nations, this being the body of rules which applies to both Roman and non-Roman citizens and which is thought to be common practice among civilised nations.[29] The focus of this categorisation seems to be public use (as opposed to ownership), not impossibility of appropriation. Rights over *res publicae* relate to navigation and fishing, reflecting their importance for trade, travel and defence.

2-12. However, the jurisdictions of the law of nature and nations are not mutually exclusive and thus may overlap which may be the cause of confusion such as concerning the categorisation of the shore which is described as both *res communes* and *res publica*.[30]

2-13. Despite the lack of clarity as to the details of the scheme of Division of Things, there are two important principles of Roman law which can be deduced from the various classifications. Firstly, there is recognition of the limitations of ownership over certain essential natural resources which cannot be physically appropriated. These things are available for the use of all. Secondly, there is an emphasis on public rights of use over certain vital objects of trade, travel and defence.

C. CRAIG AND STAIR'S DIVISION OF THINGS

2-14. Between the reign of Justinian in the 6th century and the writing of the first Scottish institutional work at the turn of the 17th century,[31] the categories of *res communes* and *res publicae* were subject to substantial interpretation and alteration in the western legal tradition. An attempt at forging a meaning for *res communes* (as distinct from *res publicae*) had been made by the glossators and commentators. As Perruso shows, many interesting arguments were developed during this period but no consensus was reached on the precise content of the categories.[32] In addition, as Van der Vyver has

---

[28] B Nicholas, *An Introduction to Roman Law* (1965) 55.

[29] Nicholas, *Roman Law* (n 28) 57.

[30] As the shore is capable of appropriation it is perhaps better regarded as *res publicae* but it may have been regarded as an accessory to the sea and therefore also *res communes*.

[31] This being Craig, *Jus Feudale* written c1600.

[32] See Perruso, 'Res Communes' for a full account of the jurisprudence of the glossators and commentators.

demonstrated, the category of *res publicae* became intermingled with the development of the idea of the *regalia*. The *regalia* were competences and property rights accorded to the King/Emperor. A consolidated list was declared by Frederick Barbarossa, ruler of the Holy Roman Empire, in 1158,[33] although the concept was far older.[34] This list came to be attached to the *Libri Feudorum* and so connected to the feudalism which was accepted in many parts of Europe.[35] Some things which were *res publicae* in Roman law were included in the list of *regalia* and either definitively declared as state property and owned by the Crown or subject to the Crown's jurisdiction and control.[36]

2-15. It is against this background that the Division of Things found its way into Scottish jurisprudence. The institutional writers consider the categories in detail. Of all the writers, it is Craig and Stair who provide the most interesting accounts of how the Division of Things of Roman law applies to Scots law.

(1) Craig

(a) Craig's Division of Things

2-16. Craig's *Jus Feudale* was written at the turn of the 17th century but not published until 1655.[37] The glossators and commentators of previous centuries had discussed the categories of *res communes* and *res publicae* in abstract terms in an attempt to discover the true meaning of the Roman texts and create a coherent system from the fragments of the *Digest* and the *Institutes*. In contrast, Craig discusses the categories for practical purposes.[38]

2-17. The Division of Things can be found in a chapter on 'What Kinds of Property May be Subject to Infeudation'[39] but, as will be shown below, this chapter's coverage is broader than its title suggests. Craig restates the various Roman divisions and rationalises them by starting with the division between things governed by divine law and human law. Things governed by divine law are, Craig says, largely incapable of infeudation.[40] Thus, the category of *res extra commercium*, or things outwith commerce, is mostly associated with divine things. Things which are governed by human law are said to include public things, things belonging to corporations, ownerless things, and things owned by private individuals.[41] *Res communes* drop out of

---

[33] Van der Vyver, 'Étatisation' at 266–267; H J Berman, *Law and Revolution* (1983) 488–491; R Hübner, *History of Germanic Private Law* (F S Philbrick (trans), 1968) 286.

[34] Hübner, *History of Germanic Private Law* (n 33) 279–280.

[35] Van der Vyver, 'Étatisation' 267.

[36] Van der Vyver, 'Étatisation' 267–268.

[37] Craig, *Jus Feudale* (1655; J A Clyde, Lord Clyde (trans), 1934) xvi and xix.

[38] Lord Clyde's translation of Craig can be misleading in this area. I will indicate where I am working from the Latin text and where my interpretation deviates from Lord Clyde's translation. My thanks go to Dr Paul du Plessis for assistance with the Latin text.

[39] Craig, *Jus Feudale* (n 37) Title 15.

[40] Craig, *Jus Feudale* (n 37) 1.15.2–12.

[41] Here I am working from the Latin text: Craig, *Jus Feudale* (1655) 1.15.1 and again at 1.15.13. The Latin text at 1.15.13 reads '*Juris autem humani Res rursus subdividuntur, ut quaedam*

Craig's classification even though the category is mentioned when he summarises Roman law at the beginning of the chapter.[42] As a result, some of the things which were communal in Roman law are either not considered at all or are transformed by Craig into public things. Thus, running water is not mentioned by Craig, while the air, the sea and the shore, which were categorised as *res communes* in Roman law, are described as public things. The transformation of communal things into public things foreshadows later developments in the law of Scotland and other countries. A consequence of not considering the category of communal things is that Craig does not explore possible limits of ownership over natural resources.

(b) Public Things

2-18.   Public things, Craig says, are common either to all men or to all nations, a definition similar to the Roman concept of *res communes*.[43] Craig's discussion focuses on public rights of use rather than on whether or not the things are capable of ownership or infeudation. Thus, the importance of public rights over certain objects for navigation and fishing, which is emphasised in Roman law, is maintained by Craig in Scots law.

2-19.   Craig's list of public things includes the air, the sea, ports and harbours, the shore, navigable rivers and highways. He deals with each in turn. Although Craig defines the air as public, and not as communal as in Roman law, there is a shadow of the category of communal things as air is also the only public thing which Craig identifies as incapable of being owned.[44] It is said to be impossible to stop anyone from using the air.

2-20.   Craig does not say that the sea is incapable of being owned. Everyone is entitled to navigate upon the sea but 'the princes of the world make a kind of division of the whole ocean among them, each reckoning that part of it his own which most conveniently adjoins his own territory'.[45] It is not clear whether Craig is discussing ownership of the waters of the sea, the sea-bed or both.[46] This statement is a reflection of the events of the time, with, for example, the Venetians and Genoese claiming large areas of the sea as their

---

sint publicae Res, quaedam universales, quaedam nullius, quaedam privatae, sive singulorum.' Lord Clyde's translation differs between 1.15.1 and 1.15.13 although the Latin text is almost identical. His translation for 1.15.13 is 'Things governed by the laws of man subdivide into those which belong to all men, those which belong to communities or corporations, those which belong to no man, and those which belong to private individuals.'

[42] This omission is not reflected in the English translation of 1.15.13 where *res publicae* is translated as 'things which belong to all men'.

[43] Justinian's *Institutes* 2.1.

[44] Craig, *Jus Feudale* (n 37) 1.15.13.

[45] Craig, *Jus Feudale* (n 37) 1.15.13. This quote is Lord Clyde's translation.

[46] It is also not clear, as is often the case, whether Craig is discussing *imperium* (jurisdiction) or *dominium* (ownership). Craig's analysis of coal-mining and islands suggests that he considered the sea-bed to be in Crown ownership. Although islands more than 100 miles from any mainland are said to be open to occupation which suggests the sea-bed underneath is ownerless. See below, paras 3-08 and 4-09.

own.[47] Although it seems that Craig accepts the sea is vested in the Crown, he does not mention the sea when discussing the *regalia*.

2-21. Craig adds that a state can also acquire a prescriptive right of ownership to a portion of the sea against another state. This reflects jurisprudence developed by the commentators, such as Caepolla and Baldus.[48] Fishing in the sea, according to Craig, belongs to the adjacent country and can also be acquired by prescription. This is consistent with attempts at excluding foreign nationals from fishing for herring in Scottish waters.[49]

2-22. Concerning ports and harbours,[50] Craig makes clear that the public has rights of use even though the ports or harbours may have passed into the ownership of the burgh. Thus, it is said that any member of the public may load and unload a ship upon payment of port-dues.[51]

2-23. The shore is briefly mentioned by Craig as a public thing but the rights of use which the public may have over the shore are not enumerated. Similarly, highways are described as public things without explanation of the rights over them.

2-24. Finally, Craig states that everyone can use navigable rivers for navigation and fishing[52] (except salmon fishing[53]). It will be remembered that in Roman law perennial rivers were *res publicae*. However, only navigable rivers were mentioned as *inter regalia* in the list of 1158.[54] Further, the Roman definition of a public river was based on the climate of the Mediterranean. To apply the Roman test to the water-rich countries of Northern Europe, would have meant defining practically all rivers as public. Therefore, navigability was adopted as a requirement. In arid countries, such as South Africa and Sri Lanka, the perennial test has remained for public rivers.[55]

(c) Public Things and the Regalia

2-25. In *Jus Feudale*, the interaction between public things and the *regalia* is complex. Later Erskine was to claim that the *res publicae* of Roman law became the *regalia* of the modern law.[56] This, however, is an over-simplification, for

---

[47] Craig, *Jus Feudale* (n 37) 1.15.13; Perruso, 'Res Communes' 81–82; F S Lane, *Venice: a Maritime Republic* (1973) 61–65.

[48] See the summaries of the arguments of these jurists by Perruso, 'Res Communes' 82.

[49] Whitty, 'Water' 430.

[50] J A Clyde, Lord Clyde translates *portus* as both sea-ports and harbours at different points (compare 1.15.15 and 1.16.12) which suggests that each is subject to a different classification. No difference of classification is indicated by the Latin text.

[51] Craig, *Jus Feudale* (n 37) 1.15.15.

[52] Craig, *Jus Feudale* (n 37) 1.16.11.

[53] See below.

[54] Craig, *Jus Feudale* (n 37) 1.16.8.

[55] Badenhorst et al para 3.3.1.1; G L Peiris, *The Law of Property in Sri Lanka* (2nd edn, 1983) 9–10.

[56] Erskine, *Institute* II.1.6.

the two concepts co-existed in Scots law for a period and had different objectives. The main principle behind *res publicae*, as shown by Craig, is public use regardless of ownership, while the core idea of the *regalia* is Crown ownership or control. Thus, the Crown either owns the *regalia* or has certain rights over them such as the right to impose taxes and customs or to require that licences are acquired for works. Discerning whether ownership or control is being referred to is often difficult especially as regards navigable rivers.

2-26.   Craig's theory of the *regalia* is that some things or rights are part of the annexed patrimony of the Crown and therefore inalienable[57] – the *regalia majora*. The *regalia majora* are closely connected to government and, where appropriate, the Crown holds them in the public interest,[58] resulting in public rights of use. However, in contrast to Craig's concept of public things, these rights of use may be limited to nationals, with foreign nationals having to make payment or ask the permission of the Crown. In Craig's view this at least was the case for navigable rivers.[59] Things being categorised as *regalia* can also result in exclusive use; as indicated by Craig there are some rights which are *inter regalia* but which are not held by the Crown for the public and can be disponed to private persons – the *regalia minora*.[60] Although fishing in navigable rivers is usually open to all nationals, salmon fishing is listed as *inter regalia minora*.

2-27.   The categories of public things and *regalia* may overlap and, when this happens, the concept of *regalia* takes precedence. Navigable rivers and highways are described as both public and *inter regalia* by Craig and so use is restricted to nationals. Thus, there are things which are public and owned by the Crown or subject to Crown control but there can also be things which are subject to public rights and not *inter regalia*. This is demonstrated by the shore which Craig describes as public but not *inter regalia* as it was not in the list of *regalia* declared in 1158. Therefore, the Roman category of *res publicae* and its associated emphasis on public use was still of importance in Scotland after the introduction of the *regalia* for the purpose of establishing public rights over objects not included in the original list of *regalia*.

(d) Omissions from The Division

2-28.   In contrast to Roman law, lakes or lochs are not mentioned by Craig as subject to public rights of use. As with the change in the definition of public rivers, the omission of lochs from the category of public things is perhaps an acknowledgment of the generosity of the Roman classification which was necessary in the more arid Mediterranean but not required in the Scottish climate. In Sri Lanka but not in South Africa, lakes are still defined as public things.[61]

[57] Craig, *Jus Feudale* (n 37) 1.16.5 and 1.16.7.
[58] Craig says that the Crown holds navigable rivers as a 'guardian of public rights': *Jus Feudale* (n 37) 1.16.11
[59] Craig, *Jus Feudale* (n 37) 1.16.11.
[60] Craig, *Jus Feudale* (n 37) 1.16.43
[61] Peiris, *The Law of Property in Sri Lanka* (n 55) 9.

(2) Stair

(a) Stair's Adaptation of the Division of Things

2-29.   The first edition of Stair's *Institutions* was published in 1681,[62] and a second, much revised, edition in 1693. In contrast to Craig's treatise on feudal law, Stair's *Institutions* was the first general and systematic account of the law of Scotland. In addition, Stair's work is rooted in the natural law tradition and in particular shows the influence of another prominent natural lawyer, Grotius. Stair's discussion of the categories of the Division of Things in the *Institutions* is, however, innovative and distinct from both Craig and Grotius.

2-30.   Stair takes the categories of the Roman Division of Things and adapts and develops them into an account of property which is also blended together with theology and history. There is, however, no general classification of things,[63] and Stair makes no explicit mention here of the broad category of *res extra commercium*, a term which is also missing from Grotius and Voet.[64]

(b) The Real Right of Commonty

2-31.   Stair's starting point is that God gave the world to humankind. Humankind did not receive ownership as such but only the right to take and make use of things for 'necessity, utility and delight'.[65] Over time the concept of ownership was developed so that things which anyone appropriated could not be taken from them. However, there are some things which cannot be appropriated in their natural state and thus remain in a state of 'community'. Running water, the open sea and the air are listed as incapable of being owned when in their natural state. Running water is constantly moving and without bounds, but when standing, Stair writes, water is capable of ownership.[66] The sea – meaning the water – is incapable of being owned due to being so vast and, like the air, without bounds.[67] Thus, Stair maintains an important aspect of Roman law which recognises the limitations of ownership over natural resources.

2-32.   Although incapable of being owned, these things are brought within the realm of property by being made subject to what Stair describes as the real right of commonty. 'Commonty' has a technical meaning in Scots law

---

[62] Stair, *The Institutions of the Law of Scotland* (1681).

[63] Later, Bankton was to state that he improved on Stair's work by providing a Division of Things, Bankton, *Institute* vii.

[64] Although Stair does refer to the category at *Institutions* II.12.10. One reason for the omission by Grotius could be that he saw public things as owned by the people of a country and thus not *res extra commercium*. See H Grotius, *The Jurisprudence of Holland* (R W Lee (trans), 1926–1936) II.1.1-60; J Voet, *The Selective Voet being the Commentary on the Pandects* (P Gane (trans) 1955) on 1.8.1 (Gaius). See also Van der Vyver, 'Étatisation' 272 and 277.

[65] Stair, *The Institutions of the Law of Scotland* (6th edn, D M Walker (ed), 1981) II.1.1.This edition is based on the 2nd edition of 1693 and will be the edition referred to unless otherwise indicated.

[66] Stair, *Institutions* II.1.5.

[67] Stair's analysis of islands suggests that he may have considered the sea-bed to be ownerless. See below, para 4-11.

which is distinct from the right Stair is discussing here.[68] Furthermore, Stair uses the words 'commonty', 'community' and 'common things' interchangeably. It can be argued that Stair is developing the Roman category of *res communes* for practical application in Scots law. The precise content of the real right with regard to air and water is not made explicit but in essence it is a right of use which everyone holds.[69] Of course, for some things to use is to consume, so that they are exhausted by use. What right does commonty give over such things? Wild animals are an example. Stair explains that such creatures are 'in some sort common to all, as fishes, fowls, bees, &c. so as to that common right of appropriation by subduing and possession'.[70] Air and water are also consumed by use and with regard to these subjects it is possible that commonty is primarily a right of appropriation for consumption.

2-33.   It seems paradoxical to suggest that commonty gives a right of appropriation to things which, by definition, cannot be appropriated. However, common things are only incapable of appropriation due to their natural state. Once running water stops moving, a portion of it can be possessed and taken into ownership through *occupatio*. Therefore, commonty gives the right to put water into a state in which it is possible to possess it and therefore own it.

(c) The Limitation on Appropriation

2-34.   A passage found only in the first edition of Stair's *Institutions* gives more information about commonty. The right of appropriation is limited to need and the interest of the community. Everyone, it is said, has an equal right to use common things but:

> 'this equality is not exact in the use but that which is enjoyed in common may freely be made use of for the ends of the community, though some make use of more, and others less, according to their need or satisfaction; as when two persons have a universal society of all their means, if the one be taller than the other, he is not to go naked, in so far as he exceeds his fellow…so that in universal societies, there is not an arithmetical quality, but a geometrical proportion, to the need and use of the parties observed.'[71]

This limitation on the right of appropriation elegantly addresses the modern law-and-economics argument of the 'Tragedy of the Commons'[72] – that communal property leads to degradation of the resource. In placing control over the use of the resource in the form of restriction in the interests of the community, the tragedy has been remedied and the resource is protected.[73]

---

[68] Reid, *Property* para 37.

[69] This is contrary to the analysis employed throughout this book that as water cannot be owned, it cannot be subject to subordinate real rights. However, this real right is held by everyone and as such it is similar to the public right of the modern law.

[70] Stair, *Institutions* II.1.5.

[71] Stair, *The Institutions of the Law of Scotland* (1681) II.1.5.

[72] G Hardin, 'Tragedy of the Commons' (1968) 162 Science 1243.

[73] This solution is recognised in R Barnes, *Property Rights and Natural Resources* (2009) 48.

Such restriction is not inconsistent with things remaining *res communes* as these things are outwith ownership but not regulation.[74] In Scotland, this analysis of *res communes* with regard to things exhausted by use is unique to Stair, although other natural law writers of the *jus commune* make similar comments. Grotius, for example, also provides a history of property rights beginning with when man was given the earth by God. All things were communal in the beginning and could be appropriated according to need. After the introduction of ownership, the original community remained for things which could not be appropriated in their entirety due to their natural state, such as running water.[75] Likewise Voet also states that a private person cannot appropriate communal things wholesale but only his or her share.[76]

2-35. As already mentioned, the passage quoted above appears only in the first edition of the *Institutions*. The reason for its exclusion from the second edition is unclear. Perhaps the passage had been criticised because a limitation on the right of appropriation stands in opposition to some of the individualistic qualities of property law.

2-36. Whether the omitted passage reflects Scots law or has institutional authority is open to question. It is not contradicted by anything in the second edition of Stair, nor by any later institutional writer. In the third edition of Stair, published in 1759, the editors suggest that Stair's statements on the limitation of appropriation based on need are purely historical and do not reflect the modern law.[77] However, this is not indicated by the first edition itself and in the omitted passage Stair writes mostly in the present tense.

(d) Commonty and the Sea

2-37. Stair's account of the sea also stands out from previous literature. Fulton claims that during the 16th century it was generally accepted by jurists that the sea was capable of appropriation and had indeed mostly been appropriated by adjoining countries.[78] This is demonstrated by Craig's statement that the princes of the world have divided the sea among them.[79] In 1609, the publication of Grotius' *Mare Liberum*, which argued that the open seas could not be appropriated and that no one could be prevented from navigating and fishing there, marked the beginning of furious debate reflecting the commercial interests of the participants. This was largely conducted between the Dutch on the one hand, who argued for freedom of

---

[74] K Gray, 'Property Law in Thin Air' (1991) 50 *CLJ* 252 at 268 n 4.

[75] H Grotius, *The Free Sea* (R Hakluyt (trans), 2004) 32–33. See also T W Fulton, *The Sovereignty of the Sea* (1911) 186–196.

[76] Voet, *Commentary on the Pandects* (n 64) on 1.8.3 (Florentinus).

[77] See Stair, *The Institutions of the Law of Scotland* (3rd edn, J Gordon and W Johnstone (ed), 1759) II.1.5. and II.1.33. Insertions are indicated by italics.

[78] Fulton, *Sovereignty of the Sea* (n 75) 338.

[79] Craig, *Jus Feudale* (n 37) 1.15.13.

the seas, and the British, Spanish and Portuguese on the other who argued for ownership of the seas.[80]

2-38. The debate was still in progress when Stair published his *Institutions*. Remarkably, the open seas are said to be incapable of bounds which suggests that Stair saw the sea as mostly incapable of being appropriated.[81] Meanwhile, commonty gives the right to use the unappropriated sea for navigation and fishing. Of course, as Craig shows, the belief that the sea can be appropriated does not of itself prevent it from being open to all as to navigation.[82] Yet, after the time in which Craig was writing, arguments about ownership of the seas were used by Spain and Portugal in an attempt to prevent all navigation to Latin America and the East Indies.[83] Therefore, the views that the sea is incapable of appropriation and that navigation and fishing are open to all became almost synonymous.

2-39. Stair continues that, although the open sea is incapable of appropriation, the position is different where the sea is enclosed in bays, between points of land or within sight of the shore. The appropriator here is likely to have been the Crown. Whitty shows that this reflects the reserved waters or the area of sea within land kenning, a distance of 14 miles from the shore.[84] The appropriation of these reserved waters was consistent with Grotius' views, which were not concerned with waters within sight of the shore.[85] Thus, there is a distinction made between reserved waters – now called territorial waters[86] – which are capable of being owned, and the open seas which are incapable of being owned.

2-40. The reserved waters were important for fishing.[87] As Fulton shows there is clear evidence that for centuries the Scots, in contrast to the English, jealously guarded the right to fish against foreigners in reserved waters especially in regard to herring upon which there was a tax called 'assize-herring'.[88] However, the juridical basis for this claim to exclusive fishing and the tax upon herring could not be discovered by Fulton.[89] Craig, as noted above, claimed exclusive fishing in the sea could be acquired through prescription. Moreover, in 1609, King James VI and I issued a proclamation preventing all foreigners from fishing on the British coasts.[90] Yet, it is unclear from reading the *Institutions* whether fishing by foreigners in the reserved

---

[80] See the summary in Fulton, *Sovereignty of the Sea* (n 75) 338–377; M J van Ittersum, 'Mare Liberum versus the Propriety of the Seas?' (2006) 10 *Edin LR* 239. This debate generally centred on the application of private law doctrines to matters of international interest.

[81] Stair, *Institutions* II.1.5.

[82] Craig, *Jus Feudale* (n 37) 1.15.13.

[83] Fulton, *Sovereignty of the Sea* (n 75) 339.

[84] Whitty, 'Water' 430. See also A D M Forte, 'Kenning be Kenning and Course be Course: Maritime Jurimetrics in Scotland and Northern Europe 1400–1600' (1998) 2 *Edin LR* 56.

[85] Grotius, *The Free Sea* (n 75) 32–33. See also Fulton, *Sovereignty of the Sea* (n 75) 347.

[86] See further below, para 2-86.

[87] Whitty, 'Water' 430.

[88] Fulton, *Sovereignty of the Sea* (n 75) 75–85.

[89] Fulton, *Sovereignty of the Sea* (n 75) 82.

[90] Reproduced in Fulton, *Sovereignty of the Sea* (n 75), Appendix F.

waters could be prevented entirely. At first Stair suggests that, even in reserved waters, everyone is entitled to fish except for certain types of fish such as herring,[91] while at a later point he states that 'other nations may be excluded from fishing, so far as bounds can be perceived in the sea'.[92] This may be due to the appropriated sea being a public thing.[93]

(e) The Right of Passage

2-41. Stair continues by discussing things which have been appropriated and rights to use them. It is said it has been established through tacit agreement and custom that there is a universal right to use the 'common ways and passages'[94] through land and water. Thus, no nation may be refused navigation through Scotland's reserved waters except in the event of war against that nation. This right cannot be directly equated to the category of *res publicae*, which also appears in some form in Stair's *Institutions*, because, as shown below, it seems that Stair sees the use of 'public' things as limited to Scottish nationals whereas this right of passage is open to people of all nations. Instead, the right may be an amalgamation of two separate ideas. One is the Roman categorisation of highways as *res publicae*;[95] the other is Grotius' right of innocent passage over land and sea which, although discussed within a chapter on things common to all men, is explained as a reservation of use agreed upon when the concept of ownership was first developed by mankind.[96]

2-42. When discussing the shore, Stair again focuses on use. It is possible he thought the shore capable of private ownership but it is also subject to rights of use which can be seen as ancillary to the right of passage.[97] Thus, everyone is entitled to cast anchor, take in ballast, disload goods, dry nets and erect tents. Any natural stations or harbours on rivers are also available to everyone as ancillary to the right of passage.[98]

(f) Public Things and The Regalia

2-43. Neither public things nor the *regalia* play a central role in the *Institutions* and Stair keeps the categories relatively distinct with little overlap between them. Stair's account of both concepts is, however, brief and unclear which makes analysis difficult.

2-44. Everyone has a right to navigate on the reserved waters and navigable rivers and to use natural stations and harbours due to the right of

---

[91] Stair, *Institutions* II.1.5.
[92] Stair, *Institutions* II.3.76.
[93] See discussion below.
[94] Stair, *Institutions* II.1.5.
[95] D.43.8.2.22 (Ulpian). See also Stair, *Institutions* II.7.10.
[96] H Grotius, *De Jure Belli Ac Pacis Libri Tres* (F W Kelsey (trans), 1925) II.II.XIII.
[97] Stair, *Institutions* II.1.5. See also below, para 3-16.
[98] Stair, *Institutions* II.1.5.

passage. However, the reserved waters, 'lochs and creeks',[99] banks of rivers, as well as ports or stations which have been created by men are 'public to their own people'.[100] It is unclear what Stair means by this phrase. As ports are often said to belong to private persons,[101] and as it is implied in a section on alluvion that river banks belong to the adjacent proprietors not the Crown,[102] Stair cannot be concerned here with ownership; rather he seems to mean that only the people of Scotland have rights of use. Indeed Stair only refers to the reserved waters as being public as to fishing; lochs and creeks are only public as to sailing and fishing.[103] If this is correct, Stair in a limited way maintains the category of *res publicae* as a source of public rights of use but unlike Craig does not seem to see these things as open to the use of all.

2-45.   When discussing the *regalia*, Stair focuses mostly on the *regalia minora*, though he does not name them as such. The only seeming overlap between public things and the *regalia* is man-made ports, briefly mentioned by Stair as *inter regalia*.[104] However, this merely indicates that the Crown has a monopoly over the establishment of ports and does not concern public rights of use or ownership. Although it is said that anyone is entitled to fish in the sea or rivers for common fish, salmon fishing in navigable rivers is included in the list of property belonging to the Crown but which can be disponed to private persons.[105] Stair cites *Lesley v Ayton*[106] as authority for the statement that salmon fishing is only *inter regalia* in navigable rivers. However, this case holds that salmon fishing is only included in the *regalia* in salt water or where fishing is with a coble and trail net.[107]

(g) Omissions From The Division

2-46.   Stair does not seem to include all lochs within the category of public things. Instead, at a later stage in the *Institutions* it is said the owner of land within which a (perhaps non-navigable) loch lies has the right to the water in that loch, and the *alveus* of lochs is explicitly mentioned as included as part and pertinent of a disposition.[108]

(3) Comparison of Craig and Stair

2-47.   The accounts of the Division of Things provided by Stair and Craig are very different, with each writer emphasising different categories of the Division. Craig does not consider communal things at all but provides a

---

[99] Stair, *Institutions* II.3.76.
[100] Stair, *Institutions* II.1.5 and II.3.76.
[101] Stair, *Institutions* II.1.5.
[102] Stair, *Institutions* II.1.35.
[103] Stair, *Institutions* II.3.76.
[104] Stair, *Institutions* II.3.61.
[105] Stair, *Institutions* II.3.69.
[106] (1593) Mor 14249.
[107] See also *Gairlies v Torhouse* (1605) Mor 14249.
[108] Stair, *Institutions* II.3.73.

detailed consideration of public rights of use. These rights have the Roman law category of *res publicae* as their source. However, where the categories of *res publicae* and *regalia* overlap, public rights of use in the *regalia* may be limited to nationals, with foreign nationals having to make a payment or ask the permission of the Crown.

2-48.   Stair, on the other hand, analyses the category of *res communes* in depth. The bare classification of Roman law is transformed into a real right to use certain natural resources which are incapable of being owned. Limitations of ownership over natural resources are recognised and appropriation is regulated. The category of *res publicae* plays a relatively minor role. This is perhaps due to Stair's separate consideration of the right of passage which allows use of land and water for travel. In contrast to Craig's concept of public things, Stair seems to limit the use of public things to nationals.

2-49.   Despite their differences, taken together Craig and Stair uphold two important principles from the Roman Division of Things. Firstly, some natural resources are exempt from ownership and as a result are available for the use of all. Secondly, there are public rights of use over certain vital objects of trade, travel and defence regardless of the ownership of such things. However, despite the maintenance of these principles, Scots law at this time was far from having an established doctrine of the Division of Things.

D. LATER INSTITUTIONAL WRITERS

(1) Mackenzie, Forbes, Bankton and Erskine

2-50.   The originality of Stair's interpretation of *res communes* and the breadth of Craig's public rights of use are scarcely matched by any of the later institutional writers, whose accounts are based on a more traditional, less innovative, interpretation of the Roman sources. Mackenzie, Forbes, Bankton and Erskine reach a consensus on the meaning of the category of *res communes* but the meaning of *res publicae* remains unclear.[109] In particular there is a difficulty determining the relationship between *res publicae* and the *regalia*.

2-51.   During this period, the Division of Things began to lose significance. Forbes' *Institutes* does not consider the categories of the Division of Things at all. Mackenzie[110] and Erskine,[111] who adopted Mackenzie's model, focus on the 'Division of Rights' rather than the 'Division of Things'.[112] This marks a

---

[109] The first edition of Mackenzie's *Institutions* was published in 1684 with a second edition in 1688, the latter being the edition used in this book. Forbes wrote his *Great Body* at the beginning of the 18th century but it was never published and his *Institutes* was published between 1722 and 1730. Bankton published his *Institute* between 1751 and 1753. Erskine's *Institute* was published posthumously in 1773.

[110] Mackenzie, *Institutions* II.1.

[111] Erskine, *Institute* II.1.

[112] Bankton has both a Division of Things and Division of Rights, Bankton, *Institute* I.3 and II.1.

shift from the discussion of whether things are subject to ownership to the definition of ownership and other real rights. The categories of *res communes* and *res publicae* are still discussed but they are no longer of primary importance. Instead, the right of ownership is now the starting point for the discussion of property.

2-52.   In addition to this change in emphasis, an increasing secularisation of law can be noted. Stair's discussion of the Division of Things blended law with history and theology but later writers, with the exception of Forbes who followed Stair's example,[113] do not refer to any religious dimension of the Division of Things. As *res communes* had been connected with the original state of nature when God gave the world to humankind, this increasing secularisation may have contributed to the diminishing importance of this category and so to the general decline in debate about the Division of Things.

(a) Common Things

2-53.   'Common things' are said to be physically incapable of ownership, and these things include light, air, the open seas and running water.[114] Light is an addition to this otherwise traditional Roman law list. A distinction, initially outlined in Stair, is maintained between the open sea, which is a common thing, and the reserved or territorial waters over which the Crown has certain rights.[115] However, the content of these rights is not clear. To the extent that no one can own common things, no one can be prevented from using them. The difference between *res communes* and *res nullius* appears to be that the latter are things which are potentially capable of ownership but have not yet been reduced to property while the former cannot be appropriated in their natural state.[116] There is no reference to a limitation on the appropriation in the interests of the community as outlined by Stair, or indeed to any other limitations on the use of common things.

2-54.   There remains some confusion regarding the shore. Bankton says that the shore was defined as common in Roman law[117] and that this position has been altered by law and custom in Scots law[118] but how the shore is now to be classified is left unclear. Erskine prefers the interpretation of Roman law that the shore is public.[119]

---

[113] Forbes, *Great Body* Vol 1, 338–341.

[114] Mackenzie, *Institutions* II.1; Forbes, *Great Body* Vol 1, 341–342; Bankton, *Institute* I.3.2; Erskine, *Institute* II.1.5–6.

[115] Mackenzie, *Institutions* II.1; Forbes, *Great Body* Vol 1, 341–342; Bankton, *Institute* I.3.2–3; Erskine, *Institute* II.1.6. Forbes also mentions, like Craig, that parts of the sea have been acquired through immemorial possession citing J Selden, *Mare Clausum* (1635).

[116] Erskine, *Institute* II.1.4–5; Bankton refers to the 'double sense' of *nullius*, Bankton, *Institute* I.3.11 and 14. However, Forbes regards the *res divini juris* as *res nullius, Great Body* Vol 1, 342.

[117] Bankton, *Institute* II.1.5.

[118] Bankton, *Institute* I.3.2.

[119] Erskine, *Institute* II.1.6.

(b) Public Things

2-55. Public things include navigable rivers, harbours, bridges, highways and perhaps the shore.[120] For rivers it is often unclear whether the *alveus*, the river as a separate entity, or the water is being referred to, and there are conflicting accounts of the meaning of the category. Erskine says that public things are physically capable of ownership but exempted from commerce in respect of the uses to which they are destined and owned by the state in which they lie.[121] However, it seems that some public things like the shore and river banks may be privately owned.[122] This indicates that the purpose of the classification of public things is still public rights.

2-56. Mackenzie, Bankton and Erskine suggest the use of public things is restricted to citizens of the state and, according to Bankton and Erskine, to others by permission.[123] However, Forbes considers public things can be used by all.[124] This view may be due to the influence of Craig's broad interpretation of public things but it is more likely that Forbes was influenced by Stair and is merely clumsily replicating Stair's right of passage. He shows further influence of Stair when he states that river banks and man-made ports can only be used by the members the nation.[125]

2-57. Uncertainty is caused due to the interaction between public things and the *regalia*. Bankton's view is that public things are *inter regalia* and owned by the Crown.[126] Erskine also states that the subjects which were public by Roman law are 'by our feudal plan deemed *regalia*, or rights belonging to the crown'.[127] However, it cannot be said that, when Erskine describes public things as *inter regalia*, this means these things are necessarily owned by the Crown, for some of them are in private ownership.[128] Instead, by categorising these things as *regalia* Erskine seems to be explaining the interest the Crown has in these things for the purpose of protecting public rights.[129]

2-58. Despite the diminishing importance of the Division of Things, the two important facets of Roman law outlined above concerning the limitations of ownership over natural resources and public rights of use are still maintained by Mackenzie, Forbes, Bankton and Erskine.

---

[120] Mackenzie, *Institutions* II.1; Forbes, *Great Body* Vol 1, 343–344; Bankton, *Institute* I.3.4; Erskine, *Institute* II.1.5.

[121] Erskine, *Institute* II.1.5. See also Forbes, *Great Body* Vol 1, 343.

[122] Erskine, *Institute* II.1.5–6.

[123] Mackenzie, *Institutions* II.1; Bankton, *Institute* I.3.4; Erskine, II.1.5.

[124] Forbes, *Great Body* Vol 1, 343–344.

[125] Forbes, *Great Body* Vol 1, 344.

[126] Bankton, *Institute* I.3.4. Although it is only the monopoly of establishing harbours which is held by the Crown.

[127] Erskine, *Institute* II.1.6.

[128] Like Bankton, only the right to establish harbours is held by the Crown, Erskine, *Institute* II.6.17.

[129] See further below, para 3-22.

(2) Kames

2-59.   Kames does not consider the Division of Things but he does use the concept of *res communes* and the authority of Justinian's *Institutes* to establish the theory of common interest both through his influence as an advocate and judge in formative cases, and also as a jurist with the *Principles of Equity*.[130] The essence of his theory is that, as water is common to all mankind and everyone can use it, no one is entitled to divert a river as this would be depriving others of their rights of use. This novel interpretation of *res communes* concerned the creation of a regime of water rights instead of the classification of things generally and thus will be considered in the context of common interest,[131] not in the present chapter.

(3) Hume and Bell

(a) The Withering of Res Communes[132]

2-60.   During the 19th and 20th centuries there was a tendency in a number of jurisdictions for some things which were previously communal to be re-classified as public things owned by the state. During the last quarter of the 19th century, for example, the Louisiana legislature passed statutes which asserted state ownership over a number of communal things, with the result that in the 1978 revision of the Louisiana *Code civil*, running water, the territorial sea and the shore were declared state property.[133] In South Africa, the case of *Surveyor-General (Cape) v Estate De Villiers*,[134] decided in 1923, held that the shore was state property. The Sea-shore Act of 1935 then declared the President of South Africa as the owner of the shore, the territorial sea-bed and the waters of the territorial sea.[135] In addition, in Civil law countries, consideration of the category of *res communes* began to disappear. In Germany, *res communes* are not seen as falling within the technical definition of 'things' as they cannot be possessed or controlled and are determined wholly by public law.[136] The drafters of the *Bürgerliches Gesetzbuch* deleted provisions on *res extra commercium* on the basis that they would be superfluous since such things are exempted from legal relations.[137] Communal things are therefore not considered in the *Bürgerliches Gesetzbuch*, and the Division of Things is now only found in academic commentaries.[138] The French *Code civil* has an allusion

[130] Kames, *Principles* 50–51. Kames' *Principles of Equity* was first published in 1760 but it is his third edition of 1778 which contains the first full discussion of water rights and will be the edition referred to unless otherwise indicated.

[131] See below, Chs 5, 6 and 7.

[132] This title is inspired by Whitty, 'Water' 431.

[133] Louisiana *Code civil* Art 450.

[134] 1923 AD 588.

[135] South Africa Sea-shore Act 1935 s 2(1). This trend was also foreshadowed in Scotland. See the analysis of Craig and Stair above.

[136] D Medicus, *Allgemeiner Teil des BGB* (2002) para 1174.

[137] M Schmoeckel, J Rüchert and R Zimmermann (eds), *Historisch-kritischer Kommentar zum BGB* Vol 1 (2003) 313.

[138] See, for example, L Enneccerus, *Allgemeiner Teil des Bürgerlichen Rechts* (1959) 824–828.

to *res communes* but the category is not considered in detail.[139] The new Dutch *Burgerlijk Wetboek* does not consider the Division of Things or the category of *res communes*.[140] Instead, there is focus on the definition of a thing which excludes those which are *extra commercium*. This code has been heavily influenced by its French and German counterparts rather than by the Roman-Dutch tradition. Thus, there was a general trend in Civilian and Mixed Legal Systems by which the category of communal things faded in importance.

2-61. This trend was also found in Scots law. By the time of Hume[141] and Bell[142] in the first decades of the 19th century, the category of communal things was hardly mentioned. Neither Hume nor Bell has a Division of Things and Bell makes only a brief allusion to the category of communal things by stating that the 'main ocean is common to all nations'.[143]

2-62. The reason for the withering of communal things from Scottish literature may be multi-faceted. In addition to the general decrease of importance of the category in Europe and European-inspired legal systems, Scottish lawyers may have been questioning aspects of Civilian learning which had previously been broadly accepted. In 1824 Lord Elchies, in his annotations to Stair's *Institutions*, noted with regard to the Division of Things: 'In this title, our author first goes through some metaphysical points anent the beginning of property or dominion, which curious in themselves, are of no use to us.'[144] Further, it is stated particularly in regard to commonty: 'He next proceeds, in the fifth section, to things common by the law of nature or nations, which, being borrowed entirely from the civil law, and of no great use in our practice, there needs nothing to be added.'[145] These sentiments reflect a belief that the category of *res communes* was superfluous with no practical importance to lawyers. Another factor may be that, with the rise of English influence in Scotland, the elucidation of general principles and broad classifications became less valued.[146]

---

[139] France *Code civil* Art 714. For arguments in favour of developing the concept of *res communes* in French law in light of environmental concerns see F Barrière, 'Turbulence over Wind Turbines: *Res Communis* under the Spotlights' (2012) 20 European Review of Private Law 1149.

[140] The Netherlands *Burgerlijk Wetboek* Book 3, Art 2. See also J M J Chorus, P H M Gerver and E H Hondius (eds), *Introduction to Dutch Law* (4th edn, 2006) 107–108; F Nieper and H D Ploeger 'Niederlande' in C von Bar (ed), *Sachenrecht in Europa* (1999) Band 3 162–163.

[141] Hume's *Lectures* were delivered to students between 1786 and 1822.

[142] The first edition of Bell, *Principles of the Law of Scotland* was published in 1829. The fourth edition of 1839 is the last which Bell edited and will be the edition referred unless otherwise indicated.

[143] Bell, *Principles* para 639.

[144] P Grant, Lord Elchies, *Annotations on Lord Stair's Institutions of the Law of Scotland* (1824) 104.

[145] Elchies, *Annotations on Lord Stair's Institutions* (n 144) 104–105.

[146] Although early English jurists did mention the categories, it cannot be said that there remains a tradition of the Division of Things in English law. For a summary of references to the categories see S C Wiel, 'Running Water' (1908–09) 22 *Harv L Rev* 190.

(b) The Rise of Regalia

2-63.   In addition to the disappearance of the consideration of communal things, the category of *res publicae* became almost completely submerged within the concept of the *regalia*. Both Bell and Hume mention the words '*res publicae*' when discussing Crown property. Bell states that some things are exempted from the 'ordinary rules of appropriation'[147] – suggesting they are exempt from commerce – and are vested in the Crown in trust for the public. Hume enumerates the *regalia* as including highways, ports, bridges, ferries, navigable rivers and the shore.[148] Bell adds the territorial sea to this list.[149]

2-64.   There is, however, one exception to the conflation of *res publicae* and the *regalia*. Bell states that navigable lakes do not appear to be *inter regalia* and instead belong to the adjacent landowners, but 'if such lakes form great channels of communication in a district of country, there seems to be some reason to regard them as *res publicae*.'[150] This statement is not only indicative of the previous position of Scots law where the concepts of *regalia* and *res publicae* co-existed but also of the Roman classification of lakes which does not appear to have been broadly accepted by the institutional writers.[151]

2-65.   However, it does not appear to be the case that these things are necessarily *inter regalia majora* as to ownership.[152] Like Erskine's analysis, despite it being suggested that such things are exempt from commerce, some of the objects listed, such as the shore, are said to be capable of being owned by private persons.[153] Hume and Bell put forward different views as to how public rights can then continue. Hume states the disponee is bound by obligations of guardianship with regards to facilitating public use and maintaining the subject.[154] Bell's view is that a trusteeship as to public rights remains with the Crown.[155] Thus, under the latter analysis, it is the public rights over the objects that are *regalia majora*, not ownership itself. This analysis combined the category of public things, which was focused on public rights of use, with the *regalia* which centred on Crown ownership or control, albeit, in the view of some, with awkward doctrinal results.

2-66.   At the end of the institutional period, then, the limitations of ownership over natural resources were barely recognised, while public

---

[147] Bell, *Principles* para 638. See also Hume, *Lectures* IV 238–239. Bell does not explicitly state that he is discussing the *regalia*. However, it is suggested the Crown property discussed in paras 638–666 is mostly amongst the *regalia*, see Bell: *Principles* para 648.

[148] Hume, *Lectures* IV 239 and 256–257. However, it is the monopoly of establishing ports and ferries which is *regalia* and not the actual things themselves.

[149] Bell, *Principles* para 638.

[150] Bell, *Principles* para 648.

[151] Except Stair, see above, para 2-44.

[152] For more discussion of this, see below, Ch 3.

[153] Bell, *Principles* para 643; Hume, *Lectures* IV 256–257. The position as to river banks is difficult to rationalise. They are subject to public rights and owned by the adjacent proprietors but it is unclear to what extent they are *inter regalia* if at all. See Hume, *Lectures* IV 244–245; Bell, *Principles* para 650.

[154] Hume, *Lectures* IV 241–242. See further below, para 3-26.

[155] Bell, *Principles* para 643.

rights of use were still present, although were being rationalised in a convoluted way.

E. MODERN SCHOLARSHIP

2-67.   There was to be no return to the Division of Things. Among the modern writers, only Rankine and Paisley discuss the categories of communal things and public things in any depth. Meanwhile, a theory of the *regalia* has become established.

2-68.   When discussing ownership and which things are capable of being owned, Rankine writes that among the *res communes* are things 'the property of which belongs to no person, but the use to all.'[156] Such things include the high seas,[157] light, air and running water. The category of *res publicae* is briefly mentioned[158] but is unimportant because, as Rankine explains, the feudal law, which demanded an owner for everything, placed the *res communes* and *res publicae* capable of appropriation within the ownership of the Crown as *regalia*.[159] The *regalia* are considered within a discussion of the restrictions on ownership, these being either restrictions on Crown ownership or restrictions on the ownership of others in favour of the public.[160] The *regalia* include the territorial sea, the shore, navigable rivers and highways.[161]

2-69.   Paisley, adopting the categorisation of Roman law, states that certain things and rights can be classified as *extra commercium* or *intra commercium*.[162] Things outwith commerce are divided into two sub-categories: things unsusceptible of any kind of ownership and things which are held in a form of public ownership. The former sub-category includes *res communes* such as the waters of the territorial sea, running water and air in its natural state. It is said this sub-category 'probably also extends to clouds and natural rainfall and this issue may arise if it becomes possible to alter weather patterns by human action'.[163] The latter, it is suggested, may include property held by local authorities or other public bodies and rights held by the Crown as part of the *regalia*. The effect of this property being outwith commerce is to prevent any legal dealings inconsistent with the public purpose for which the thing or right is being held. This analysis attempts to preserve the concept of *res publicae* despite the rise of the *regalia*. This is one approach to the Division of Things that can be taken. As can be seen below, this approach is not adopted in this book. One reason for this is that historically the Division of Things has been concerned with classifying physical things rather than incorporeal

[156] Rankine, *Landownership* 98–99.
[157] Considered separately at 251.
[158] Rankine, *Landownership* 99.
[159] Rankine, *Landownership* 251. Rankine strangely considers navigable rivers as well as the sea and the shore as *res communes*.
[160] Rankine, *Landownership* 247–248.
[161] The ownership of these things is considered further below, Ch 3.
[162] R R M Paisley, *Land Law* (2000) paras 1.24–1.27.
[163] Paisley, *Land Law* para 1.25.

rights – although development in this direction is not infeasible. Secondly, the concepts of *res publicae* and the *regalia* are different. Although the modern doctrine of the *regalia* means that there are public rights over certain property, this is not the necessary result of the regalian concept.[164] It is suggested that it is not essential to maintain *res publicae* as a sub-category of *res extra commercium*[165] in light of the dominance of the *regalia*. It is perhaps simpler merely to define *res extra commercium* as generally being physical things which are exempt from commerce and, separately, to accept that there are public rights over certain objects which are central to trade, travel and defence.

2-70.   Paisley's analysis of communal things, like that of Rankine, highlights that such things are outwith legal relations due to the impossibility of appropriation and also indicates future development of the category but such a discussion is rare among modern scholars. A list of communal things is given in the first edition of Gloag and Henderson, published in 1927, and it is said, without explanation, that one cannot own such things.[166] In other works, if the category of communal things is mentioned at all, it is often questioned or even misunderstood. Ferguson interprets Stair's statement that running water is common to all men as being a reference to common interest.[167] This conflation may be a result of the similarity of the names 'common interest' and 'common thing' but also reveals a lack of historical understanding.

2-71.   Gordon states that defining running water, like the sea, as among the *res communes* 'requires considerable explanation and qualification, so much indeed, that doubt is cast on the validity of the proposition as representing Scots law'.[168] The explanation and qualification referred to include the extensive rights and obligations of landowners arising from common interest. However, whilst it is true that landowners have a better opportunity than the public at large to use water running over their lands, it is undisputed that these proprietors do not own the actual water and cannot do so until it is put into a state where it is capable of possession. The *regalian* rights of the Crown are also mentioned as a limitation on the principle that the sea cannot be appropriated. Yet, while the sea-bed may be capable of appropriation, it is open to question whether the actual waters of the sea can be said to be owned by the Crown either within or beyond the territorial limit of 12 nautical miles. Gordon suggests that modern technology and developments since the time that Stair was writing permit appropriation of the high seas.[169] It is unclear which technological advances are being referred to but it may be argued that the waters of the sea are still as incapable of

---

[164] See above, para 2-26.

[165] If, indeed, it ever was such a sub-category.

[166] W M Gloag and R C Henderson, *Introduction to the Law of Scotland* (1927) 381.

[167] Ferguson 169.

[168] Gordon & Wortley, *Land Law* para 6-17.

[169] Gordon & Wortley, *Land Law* para 6-03. It is unclear whether Gordon is referring to the sea-bed or waters of the sea.

being appropriated, in the absence of extensive occupation through containment, as they were in the 17th century.

2-72.   Reid also refers to Stair's comment that running waters are common to all and interprets this as meaning that such water is ownerless.[170] As can be seen from the foregoing discussion, this is a simplification of complex intellectual history of the category of communal things. Whitty's view is that *res communes* has 'scarcely (if at all) influenced the development of Scottish private law'.[171] This statement overlooks the role of *res communes* in the development of common interest[172] and the common good (albeit the latter is not the subject of this book).

2-73.   Through case law and juristic writing, a settled theory of the *regalia minora* and *majora* has developed. The sea-bed, the *alveus* of public rivers and lochs,[173] and the right of establishing a port or harbour all belong to the Crown as *regalia minora* and may be alienated to private persons.[174] The foreshore is not *regalia minora* as such but, like all land, is originally owned by the Crown.[175] The *solum* of highways is also not *regalia minora* and is often owned by the adjacent landowners.[176] Public rights over these objects are held by the Crown for the public and these are *regalia majora* and thus inalienable.[177] This convoluted theory merges the category of *res publicae*, which is centred on public use, and the concept of the *regalia* which is focused on Crown ownership or control. It is an unnecessarily complex theory and Reid states that it is disregarded in practice.[178] The Crown's position as trustee has been called 'anomalous, and appears to have no modern analogue on dry land'.[179] It is suggested that the current law of public rights can be better understood by appreciating how the category of *res publicae* has interacted with the *regalia* over time.[180]

F. THE MODERN DIVISION OF THINGS

2-74.   After these historical deliberations, the question must be posed, what is the modern Scots Division of Things? Despite the absence of discussion of the Division in modern scholarship, it is clear that whether things are within

---

[170] Reid, *Property* para 274.

[171] Whitty, 'Water' 432.

[172] To be explained below, Chs 5 and 6.

[173] Now defined as those which are tidal, see below, para 2-94.

[174] Gordon, *Land Law* para 27-07.

[175] See below paras 3-22–3-40.

[176] Cusine & Paisley para 18.06.

[177] Reid, *Property* paras 335 and 514; Gordon, *Land Law* para 27-06.

[178] Reid, *Property* para 514.

[179] *Burnet v Barclay* 1955 JC 34 at 39. The substance of this quotation is inaccurate and overlooks, *inter alia*, the Crown's position in relation to public rights of way, public rights of highway, fortalices, markets and rights in graves. It is fair to say, however, that the preponderance of regalian rights encountered in modern Scots law relate to water.

[180] As is recognised by Paisley's approach in *Land Law* (n 162) paras 1.24–1.27. For further discussion of the interaction between the concept of the *regalia* and ownership see below, Ch 3.

or outwith private ownership is a crucial issue. Gray states: 'Contrary to popular perception the vast majority of the world's human and economic resources still stand *outside* the threshold of property and therefore remain unregulated by any proprietary regime.'[181] When a thing is not subject to private ownership, its use is regulated by different principles both within and outwith property law. As many of the things outwith ownership are natural resources which are essential for life and also central to trade, commerce and recreation, the use of such things is a matter of relevance to everyone. Greater debate on this topic would therefore be welcomed.

2-75.   From the foregoing discussion, it can be seen that there is a tradition of considering whether things are subject to, or exempt from, private ownership in Scots law. Every institutional writer discusses the issue to some extent. Further, taken together, Craig and Stair provided the dual tenets of the underlying rationalisation of the Division of Things during the institutional period. These are that certain natural resources are excluded from private ownership due to their physical characteristics, and that there are inviolable public rights over some objects which are beneficial to human co-existence. Moreover, Mackenzie, Forbes, Bankton and Erskine are in broad agreement about the enumeration of communal things and public things even though the meaning of the latter category is unclear. However, due to various historical developments, such as the rise of the *regalia* and recent legal reform, the Division of Things now needs to be updated to take into account changes which have affected the justification for, and structure and content of, the traditional categories. Inspiration for a modern Division of Things can be drawn from other Mixed Legal Systems where the categories of the Division are maintained in their fullest form.

(1) Things Exempt From Commerce

2-76.   *Res extra commercium* is a convenient overarching category denoting things which are exempt from commerce.[182] In Scotland, the category of things outwith commerce is found in institutional writing,[183] case law[184] and even legislation.[185] In the modern law, things exempt from commerce is a

---

[181] K Gray, 'Property Law in Thin Air' (1991) 50 *CLJ* 252 at 256.

[182] This category is also used in South Africa and Sri Lanka. See Van der Merwe, 'Things' para 22; Badenhorst et al para 3.3.1.1; Peiris, *The Law of Property in Sri Lanka* (n 55) 5. In Louisiana, Yiannopoulos uses the category of 'things not susceptible of ownership', see A N Yiannopoulos, 'Common, Public, and Private Things in Louisiana: Civilian Tradition and Modern Practice' (1960–1961) 21 *La L Rev* 697; Louisiana *Code civil* Art 448. (Yiannopoulos's statements must be considered in light of the 1978 revisions of the Louisiana *Code civil*, see above, para 2-60.) The category of things exempt from commerce is broader than Yiannopoulos's category and can also include things which can be owned but not alienated.

[183] Stair, *Institutions* II.12.10; Bankton, *Institute* I.3.11; Erskine, *Institute* III.7.14.

[184] *Presbytery of Edinburgh v University of Edinburgh* (1890) 28 SLR 567 at 573 regarding presbytery records; *Earl of Lauderdale v Scrymegeour Wedderburn* 1910 SC (HL) 35 at 43 regarding the right to heritable office; *Assessor for Kincardineshire v Heritors of St Cyrus* 1915 SC 823 at 829 and 831 regarding churches.

[185] Prescription and Limitation (Scotland) Act 1973 Sch 3, para (d). See also Johnston, *Prescription* paras 3.19–3.22; Paisley, *Land Law* (n 162) para 1.26.

broad category which includes things which cannot be owned by private persons for a variety of different reasons.

2-77. Although some institutional writers rationalise the category of things exempt from commerce as containing the sub-categories of communal things and public things, the latter did not seem to be incapable of private ownership. Thus, communal things comprise the main sub-category within the overarching category.[186] This could mean that the broad category of things exempt from commerce is redundant in the modern law, or that it contains further sub-categories of things which are outwith commerce but are not governed by the principles of communal things. Consideration of the possible sub-categories which could be recognised is outwith the scope of this book. However, examples of prospective inclusions are human bodies and body parts. These things are exempt from private ownership but not subject to the general rights of use which the public enjoy in respect of communal things.[187]

(2) Communal Things

2-78. Communal things, the *res communes* of Roman law, form a sub-category of things exempt from commerce. The label 'communal' is used here, despite the preference among the institutional writers to use the phrase 'common things', in order to avoid confusion with common property.

2-79. The things in this category are traditionally said to be incapable of private ownership for the reason that they cannot be appropriated in their entirety due to their natural state.[188] This is the practical result of the physical characteristics of these things as they often lack the bounds required to identify them as an object of property rights or they cannot be subject to the level of control required for ownership. Thus, exempting these unidentifiable and uncontrollable things from private ownership could be seen as a reflection of the principles of specificity and publicity in property law.[189] Accepted things in this category are air, light, the waters of the sea, and running water.[190]

---

[186] For a different approach to the category of *extra commercium* see Paisley, *Land Law* (n 162) paras 1.24–1.27.

[187] See discussion in J K Mason and G T Laurie, *Mason and McCall Smith's Law and Medical Ethics* (9th edn, 2013) Ch 14. The law on property and the human body has been thrown into flux by *Yearworth v North Bristol NHS Trust* [2010] QB 1. See also S H E Harmon and G T Laurie, '*Yearworth v North Bristol NHS Trust*: Property, Principles, Precedents and Paradigms' (2010) 69 *CLJ* 476 and the discussion in *Holdich v Lothian Health Board* 2014 SLT 495.

[188] Stair, *Institutions* II.1.5; Forbes, *Great Body* Vol 1, 341; Erskine, *Institute* I.2.5. The difference between *res nullius* and *res communes* is that while the former are merely unowned things, the latter are things which are incapable of being owned in their entirety in their natural state and which are open to general use, Bankton, *Institute* I.3.11 and 14.

[189] On which see B Akkermans, *The Principle of* Numerus Clausus *in European Property Law* (2008) 5.

[190] For the suggestion of also including clouds and natural rainfall in this category see Paisley, *Land Law* (n 162) para 1.25.

2-80.   These things also have a crucial role in many aspects of life and are susceptible to general use. Being outwith ownership, they are available for the use of everyone.[191] The use to which they can be put is dependent on their inherent nature and characteristics. For some of the communal things, such as air and water, to use them is to appropriate them and consume them. Although communal things are incapable of appropriation in their entirety and in their natural state, portions of some communal things can be appropriated by acquiring the requisite control over them. However, the process of achieving this control often changes the nature of the resource.[192] The right to use communal things consumed by use is therefore primarily a right of appropriation. This is a public right.

2-81.   Large-scale or repeated appropriation is obviously problematic for finite resources like water which are exhausted by use. If communal things are not subject to some form of regulation, the 'Tragedy of the Commons'[193] argument may be realised when a few people exhaust a resource without consideration for others. Stair provided a solution to this by placing a limitation on appropriation based on the need of the appropriator and the interests of the community.[194] This innovative limitation provided control over communal things and aimed to ensure they remained available for the use of all.

2-82.   For water, an extension of the form of regulation that Stair envisaged exists both at common law and in legislation. The doctrine of common interest, which regulates the use of running water in rivers and lochs by landowners, permits the appropriation of water for the domestic purposes of the adjoining land but further appropriation must not materially interfere with the natural flow of the water.[195] This therefore limits appropriation to the needs of the occupier of land. Further, the Water Environment and Water Services (Scotland) Act 2003, which implements the European Water Framework Directive,[196] also places far-reaching restrictions on the appropriation of water[197] in the interests of 'promoting sustainable water use based on the long-term protection of available water resources'.[198] The Directive reaffirms the status of water as a communal thing by stating that

[191] Forbes, *Great Body* Vol 1, 341; Bankton, *Institute* I.3.2; Erskine, *Institute* II.1.5. See also the discussion of communal things in S Buckle, *Natural Law and the Theory of Property* (1991) 94–96.

[192] The category of communal things is similar to Gray's category of physically non-excludable resources: K Gray, 'Property Law in Thin Air' (1991) 50 *CLJ* 252 at 269–273. However, Gray's analysis is not wholly adopted here due to his emphasis on the right of exclusion as the mark of private property which may require reconsideration in light of other developments in Scots law. See J A Lovett, 'Progressive Property in Action: The Land Reform (Scotland) Act 2003' (2011) 89 *Neb L Rev* 739.

[193] G Hardin, 'Tragedy of the Commons' (1968) 162 *Science* 1243.

[194] Stair, *The Institutions of the Law of Scotland* (1681) II.1.5. See discussion above, paras 2-34–2-36.

[195] See below, Ch 7.

[196] Directive 2000/60/EC (23 Oct 2000).

[197] See Water Environment (Controlled Activities) (Scotland) Regulations 2011.

[198] Water Environment and Water Services (Scotland) Act 2003 s 1(2)(b).

water 'is not a commercial product like any other but, rather, a heritage which must be protected, defended and treated as such'.[199] Thus, the limitations on appropriation for water have now been entrenched in legislation which will ensure that water will not succumb to the 'Tragedy of the Commons' and instead remain communal and available for general use in the future.[200]

2-83.   Each of the communal things will now be considered individually.

(a) Air

2-84.   Air circulating in the atmosphere cannot be seen or touched and has no bounds. In its natural state one cannot exert sufficient control over it to acquire ownership. Air is perhaps the most uncontroversial exclusion from ownership and it is a matter of consensus among the institutional writers in Scotland[201] and in the jurisprudence of other Mixed Legal Systems.[202] Portions of air can be captured and placed within containers and therefore be appropriated through *occupatio*.[203] Predictably, though, this often changes the nature of the resource as in the case of compressed air or the creation of oxygen.[204] If air which has been compressed escapes, it is no longer subject to sufficient control and will regain its status as a communal thing.[205]

(b) Light

2-85.   Light is not contained in the original Roman law list of *res communes*. However, later institutional writers in Scotland included it as an object incapable of ownership.[206] Natural light is not a physical thing which can be identified as the object of ownership. Further, little control can be placed over who has the advantage of light.[207] Gray uses light as the classic example of a

---

[199] Directive 2000/60/EC (23 Oct 2000) preamble, para 1.

[200] For arguments regarding the need to develop the concept of *res communes* due to climate change and increased demand for renewable energy see F Barrière, 'Turbulence over Wind Turbines: *Res Communis* under the Spotlights' (2012) 20 *European Review of Private Law* 1149.

[201] Stair, *Institutions* II.1.5; Forbes, *Great Body* Vol 1, 341; Bankton, *Institute* I.3.2; Erskine, *Institute* II.1.5.

[202] Louisiana *Code civil* Art 449; A N Yiannopoulos, *Louisiana Civil Law Treatise: Property* (4th edn, 2001) para 47; Quebec *Code civil* Art 913; Van der Merwe, 'Things' para 23; Badenhorst et al para 3.3.1.1; Peiris, *The Law of Property in Sri Lanka* (n 55) 6.

[203] See Quebec *Code civil* Art 913.

[204] A portion of air in a container without a change in its state in the form of pressure or composition is arguably subject to ownership yet it is of little economic value.

[205] An analogy can be made here with wild animals which are ownerless until captured and become ownerless again in the event of escape, Reid, *Property* para 542. Indeed, wild animals could potentially be considered within the category of communal things for Stair describes them as 'in some sort common to all', Stair, *Institutions* II.1.5.

[206] Forbes, *Great Body* Vol 1, 341; Bankton, *Institute* I.3.2; Erskine, *Institute* II.1.5.

[207] However, in November 2010, Angeles Duran claimed ownership of the sun and aimed on charging people for use of its rays. As this article points out, Duran has not yet figured out how to enforce this charge. Available at: http://www.dailymail.co.uk/news/article-1333776/Spanish-woman-Angeles-Duran-claims-owns-sun—plans-start-charging-ALL-users.html.

resource outwith ownership, the use of which is open to all as the benefits of light are 'distributed indiscriminately'.[208]

(c) The Sea

2-86.   The inclusion of the sea in the category of communal things is a more complicated issue than air or light despite the consensus as to its status as such in the institutional writers.[209] It is now settled law that the Crown owns the sea-bed under the territorial waters of the sea,[210] which extend 12 international nautical miles from defined baselines.[211] The Crown also owns the sea-bed under tidal waters which are *inter fauces terrae*.[212] The sea-bed can be disponed to private persons and thus is not a communal thing.

2-87.   The waters of the sea within and outwith this territory, however, remain communal. The waters of the sea are vast, constantly moving and are without the physical bounds or susceptibility to control which is required for private ownership. Further, the waters of the sea are of fundamental political, social, economic and environmental importance, as was emphasised during the debate on the freedom of the seas during the 17th century.[213] Thus, it is important for them to remain open to general use of navigation and fishing.[214] Similar reasoning applies to the sea-bed outwith territorial waters, or the high seas, which can also be placed in the category of communal things.[215] Indeed, in a statement reflecting the *res communes* concept, the United Nations Convention on the Law of the Sea declares the sea-bed beyond the limits of national jurisdiction to be the common heritage of mankind.[216]

(d) Running Water

2-88.   Running water encompasses the water flowing in rivers and over or through the surface of the earth, distinct from the mass of salt water which comprises the sea. In its natural state, running water is accepted as a communal thing by the institutional writers.[217] In South Africa and Sri Lanka

---

[208] K Gray, 'Property Law in Thin Air' (1991) 50 *CLJ* 252 at 269.

[209] Stair, *Institutions* II.1.5; Bankton, *Institute* I.3.2; Erskine, *Institute* II.1.6.

[210] *Shetland Salmon Farmers Association v Crown Estate Commissioners* 1991 SLT 166 at 174 (Lord Justice-Clerk Ross). See discussion on ownership below, paras 3-08–3-13.

[211] Territorial Sea Act 1987 s 1(1)(a).

[212] 'Between the jaws of the land'.

[213] See above, paras 2-37–2-40.

[214] Of course, use may be subject to restrictions in the interests of conservation.

[215] In South Africa and Louisiana, the territorial sea is defined as public. See Louisiana *Code civil* Art 450; South Africa Sea-shore Act 1935 s 2(1); Van der Merwe, 'Things' para 24; Badenhorst et al para 3.3.1.1 and discussion above, para 2-60. But the high seas remain communal in Louisiana, Louisiana *Code civil* Art 449 and it could be argued that this is also the position in South Africa.

[216] United Nations Convention on the Law of the Sea 1982 Art 136.

[217] Stair, *Institutions* II.1.5; Forbes, *Great Body* Vol 1, 341; Bankton, *Institute* I.3.2; Erskine, *Institute* II.1.5.

it is also defined as such.[218] As a naturally occurring resource which is constantly moving, its bounds are not sufficiently specific nor can it be suitably controlled to be defined as a thing capable of ownership. By placing water in a container, its extent is then adequately precise to allow it to pass into private ownership through *occupatio*.[219] However, then its natural state has been changed as it has become still, not running water. Further, as highlighted above, there are many limitations on the appropriation of water in Scots law.

(e) Standing Water?

2-89. Although there is ample authority on the legal status of running water, there is little authority on standing water. Water percolating through the earth, which is indistinguishable from the earth itself, has been defined as *pars soli* and owned by the owner of the land.[220] Water in a definable pool lying on or beneath the surface has sufficient bounds to allow physical appropriation.[221] However, the mere fact that water has stopped moving does not mean that the requisite level of control has been achieved over it for it to pass into private ownership of the owner of land on which it stands. It is suggested, therefore, that standing water could also be defined as a communal thing. This classification may be further justified by recognising that water in its many forms is part of a natural and inter-dependent cycle – a fact which is highlighted in South Africa's National Water Act 1998[222] and the European Water Framework Directive.[223] Thus, it is logical to place water at all stages in this cycle within the same classification of a communal thing.[224]

2-90. Defining standing water as a communal thing would also reaffirm that water is available for the use of all, for, as Reid states 'water, like air and light, is regarded as a natural resource which should not be the property of any one person'.[225]

(3) Public Rights and Communal Things

2-91. Navigable rivers, highways, the shore, ports and harbours were at one stage defined as *res publicae*, or public things, a term which was interpreted by Erskine and Bell as implying exemption from commerce due to public

---

[218] Van der Merwe, 'Things' para 23; Badenhorst para 3.3.1.1; Peiris, *The Law of Property in Sri Lanka* (n 55) 5. In Louisiana, running water has been redefined as public: see Louisiana *Code civil* Art 450 and discussion above, para 2-60.

[219] See Quebec *Code civil* Art 913.

[220] *Crichton v Turnbull* 1946 SC 52. See also Reid, *Property* para 274.

[221] Stair, *Institutions* II.1.5. This discussion does not apply to lochs which, by definition, have a perennial outflow and therefore consist of (albeit slowly) moving water, see below, para 7-27.

[222] South African National Water Act 1998 preamble.

[223] Directive 2000/60/EC (23 Oct 2000) preamble, para 34

[224] This view is shared by B Clark, 'Water Law in Scotland: the Water Environment and Water Services (Scotland) Act 2003 and the European Convention on Human Rights' (2006) 10 *Edin LR* 61 at 66.

[225] Reid, *Property* para 274.

rights of use. However, in these writers' accounts some of these things also appear to be privately owned. This showed that this classification is not focused on ownership but on public rights. Following the submersion of the category of public things within the *regalia*, it has been established that it is not the things themselves which are inalienable but the public rights over them which are held by the Crown as *regalia majora*. Thus, the principle of protecting public rights over important objects for trade, travel and defence is maintained without requiring the things themselves to be exempt from private ownership. These public rights are relevant to the Division of Things, for they also contribute to the realisation of the general use of communal things. The use of a communal thing is dependent on acquiring lawful access to it. If a communal thing is surrounded by, or located on, land which is in private or Crown ownership, the use of that communal thing can be factually monopolised despite its legal status as a thing available for the use of all. Although everyone may breathe the air, to walk onto another's property to breathe air may be trespass. Many of the common law public rights allow access to the water via ports, harbours or the shore and allow use of the sea and public rivers and lochs[226] which could otherwise be prejudiced by private or Crown ownership of the *alveus* or sea-bed. This complementary relationship between *res communes* and *res publicae* of Roman law was always present and still exists between communal things and public rights in Scots law. In addition to these common law rights, recent reform has created the statutory public rights contained in the Land Reform (Scotland) Act 2003. This radical piece of legislation greatly extends public rights of access over land and inland water which further increases access rights to communal things.

(a) Common Law Public Rights

(i) Rights over the Sea

2-92.   The waters of the sea are communal but the sea-bed under territorial waters is owned by the Crown and can be alienated to private individuals.[227] As ownership of the sea-bed gives rights to use the air-space above the sea-bed, public rights over the sea exist to protect the use of the communal waters of the sea. These rights are held by the Crown for the public and cannot be prejudiced by private or Crown ownership of the sea-bed. The public have a right of navigation over the sea which is primarily for the purpose of passage,[228] a right to fish for white fish and shellfish[229] and, Reid also suggests, a right of recreational swimming.[230]

---

[226] For the inclusion of lochs here see below.

[227] See below, paras 3-08–3-11 for discussion.

[228] *Crown Estate Commissioners v Fairlie Yacht Slip* 1979 SC 156. See also Reid, *Property* paras 519–520; Discussion Paper on the Law of the Foreshore and Seabed (Scot Law Com DP 113, 2001) para 4.11.

[229] *McDouall v Lord Advocate* (1875) 2 R (HL) 49; *Duke of Argyll v Robertson* (1859) 22 D 261. See also Discussion Paper on the Law of the Foreshore and Seabed (n 228) para 4.2. White fish are all floating fish excluding salmon, and shellfish excludes oysters and mussels, both of which are separate tenements: Reid, *Property* paras 320–330, 331–333 and 521.

[230] Reid, *Property* para 518.

(ii) RIGHTS OVER PUBLIC RIVERS AND LOCHS

2-93. In contrast to Roman law, which used the test of whether a river was perennial, Scots law included only navigable rivers within the category of public things.[231] Further, it was not broadly accepted that navigable lochs were public things.[232] Following the intermingling of the concepts of public things and the *regalia*, it became established that the Crown owned the *alveus* of navigable rivers and could dispone it to private parties.[233] However, the public rights over such rivers held by the Crown were not alienable.

2-94. In 1877, the test of navigability was changed to the test of tidality by *Colquhoun's Trs v Orr Ewing*.[234] As only tidal rivers were now public, the public were deprived of the tacit rights they had previously held over non-tidal navigable stretches of water.[235] Following this change, the ownership of the *alveus* of both tidal rivers and lochs is analysed in the same way as the sea-bed. The public rights over tidal rivers and lochs are also similar to those enjoyed over the sea and include rights of navigation[236] and fishing for white fish and shellfish[237] which cannot be prejudiced by Crown or private ownership of the *alveus*.[238]

2-95. The public can acquire rights of navigation over private, non-tidal rivers (and perhaps also non-tidal lochs) through immemorial use.[239] The public do not appear to have tacit rights to use river banks for purposes ancillary to navigation, although again such rights can be acquired.[240] Further public rights over inland waters were created by the Land Reform (Scotland) Act 2003, considered below.

(iii) RIGHTS OVER THE FORESHORE

2-96. The shore, or the 'foreshore' as it is now more commonly named in Scots law, is defined as the area between the high and low water mark of ordinary spring tides. In Roman law the status of the shore was unclear as it was described as both *res communes* and *res publicae*.[241] This confusion was continued in Scots law as Bankton describes the shore as common[242] whereas Erskine states the shore is public. Further, there was great debate in the 19th century as to the Crown's interest in the shore. Eventually it was established

---

[231] Bankton, *Institute* I.3.4; Erskine, *Institute* II.1.5.

[232] Except Stair, *Institutions* II.3.76; Bell, *Principles* para 648.

[233] See below, paras 3-46–3-49.

[234] (1877) 4 R 344 (reversed on a different point in (1877) 4 R (HL) 116). See further below, para 3-50.

[235] See Whitty, 'Water' 441.

[236] *Colquhoun v Duke of Montrose* (1793) Mor 12827.

[237] *Grant v Henry* (1894) 21 R 358. See also Whitty, 'Water' 444–446.

[238] Reid, *Property* paras 310–311

[239] See Reid, *Property* para 523; *Wills' Trs v Cairngorm Canoeing and Sailing School Ltd* 1976 SC (HL) 30.

[240] Reid, *Property* para 528.

[241] Compare D.1.8.2.1 (Marcian) and D.43.8.3.pr. (Celsus).

[242] Although this is said to be altered by law and custom. See Bankton, *Institute* I.3.2.

that the shore is no different from ordinary land, that is to say that it is originally owned by the Crown and is not *inter regalia* as to ownership.[243]

2-97.   There remain, however, inalienable public rights held by the Crown which allow access to the sea including the right of navigation, and of fishing for white fish and shellfish from the foreshore.[244] There is also a right of recreation but its extent is unclear.[245]

(IV) RIGHTS OVER THE PORTS AND HARBOURS

2-98.   Classified as *res publicae* in Roman law, ports and harbours were listed by the institutional writers in Scotland as *inter regalia*.[246] However, it was not the things themselves but the monopoly of establishing a port or harbour open for use by the public which was, and still is, held by the Crown and can be granted to private individuals.[247] The right of port and harbour is now viewed as a separate legal tenement.[248] A grant of port or harbour carries with it the obligation on the grantee to allow 'free' use of the port and the corresponding public right is held by the Crown.[249] The public right of 'free' use consists of a right of unimpeded access to the harbour, not use free of charge.[250]

(V) RIGHTS OF HIGHWAY

2-99.   Finally, and for the sake of completeness, it should be mentioned that highways, said to be among the *res publicae* in the *Digest*,[251] are described by the institutional writers as public things and as *inter regalia*.[252] However, unlike the other *res publicae*, where ownership often remains – as originally – with the Crown, the *solum* of highways frequently belongs to the owners of adjacent land,[253] and the public right of highway is held by the Crown as *regalia majora*.[254] The right is primarily one of passage between public places but may also include some ancillary rights to stay or hunt on the land.[255]

[243] See below, paras 3-22–3-40.
[244] Stair, *Institutions* II.1.5; *Earl of Stair v Austin* (1880) 8 R 183; *Duke of Argyll v Robertson* (1859) 22 D 261. See also Reid, *Property* para 525; Discussion Paper on the Law of the Foreshore and Seabed (n 228) paras 4.2 and 4.19.
[245] Discussion Paper on the Law of the Foreshore and Seabed (n 228) para 4.25.
[246] Bankton, *Institute* II.3.107–108; Erskine, *Institute* II.6.17; Bell, *Principles*, para 654. See also *Shetland Islands Council v Lerwick Port Authority* [2007] CSOH 5.
[247] Gordon & Wortley, *Land Law* para 7-04.
[248] Reid, *Property* paras 334–336.
[249] *Crown Estate Commissioners, Petitioners* 2010 SLT 741.
[250] *Crown Estate Commissioners, Petitioners* at 764.
[251] D.43.8.2.22 (Ulpian)
[252] Craig, *Jus Feudale* (n 37) 1.16.10; Erskine, *Institute* II.1.5 and II.6.17; Bell, *Principles* paras 638 and 659.
[253] Cusine & Paisley para 18.07. See also J Ferguson, *The Law of Roads, Streets and Rights of Way in Scotland* (1904) 8; *Galbreath v Armour* (1845) 4 Bell's App 274.
[254] Gordon, *Land Law* para 27-06.
[255] Cusine & Paisley para 18.09. See also *Hamilton v Dumfries and Galloway Council* 2009 SC 277 at 288–291.

This right would have been important for access to public rivers and the foreshore in the past. General access rights, however, are now contained in the Land Reform (Scotland) Act 2003.

(b) Statutory Public Rights

2-100. The Land Reform (Scotland) Act 2003[256] aims to 'establish statutory public rights of access to land for recreational and other purposes'[257] and it gives everyone the rights to cross land and to be on land for specified purposes.[258] Unlike common law rights, the statutory rights are held directly by the public.[259] These rights must be exercised responsibly.[260] All land is subject to the public rights except that specially excluded by section 6 of the Act. 'Land' is defined as including the foreshore and inland waters,[261] the latter being inland, non-tidal rivers and lochs as well as the banks and shores of such bodies of water.[262] The Act, therefore, does not confer rights over tidal rivers and lochs, the sea or the sea-bed.

2-101. The public rights contained in the 2003 Act co-exist and overlap with the common law public rights.[263] However, statutory public rights are different in scope. The 2003 Act gives a right of navigation over non-tidal rivers and lochs which is not merely for the purpose of passage but can also be recreational.[264] The banks of inland waters can also be used for purposes incidental to navigation. However, any vessel used may not be motorised.[265] The right to use inland waters and their banks for recreation allows swimming,[266] but unlike the common law, the Act does not give a right to fish for white fish or shellfish in inland waters[267] and it prohibits taking away

---

[256] On the 2003 Act generally see T Guthrie, 'Access Rights' in R Rennie (ed), *The Promised Land: Property Law Reform* (2008); M M Combe, 'Access to Land and Landownership' (2010) 14 *Edin LR* 106; J Fordyce, 'Land Reform (Scotland) Act 2003 – Pushing the Boundaries' 2010 *Jur Rev* 263; J A Lovett, 'Progressive Property in Action: The Land Reform (Scotland) Act 2003' (2011) 89 *Neb L Rev* 739.

[257] Land Reform (Scotland) Act 2003 preamble.

[258] Land Reform (Scotland) Act 2003 s 1(2)(a) and (b).

[259] Section 28 of the 2003 Act provides for the judicial determination of the extent and existence of the statutory public rights. In contrast, the common law rights can be enforced by a member of the public in an *actio popularis* or by the Crown as a trustee of the public right. See Reid, *Property* para 515.

[260] Land Reform (Scotland) Act 2003 s 2.

[261] Land Reform (Scotland) Act 2003 s 32.

[262] Land Reform (Scotland) Act 2003 s 32.

[263] Public rights of access and public rights over the foreshore are specifically mentioned as being unaffected by the 2003 Act: s 5(3) and (4). See generally Discussion Paper on the Law of the Foreshore and Seabed (n 228) Part 4 for discussion.

[264] Land Reform (Scotland) Act 2003 s 1(3).

[265] Land Reform (Scotland) Act 2003 s 9(f). An exception to this is that a vessel may be motorised if constructed or adapted for use by a person who has a disability and is being used by such person.

[266] Discussion Paper on the Law of the Foreshore and Seabed (n 228) para 4.22.

[267] Land Reform (Scotland) Act 2003 s 9(c).

anything on the land for commercial purposes or profit.²⁶⁸ With respect to the foreshore, the 2003 Act gives the right to cross the foreshore, remain on it and use it for recreational purposes. Again, however, there is no statutory right to fish for white fish or shellfish.²⁶⁹ As can be seen, the new public rights greatly increase the access of the public to communal things and extend the common law rights over the foreshore and non-tidal rivers.

2-102.   The co-existence of the statutory and common law public rights and the potential confusion this may cause have resulted in the Scottish Law Commission proposing that common law rights be abolished and replaced by statutory public rights.²⁷⁰ This would also put an end to the awkward theory of the Crown's trusteeship of certain public rights, which is a result of the historical interaction between *res publicae* and the *regalia*. Instead, the public would hold the rights directly. The new statutory public rights which the Scottish Law Commission proposes would maintain, or even extend, the existing common law rights²⁷¹ and so further entrench the rights of the public to access and use communal things.

G. CONCLUSION

2-103.   In response to Gray's criticism that an insufficient number of property lawyers consider the core issue of which objects are exempt from private ownership and why, this chapter has attempted to revive the discussion of this issue in Scots law. In tracing the development of the Division of Things from Roman law through the institutional writers to the present day, it becomes clear that there is a historical framework on which to build a modern Division of Things. Yet, the modern exposition of the Division provided above is only a starting point for a broader debate which cannot be pursued in this book. To demonstrate the possible scale of the issue, Gray provides a list of things which are potentially outwith ownership, ranging from 'human body parts and cells to fecundity, reproductive capacity and live babies; from the exploitable aspects of the human persona to the asset of commercial product goodwill; from leisure options to the eventual cure for AIDs and cancer; from Antarctica to outer space'.²⁷² Inevitably, the analysis presented here is only a partial representation of things which are exempt from private ownership in Scots law.

2-104.   Any discussion of a modern Division of Things must respect the two principles which have been regarded as paramount throughout this chapter and which were evident from Roman law to the present day, although the

²⁶⁸ Land Reform (Scotland) Act 2003 s 9(e).
²⁶⁹ Land Reform (Scotland) Act 2003 s 9(c).
²⁷⁰ Report on the Law of the Foreshore and Seabed (Scot Law Com No 190, 2003) para 3.7. See also Land Reform Review Group, *The Land of Scotland and the Common Good* (2014; http://www.scotland.gov.uk/Resource/0045/00451597.pdf) paras 29.16-29.22.
²⁷¹ See Report on the Law of the Foreshore and Seabed (n 270) Appendix A: Draft Sea, Shore and Inland Waters (Scotland) Bill.
²⁷² K Gray, 'Property Law in Thin Air' (1991) 50 *CLJ* 252 at 299.

manner in which these principles are maintained has changed over time: the recognition of the limitations of ownership over certain essential natural resources, and the protection of public rights over objects which have a valuable role in society. Further, these principles are interdependent as public rights are necessary to access communal things. From both of these principles, the golden thread which underlies this book can be deduced. Water is a resource which, due to its critical importance to humankind, should, in general, be exempt from private ownership, and the focus of water law should instead be on ensuring the availability of water for general use.[273]

[273] These principles are explicitly recognised in South Africa where private ownership of water has been abolished and the state is the public trustee of water. See the South Africa National Water Act 1998 s 3 and Fundamental Principles and Objectives for a New Water Law in South Africa (1996) Principle 3.

3 The Ownership of Land Beneath Water

A. INTRODUCTION

3-01.   In the previous chapter, it was established that water in its natural state is a communal thing incapable of ownership. Being incapable of ownership, it also cannot be subject to subordinate real rights. The only right which anyone has, and indeed everyone does have, to water in its natural state is the right of appropriation. Therefore, landowners have no rights to water beyond those held by the public, although in practice they have the best opportunity to use water and exercise the right of appropriation because they are not reliant on public rights to access water.[1] However, ownership of land beneath water is burdened by certain obligations enforceable by other landowners regarding the use of water.

3-02. Establishing the ownership of land beneath water is an essential precursor to discussions about these obligations and correlative rights. Despite this, for a prolonged period of time, the law was unclear. Determining the ownership of the sea-bed, foreshore, and the *alveus* of public rivers and lochs was intimately connected with the categories of the Division of Things. The ownership of the *alveus* of private rivers and lochs was also the subject of confusion but this was due to the developing doctrine of common interest – which will be the subject of three chapters later in this book. This chapter seeks to undertake a comprehensive investigation of the history of the ownership of land under water and to outline the modern law.

B. ROMAN LAW

3-03. The Roman texts on the Division of Things were discussed in the previous chapter. There are few direct and clear statements on the ownership of land beneath water. Lakes and perennial rivers were enumerated among the *res publicae*.[2] Various interpretations of what this might mean were discussed earlier.[3] It is unclear whether the categorisation related to ownership of the *alveus*, of the body of water as a separate entity, or merely to public rights of use. It is likely that the focus of the classification was public rights of use and, therefore, that the ownership of the *alveus* of rivers and lakes was unresolved. Although it was clear that river banks were owned by the adjacent landowners,[4] the *alveus* may have been owned by adjacent landowners, by the state, or have been ownerless.

3-04. In Roman law, under the doctrine of alluvion, which is considered in the following chapter, the swelling of a public (perennial) river or the drying up of a river-bed resulted in a change of ownership of land.[5] In the former case the adjacent landowners lost the part of their land which became covered by water;[6] in the latter case the newly dry land 'becomes the property of the neighbouring owners'.[7] These rules fit well with the *alveus* of public rivers being either ownerless or state-owned[8] for if the bed of a public river was already owned by adjacent landowners, alluvion would only effect a change in status – from dry land to *alveus* and *vice versa* – rather than in

---

[1] See the comments in *Patrick v Napier* (1867) 5 M 683 at 698–699.

[2] D.1.8.5.pr. (Gaius) on rivers; D.43.14.1.pr.-3 (Ulpian) on lakes.

[3] See above, paras 2-07–2-08.

[4] D.1.8.5. pr. (Gaius); D.43.12.3.pr. (Paul).

[5] See below, para 4-03.

[6] D.41.30.3 (Pomponius).

[7] D.41.1.30.1 (Pomponius).

[8] See D.41.1.7.5 (Gaius); D.41.1.30.1 (Pomponius); D.41.1.38 (Alfenus Varus); D.7.4.23 (Javolenus) regarding the loss of a usufruct of ground covered by a river.

ownership. However, when the ownership of islands arising in public rivers was discussed, it was stated that such islands belonged to the adjacent landowners in accordance with the position of the *medium filum* of the river, which seems to contradict the idea that the *alveus* was state-owned or ownerless. De Zulueta suggests the rules as to islands are the result of a kind of 'dormant ownership' of the adjacent landowners in the *alveus*[9] while Buckland concludes that the classical lawyers were reaching a consensus that the *alveus* of public rivers was owned by the adjacent landowners.[10]

3-05.   The sea was described as *res communis*, which the previous chapter interpreted as meaning incapable of private ownership while questioning whether this categorisation applied to the mass of water or the sea-bed or both. Islands rising in the sea were ownerless, which may indicate that the sea-bed belonged to no one.[11] The shore, which was mentioned as being both *res communes* and *res publicae*, was bluntly described as ownerless.[12]

3-06.   A private river – being in Roman law one which was not perennial – was said to be no different from other private property.[13] This implies that the *alveus* of private rivers was owned by the adjacent landowners but gives no guidance as to the extent of the ownership when a river is a boundary between two estates.

C. SCOTS LAW

3-07.   In Scots law also, the collection of often sparse and contradictory authority makes the task of determining the ownership of land beneath water a challenging one. An added difficulty is the concept of regalian rights. As explained in the previous chapter, the *regalia* are competences and property rights historically accorded to the King. Yet, not everything the Crown owns is *inter regalia*: for example, the Crown is taken to have been the original owner of all land but most land is not *inter regalia*.[14] Further, there is a difference between rights which are *regalia majora* and inalienable, and those which are *regalia minora* and capable of alienation provided this is through express grant.[15] The theory of the *regalia* outlined by Craig suggests that the

---

[9] F de Zulueta, *Digest 41, 1 & 2* (1950) 48.

[10] W W Buckland, *Textbook of Roman Law from Augustus to Justinian* (3rd edn, P Stein (ed), 1963) 212.

[11] D.41.1.73 (Gaius); Justinian's *Institutes* 2.1.22. However, as the rules on islands are contradictory with respect to public rivers, this perhaps should not be relied upon.

[12] Justinian's *Institutes* 2.1.5.

[13] D.43.12.1.4 (Ulpian).

[14] See also Gordon, *Land Law* para 27-08 and, for example, the overview of the urban estate owned by the Crown which is managed by the Crown Estate Commissioners in Crown Estate, Annual Report and Accounts (2014; http://www.thecrownestate.co.uk/media/300059/annual-report-and-accounts-2014.pdf) 6.

[15] This distinction was established at an early stage, Craig, *Jus Feudale* 1.16.43–45. On the requirement of an express grant see Stair, *Institutions* II.3.60; Bankton, *Institute* II.3.107; Erskine, *Institute* II.6.13; Bell, *Principles* para 737. The need for an express grant may have been subject to an exception regarding barony titles at one point, see Stair, *Institutions* II.3.61; Bankton, *Institute* II.3.86.

regalia majora are closely connected to government and, where appropriate, such as with respect to highways and navigable rivers, the Crown holds them in the public interest, resulting in public rights of use.[16] By contrast, the *regalia minora*, such as salmon fishings, can be exploited by the Crown for financial gain.[17] Some things can be *inter regalia minora*, or even not regalian at all, as to ownership but subject to public rights which are *inter regalia majora*.[18]

(1) Sea-Bed

(a) A Dearth of Authority

3-08.   When the institutional writers discuss the sea in the context of the Division of Things, some make comments which may be interpreted as meaning that the sea is owned by the Crown[19] but, as with the Roman jurists, it is unclear whether they are referring to the water or the sea-bed. In truth, these writers seem more concerned with public rights than with ownership. In considering coal-mining and islands arising in the sea, Craig seems to imply that the Crown owns the sea-bed.[20] Bankton's analysis of islands may also suggest Crown ownership whereas Stair may consider the sea-bed to be ownerless.[21]

3-09.   There is little discussion in case law. Rankine commented on the 'almost entire absence of litigation, both here and in England, in regard to rights in the sea, except as incidental to questions respecting the foreshore. This is all the more extraordinary, inasmuch as it has been found possible and profitable in many parts of both countries to extend mines for long distances beyond the foreshore.'[22] The view in the case law that did emerge was fairly unanimously in favour of ownership by the Crown.[23] In *Officers of*

---

[16] Craig, *Jus Feudale* 1.16.10–11.

[17] Craig *Jus Feudale*1.16.38. This appears to be contrary to the *jus commune* understanding, Van der Vyver, *Étatisation* 267–268.

[18] See Gordon, *Land Law* paras 27-06–27-07 (caution should be exercised regarding Gordon's classification of the foreshore) and discussion further below.

[19] Craig, *Jus Feudale* 1.15.13; Mackenzie, *Institutions* II.1; Forbes, *Great Body* Vol 1, 342; Bankton, *Institute* I.3.3; Erskine, *Institute* II.1.6.

[20] Craig, *Jus Feudale* 1.15.14 and 2.8.20, and below, para 4-09.

[21] Bankton, *Institute* II.1.10; Stair, *Institutions* II.1.33.

[22] Rankine, *Landownership* 253.

[23] *Ramsay v York Building Company* (1763) 5 Brown's Supp 557; *Officers of State v Smith* (1846) 8 D 711 at 723; (1851) 13 D 854 at 873 (aff'd by the House of Lords (1859) 3 Macq 419); *Duchess of Sutherland v Watson* (1868) 6 M 199 at 209, 213 and 215; *Agnew v Lord Advocate* (1873) 11 M 309 at 322 and 327; *Lord Advocate v Clyde Navigation Trs* (1891) 19 R 174; *Lord Advocate v Wemyss* (1899) 2 F (HL) 1 at 8–9; *Crown Estate Commissioners v Fairlie Yacht Club* 1976 SC 161 at 163–165; *Argyll and Bute District Council v Secretary of State for Scotland* 1977 SLT 33 at 35; *Shetland Salmon Farmers Association v Crown Estate Commissioners* 1991 SLT 166. However, see Lord Justice-Clerk Hope's opinion in *Gammell v Commissioners of Woods and Forests* (1851) 13 D 854 at 868: 'where, I ask, is the authority for this very novel and dangerous doctrine, which obliterates at once the whole doctrine of *jus regale*, and treats not only the whole land, but the bed of the sea, as the private property of the Crown, and the right of fishing in the sea as a source of profit or revenue to the Crown?'

State v Smith,[24] discussed further below in relation to the foreshore, it was said by Lord Cockburn: 'I know of nothing which I should think might be predicted with greater safety, or that less requires formal proof, than that the bed of the British sea belongs in property to the British Crown.' Initially it was thought that the Crown's ownership rested on feudal principles[25] but the modern view, established in *Shetland Salmon Farmers Association v Crown Estate Commissioners*,[26] is that it is based on the royal prerogative.[27] As a result it is unaffected by the abolition of feudal tenure in 2004.[28]

3-10.   Erskine and Bell state that the 'sea' is *inter regalia* and held in trust for the public[29] but it is unclear whether this relates to ownership of the sea-bed or public rights. At one point case law suggested that the sea-bed was *inter regalia majora* as to ownership and therefore could not be disponed to private persons.[30] However, it has since been indicated that the sea-bed can be alienated, making it *inter regalia minora*.[31] It is rather the public rights over the sea-bed that the Crown holds in trust for the public which are *inter regalia majora* and cannot be disponed.[32] As Rankine noted, the lack of detailed authority is surprising due to the economic value of the sea-bed which has been realised over the centuries.[33]

(b) Modern Law

3-11.   The Crown owns the sea-bed under territorial waters,[34] which reach 12 international nautical miles from the baselines from which they are measured,[35] and inwards *inter fauces terrae*.[36] As the sea-bed is *inter regalia minora*

---

[24] (1846) 8 D 711 at 723.

[25] At 723; Rankine, *Landownership* 251 and 253.

[26] 1991 SLT 166. See also *Lord Advocate v Clyde Navigation Trs* (1891) 19 R 174 at 183.

[27] For consideration of this see G Marston, *Marginal Seabed* (1981) 272–285.

[28] Abolition of Feudal Tenure etc (Scotland) Act 2000.

[29] Erskine, *Institute* II.1.6; Bell, *Principles* paras 638–639. See below, paras 3-22–3-27.

[30] *Agnew v Lord Advocate* (1873) 11 M 309 at 322; *Lord Advocate v Wemyss* (1899) 2 F (HL) 1 at 8–9.

[31] *Crown Estate Commissioners v Fairlie Yacht Club* 1976 SC 161 at 163–166; *Shetland Salmon Farmers Association v Crown Estate Commissioners* 1991 SLT 166 at 174 and 178. Before this see *Erskine v Magistrates of Montrose* (1819) Hume 558 (which may concern a disposition of the sea-bed); *Officers of State v Smith* (1846) 8 D 711 at 723; *Duchess of Sutherland v Watson* (1868) 6 M 199 at 213.

[32] Rankine, *Landownership* 248 and 252; Reid, *Property* para 310; Gordon, *Land Law* paras 27-06–27-07.

[33] Whitty comments the sea-bed was important for harbours, oyster-beds, mussel-beds and coal mining as early as the 16th century, Whitty, 'Water' 436. For consideration of controversy in cases south of the border see Whitty, 'Water' 436–437; G Marston, *The Marginal Seabed* (1981).

[34] *Shetland Salmon Farmers Association v Crown Estate Commissioners* 1991 SLT 166 at 174 (Lord Justice-Clerk Ross).

[35] Territorial Sea Act 1987 s 1(1)(a). See the map showing the 12-mile boundary reprinted on the front cover of Land Reform Review Group, *The Land of Scotland and the Common Good* (2014; http://www.scotland.gov.uk/Resource/0045/00451597.pdf). See also Gordon & Wortley, *Land Law* para 6-02. For a historical discussion of the extent of territorial waters see Ferguson 10–14.

as to ownership, it will not pass as a pertinent to sea-board property and an express grant is required. If an *a non domino* disposition is presented for registration in the Land Register, the Crown must be notified, and its objection is then sufficient to prevent registration.[37] In the event that registration proceeds, the applicant's title is put beyond challenge by possession for 20 years against the Crown and 10 years against private parties.[38] Until that time, the entry in the title sheet will be marked as provisional.[39] It is suggested that possession may involve operations like mining and the erection of piers or harbours.

3-12.   Section 113(1) of the Land Registration etc (Scotland) Act 2012 clarifies the previous doubt about operational extent of the Land Register in defining 'land' as including the sea-bed.[40] To enable mapping of a sea-bed plot the deed inducing registration must include (i) a verbal description of the plot, (ii) a description of the plot using the projected coordinate system OSGB 1936 | British National Grid (EPSG:27700) to provide the coordinates of the plot, preferably in the form of a table, which will then be used in the property description on the title sheet, and (iii) a plan defining the boundaries of the plot including a location plan showing how the plot relates to the coast of Scotland.[41]

3-13.   The sea-bed, for many years exploited for coal and then offshore oil and fish farming, is now becoming central in the creation of renewable energy in the form of wind and tidal power. The Crown owns almost all of the sea-bed around Scotland, and it is managed on its behalf by the Crown Estate Commissioners.[42] The Crown Estate has a policy to lease rather than sell the

---

[36] 'Between the jaws of the land': *Lord Advocate v Clyde Navigation Trs* (1891) 19 R 174. See also Scottish Law Commission Report on the *Law of the Foreshore and Sea Bed* (Scot Law Com No 190, 2003) paras 2.3–2.7. The Scottish Law Commission has proposed that a clear statutory statement of the extent of the Crown's ownership of the sea-bed would be desirable. Rivers and lochs will be treated separately below, paras 3-45–3-86.

[37] Land Registration etc (Scotland) Act 2012 ss 43(4) and 45.

[38] Prescription and Limitation (Scotland) Act 1973 s 1. See also Reid, *Property* para 316; Gordon & Wortley, *Land Law* paras 3-27–3-28 on the foreshore.

[39] Land Registration etc (Scotland) Act 2012 s 44(1).

[40] Regarding the lack of clarity in the previous law, see Report on Land Registration Vol 1 (Scot Law Com No 222, 2010) paras 4.61–4-62. Interestingly, the definition of 'land in Scotland' in s 4(3) of the Land and Buildings Transaction Tax (Scotland) Act 2013 excludes land below the mean low water mark with the result that no LBTT will be chargeable on transactions regarding the sea-bed. I am indebted to Bob Langridge for this observation.

[41] Registers of Scotland, General Guidance, *The Cadastral Map: The Land Register and Land Covered by Water* (2014; http://2012act.ros.gov.uk/guidance/General_Guidance_CM_water_boundaries.pdf).

[42] Crown Estate Act 1961. See Crown Estate, *Scotland Report* (2014; http://www.thecrownestate.co.uk/media/300060/scotland-report-2014.pdf) 3. The operation of the Crown Estate in Scotland has been under significant scrutiny in recent years after its profile was raised during the Calman Commission 2007–2009. For criticism and recommendations as to devolution, see Scottish Affairs Committee of the UK Parliament, *The Crown Estate in Scotland*, Seventh Report of Session (2010–12) (2012) 63 and *The Crown Estate in Scotland: follow up*, Fifth Report of Session (2013–14) (2014) 21–23. See also the proposals in Land Reform Review Group, *The Land of Scotland and the Common Good* (n 35) paras 11.1–11.40.

sea-bed and projects have included leasing a number of sites for harnessing wave and tidal power in the Pentland Firth and Orkney waters.[43] Following the report of the Smith Commission in November 2014, it is expected that the management of the sea-bed and other parts of the Crown Estate's economic assets will be transferred to the Scottish Parliament and then further devolved to local authorities.[44]

(2) Foreshore

3-14.   Ownership of the foreshore has been a matter of prolonged controversy in Scotland.[45] In Roman law the shore was described as both *res publicae* and *res communes*,[46] indicating indecision about whether to classify the shore as incapable of ownership – like the air or the sea – or subject to public rights of use – like harbours and public rivers. Uncertainty is also encountered in Scots law but the debate centred on whether the shore was owned by the Crown or by adjacent proprietors. The shore takes an intermediate place between dry and submerged land. It is necessary for access to the sea – hence the need for public rights thereon – but capable of occupation and cultivation by adjacent landowners. Should it therefore be treated in the same way as the sea-bed or as a pertinent of the adjacent land?

(a) Craig, Stair, Forbes and Bankton

3-15.   Craig defines the shore as the area covered by the highest winter tides,[47] a view drawn from Roman law.[48] Stair adds that the greatest winter tide 'must be understood of the ordinary tides, and not of extraordinary spring tides'.[49] Although this statement is potentially ambiguous, it is suggested that, because Stair is clarifying what the 'greatest tide' means, he is referring to ordinary spring tides[50] and not ordinary neap tides.[51] Forbes

[43] See Crown Estate, *Wave and Tidal Energy in the Pentland Firth and Orkney Waters: How the Projects Could Be Built* (2011; http://www.thecrownestate.co.uk/media/71431/pentland_firth_how_the_projects_could_be_built.pdf).

[44] *Report of the Smith Commission for further devolution of powers to the Scottish Parliament* (2014; www.smith-commission.scot) paras 32–35. This has been accepted by the UK Government: see *Scotland in the United Kingdom: An enduring settlement* (Cm 8990, 2015) para 5.5 and is being implemented in the Scotland Bill.

[45] Its management is still a topic of debate, see n 42.

[46] See above, para 2-12; *res communes*: D.1.8.2.1 (Marcian); *res publicae*: D.39.2.24.pr. (Ulpian).

[47] Craig, *Jus Feudale* 1.15.15.

[48] Justinian's *Institutes* 2.1.3; D.50.16.112 (Javolenus). There is authority which is earlier than Craig. Balfour, *Practicks* 626 discusses cases 'Anent the flude mark' and in J Skene, *De Verborum Significatione* (1597) 'Ware' 141–142 there are comments relating to the shore. However, the statements are so vague and open to interpretation that little can said about them with certainty and they will not be considered here.

[49] Stair, *Institutions* II.1.5.

[50] 'Spring' tides here does not refer to the season but to the bi-monthly alignment of the sun, earth and moon which results in the maximum range of the tide.

[51] The neap tides are when the sun and moon are separated by 90 degrees and the tide's range is at a minimum. Erskine defines the shore as 'the sand over which the sea flows in common tides', Erskine, *Institute* II.6.17, but this could mean the neap or spring tides.

explicitly states that the shore is that which is covered by the ordinary spring tides.[52]

3-16.   As with the sea, early institutional writers are more concerned with public rights than with ownership. Craig does not mention the shore as *inter regalia* and categorises it instead as a public thing and subject to public rights of use.[53] Stair says that the shore is open to all 'common uses' such as casting anchors, unloading goods and drying nets but that it remains 'proper, not only as to jurisdiction, but as to houses, or works built thereupon; and as to minerals, coals, or the like found therein, and so is not in whole common, but some uses thereof only'.[54] This may mean only that houses and minerals are capable of private ownership or, more likely, that the *solum* of the shore can be privately owned. [55] Forbes reproduces Stair's view despite including the shore within the category of 'Things Which Cannot Be Appropriated'.[56] Bankton says that the shore was defined as common in Roman law[57] and that this position has been altered by law and custom in Scots law[58] but the implications for ownership are left unexplored. Mines, minerals, sea-ware and stones are said to belong to the adjacent proprietor if this privilege is granted by the Crown but this may merely be a reference to the right to gather or mine such things.[59]

(b) Battles Over the Right to Kelp

3-17.   Early litigation mostly concerned the right to collect sea-weed. The harvesting of kelp was to become a significant industry in Scotland between 1750 and 1850 and establishing who had the right to collect it was an important issue.[60] However, the cases are often unclear as to whether the point being decided concerns the ownership of the shore or the servitude of wreck and ware.[61] In *Fullerton v Baillie*,[62] decided in 1697, the issue was whether

---

[52] Forbes, *Great Body* Vol 1, 342

[53] Craig, *Jus Feudale* 1.15.15. The shore was not on the list of *regalia* of Emperor Barbarossa from 1158.

[54] Stair, *Institutions* II.1.5.

[55] In Roman law, whatever was built on the shore belonged to the builder, D.41.1.14.pr. (Neratius).

[56] Forbes, *Great Body* Vol 1, 342.

[57] Bankton, *Institute* II.1.5.

[58] Bankton *Institute* I.3.2.

[59] Bankton *Institute* II.1.5. The right to wreck goods is said to be a consequence of the right of admiralty in the Crown, Bankton *Institute* I.3.3.

[60] On the kelp industry see M Gray, 'The Kelp Industry in the Highlands and Islands' (1951) 4 *Economic History Review* 200; J MacAskill, ' "A Silver Fringe?" The Crown, Private Proprietors and the Scottish Kelp Shores and the Scottish Foreshore Generally c1800–c1940.' Unpublished PhD Thesis (University of Aberdeen, 2003) (hereafter 'MacAskill, *Silver Fringe*').

[61] This servitude, which encompasses the right to take seaweed, is to be distinguished from the regalian right of wreck relating to shipwrecks. On the latter right see the leading case of *Lord Advocate v Hebden* (1868) 6 M 489 as well as Craig, *Jus Feudale* I.16.42–43; Stair, *Institutions* III.3.27; Bankton, *Institute* I.3.3; Erskine, *Institute* II.1.13; Bell, *Principles* para 670; Reid, *Property* paras 213 and 554–557. For discussion of the servitude see Cusine & Paisley para 3.88.

[62] (1697) Mor 13524.

the pursuer, who was infeft of a barony with the right of wreck and ware, had the right to exclude his neighbour from gathering sea-weed. The court made the reservation 'whatever the King might say against this pursuer'[63] before deciding that the pursuer had the right to exclude the defender unless the defender proved a servitude of wreck and ware. The court's reservation indicates that the Crown may have had some form of interest in the shore but this would not be considered further as the Crown was not a party to the litigation. However, it was not clear whether this decision was based on the pursuer having ownership of the shore or merely the servitude of wreck and ware.[64]

3-18.   Two further cases followed in the 1760s. *Earl of Morton v Covingtree*[65] concerned the right of the Earl's tenants to take kelp on the shores adjacent to Covingtree's land. Covingtree sought declarator of ownership of the shore and argued that, although the shore was *inter regalia*, it could be conveyed to private individuals. Indeed, a grant of land with wreck and ware adjacent to a shore implied 'an exclusive right to the shores adjacent to the lands, with the whole produce thereof, subject only to the uses of navigation, without the necessity of prescription to support it'.[66] Thus, no express grant of the shore was required.[67] The court decided that the Earl had no right to cut kelp on Covingtree's land but found a servitude established for taking kelp which had washed up on the shore. No mention was made of the ownership of the shore in the interlocutor of the court.

3-19.   In *Magistrates of Culross v Earl of Dundonald*[68] the Magistrates sought to establish their ownership of, and exclusive right to wreck and ware on, the shore beside their land which was bounded by the sea. They argued that the shore was a communal thing and was not *inter regalia* but, without much regard for consistency, that the Crown could convey the shore as far as was compatible with public rights. The court found that the Magistrates had the exclusive right to wreck and ware, but again whether this decision was based on ownership, or what the requirements of transfer might be, was not specified. Lord Gardenston acknowledged the economic significance of the question by saying that if a grant of lands bounded by the sea and followed by possession 'does not comprehend the shore, there is a valuable property still in the hands of the crown, which is supposed to be in the subjects having estates on the coast; I mean the whole seaware all over Scotland'.[69] Lord Monboddo indicated that the shore was *inter regalia* as we 'follow the

---

[63] At 13524.
[64] At this time there was the possibility of arguing that a barony carried the shore with it as a pertinent if the shore was seen to be *regalia minora*: Stair, *Institutions* II.3.61; Bankton, *Institute* II.3.86.
[65] (1760) Mor 13528. It is noted (at 13528): 'Of late, the manufacture of kelp was introduced into that country.'
[66] At 13529.
[67] This was contrary to authority which suggested that an express grant was required to convey the *regalia minora* in the absence of a barony: Stair, *Institutions* II.3.60; Bankton, *Institutes* II.3.107.
[68] (1769) Mor 12810, Hailes 291.
[69] (1769) Hailes 291 at 291.

constitution of the Emperor Frederic I'.[70] The shore was, however, not mentioned on this list of *regalia* from 1158.[71] The Magistrates interpreted the decision as meaning they had ownership because they later sold and leased areas of the shore.[72]

3-20.   Although these cases recognise the Crown's interest in the shore, other cases show less deference. In *Duke of Roxburgh v Magistrates of Dunbar*[73] from 1713 it was found that the Duke could not build a wall on the shore which hindered public passage but the court declared the Duke's right of property in the shore without debate. Further, *Hall v Dirleton* in 1772, briefly noted by Tait, makes no mention of the Crown's interest. It is said 'as to the shore, within the flood-mark, covered at flood, and bare at ebb, it would appear that it remains the property of the contiguous heritor, subject to the common uses of navigation'.[74]

3-21.   The developments up to this point show a lack of clarity about whether the Crown owned the shore as *regalia*[75] or upon some other basis, and what the requirements were for transfer to private persons. The possibility that the Crown owned the shore as *regalia majora* which is incapable of transfer does not seem to have been considered. Although the cases often begin with consideration of the wording of Crown charters, the emphasis on the Crown's potential interest has notably diminished by the end of the 18th century.

(c) The Extent of Regalian Rights

3-22.   Erskine is the first institutional writer to describe the shore as *inter regalia*.[76] In his view the shore should not be defined as a communal thing because it is capable of appropriation. He continues:

'If our kings have that right of sovereignty in the narrow sea, which is affirmed by all our writers, and consequently in the shore as an accessory of the sea, it must differ much in its effects from private property, which may be disposed of or sold at the owner's pleasure; for the king holds both the sea and its shore as a trustee for the public. Both therefore are to be ranked in the same class with

---

[70] At 291.

[71] See above, para 2-14.

[72] See *Magistrates of Culross v Geddes* (1809) Hume 554.

[73] (1713) Mor 10883.

[74] (1772) 5 Brown's Supp 557.

[75] An odd case around this time which does not concern kelp is *Bruce v Rashiehill* (1714) Mor 9342. This involved 'sea-greens'. Although sea-greens have been more recently described as saltings or strips of pasture covered only by occasional tides in *Aitken's Trs v Caledonian Railway Co* (1904) 6 F 465, in *Bruce* the area in question was 'for the most part every tide, and in spring and high tides, entirely overflown' (at 9344). Thus, the area was part of the shore but the court did not seem to regard it as such. As a result, there is little guidance to be taken from the decision that this area was not *inter regalia* and was carried as part and pertinent of the adjacent land.

[76] Contrary to Whitty, 'Water' 433–434, the shore was not always described as *inter regalia* and Erskine does not state that the shore is *regalia minora*.

several other subjects which by the Roman law were public but are by our feudal plan deemed *regalia*, or rights belonging to the crown.'[77]

The primary role of the Crown, on this view, is as guardian of public rights. Subsequent case law considered the meaning of this account.[78] Crown trusteeship is not necessarily inconsistent with private ownership.[79] Earlier in the same passage, Erskine makes an analogy between the shore and river banks[80] – the latter being owned by the adjacent landowners – and adds at a later point in his *Institute* that landowners next to the sea 'inclose as their own property grounds far within the sea-mark'.[81] In the passage quoted above, Erskine could be using the word 'trustee' not literally but as a metaphor for an interest which is limited to protecting public rights. Such an interest would seem to be *inter regalia majora* and incapable of alienation despite the transfer of the foreshore itself to private parties. This analysis allowed public rights to continue over the shore after alienation to private parties which is consistent with *Duke of Roxburgh v Magistrates of Dunbar*,[82] discussed above at para 3-20.

3-23.   Even if the Crown's trusteeship of public rights was accepted to be *inter regalia majora*, it did not follow that its ownership rights in the foreshore – those rights which were freely transferrable – were likewise regalian. The foreshore might be owned by the Crown as 'ordinary' property in the same way as dry land. The distinction was important mainly for conveyancing. If the foreshore was *inter regalia minora*, it could be carried only by express grant; if not, it was capable of being carried without express mention as a part and pertinent.

3-24.   In case law, there is little evidence that the shore is *regalia minora* as to ownership. *Innes v Downie*[83] concerned a shelly bank which was uncovered only at the low ebb of the spring tides. The owner of the adjacent dry land wished to prevent the public from taking the shells (which were used as fertiliser).[84] Lord President Campbell found the shelly bank to be owned by the adjacent landowner. To the Lord President it was beyond doubt that the shore was Innes' property and that the bank was owned through alluvion.[85] This case was later relied on by the Lord Ordinary in *Kerr v Dickson*[86] where

---

[77] Erskine, *Institute* II.1.6.

[78] In *Smart v Magistrates of Dundee* (1797) 3 Pat 606 at 608 it was argued that the Crown was trustee of the shore. For further consideration in case law see below.

[79] Contrary to Reid, *Property* para 514, it was not clear that the shore was *regalia majora* in property at this time. See also the discussion by the Lord Ordinary in *Paterson v Marquis of Ailsa* (1846) 8 D 752 at 757–758.

[80] Erskine, *Institute* II.1.6.

[81] Erskine *Institute* II.6.17; Ae MacKay 'The Foreshore Question' (1867) 11 *Journal of Jurisprudence* 75 at 81 states: 'The supposition that Erskine is here stating a practice contrary to law is unreasonable.'

[82] (1713) Mor 10883.

[83] (1807) Hume 552.

[84] Although not mentioned in the case, as the bank was only uncovered in exceptional tides, it was really part of the sea-bed and should have been found to be property of the Crown.

[85] (1807) Hume 552 at 553. Alluvion will be discussed below in Ch 4.

[86] (1840) 3 D 154 at 160. This statement was *obiter dictum* but not explicitly mentioned by their Lordships on appeal who affirmed the judgment of the Lord Ordinary.

it was said that 'the sea-beach or rocks within the flood-mark are not inter jura regalia, but subjects of private property for all purposes not inconsistent with the public uses'. Such confident views are striking in light of the preceding uncertainty about the Crown's interest. *Innes v Downie* was decided when the price of kelp was at its peak and so the Lord President's comments may have had an economic agenda to support landowners who had coastal estates on which kelp was being harvested to great profit. Other judges in the same case were more cautious, emphasising that this was a grant of barony which included the lesser *regalia* by implication[87] or expressing doubt as to Innes' title to the shore.[88]

3-25.   A number of cases tackled the conveyancing implications of this debate. On orthodox principles a piece of land bounded by the 'sea' or a 'river' would include the foreshore.[89] However, it was also established at an early stage that a 'sea-shore' boundary also carried the shore.[90] This is unexpected because, when property is said to be 'bounded by' an object, the object is generally taken to be excluded.[91] These examples cannot be classified as instances of express grant in a strict sense – because the foreshore is not mentioned – but as an application of a rule of construction that using certain words conveys the shore by implication.[92] In *Macalister v Campbell*[93] the court went further, deciding that even where property next to the sea was conveyed without any mention of a boundary of the sea or shore, this was sufficient to convey the shore. Lord Gillies said 'the conveyance of an estate, which is notoriously bounded by the sea, conveys the shore as effectually as if the words "bounded by the sea" were in the charter.... I think it is probable

---

[87] Lords Hermand and Bannatyne.

[88] Lord Meadowbank.

[89] See *Magistrates of Culross v Earl of Dundonald* (1769) Mor 12810, Hailes 291; *Magistrates of Culross v Geddes* (1809) Hume 554; *Campbell v Brown* 18 Nov 1813 FC.

[90]*Magistrates of Culross v Geddes*; *Boucher v Crawford* 30 Nov 1814 FC; *Cameron v Ainslie* (1848) 10 D 446 (a boundary by 'sea-beach' here was said to be the same as the 'sea-shore'); *Hunter v Lord Advocate* (1869) 7 M 899 at 912–913. Although regarding *Boucher*, Bell mentions that the case was appealed to the House of Lords and was to be reversed but on the death of one of the parties, the judgment was not signed: Bell, *Illustrations from Adjudged Cases of the Principles of the Law of Scotland* (1836–1838) Vol 2, 2. Thus, the case should not be relied on as authority. In *Gordon v Suttie* 1837 15 S 1037 the shore was excluded due to being outwith the measurements provided in the conveyance. See other cases of limited grants excluding the shore: *Kerr v Dickson* (1840) 3 D 154 (aff'd (1842) 1 Bell's App 499) (bounded by the 'sea-wall'); *Magistrates of St Monance v Mackie* (1845) 7 D 852 (bounded by 'the common passage and full sea' and 'the full sea, the High Street intervening').

[91] *Smart v Magistrates of Dundee* (1797) 3 Pat 606, 8 Bro PC 119, 3 ER 481 where a property was bounded by tenements; Ae MacKay 'The Foreshore Question' (1867) 11 *Journal of Jurisprudence* 75 at 78–79; A M Bell, *Lectures on Conveyancing* (3rd edn, 1882) Vol 1, 599–600. Generally, property bounded by the sea-flood did not include the shore: see *Smart v Magistrates of Dundee*; *Berry v Holden* (1840) 3 D 205. However, see *Leven v Magistrates of Burntisland* (1812) Hume 555 but it is unclear whether this case is based on ownership or on the right to wreck and ware.

[92] Compare Gordon, *Land Law* para 4-26.

[93] (1837) 15 S 490.

that the titles of many of the largest proprietors there may contain no words whatever expressly stating that the sea is their boundary, which is nevertheless notoriously the fact.'[94] Other judges, however, were less bold and suggested that possession of the shore was a factor to be considered in deciding whether Macalister's boundary extended to the shore.[95]

3-26.   There were differing opinions in the later institutional writers. Both Bell and Hume seem to regard the shore as *inter regalia* and describe the shore as held in trust for public uses[96] but both give these terms their own interpretation with regard to the shore. Hume apparently regards the shore as *inter regalia minora*. He describes the Crown's interest as 'not exclusive of a power of disposal in his Majesty, under the provision that it is exercised with sound discretion, and so as not to hinder or impede those uses in which the public have a material concern'.[97] The Crown owns the shore and can dispone it but the new owner is then burdened with the same obligations of guardianship as regards facilitating public use and maintaining the subject.[98] To acquire ownership, Hume says there needs to be an express grant or the land needs to be declared as 'bounded by the sea, or the flood,[99] or the sea shore'.[100] However, he continues: 'If, on the contrary, his charter do not contain these or the like favourable expressions – or if it directly and *nominatim* give him such shores and sands (rocks and crags) – this grant shall be valid if confirmed and protected by long possession'.[101] This suggests even when the titles are silent, the shore can be acquired through prescription. 'In short the proper shore is *inter regalia*, but still in this qualified sense that his Majesty by his charters bearing the suitable words, may bestow the exclusive privilege of such portions and articles of its produce as may be profitable to an individual, under provision always that possession follow, and that the public uses of the strand for navigation and passage, and so forth, are not impeded or interfered with.'[102] This provides a neat compromise between the interests of the Crown and the adjacent landowners.

---

[94] At 493.

[95] Lord President Hope and Lord Mackenzie.

[96] Hume, *Lectures* IV 258; Bell, *Principles* para 638. Hume seems to suggest that the shore is only that which is covered by the neap tides: Hume, *Lectures* IV 256. This definition was not accepted by the courts: see below, para 3-40.

[97] Hume, *Lectures* IV 258.

[98] Hume, *Lectures* IV 241–242. This solution offered by Hume is said to be the 'simplest course' by Reid but it has not been adopted in the modern law: Reid, *Property* para 514.

[99] This is an even more generous interpretation than is developed through case law: see below, para 3-40.

[100] Hume, *Lectures* IV 255.

[101] Hume, *Lectures* IV 257. This sentence would be clearer if it read, 'or if it does not directly and *nominatim*'. That the present interpretation of Hume is correct is corroborated by a statement of Lord Cowan in *Agnew v Lord Advocate* (1873) 11 M 309 at 327. He says: 'Having attended [Hume's] lectures, of which I have preserved full notes, I can safely say that he held it indispensable, where the proprietor had only a general title from the Crown, that to give him a right to the shore he should have enjoyed immemorial and undisputed possession.'

[102] Hume, *Lectures* IV 258.

3-27. Bell's analysis is slightly different.[103] The shore is owned by the Crown and can be disponed after which 'nothing remains in the Crown but the public trust'.[104] This would suggest that the trusteeship as to public rights is *inter regalia majora*. The requirements for transfer of ownership are clarified over several editions of the *Principles*. Bell begins conservatively by stating in the first edition of 1829 that the shore 'is carried by the King's grant, subject to public use'.[105] This could mean that an express grant of the shore is required. However, by the third edition of 1833 Bell's view is that the shore is presumed to be granted as part and pertinent of the adjacent lands, unlike in English law.[106] This statement may be a reflection of a growing sense that the shore is not *inter regalia* as to ownership and should be viewed as an accessory to the adjacent land.

(d) Summary of Potential Status of the Shore

3-28. Following such a variety of views, it is useful to summarise the possible positions regarding the status of the shore:

- The shore is *inter regalia majora* as to trusteeship for public rights, but possibly also *inter regalia minora* as to ownership and so would require an express grant to be transferred to private persons.[107]
- The shore is *inter regalia majora* as to trusteeship for public rights. It is not *inter regalia minora* as to ownership but is carried as a part and pertinent with a grant of the adjacent lands.[108]
- The shore is *inter regalia minora* as to ownership with continuing obligations on the transferee in respect of public rights. Transfer requires either an express grant, an appropriate bounding description or a *habile* title plus possession for the period of positive prescription.[109]
- The shore is not *inter regalia* in any sense and is carried as a part and pertinent of adjacent lands but the owner cannot interfere with public rights.[110]

3-29. This variety of views is not surprising when put in comparative context. Van der Vyver has shown that there was also debate in French, German and Dutch jurisprudence as to whether the State owned the *regalia*, in what capacity, and whether the *regalia* were capable of alienation.[111] It is

---

[103] Bell does not explicitly state that he is discussing the *regalia*. However, it is suggested the Crown property discussed in paras 638–666 is mostly amongst the *regalia*: see Bell, *Principles* para 648.

[104] Bell, *Principles of the Law of Scotland* (1829) para 153.

[105] Bell, *Principles of the Law of Scotland* (1829) para 153.

[106] Bell, *Principles of the Law of Scotland* (3rd edn, 1833) para 642. It is said in *Officers of State v Smith* (1846) 8 D 711 at 722 that Bell changes his view as to the King being trustee of the shore between the first and second edition. However, in the first edition, Bell states that the shore is held in trust for the public.

[107] Erskine's view.

[108] Bell's view.

[109] Hume's view.

[110] The view which seemed to be developing in the case law.

[111] Van der Vyver, *Étatisation* 271–272.

interesting to note that it seems to be the institutional writers who were concerned with the concept of *regalia*. The courts, continuing the trend from the end of the 18th century, were still failing to give detailed consideration to the Crown's interest.

(e) The Crown Asserts its Rights

3-30. In light of the extensive use of the shore by adjacent landowners during the rise and fall of the kelp industry, a view grew up that the shore was owned by adjacent landowners as a pertinent of their land. Case law, such as it was, rather supported this position. MacAskill has outlined this view in detail.[112] Evidence ranges from contemporary sources,[113] leases of the shore, and methods of control used by landowners as well as kelp farmers seeking protection of their interests by government intervention during the decline of the industry in the 1820s.[114]

3-31. Just at the same time, however, the Crown began to assert its rights. The beginning of this period is marked by the Crown Lands Act 1829 which transferred authority for Crown possessions in England and Wales into the hands of the Commissioners of Woods, Forests and Land Revenues. This was followed by the Crown Lands (Scotland) Act 1833 which effected the same change for Scotland. The Crown was emboldened during this period by the publication in 1830 of Hall's *Essay on the Rights of the Crown and the Privileges of the Subject in the Sea Shores of the Realm* which argued strongly in favour of the Crown's ownership of the shore in England.[115] MacAskill states that 'there was certainly an underlying understanding on the part of the Crown, and in particular the Commissioners of Woods, that the Crown's interest in the foreshore generally extended beyond merely a right as trustee for the public'.[116] The Crown wished to establish that its role was not limited to a conservator for public rights and that the foreshore was not carried as part and pertinent of the adjacent land; instead it had a full patrimonial interest in the shore and proprietors required an express Crown grant to obtain ownership. These claims regarding the foreshore were only part of a more general effort by the Crown to establish ownership with regard to property including the sea-bed[117] and the *alveus* of navigable rivers.[118]

---

[112] MacAskill, *Silver Fringe*.

[113] These being J Carr, *Caledonian Sketches on a Tour Through Scotland in 1807* (1809); J MacCulloch, *A Description of the Western Islands of Scotland* (1819); B Botfield, *Journal of a Tour Through the Highlands of Scotland During the Summer of 1829* (1830).

[114] MacAskill, *Silver Fringe* 6–16.

[115] R G Hall, *Essay on the Rights of the Crown and the Privileges of the Subject in the Sea Shores of the Realm* (1830). MacAskill and Marston see these events as significant: MacAskill, *Silver Fringe* 64; G Marston, *The Marginal Seabed* (1981) 22–23. Rankine notes that 'the Crown began to assert its rights only about the middle of the present [19th] century': Rankine, *Landownership* 257.

[116] MacAskill, *Silver Fringe* 64.

[117] However, this did not result in many cases being brought before the courts regarding the sea-bed.

[118] See Anon 'Title of the Crown to the Seashore' (1859) 6 *Law Magazine and Law Review* 99 at 99; Ae MacKay, 'The Foreshore Question' (1867) 11 *Journal of Jurisprudence* 75.

3-32. It may be asked why the Crown should suddenly become so active in the assertion of its rights. The role of the Crown was changing significantly as society moved from being based on feudalism and agriculture to being industrialised. Instead of being dependent on the Crown for protection and the grant of privileges,[119] some individuals at least began to make huge profits through the exploitation of natural resources. Perhaps the Crown was inspired by such exploitation and sought to share in some of the riches. Further, as a result of the Industrial Revolution, there was a lot of activity on the assets to which the Crown had a potential claim, such as the building of railways along the coast,[120] improvement of navigation of rivers[121] and coal-mining under the sea.[122] To assert its rights would be to claim payment for all of these activities.

3-33. This increased assertiveness by the Crown was accompanied by a new deference in the courts. This change of attitude is evident in *Officers of State v Smith*[123] and *Paterson v Marquis of Ailsa*,[124] decided in the same court – the Second Division – and in the same year – 1846. In the first case, the Officers of State were objecting to the erection of a wall on the foreshore which interfered with public uses by Smith, whose land was bounded by the 'sea-shore'. In the second case, Paterson sought declarator of the right to gather wreck and ware *ex adverso* the lands of the Marquis, whose title had been granted by the Crown with no express sea-boundary. The Lord Ordinary in *Paterson* states what he, and probably many others, thought the law to be regarding the foreshore:

> 'it was, as the date of Mr Macalister's case,[125] held to be the law of Scotland, as settled by authority and prior decisions, that the sea-shore – except for the purposes of navigation and commerce – with the benefits that may be derived from coal and minerals under them, or from the sea-weed or ware found on their surface, are not to be accounted res communes, but are capable of being appropriated and acquired in individual property, like other heritable subjects, – that if they can in any respect be classed as inter regalia, they are merely held by the sovereign for the public uses, and may be acquired and transmitted as private property, either by special grant from the Crown, or without special grant, as parts and pertinents of the adjoining lands;- and that where lands contiguous to the sea are, in the Crown titles, conveyed with parts and pertinents, and expressly described as being bounded by the sea, a right to the shore, and to wreck and ware, and other secondary uses, is presumed, without any special conveyance, to be granted along with the lands, under burden always of the Crown's right as trustee for the public uses...[In *Macalister v Campbell* it was held] that the law being, that a grant of land described as bounded by the sea

---

[119] Van der Vyver, *Étatisation* 269.

[120] See *Hunter v Lord Advocate* (1869) 7 M 899; *Blyth's Trs v Shaw* (1883) 11 R 99; *Young v North British Railway* (1887) 14 R (HL) 53.

[121] See *Todd v Clyde Trs* (1840) 2 D 357 (aff'd by the House of Lords in (1841) 2 Rob 333); *Lord Advocate v Hamilton* (1852) 15 D (HL) 1; *Lord Advocate v Lord Blantyre* (1879) 6 R (HL) 72; *Lord Advocate v Clyde Navigation Trs* (1891) 19 R 174.

[122] See *Cuninghame v Assessor for Ayrshire* (1895) 22 R 596.

[123] (1846) 8 D 711.

[124] (1846) 8 D 752.

[125] *Macalister v Campbell* (1837) 15 S 490.

comprehended the sea-shore, which was not reserved from the grant, the same rules must apply where the grant was one of lands on the sea-coast, actually bounded by the sea, although the boundary was not set forth in the titles.'[126]

3-34.   The Second Division in both cases took a different view of the law. According to Lord Medwyn, Lord Cockburn and Lord Justice-Clerk Hope, the Crown had a full patrimonial interest in the shore[127] and an express grant was needed to transfer ownership.[128] This would suggest that the shore was *inter regalia* as to ownership although this was not explicitly stated.[129] Little authority was cited. Lord Cockburn provided the doctrinal justifications that the Crown's interest was based both on the prerogative (another indication that the shore is *inter regalia*) and on the fact that the King was the ultimate feudal superior.[130] One justification offered in *Officers of State* was that there was no previous (reported) case where the Crown was a party to the dispute.[131] Lord Hope's position may be partly explained by the admission in a later case that he was at one point an adviser to the Crown on the vindication of its rights.[132] Only Lord Moncreiff, in *Paterson*, put forward the view that the shore was *inter regalia* merely with regard to public rights,[133] rights which were inalienable and therefore *regalia majora*.[134]

3-35.   The *dicta* in *Paterson* and *Officers of State* largely contradicted both the trends in previous case law and also the beliefs held by adjacent proprietors.[135] The result was even more confusion and uncertainty. It would be surprising if the change of view seen in the courts was purely a reaction to increased activism on the part of the Crown; yet a different explanation is difficult to discern.[136]

---

[126] *Paterson v Marquis of Ailsa* (1846) 8 D 752 at 757 and 760.

[127] *Officers of State v Smith* (1846) 8 D 711 at 718 (Lord Justice-Clerk Hope) and 722 (Lord Cockburn); *Paterson v Marquis of Ailsa* (1846) 8 D 752 at 767 (Lord Medwyn), 770 (Lord Cockburn) and 772 (Lord Justice-Clerk Hope).

[128]*Officers of State v Smith* (1846) 8 D 711 at 715–716 (Lord Justice-Clerk Hope) and 723–724 (Lord Cockburn); *Paterson v Marquis of Ailsa* (1846) 8 D 752 at 767 (Lord Medwyn).

[129] Lord Moncreiff states that the shore is *inter regalia* as to public rights rather than ownership: *Paterson v Marquis of Ailsa* (1846) 8 D 752 at 770.

[130] *Officers of State v Smith* (1846) 8 D 711 at 723 (Lord Cockburn). See also Lord Justice-Clerk Hope at 718 in relation to the prerogative.

[131] At 715 (Lord Justice-Clerk Hope) and 722 (Lord Cockburn).

[132] See *Gammell v Commissioners of Woods and Forests* (1851) 13 D 854 at 871. This is perhaps not surprising as many judges were Lord Advocate before being appointed to the bench. However, in *Gammell*, Lord Hope also appears to change his mind: see below.

[133] *Paterson v Marquis of Ailsa* (1846) 8 D 752 at 768–770.

[134] These statements were *obiter* and largely irrelevant to the decisions made. In *Officers of State*, the court decided that the Crown could challenge the encroachment on the shore which interfered with public rights. In *Paterson*, it was decided that the Marquis had 'sufficient title' to defend the action against Paterson. However, it is unclear precisely what this means and it may be that the court was merely trying to avoid deciding the issue on the basis of the right of wreck and ware or ownership of the shore.

[135] The decision in *Officers of State* was affirmed by the House of Lords (1849) 6 Bell's App 487. Although Lord Brougham expressed disagreement with the opinion of Lord Justice-Clerk Hope, preferring the 'great clearness' of Lord Moncreiff at 496.

[136] In both cases R G Hall's *Essay on the Rights of the Crown and the Privileges of the Subject in the Sea Shores of the Realm* (1830) is cited by counsel.

3-36. Following these cases, the Office of Woods became ever more active in granting rights to third parties for use of the foreshore. MacAskill claims that some proprietors paid for such rights merely to avoid the expense of litigation against the Crown.[137] However, some adjacent proprietors were unwilling to have their property, as they believed, expropriated.[138] To combat these claims an Association of Sea-board Proprietors was established in 1861 to create 'a common fund, by means of which to meet the expenses of such law proceedings as shall, on consideration, seem best adapted to raise and try the question fairly and fully between the Crown and Sea Coast Proprietors'.[139]

3-37. The Association acted on behalf of its members in several cases, such as those for the Duke of Argyll and Stuart Munro of Teaninich which were undefended by the Crown,[140] and *HM Advocate v MacLean*,[141] but these cases did not achieve a definitive statement as to ownership of the shore, and there continued to be a variety of opinion present in the case law.[142] Some judges erred on the side of caution and reserved their opinion with regard to ownership.[143] Authority could also be found which was favourable to adjacent proprietors. In *Hunter v Lord Advocate*,[144] Lord Kinloch said when 'the Crown gives off lands locally situate on the sea-shore, I am of the opinion that, whether the title declares the sea to be the boundary or not, there is thereby given off a right to the sea-shore as part and pertinent of the land'.[145]

3-38. Indeed, even Lord Justice-Clerk Hope, who had so strongly supported the Crown in *Officers of State*, stated in *Lord Saltoun v Park*[146] that there was 'no doubt that a royal grant of lands *de facto* bounded by the sea, gives the vassal rights, as the Lord Ordinary says, to the sea-shore'. The suggestion here that no express grant was required may, however, be due to the fact that the grant was of a barony which on one view carried the *regalia minora* by implication.[147]

---

[137] MacAskill, *Silver Fringe* 66; J MacAskill, ' "The Most Arbitrary, Scandalous Act of Tyranny": The Crown, Private and the Ownership of the Scottish Foreshore in the Nineteenth Century' (2006) 85 *Scottish Historical Review* 277 at 281.

[138] For a summary of the arguments in favour of the adjacent proprietors see Ae MacKay, 'The Foreshore Question' (1867) 11 *Journal of Jurisprudence* 75.

[139] Circular of June 1861 sent to potential members of the Association, cited in MacAskill, *Silver Fringe* 72.

[140] See discussion in MacAskill, ''The Most Arbitrary, Scandalous Act of Tyranny' (n 137) at 286; MacAskill, *Silver Fringe* 102.

[141] (1866) 38 SJ 584, 2 SLR 25. This case decided that a barony title was sufficient to transfer *regalia minora*, if shore was *inter regalia*.

[142] See the difference of opinion between the Lord Ordinary and Lord Neaves in *Duchess of Sutherland v Watson* (1868) 6 M 199 at 202 and 213.

[143] See *Lord Saltoun v Park* (1857) 20 D 89, (1857) 20 SJ 54; *Nicol v Hector* (1859) 32 SJ 134. See also the uncertainty demonstrated in *Scrabster Harbour Trs v Sinclair* (1864) 2 M 884 at 889; *Baillie v Hay* (1866) 4 M 625 at 629.

[144] (1869) 7 M 899.

[145] At 911.

[146] (1857) 20 SJ 54 at 56. The issue as to ownership in *Lord Saltoun* was reserved in the interlocutor due to the explicit doubts of the other judges.

[147] See n 64 above.

The other judges reserved their opinion as to ownership. Further evidence that Lord Hope had changed his mind can be found in *Gammell v Commissioners of Woods and Forests*.[148]

3-39. This period of uncertainty and conflicting authority ended with *Agnew v Lord Advocate*[149] in 1873 where it was decided by the Second Division that the shore was not *inter regalia* as to ownership.[150] The public rights over the shore were, however, *inter regalia* and could not be alienated.[151] As to the requirements for transfer, a compromise was struck between the views of the Crown and of the adjacent proprietors. The shore was included in a grant when a boundary description was used which included the shore or when the foreshore was expressly mentioned. In the absence of these elements, Lord Neaves said, the shore's liability to public use precluded it from being implied in a grant.[152] However, the shore could be acquired after possessing for the period of positive prescription on a *habile* title.[153] This was an important concession because, due to the extensive use of the foreshore for the purposes of the kelp industry, most adjacent proprietors could prove prescriptive possession.[154] This outcome is similar to Hume's analysis of the requirements of transfer and indeed Lord Cowan mentioned that he was a student of Hume.[155] The Board of Trade (the successor of the Office of Woods[156]) considered appealing this judgment to the House of Lords but this idea was rejected for fear that the House of Lords would take a position more favourable still to adjacent proprietors, which may then have an effect on title to the foreshore in England.[157] *Agnew* was seen as settling the law and has been followed in subsequent cases.[158]

---

[148] See (1851) 13 D 854 at 868. See also Ae MacKay, 'The Foreshore Question' (n 138) at 86.

[149] (1873) 11 M 309. The Association supported Agnew in this case and there is mention of the body in the Crown's pleadings (at 319).

[150] At 323. Contrary to the suggestion in Law of the Foreshore and Seabed (Scot Law Com DP113, 2001) para 3.3, Lord Justice-Clerk Moncreiff is not suggesting that the foreshore is *inter regalia* as to ownership. Interestingly, the case of *Officers of State v Smith* (1846) 8 D 711 (aff'd (1849) 6 Bell's App 487) is barely mentioned in subsequent cases despite its appeal to the House of Lords. However, the comments made by their Lordships in the House of Lords in reference to ownership of the shore were sparse and *obiter dicta*.

[151] (1873) 11 M 309 at 331.

[152] At 332.

[153] At 321. It is odd for the title required for an initial grant to be different from the title suitable for prescription. However, see the law regarding salmon fishings in Reid, *Property* paras 323–325.

[154] This is noted by Lord Justice-Clerk Moncreiff at 324. See also MacAskill, *Silver Fringe* 181 and generally on this case 169–176.

[155] (1873) 11 M 309 at 327.

[156] Responsibility was transferred in 1866: MacAskill, *Silver Fringe* 105.

[157] MacAskill, "The Most Arbitrary, Scandalous Act of Tyranny'(n 137) at 93.

[158] See *Magistrates of Montrose v Commercial Bank of Scotland* (1886) 13 R 947; *Mather v Alexander* 1926 SC 139; *Luss Estates Co v BP Oil Grangemouth Refinery Ltd* 1982 SLT 457; Rankine, *Landownership* 274–277; Ferguson 49.

(f) The Modern Law

3-40. In the modern law, the foreshore is the ground between the high and low water marks of ordinary spring tides.[159] Although not *inter regalia* as to ownership[160] it is considered to have been originally owned by the Crown, like all land.[161] The shore can be alienated to private persons, and is conveyed when mentioned in a grant, whether by words or by reference to a plan, or when the boundary is said to be the 'sea'[162] or the 'river'.[163] The shore is also included in a grant bounded by the 'sea-shore',[164] contrary to the general rule that a bounding feature is excluded from the conveyance.[165] When land is bounded by the 'sea-flood' or 'flood-mark' the foreshore has generally been found to be excluded but there is contrary authority.[166] In light of this conflicting authority the Scottish Law Commission considered whether reform would be desirable in this area.[167] However, no reform was proposed and the primary motivating factor behind this decision may have been the

---

[159] *Bowie v Marquis of Ailsa* (1887) 14 R 649; *Fisherrow Harbour Commissioners v Musselburgh Real Estate Co Ltd* (1903) 5 F 387. This is a different rule from that in England and under Udal law: D J McGlashan, 'Udal Land and Coastal Land Ownership' 2002 *Jur Rev* 251; D J McGlashan, R W Duck and C T Reid, 'The Foreshore: Geographical Implications of the Three Legal systems in Great Britain' (2004) 36.4 *Area* 338. Exactly how the tide is determined is unclear. In *Bowie v Marquis of Ailsa* (1887) 14 R 649 at 667 reference was made to the Ordnance Survey Maps but these are infrequently updated. The suggestion that the Ordnance Survey map should be definitive of boundaries was rejected by the Report on the Law of the Foreshore and Seabed (n 36) para 2.10.

[160] Despite the assertions in Report on the Abolition of the Feudal System (Scot Law Com No 168, 1999) para 2.21; Gordon & Wortley, *Land Law* para 3-25.

[161] Except land governed by Udal law on which generally see J Ryder, 'Udal Law' in SME (Vol 24, 1989).

[162] See, for example, *Magistrates of Culross v Earl of Dundonald* (1769) Mor 12810, 1 Hailes 29; *Magistrates of Culross v Geddes* (1809) Hume 554; *Campbell v Brown* 18 Nov 1813 FC; *Young v North British Railway* (1887) 14 R (HL) 53; Gordon & Wortley, *Land Law* para 3-26; Reid, *Property* para 315.

[163] *Campbell v Brown* 18 Nov 1813 FC.

[164] Cases in favour of inclusion include *Magistrates of Culross v Geddes* (1809) Hume 554; *Cameron v Ainslie* (1848) 10 D 446 (regarding the 'sea-beach'); *Hunter v Lord Advocate* (1869) 7 M 899 at 912–913; *Lockhart v Magistrates of North Berwick* (1902) 5 F 136 at 145–146; *Luss Estates Co v BP Oil Grangemouth Refinery Ltd* 1987 SLT 201. See also Rankine, *Landownership* 106; Ferguson 88; Reid, *Property* para 315. However, there is contrary *dicta* in *Musselburgh Magistrates v Musselburgh Real Estate Co Ltd* (1904) 7 F 308 at 313–317 and 321. This case involved the boundary by the sea-beach which should not be treated differently from a boundary by the sea-shore. See also Ferguson 76–88; Gordon & Wortley, *Land Law* para 3-26.

[165] Reid, *Property* para 315; Gordon & Wortley, *Land Law* para 3-26.

[166] *Smart v Magistrates of Dundee* (1797) 3 Pat 606, 8 Bro PC 119, 3 ER 481; *Berry v Holden* (1840) 3 D 205; *Keiller v Magistrates of Dundee* (1886) 14 R 191. See also Rankine, *Landownership* 109; Reid, *Property* para 315; Gordon & Wortley, *Land Law* para 3-26. However, see *Leven v Magistrates of Burntisland* (1812) Hume 555 (it is unclear whether this is a decision on ownership or the right of wreck and ware); *Hunter v Lord Advocate* (1869) 7 M 899 at 912–913; *Magistrates of Montrose v Commercial Bank of Scotland* (1886) 13 R 947.

[167] Discussion paper on Law of the Foreshore and Seabed (Scot Law Com DP 113, 2001) paras 8.8–8.10

human rights considerations of a retrospective change in the rules of interpretation for boundaries.[168]

3-41. The foreshore can also be acquired by positive prescription. For property still in the Register of Sasines this requires a *habile* title and possession for 20 years against the Crown and 10 years between private parties.[169] The foreshore needs to have been possessed openly, peaceably and without judicial interruption.[170] Sufficient acts of possession have included grazing cattle, cutting reeds, harvesting kelp, taking sand for building purposes, depositing rubbish, and enclosing sections of the foreshore.[171] Possession does not have to be exclusive, as there are still public rights to use the shore and it has been suggested that exclusivity would be difficult or impossible to achieve.[172] Acts carried out by the public without title do not interrupt prescription.[173] Contrary possession by the Crown would perhaps have to entail activities such as mining in an exclusive manner or granting of licences to third parties. Although the Crown Estate Commissioners estimate that only 50 per cent of the foreshore is privately owned in Scotland,[174] it is unclear how this figure can be arrived at without extensive investigation of titles and possession. Due to the history of the kelp industry, it is suggested that much of the shore will have been subject to sufficient prescriptive possession.[175]

3-42. Under the Land Registration etc (Scotland) Act 2012, as the Act operates on a 'negative' system of land registration,[176] until prescription has run (assuming absence of title) the person on the title sheet will not be owner. Presumably, therefore, those titles which are *habile* to include the shore will be mapped accordingly[177] and after a period of 10 or 20 years' possession, ownership will be acquired. The provisions regulating *a non domino* dispositions on the Land Register were outlined above.[178]

[168] Report on the Law of the Foreshore and Seabed (n 36) paras 6.6–6.7. Although it was said that a non retrospective changing of the law would not be useful, some clear guidance on the meaning of bounding descriptions would aid future conveyancing.

[169] Prescription and Limitation (Scotland) Act 1973 s 1; Reid, *Property* para 316; Gordon & Wortley, *Land Law* paras 3-27–3-28.

[170] Prescription and Limitation (Scotland) Act 1973 s 1(1).

[171] See the summary by the Lord Ordinary in *Lord Advocate v Lord Blantyre* (1879) 6 R (HL) 72 at 75–76.

[172] *Buchanan v Geils* (1882) 9 R 1218; *Young v North British Railway* (1887) 14 R (HL) 53; *Marquess of Ailsa v Monteforte* 1937 SC 805; Gordon & Wortley, *Land Law* para 3-29; Reid, *Property* para 316.

[173] *Buchanan v Geils* (1882) 9 R 1218; *Young v North British Railway* (1887) 14 R (HL) 53.

[174] Crown Estate, Scotland Report (2014; http://www.thecrownestate.co.uk/media/300060/scotland-report-2014.pdf) 3. See also the map reprinted in Land Reform Review Group, *The Land of Scotland and the Common Good* (n 35) 49 Fig 5.

[175] See the comments of Lord Moncreiff in *Agnew v Lord Advocate* (1873) 11 M 309 at 324.

[176] For further explanation see Report on Land Registration Vol 1 (Scot Law Com No 222, 2010) paras 13.9–13.36.

[177] There may be difficulties in establishing exactly where the shore is. In contrast to its proposals on the extent of tidal rivers, the Scottish Law Commission did not propose to create any presumption regarding the Ordnance Survey Map and the extent of the foreshore: Report on the Law of the Foreshore and Seabed (n 36) para 2.10.

[178] See para 3-11 above.

3-43. In the absence of contrary intention, the boundaries between two adjacent owners of the shore are established as a line which is perpendicular to the straight average line of the coast and which touches the edge of the piece of land at the high water mark.[179] In the case of tidal rivers, rather than the average line of the coast, the average *medium filum* of the river at low tide is taken.[180] Where there is a curve in the coast or river, a circle is drawn following the average line of the curve and a line is drawn perpendicular to the tangent of the circle which joins the edge of the plot of land and the centre of the circle.[181]

3-44. When ownership remains with the Crown, the Crown Estate Commissioners are responsible for the management of the foreshore.[182] Regardless of ownership, there are common law public rights over the shore held by the Crown as *regalia majora*.[183] The public also have rights to use the foreshore under the Land Reform (Scotland) Act 2003.[184]

(3) Rivers

(a) Public Rivers

3-45. Discussion concerning public rivers follows a pattern which by now has become familiar. There is little early authority regarding ownership. The first institutional writers focus less on ownership than on public rights. Finally, the Crown asserts its rights of ownership and power of alienation.

(I) NAVIGABLE RIVERS: INSTITUTIONAL WRITERS AND CASE LAW

3-46. As with the Roman jurists, when early institutional writers discuss the classification of navigable rivers, it is unclear whether they are referring to the *alveus* or the river as a separate entity. Craig includes navigable rivers as *inter regalia* and seems to imply that they are part of the annexed property of the Crown and inalienable.[185] The Crown is said to act as the 'guardian of public rights'.[186] It is open to question whether this means that the Crown owns the *alveus* or merely that it has an interest in protecting public rights. Bankton similarly describes navigable rivers as *inter regalia* but with the

---

[179] *McTaggart v McDouall* (1867) 5 M 534; *Fraser v Anderson* (1951) 67 Sh Ct Rep 110. The court determines the two points between which the average line should be drawn.

[180] *Campbell v Brown* 18 Nov 1813 FC. This involves taking account of the whole estuary: see *Laird's Tr v Reid* (1871) 9 M 1009. The Professor Rankine referred to is not the jurist but an engineer.

[181] *Darling's Trs v Caledonian Railway* (1903) 5 F 1001. See the useful diagram at 1009. Generally on mapping boundaries see Rankine, *Landownership* 109–110; Ferguson 89–93; Gordon & Wortley, *Land Law* para 3-30.

[182] Crown Estate Act 1961 s 1. See also Discussion Paper on the Law of the Foreshore and Seabed (n 167) paras 3.9–3.19.

[183] Reid, *Property* paras 524–526.

[184] See above, paras 2-96–2-97.

[185] Craig, *Jus Feudale* 1.16.11.

[186] Craig, *Jus Feudale* I.16.11.

implied suggestion that they are not among the *regalia majora* and could be disponed.[187] This may suggest that Bankton is discussing the *alveus* rather than public rights, and this is further suggested by his analysis of islands and deserted river-beds.[188] When alluvion is discussed by Forbes, his comments could be interpreted as meaning that public river-beds are owned either by adjacent landowners or by the Crown,[189] whereas Stair does not mention that rivers are *inter regalia* and it may be that he thought the *alveus* was ownerless.[190]

3-47.   That the position was unclear is reflected in the case law. In *Grant v Duke of Gordon*,[191] from 1781, it was argued that the Duke of Gordon's right of cruive fishing[192] impeded navigation on the river. Counsel for Grant discussed the public's right of navigation and stated that by 'the feudal law, the principles of which are adopted in Scotland, these rights, which were deemed public by the Roman law, are vested in the person of the King, not as a patrimonial interest and alienable by him, but as a trust for the good of the community. Such are public rivers and highways.'[193] The court, however, considered 'a river, by which the produce of the country could be transported to the sea, to be a public benefit, entrusted to the King, as *pater patriae*, for the behoof of his subjects in general, which could neither be given away nor abridged by him; and that this transportation, as the chief and primary use of the river, if incompatible with the cruive fishing, would prevail over it'.[194] As reported, this decision by the court seems more in line with the *alveus* being *regalia majora*.[195]

3-48.   Erskine, Hume and Bell defined navigable rivers as *inter regalia* and held in trust for the public[196] with little further explanation. Erskine's account of deserted river-beds implies Crown ownership but this is not made explicit.[197] As with the foreshore, Hume discusses navigable rivers along with other *regalia minora* which suggests that the *alveus* can be alienated,[198] in which

---

[187] Bankton, *Institute* I.3.4 and II.3.107–108.

[188] Bankton, *Institute* II.1.10.

[189] Forbes, *Great Body* Vol 1, 496. See also 343–344.

[190] Stair, *Institutions* II.1.5 and II.1.33. See also below, para 4-11.

[191] (1781) Mor 12820.

[192] A cruive is defined in the Oxford English Dictionary as a 'coop or enclosure of wickerwork or spars placed in tide-ways and openings in weirs, as a trap for salmon and other fish'.

[193] (1781) Mor 12820 at 12821. See *Wills' Trs v Cairngorm Canoeing and Sailing School Ltd* 1976 SC (HL) 30 where the session papers of this case are investigated to determine whether the decision was made on the basis of a public or servitude right. The judges in this case erroneously presume that the Crown's ownership of the *alveus* of public rivers was settled at the time, see at 78 (*per* Lord President Emslie in the Inner House) and 142 (*per* Lord Hailsham).

[194] *Grant v Duke of Gordon* (1781) Mor 12820 at 12822. This interlocutor of the Court of Session was affirmed by the House of Lords in (1782) 2 Pat 582.

[195] See also *Dick v Earl of Abercorn* (1769) Mor 12813 at 12815 where it was suggested that the *alveus* of public rivers could not be transferred by the Crown.

[196] Erskine, *Institute* II.1.5, II.6.17; Hume, *Lectures* IV 243 and 258; Bell, *Principles* para 648.

[197] Erskine, *Institute* II.1.5.

[198] Hume, *Lectures* IV 243–245.

case the purchaser is then bound by the guardianship obligations which had previously been on the Crown.[199]

3-49. When subsequent case law emerged on the topic, it was established that the Crown had a full patrimonial interest in the *alveus*. In *Todd v Clyde Trs*,[200] the first of several cases involving the Clyde Trustees,[201] the court said that the 'Crown is not only conservator of the stream for…in the case of a navigable river, the alveus of that river is, in truth, the property of the Crown'. Similar comments were made in *Lord Advocate v Clyde Trs*[202] where Lord President Boyle stated: 'No doubt the Crown cannot be permitted to exercise its proprietary rights in such a way as to obstruct the navigation. The Crown must act as conservator of the public interest. But I see no authority for saying that the Crown is not absolute proprietor of the *alveus*.' In this case it was also suggested that ownership could be transferred to other parties.[203] Thus, as with the sea, two regalian rights coexist in navigable rivers: the *alveus* is *inter regalia minora*;[204] the public rights which are held by the Crown in trust for the public are *inter regalia majora*.[205]

(II) TIDAL RIVERS AND THE MODERN LAW

3-50. Although for centuries the test for public rivers was navigability, in 1877 this was changed by *Colquhoun's Trs v Orr Ewing*[206] to a test of tidality. This case is surprising on many counts. Firstly, the tidality test has no grounding in Scottish authority. The defenders cited Craig and Stair,[207] who did not support their argument in favour of tidality, as well as English and American sources, which did.[208] The judges do not cite any authority for their decision on this point. Indeed, Lord President Inglis had to explain that his

---

[199] Hume, *Lectures* IV 241.

[200] (1840) 2 D 357 at 374. This decision was affirmed by the House of Lords (1841) 2 Rob 333.

[201] See also *Lord Advocate v Hamilton* (1852) 15 D (HL) 1; *Lord Advocate v Lord Blantyre* (1879) 6 R (HL) 72; *Lord Advocate v Clyde Navigation Trs* (1891) 19 R 174.

[202] (1849) 11 D 391 at 396. The decision was affirmed by the House of Lords in (1852) 15 D (HL) 1. See also *Duke of Buccleuch v Cowan* (1866) 5 M 214 at 215; *Lord Advocate v Clyde Navigation Trs* at 184.

[203] (1849) 11 D 391 at 402. See also *Erskine v Magistrates of Montrose* (1819) Hume 558 which may concern the *alveus* of a tidal river; *Todd v Clyde Trs* (1840) 2 D 357 at 374.

[204] This proposition has more support in the views of the institutional writers, namely Bankton and Hume, regarding navigable rivers than regarding the sea-bed.

[205] See also Rankine, *Landownership* 248–249; Reid, *Property* para 310; Gordon, *Land Law* paras 27-06–27-07. The statements made in *Ross v Powrie and Pitcaithley* (1891) 19 R 314 at 321 should therefore not be relied upon. On public rights see above paras, 2-93–2-95.

[206] (1877) 4 R 344. Even though the House of Lords reversed the judgment of the Inner House, the test of tidality was accepted (1877) 4 R (HL) 116.

[207] Craig, *Jus Feudale* 1.16.11; Stair, *Institutions* II.1.5.

[208] Namely Lord Hale (ascribed to), *De Jure Maris* (date unknown); R G Hall, *Essay on the Rights of the Crown and the Privileges of the Subject in the Sea Shores of the Realm* (1830) 5; J K Angell, *A Treatise on the Law of Watercourses* (edition not given).

69 *Scots Law* **3-52**

comment in *Duke of Buccleuch v Cowan*,[209] that a navigable river was vested in the Crown whether it was tidal or not, was 'rather loosely made'.[210] Secondly, it seems to go against the impression of judicial deference to the Crown's proactive approach to asserting its rights, for the Crown was suddenly deprived of its ownership in rivers which were navigable but non-tidal, and many landowners had the extent of their land extended to the *medium filum* of such rivers. Thirdly, with the expropriation of Crown property went the loss of public fishing rights which led to much public protest.[211] Finally, the reasons for such a change seem to be a mystery. As Whitty comments, this was 'not a case in which the House of Lords imposed English law over the protests of a reluctant Court of Session. Rather it was the First Division which introduced English law despite the pursuer's protests and their decision was affirmed on appeal. ...There may have been an assimilationist climate of opinion in which it was thought that the civilian criterion of navigability stood little chance of being upheld by the House of Lords.'[212] A better explanation is yet to be offered.

3-51. A public river is a tidal body of water which is perennial and exists in a definite channel.[213] It now seems accepted that the *alveus* of tidal rivers is treated in the same way as the sea-bed,[214] with the result that the authority discussed above regarding the sea-bed is also applicable to tidal rivers. Crown ownership therefore is based on the prerogative.[215] Transfer of the *alveus* requires an express conveyance or positive prescription. When the Crown has retained ownership, the *alveus* is managed by the Crown Estate Commissioners.[216]

3-52. Landwards the extent of a tidal river is the highest point reached by the ordinary spring tides. However, the determination of the actual boundary of tidality is an issue of doubt,[217] and the Scottish Law Commission has proposed that there should be a rebuttable presumption that, to the extent that the Ordnance Survey Maps show the presence of Mean High and Low Water Spring Tides, a river is tidal.[218]

[209] (1866) 5 M 214 at 215
[210] (1877) 4 R 344 at 350.
[211] See *Grant v Henry* (1894) 21 R (HL) 116; Whitty, 'Water' 443–446.
[212] Whitty, 'Water' 441–443.
[213] For discussion of the meaning of 'perennial' and 'definite channel' see below, paras 7-20–7-21.
[214] See Reid, *Property* paras 309–311; Discussion Paper on the Law of the Foreshore and Seabed (n 167) paras 2.7 and 2.18; Report on the Law of the Foreshore and Seabed (n 36) para 2.4.
[215] See above, para 3-09.
[216] See above, para 3-13.
[217] *Bowie v Marquis of Ailsa* (1853) 15 D 853. In *Bowie*, a river was held to be non-tidal when there was substantially no salt water even though the tide influenced the height of the water. See discussion in Ferguson 107; Reid, *Property* para 276; Gordon & Wortley, *Land Law* para 6-05.
[218] Report on the Law of the Foreshore and Seabed (n 36) para 2.22.

3-53. The limit of a river seawards is much more difficult. Ferguson says that the limit 'is the point where the river reaches the level of the general line of the coast at low water, this being possibly subject to a farther extension seawards where well-defined *fauces terrae*, or the existence of a bar, present clear natural features'.[219] However, there are no decisions on the point and a glance at a map of Scotland easily demonstrates the difficulty of establishing where a river ends and the sea begins.[220]

(b) Private Rivers

3-54. The *alveus* beneath non-navigable and then, post-1877, non-tidal, rivers is in private hands, and discussion of ownership is intimately connected with the chapters on common interest which follow. However, perhaps surprisingly, the doctrine of common interest is considered in more detail and at an earlier stage than issues of ownership. Ownership is most contentious when a river is a boundary between two properties and yet there was little early authority on the topic with only Bankton and Bell giving guidance. Still, at least since the mid-17th century there seems to have been an understanding that opposite proprietors owned the *alveus* to the *medium filum* of the river or, where the river was not on the boundary, landowners owned the section of *alveus* underneath the river running through their lands. This belief was tested slightly when an attempt was made to explain common interest restrictions as a form of common property but, as we will see, this theory never became established. In the mid-19th century, separate ownership of the *alveus* was expressly approved.

(i) Early Cases

3-55. The earliest evidence as to assumptions of the ownership of the *alveus* of private rivers where the river is the boundary between two plots of land can be found in cases concerning march fences. The March Dykes Act 1661 provides that where a fence or wall is placed on the border of two plots of land, half the cost of its construction can be recovered from the neighbouring proprietor.[221] In *Earl of Crawford v Rig*[222] of 1669, the Earl wished to recover half the expenses of building a dyke. Rig argued that, because the boundary was a burn, the 1661 Act did not apply. The Earl replied that the burn was often dry and so 'cannot hinder a stone dyke to be built in the very channel of it'.[223] This suggests an understanding that the boundary was actually the

---

[219] Ferguson 107.

[220] A good example is the Clyde. Does the island of Arran lie on the sea-bed or in a tidal river?

[221] The 1661 Act reads: 'wher inclosours fall to be vpon the border of any persons inheritance the next adjacent heritor shall be at equall paines and charges in building ditching and planting that dyk which parteth their inheritance.'

[222] (1669) Mor 10475.

[223] At 10475.

middle of the *alveus*. The court found that the Act did apply and, as a compromise between the two owners, that the dyke could be built partly on one side of the burn and partly on the other.

3-56.   A similar issue was raised in *Seaton v Seaton*,[224] where the pursuer had built a dyke on his ground and sought recovery of half the cost. The defender argued 'that a strip of water running from the Lady-well, is the march between both parties, so that the pursuer's dyke is not upon the march'.[225] The Lords repelled this defence and found the defender liable.

3-57.   These cases are evidence of an early understanding that, when a river is a boundary between two plots of land, ownership extends to the *medium filum*. However, to avoid the requirement of placing a fence down the middle of a river, boundary fences could be placed on one side of the river or both. This view is confirmed and explained by later cases where the use of the 1661 Act was found inapplicable to larger rivers than those in *Earl of Crawford* and *Seaton* as the fence would be too far away from the actual boundary.[226]

3-58.   Concerning successive owners, there is a brief glimpse in *Magistrates of Dumfries v Heritors upon the Water of Nith*[227] in 1705 of what may have been taken as the accepted law. The Magistrates were building a new mill due to the river having changed course. The Heritors protested that the mill and dam would injure their fishings. The Magistrates argued that as they were 'Heritors upon both sides of the water, the *alveus* is their property'[228] and so they could do as they wished with it. Although the court granted commission to investigate the operations on the *alveus*, the works were allowed to proceed and the position as to ownership does not seem to have been disputed.

(II) COMMON INTEREST CONFUSION

3-59.   This implicit understanding of the ownership of the *alveus* of private rivers was shaken for a time when the possibility that the *alveus* was common property was entertained.[229] This was an attempt to rationalise what we now know as the common interest obligations on owners. Bankton refers to a water-course on a boundary being 'common to both'[230] owners and quotes the maxim *in re communi potior est conditio prohibentis* associated with common property. However, by 'water-course' it is unclear whether Bankton means the *alveus* or the body of water constituting the river. Arguments based on

---

[224] (1679) Mor 10476.

[225] At 10476.

[226] *Pollock v Ewing* (1869) 2 M 815; *Graham v Irving* (1899) 2 F 29.

[227] (1705) Mor 12776.

[228] At 12776.

[229] I only mention here the arguments of common property which may be referring to the *alveus* of a river. For a full discussion of these arguments and those related to the river as a separate entity see below paras 5-40–5-46 and 6-34–6-38. It must be noted that due to the fluidity of the terms in the 18th century, it is often difficult to know if reference was being made to the concept of common property as we now understand it.

[230] Bankton, *Institute* II.7.29.

common property were also used in the cases of *Gibson v Earl of Weems*[231] and *Fairly v Earl of Eglinton*[232] which concerned successive owners. The result of *Gibson* is unknown but the court did not accept the common property argument in *Fairly*.

3-60. Indeed, it appears that arguments based on common property had little purchase in the courts. In *Lyon and Gray v Bakers of Glasgow*,[233] regarding opposite owners on a river where the pursuers had argued that the *alveus* was common property, it was observed by the court that 'the *alveus* was the property of the conterminous heritors'. Thus, the consideration of common property was brief and the doctrine never became established. A rationale for the restrictions on landowners with respect to rivers running through their lands would have to be found elsewhere.[234]

(III) Separate Ownership is Established

3-61. Ferguson writes: 'After some hesitation as to whether there might in such a case be a common property in the channel, and perhaps a little tendency to find a foundation for the necessary limitations in favour of opposite riparian proprietors in the notion of such common property, it was definitely settled, as between opposite proprietors, that each is owner of the *solum* of the *alveus* to the centre line of the channel – *ad medium filum aquae*.'[235] In *Fisher v Duke of Atholl's Trs*,[236] the Lord Ordinary acknowledged that the boundary of land which was said to be bounded by the Tay was the middle of the river. This suggested that a presumption of ownership *medium filum* applied when property was described in the titles as bounded by the river even though the usual rule was that a bounding object is excluded from the conveyance. Further, Bell wrote that 'Opposite Proprietors on the banks have half the land covered by the stream, but no property in the water.'[237] However, the *medium filum* rule with regard to opposite owners was still to be given detailed consideration in the courts.

3-62. The House of Lords finally gave a direct statement on the issue in *Wishart v Wyllie*,[238] when it was said that if:

'a stream separate properties A and B – *primâ facie*, the owner of the land A, as to *his* land, on one side, and the other of the land B, as to *his* land, on the other, are each entitled to the soil of the stream, *usque ad medium aquae* – that is, *primâ facie* so…It may be rebutted by circumstances, but if not rebutted, that is the legal presumption.'

---

[231] (Unreported), Information for Gibson 27 Nov 1723 (Robert Dundas), *Gibson v Weems* WS 8:32.

[232] (1744) Mor 12780.

[233] (1749) Mor 12789 at 12790.

[234] For common interest see below, Chs 5, 6 and 7.

[235] Ferguson 170.

[236] (1836) 14 S 880.

[237] Bell, *Principles* para 1101.

[238] (1853) 1 MacQ 389 at 389–390.

This was the first explicit statement in the courts of a rule which had probably been accepted by lawyers since the mid-17th century. It was confirmed and explained by the Inner House in *Morris v Bicket*,[239] Lord Justice-Clerk Inglis stating that:

'the property of these two neighbours on the opposite sides of the stream is said to be, and is by their titles described as being, bounded by the stream. The effect in law is, that each is proprietor up to the *medium filum fluminis*, and that *medium filum* constitutes the boundary or line of the march between the two estates. It is a mistake to say that the *alveus* of the stream is the common property of the two proprietors of the banks.'

This was confirmation that the presumption of ownership to the *medium filum* applied when the properties were bounded by the river in the titles. Lords Neaves and Benholme gave judgments in a similar vein but, in the latter case, with slight inconsistencies in terminology.[240] This decision, and the principles contained in it, was affirmed by the House of Lords.[241]

3-63.   Strangely, only a couple of years later, Lords Benholme and Neaves seemed to cast doubt on the very propositions which they had expounded in *Morris*. In *McIntyre's Trs v Magistrates of Cupar*,[242] in which property was described as bounded by a river but with measurements which did not include the *alveus*, Lord Neaves questioned the presumption. The general rule was that, when property was bounded by an object, the object was excluded. However, 'I am not satisfied that there has not been a practice introduced in conveyancing which has altered the literal meaning of a stream boundary, and carried the proper limit into the middle of the water.'[243] Lord Benholme put forward his objections more strongly, saying he did:

'not think it is a universal principle, nor that the decisions lay it down, that every man who has property bounded by a stream has a right *usque ad medium filum aquae*. On the contrary, I think it is only in certain circumstances, and especially where there are conterminous properties having a stream as their common boundary, that it becomes necessary to give to each proprietor an interest in the stream to one-half of the channel.'[244]

He did not see this as a case between competing opposite owners because the Magistrates had simply retained whatever land was not disponed to McIntyre. The other judges, however, failed to share these concerns. Lord Cowan found the measurements to be demonstrative only and applied the

---

[239] (1864) 2 M 1082 at 1087.
[240] At 1092 (Lord Neaves). Lord Benholme says 'the *medium filum* is held to be the limit of the absolute property…the channel is not common property', but at 1090 it is said there is common property in the stream (later, more accurately, the term common interest is used) and that the maxim *potior est conditio prohibentis* is applicable in relation to operations on the *alveus*. The view of Lord President Inglis is preferable that the maxim is not applicable, see at 1087.
[241] (1866) 4 M (HL) 44.
[242] (1867) 5 M 780.
[243] At 787.
[244] At 786–787.

presumption that, when property is bounded by a river, the *alveus* is conveyed up to the *medium filum*. The Lord Justice-Clerk came to the same conclusion, citing D.41.1[245] and the French *Code civil* Art 561 regarding the ownership of islands.

3-64. By the time of the decision of *Gibson v Bonnington Sugar Refining Co Ltd*[246] any concerns seem to have evaporated. Again land was described as bounded by the river but the *alveus* was not included in the measurements (which were described by Lord Justice-Clerk Moncreiff as not taxative[247]). Both Lords Neaves and Benholme applied the presumption of ownership to the mid-point.

3-65. Regarding the less controversial issue of successive owners, direct authority is not available but some guidance can be taken from the case of *Fergusson v Shirreff*.[248] Fergusson raised an action to prevent Shirreff, a member of the public, from fishing in his river and it was said that the 'river Tyne flows through his estate; he is proprietor of both banks and of the *alveus*'.[249] It was undisputed that Fergusson owned the *alveus* of the river, and this ownership was the basis of his successful attempt to exclude the public from fishing in the river.

(IV) MODERN LAW

3-66. A private river is a non-tidal body of water which is perennial and runs in a definite channel.[250] Where a river is wholly contained within one person's land, the whole of the *alveus* belongs to him or her.[251] Where it runs successively through several properties, the *alveus* is owned in sections by the owner of each property.[252]

3-67. Regarding opposite owners, there are conflicting opinions in the modern law as to when the presumption of ownership to the mid-point applies. Gordon sees it applying only when the titles expressly give the boundary as the river.[253] However, the comments in the cases cited above seem to be wider than this,[254] so that where property is *de facto* bounded by a river there is a presumption that ownership extends to the *medium filum*.[255] This avoids uncertainty where titles are silent. The two cases cited by Gordon

---

[245] Mostly likely to be D.41.1.7.2 (Gaius). See also D.42.12.1.6 (Ulpian); Justinian's *Institutes* 2.1.22 and below, para 4-07.

[246] (1869) 7 M 394.

[247] At 398.

[248] (1844) 6 D 1363.

[249] At 1367.

[250] For a discussion of tidality see above, para 3-52 and the meaning of 'perennial' and 'definite channel' below, paras 7-20–7-21.

[251] Rankine, *Landownership* 536; Ferguson 170; Reid, *Property* para 278; Gordon & Wortley, *Land Law* para 6-21.

[252] *Fergusson v Shirreff* (1844) 6 D 1363; Rankine, *Landownership* 536; Reid, *Property* para 278.

[253] Gordon & Wortley, *Land Law* para 3-34.

[254] See the assumptions in the march fence cases discussed above and the original statement of the rule in *Wishart v Wyllie* (1853) 1 MacQ 389.

[255] See also *Morris v Bicket* (1864) 2 M1082 (aff'd by the House of Lords (1866) 4 M (HL) 44); *Gibson v Bonnington Sugar Refinery Co Ltd* (1869) 7 M 394; *Magistrates of Hamilton v Bent*

in support of his view – *North British Railway Co v Magistrates of Hawick*[256] and *Dalton v Turcan Connell (Trustees) Ltd*[257] – are better classified as examples of where the presumption was rebutted. In the first case, no river boundary was mentioned but the plans and the measurements of the lands – which were found to be taxative – excluded the *alveus*. In the second case, the boundary given was the 'North side of the Water of Leith' and the plans excluded the *alveus*. Thus, the presumption will be rebutted where there is evidence of a contrary intention, although it has been described as a strong presumption.[258]

3-68. Where there are subsidiary channels and islands, the *medium filum* is the centre line from bank to bank not the centre line of the main channel.[259] Establishing exactly where the *medium filum* lies may be a matter of difficulty, as shown in *McGavin v McIntyre*[260] where there were conflicting reports from engineers. Lord Justice-Clerk Macdonald stated that it 'is a very delicate and a very difficult question. I think that even though we had the evidence of fifty skilled engineers upon each side it might still be very difficult to decide where that *medium filum* was.'[261] The Lord Ordinary seemed to favour the report which was the most accurate reflection of all undulations of the stream. However, the issue will inevitably be one of fact.

3-69. On the map-based system of land registration, there are challenges in plotting the position of the *medium filum*. The *Plans Manual* of Registers of Scotland states that determination will be made with reference to the Ordnance Survey maps[262] but the policy for establishing the *medium filum* is unclear. The *Plans Manual* merely indicates that there may be problems with long and irregularly shaped rivers and also rivers in areas of mountains or moorland where the scale of the Ordnance Survey map is too small to be an accurate representation.[263]

3-70. To acquire ownership of a river-bed through prescription, taking possession may prove challenging.[264] Guidance may be taken from cases on

---

Colliery 1929 SC 686; *Scammell v Scottish Sports Council* 1983 SLT 463; Rankine, *Landownership* 110 and 536 where it is said 'where a river forms the march of two estates either *de facto* or with an express boundary in the titles of either or both of the riverain subjects "by" the river, the *medium filum* is the line of demarcation'; Ferguson 170; Reid, *Property* para 278.

[256] (1862) 1 M 200.

[257] 2005 SCLR 159 (Notes).

[258] *Magistrates of Hamilton v Bent Colliery* 1929 SC 686 at 696. See also *Jamieson v Commissioners of Police of Dundee* (1884) 12 R 300; Ferguson 172–173. However, it was not clear in this latter case whether the presumption was rebutted or there was simply not sufficient consideration of the presumption. See further Registers of Scotland, *Plans Manual* para 8.2.29.3 which reads 'in the event of a conflict between these presumptions and the titles, it is the titles which will normally prevail'.

[259] *Menzies v Breadalbane* (1901) 4 F 55.

[260] (1890) 17 R 818.

[261] At 827.

[262] See Registers of Scotland, *Plans Manual* para 8.2.3.

[263] Registers of Scotland, *Plans Manual* para 8.2.29.7.

[264] Possession is not assumed contrary to the assertion in A Brand, A J M Steven and S Wortley, *Professor McDonald's Conveyancing Manual* (7th edn, 2004) para 8.12.

land registration law. In *Safeway Stores Plc v Tesco Stores Ltd*[265] removing poles which had been placed on the *alveus* was not sufficient possession to protect against rectification of the Land Register. Neither was a bridge across the *alveus*, to which pipes were attached, in *Dalton v Turcan Connell (Trustees) Ltd*.[266] Further, any activity on the *alveus* which materially disrupts the natural flow of the river in an attempt to possess is a breach of common interest obligations.[267]

(4) Lochs

(a) Public Lochs

3-71.   Although lakes were *res publicae* in Roman law,[268] only Stair and Bell of the institutional writers treat lochs as capable of being public things. Stair states that some (perhaps only navigable) lochs are public, but it is suggested that he is not considering ownership but only public rights of sailing and fishing.[269] Bell states:

> 'Navigable lakes do not, generally speaking, appear to be inter regalia, as rivers are...But if such lakes form great channels of communication in a district of country, there seems to be some reason to regard them as res publicae; not to be held as implied in a grant of the adjacent land, but to be regulated in the conveyance, and in the exercise of the use, by the same rules which prevail with regard to a public river.'[270]

This passage suggests that the *alveus* of navigable lakes is owned by the Crown. This suggestion had some support from *MacDonell v Caledonian Canal Commissioners*,[271] where Lord Cringletie considered that the *alveus* of navigable lochs was not owned by the adjacent landowners, with the implication that it was owned by the Crown.[272] The *alveus* of the loch in question, however, was ultimately found to be owned by the owner of the land in which it lay. The law is now beyond dispute as after 1877 Crown ownership of land beneath water has been limited to tidal stretches.[273] Tidal lochs are thus treated in the same way as the sea-bed and the *alveus* is owned by the

---

[265] 2003 SC 29. For further discussion of this case see K G C Reid and G L Gretton, *Conveyancing 2003* (2004) 91–96.

[266] 2005 SCLR 159 (Notes). See also K G C Reid and G L Gretton, *Conveyancing 2004* (2005) 112. Both of these cases were decided under the Land Registration (Scotland) Act 1979.

[267] 2005 SCLR 159 (Notes). For further discussion see below Ch 7.

[268] See above, para 2-06.

[269] Stair, *Institutions* II.3.76 and above, para 2-44.

[270] Bell, *Principles* para 648.

[271] (1830) 8 S 881.

[272] At 888–889. Other judges seem to be merely discussing public rights.

[273] *Colquhoun's Trs v Orr Ewing* (1877) 4 R 344 (rev'd on a different point in (1877) 4 R (HL) 116).

Crown.[274] The public rights over tidal lochs are held by the Crown as *regalia majora*.[275]

(b) Private Lochs

3-72.   Just as there were similarities in the history of ownership of the foreshore, the *alveus* of public rivers and the sea-bed, so the position of private lochs follows a similar pattern to private rivers. The issue becomes controversial when a loch is contained within several pieces of land, and common property was briefly utilised to explain rights which are now attributed to common interest. Reid interprets the common property arguments as relating to ownership of the *alveus*. There were, he says, two theories present in the courts: firstly, that the *alveus* was common property and, secondly, that the *alveus* was severally owned.

> 'The first of these views (common property) was the earlier to become established. It is to be found in Bell and in a number of cases decided around the middle of the nineteenth century, and it remained the dominant view until the decision of the House of Lords in 1878 in the leading case of *Mackenzie v Bankes*.[276] In *Mackenzie* the House of Lords adopted the second view, the view that the loch is held in several ownership; but since the Court of Session in the same case had followed the older, common property, view without attracting comment in the higher court, it may be doubted whether the House of Lords was aware of the significance of its own adopted stance. The cases since *Mackenzie* have, however, followed the House of Lords rather than the Court of Session, and the idea of several ownership may now be regarded as established.'[277]

3-73.   However, it appears that when common property was being discussed in the 19th century, it was mostly the loch as a body of water which was being referred to rather than the *alveus*. The loch was regarded as a distinct object, separate from the constantly moving individual particles of water – which are incapable of ownership – and the *alveus* underneath. The result was the loch was treated almost like a separate tenement.[278] Common property of the loch as a body of water was used to explain the rights of fishing and sailing which could be exercised over the entire surface of the loch. The position as to the *alveus* of the loch may have been fairly stable from the time of Stair onwards.

---

[274] *Lord Advocate v Clyde Navigation Trs* (1891) 19 R 174 concerning Loch Long. Lochs are tidal to the highest point of the ordinary spring tides: *Bowie v Marquis of Ailsa* (1853) 15 D 853. For consideration of the difficulties of this definition and discussion of the seawards limit see above, paras 3-52–3-53. For the requirements of a loch to be perennial and to exist in a definite hollow see para 7-27. See discussion of reform of the ownership of the *alveus* of public lochs in Land Reform Review Group, *The Land of Scotland and the Common Good* (n 35) para 30.12.

[275] Reid, *Property* para 514.

[276] (1878) LR 3 App Cas 1324.

[277] Reid, *Property* para 305.

[278] See also below, paras 5-40–5-46 and 6-34–6-38 regarding rivers.

3-74. Stair treats the *alveus* of a loch as part of the land in which it is contained, and so owned by the owner of that land. He gives a surprisingly detailed account:

> 'All other interests of fees are carried as part and pertinent, though they be not expressed; and albeit woods and lochs used oft to be expressed yet they are comprehended under parts and pertinents; and therefore the master of the ground hath not only right to the water in lochs, but to the ground thereof, and may drain the same, unless servitudes be fixed to water-gangs of mills, or other works, and the ground of the loch, and all that is upon it, or under is, is a part of the fee: but if the loch be not wholly within the fee, but partly within or adjacent to the fee of another, then, unless the loch be expressed, it will be divided among the fiars whose land front thereupon.'[279]

Ownership of the *alveus* of a loch is thus implied in a conveyance. Where a loch is surrounded by several landowners, each will own a separate part of the *alveus* rather than it being common property. Stair also makes a distinction between the water and the *alveus*. Although he may just have meant that the owner could do as he or she wished with the water, this may be the inspiration for the separate treatment of the loch as a body of water and the *alveus* which was adopted by subsequent case law.

3-75. Bankton did not make so clear a statement: 'Woods, Lochs and Coal, within one's property belong to him as owner of the ground, as he may cut the wood, drain the loch, dig and win the coal at his pleasure. If the loch is between two contiguous heritors, it belongs to them equally, unless it is provided otherwise by the rights.'[280] Here it is uncertain whether Bankton is referring to the loch as a body of water or the *alveus* underneath; or whether shared lochs are held in separate ownership or common property. Unlike Stair's use of the word 'divided' which suggests separate ownership, Bankton's statement that a shared loch belongs 'equally' to each owner could indicate common property. Hume makes similar comments with regard to lochs within one piece of land and does not consider the ownership of shared lochs.[281]

3-76. Early case law focuses on one-estate lochs. In *Scot v Lindsay*[282] of 1635, decided before Stair published his *Institutions*, an action was raised by Scot for declarator of ownership of a loch. Scot had an express grant of the loch of Rossie and alleged possession. Lindsay had a previous grant without express mention of the Rossie loch but *'cum lacu et piscationibus'* and also alleged possession. The court found in favour of Scot without allowing proof of possession. This may be due to the fact that the loch was not seen as a pertinent of Lindsay's land and therefore required an express grant. However,

---

[279] Stair, *Institutions* II.3.73.

[280] Bankton, *Institute* II.3.165.

[281] Hume, *Lectures* III 225. There is a surprising lack of discussion of lochs by Mackenzie, Forbes and Erskine.

[282] (1635) Mor 12771.

the reasoning of the judges is not given.[283] It is also not clear whether the court was concerned with the loch as a body of water or was merely considering the ownership of the *alveus*.

(II) THE LOCH AS A BODY OF WATER AND COMMON PROPERTY

3-77.   After Stair published his *Institutions*, there is more indication of a distinction being made between the loch and the *alveus* underneath, as well as acceptance of the view that rights to both pass as a pertinent of a conveyance. In a case concerning Duddingston loch near Edinburgh, *Dick v Earl of Abercorn*,[284] Dick sought declarator of 'the sole property of the lake in question, and of the whole ground, soil and bounds thereof'. Dick had an express grant of the loch while the Earl's predecessor had renounced the right to the loch under reservation of a servitude of watering cattle and horses. The *Morison's Dictionary* report shows the Earl as arguing that although the pursuer had 'an undoubted right to the lake, considered as a body of water, yet he had no right to the soil or *alveus* of the lake'.[285] Dick responded that it was 'absurd to say that the water of the lake belonged to one person, and the *solum* to another'.[286] However, the Earl may merely have been arguing that he was entitled to the *alveus* which was exposed through the receding of the loch.[287] In the event, the court found that both loch and *alveus* were owned by the same person, holding that 'the pursuer has the sole and exclusive right of property to the loch of Duddingston, not only to the fishings and fowlings, and plants of every kind therein, but also to the soil or *alveus* thereof'.[288]

3-78.   The distinction between the loch as a body of water and the *alveus* allowed the application of common property to lochs surrounded by many landowners despite the indication from Stair that the *alveus* itself was in several ownership, but it took many years for the use of common property to become explicit. In the case of *Cochrane v Earl of Minto*,[289] Admiral Elliot (the original party to the action and predecessor of the Earl) sought to establish

---

[283] Rankine states that a proof of possession would be allowed in a case like this today: *Landownership* 196. See also Ferguson 145.

[284] (1769) Mor 12813 at 12813.

[285] At 12814.

[286] At 12815.

[287] Understanding the arguments of the Earl is not made easier by access to the session papers of the case. See Petition for the Earl of Abercorn 20 Jul 1768 (Robert McQueen), *Dick v Earl of Abercorn* Campbell Collection Vol 18, Paper 49; Answers for the Earl of Abercorn 25 Apr 1769 (Robert McQueen), *Dick v Earl of Abercorn* WS 346:20. Indeed, it appears that Dick is claiming a right to a margin of grassy land around the loch which could not be land ordinarily covered by water, see Answers for Dick 20 Sept 1768 (Henry Dundas), *Dick v Earl of Abercorn* WS 134:44a; Petition for Dick 3 Mar 1769 (Henry Dundas), *Dick v Earl of Abercorn* WS 346:20. James Boswell represented Dick in the Ordinary stage of this case, see H M Milne, *The Legal Papers of James Boswell*, (Stair Society, Vol 60, 2013) 18. My thanks go to Hugh and Odell Milne for information about this case.

[288] (1769) Mor 12813 at 12816.

[289] (1815) 6 Pat 139.

an exclusive right to a loch mainly for the purpose of obtaining marle.[290] There was nothing in the titles with respect to the loch. In 1808, the Lord Ordinary decided 'that each party's interest in the loch shall extend *ex adverso* of his lands from the shore to the middle of the loch and that each party may dig marle within his own division: Finds that the right of fishing and fowling to be common to both over the whole loch'.[291] This appears to be the first recognition that, even though the *alveus* of the loch was in several ownership, there were rights over the entire sheet of water. This interlocutor was adhered to by the Second Division. Due to the Admiral's death, the Earl was sisted to the action and he gave a new condescendence as a result of which the interlocutor of the Lord Ordinary was varied to the effect that the Earl was now found to be sole owner of the *alveus*. Cochrane reclaimed and the House of Lords reinstated the original interlocutor of the Lord Ordinary. This confirmed Stair's view as to separate ownership of the *alveus* and that rights to lochs were implied in conveyances as pertinents. However, what was not clear was the nature of these rights, of fishing and fowling, which could be exercised over the entire water of the loch.

3-79. Subsequent cases did not completely clarify the issue. In *Stirling v Dunn*,[292] where the lease of a loch was found to contravene the terms of an entail, the lessee had questioned whether a *pro indiviso* share of a loch could be subject to an entail at all. It was not specified whether this reference to common property related to the *alveus* or the loch as a body of water. However, the court seemed to think there had been a lease of the water rather than of the land underneath, indicating that the loch as a body of water was common property. In *Macdonald v Farquharson*,[293] fishing and sailing were found to be an inherent part of the ownership of the *alveus* of a loch. Further, there was an implication that the *alveus* was separately owned by the surrounding proprietors, as Lord MacKenzie stated that Macdonald was 'just one of two conterminous proprietors, and does not even allege right to the whole solum of the loch'.[294] Yet, there was no consideration of whether the rights of fishing and sailing could be exercised over the whole loch and, if so, why.

3-80. These problems were not experienced in relation to lochs which were contained wholly within the lands of one person. It was quickly accepted that such lochs and the land underneath belonged to the landowner without the requirement of express grant, but subject to common interest obligations to those down or upstream.[295]

---

[290] The Oxford English Dictionary defines 'marle' as an 'earthy deposit, typically loose and unconsolidated and consisting chiefly of clay mixed with calcium carbonate, formed in prehistoric seas and lakes and long used to improve the texture of sandy or light soil'.

[291] This interlocutor was not cited in the decision of *Cochrane v Earl of Minto* (1815) 6 Pat 139 but is quoted in *Mackenzie v Bankes* (1878) LR 3 App Cas 1324 at 1342.

[292] (1827) 6 S 272.

[293] (1836) 15 S 259.

[294] At 262.

[295] *Macdonell v Caledonian Canal Commissioners* (1830) 8 S 881; *Montgomery v Watson* (1861) 23 D 635; *Magistrates of Linlithgow v Elphinstone (No 2)* (1768) Mor 12805, Hailes 203 and see Ch 5 on common interest.

3-81. In respect of the more difficult question of lochs surrounded by different owners, Bell in the first edition of his *Principles* in 1829 stated: 'Lakes surrounded by the ground of various proprietors, are common property; but they are not under the act 1695, nor divisible otherwise than by consent of act of Parliament.'[296] It is not clear whether Bell is referring to the loch as a body of water or the *alveus* underneath. If the former, saying that lochs are common property may explain the interlocutors of the Lord Ordinary from 1808 in *Cochrane v Earl of Minto*[297] and the earlier interlocutor from 1789 cited in *Menzies v Macdonald*,[298] discussed further below, which decided that adjacent landowners can use the whole loch for sailing and fishing rather than that section of water above their section of the *alveus*. However, despite the fact that Bell made a distinction between common interest and common property,[299] how water rights relate to that distinction is not always clear.[300] If Bell was discussing common property why did he refer to the Division of Commonties Act 1695 which concerns the separate institution of commonty?[301] It may be that Bell did not intend to apply the doctrinal concept of common property as we understand it in the modern law. Distinctions between different institutions were not settled at this time and terms had not acquired the technical meaning which we attribute to them today. This should be kept in mind when considering the cases. Indeed, in the second edition of the *Principles*, published in 1830, Bell included an additional section which stated that if 'wholly within the land of one proprietor, the lake goes as a pertinent of the land. If not so, but touching the estates of various proprietors, the lake and its solum rateably belongs to them all.'[302] Stair and Bankton were cited. Bell's statement does not explicitly refer to common property and the sources cited do not offer much support to any common property argument.[303]

3-82. The application of common property was developed in *Menzies v Macdonald*.[304] Loch Rannoch was surrounded by two large properties.[305] When the owner of one disponed part of his lands, the issue was whether any rights to the loch were transmitted. The loch had been the subject of a decision in 1789, where it was found 'that both parties in this cause have a joint right or common property in the loch of Loch Rannoch, and a joint right of sailing, fishing, floating timber, and exercising all acts of property thereupon'.[306] This

---

[296] Bell, *Principles of the Law of Scotland* (1829) para 283.

[297] (1815) 6 Pat 139 discussed above.

[298] (1854) 16 D 827 (aff'd by the House of Lords (1856) 2 MacQ 463).

[299] Bell, *Principles of the Law of Scotland* (1829) paras 272 and 275.

[300] See discussion in relation to common interest below, para 6-66.

[301] On commonty see Reid, *Property* para 35.

[302] Bell, *Principles of the Law of Scotland* (2nd edn, 1830) para 648.

[303] Stair, *Institutions* II.3.73; Bankton, *Institute* II.3.12. This latter paragraph does not even refer to lochs.

[304] (1854) 16 D 827 (aff'd by the House of Lords (1856) 2 MacQ 463).

[305] There was also a landowner with a smaller plot of land who did not claim any right to the loch.

[306] Quoted in (1854) 16 D 827 at 833.

interlocutor seems to be referring to the loch as a separate body of water. Indeed the Lord Ordinary in *Menzies v Macdonald*[307] stated that a:

> 'perusal of the pleadings, and of the notes of the opinions of the judges in pronouncing that judgment, leads him to think, that in so far at least as regards the *solum* of the loch, the Court may not have intended to alter the legal character of the right of the parties under their title deeds. And as, apart from the effect of the decree in this respect, the *solum* would have vested in the proprietors adjoining the loch, so far as *ex adverso* of their several properties.'

Further, the interlocutor is not settled on the loch being common property; there may just be a 'joint right' in this loch which could have been attributed to common interest. The judges in the Inner House in 1854 continued with the view of the loch as a separate object but, perhaps influenced by Bell,[308] tended to use the words and concepts of common property, such as regulation and the possibility of subdivision. This case is probably not about ownership of the *alveus*, of which there was little discussion,[309] but ownership of the loch as a body of water. It was found that a right of common property in the loch did transmit on subdivision of the land, a decision affirmed by the House of Lords.[310]

(III) COMMON INTEREST RATHER THAN COMMON PROPERTY

3-83.   This view of common property of the loch as a separate body of water was not to persist for long. In *Mackenzie v Bankes*,[311] decided only a few years later, the Court of Session still used the term common property (and indeed common interest[312]) in relation to a loch.[313] However, the House of Lords refrained from referring to common property and the rights of fishing and sailing which landowners can exercise over the whole surface of a loch are today attributable to common interest.[314] This is a welcome change.[315] A loch

---

[307] At 832.

[308] Bell is cited by the Lord Ordinary at 831 and by Lord Deas at 852–858.

[309] Lord Deas makes reference to ownership *ad medium filum*, at 853 but dissents from the decision on the grounds that the disposition did not convey a right of common property to the defender although it is unclear whether on this point he is referring to the loch or the *alveus*.

[310] (1856) 2 MacQ 463.

[311] (1877) 5 R 278 (aff'd by House of Lords (1878) LR 3 App Cas 1324).

[312] The interlocutor mentions the 'right of common property or common interest' (1877) 5 R 278 at 289.

[313] Lord Justice-Clerk Moncreiff at 281 states 'the proprietors of the banks of a lake or loch have a right of common property in the loch itself, and a right of common interest in the ordinary uses of the loch. That arises not from the fact that they are common proprietors equally of the *solum* of the loch.'

[314] See below, para 7-75.

[315] Although there is still reference to common property at times, see *Menzies v Wentworth* (1901) 3 F 941 which was a sequel to *Menzies v Macdonald* (1854) 16 D 827 (aff'd by the House of Lords (1856) 2 MacQ 463); J Craigie, *Scottish Law of Conveyancing: Heritable Rights* (1899) 113; Rankine, *Landownership* 198; J M Halliday, *Conveyancing Law and Practice in Scotland* (2nd edn, 1997) Vol 2 para 33-11.

is a constantly moving and, by definition, perennial body of water.[316] Allowing separate ownership of a loch is artificial and potentially inconsistent with the concept of flowing water as a communal thing.[317]

3-84.   In *Mackenzie v Bankes*[318] the position as to the *alveus* was finally clarified, the House of Lords deciding that the *alveus* underneath a loch was severally owned. Lord Selborne said:

> 'So far as relates to the *solum* or *fundus* of the lake, it is considered to belong in severalty to the several riparian proprietors, if more than one; the space enclosed by lines drawn from the boundaries of each property *usque ad medium filum*; being deemed appurtenant to the land of that proprietor, exactly as in the common case of a river.'[319]

Of course, it is arguable that this had been the position all along and that the discussion of common property had only been relevant to the loch as a separate body of water. Be that as it may, this view as to separate ownership of the *alveus* has been followed in subsequent cases.[320]

(IV) MODERN LAW

3-85.   A private loch is defined as a non-tidal, perennial body of water which exists in a definite hollow.[321] The extent of a loch is determined by taking its ordinary state without variations due to flood or drought.[322] The water which a loch is composed of is a communal thing and incapable of ownership.[323] If a loch is surrounded by the land of one person, the *alveus* is wholly owned by that person unless the loch has expressly been conveyed to someone else.[324] If it is surrounded by the lands of several persons, it is presumed they each own a section of the *alveus* to the *medium filum*.[325] Ownership passes as a pertinent of the adjacent lands.[326] However, every owner of the *alveus* has a right to sail and fish over the entire loch due to common interest.[327]

---

[316] *Magistrates of Linlithgow v Elphinstone (No 2)* (1768) Mor 12805, Hailes 203 and below, paras 7-20–7-21 and 7-27.

[317] See Ch 2 and the arguments against ownership of a river as a body of water below, para 6-39.

[318] (1878) LR 3 App Cas 1324.

[319] At 1338.

[320] *Leny v Linlithgow Magistrates* (1894) 2 SLT 294; *Meacher v Blair-Oliphant* 1913 SC 417; *Kilsyth Fish Protection Association v McFarlane* 1937 SC 757.

[321] See discussion of the meaning of 'perennial' and 'definite hollow' below, paras 7-20–7-21 and 7-27.

[322] *Dick v Abercorn* (1769) Mor 12813; *Baird v Robertson* (1836) 14 S 396 and (1839) 1 D 1051; Rankine, *Landownership* 198.

[323] See discussion above, Ch 2.

[324] Rankine, *Landownership* 195; Ferguson 138; Reid, *Property* para 304; Gordon & Wortley, *Land Law* para 6-12.

[325] Rankine, *Landownership* 198; Reid, *Property* para 305; Gordon & Wortley, *Land Law* para 6-13.

[326] Rankine, *Landownership* 195; Reid, *Property* para 304.

[327] See below, para 7-75.

3-86.   The presumption of ownership to the *medium filum* can be displaced, for example by the *alveus* being excluded from the titles or where one owner can show a *habile* title to the *alveus* which has been fortified by prescription through exclusive possession. The cases on prescription were mostly decided at a time when the loch was seen as a separate object of common property and consider acts such as fishing and sailing.[328] However, arguably to acquire ownership of the entire *alveus* possession would have to be of the land rather than the water – and therefore merely the airspace which the water occupies – over it.[329] It is not clear whether a grant of land said to be 'bounded by a loch' would include the loch,[330] although in *Leny v Linlithgow Magistrates*[331] it was assumed that it did.

[328] *Baird v Robertson* (1836) 14 S 396; *Scott v Napier* (1869) 7 M (HL) 35; *Stewart's Tr v Robertson* (1874) 1 R 334 (in this case and *Baird* it was mentioned that a little water was the Sasine symbol for the lochs); *Meacher v Blair-Oliphant* 1913 SC 417. See also Ferguson 142–151.

[329] Gordon & Wortley, *Land Law* para 3-33.

[330] Reid doubts it does in *Property* para 304 n 5. However, Reid says this on analogy with the rule for non-tidal rivers. Surely such an analogy would be in favour of inclusion of the *alveus*.

[331] (1894) 2 SLT 294.

4 Alluvion and Avulsion

A. INTRODUCTION

4-01.   The ownership of land beneath water was discussed in the previous chapter. Water, however, is an unpredictable and ever-changing element. 'The boundaries between those parts of the earth's surface covered by water and those parts which are dry are in a state of constant, although gradual, flux.'[1] Under certain circumstances, these geographical changes are reflected in an alteration to the status of land – from dry land to *alveus* or from sea-bed to foreshore – and also to the ownership of land. This chapter will analyse the response of the law to the effects of water on land by considering the doctrines of alluvion and avulsion.

---

[1] Reid, *Property* para 592.

B. THE EFFECTS OF LAND ON WATER

4-02. There are several ways by which water can affect land. Due to the flowing of a river or lapping of the sea, tiny particles of soil can be eroded from one piece of land and become part of another. Large pieces of earth can become detached from the banks of a river or the foreshore through floods. Water boundaries can slowly encroach on or recede from dry land. A spate or storm can dramatically alter the *alveus* of a river or the landscape of the foreshore and adjoining dry land. Islands can rise up on the *alveus* of rivers and on the sea-bed or become accumulated from silt carried by the water. Islands can also be created when a river carves out a portion of the bank of a river or sea erosion causes the formation of sea stacks. These various changes can have different legal consequences.

C. ROMAN LAW

4-03. Roman law analysed some of these natural occurrences. In the *Digest*, Gaius explains the doctrines of alluvion and avulsion:

'what the river adds to our land by alluvion becomes ours by the law of nations. Addition by alluvion is that which is gradually added so that we cannot, at any given time, discern what is added. But if the force of the river should detach part of your land and bring it down to mine, it obviously remains yours. Of course, if it adheres to my land, over a period of time, and trees on it thrust their roots into my land, it is deemed from that time to have become part of my land.'[2]

Alluvion is an example of original acquisition and is treated as a sub-category of accession.[3] Gaius' description may bring to mind individual particles of soil being eroded from the banks of a river and transported downstream to be deposited on another's banks[4] – which is what many jurists consider the core of alluvion[5] and is primarily an issue between successive owners. Indeed, this would fit with the contrasting example of avulsion. However, Lewis has argued that alluvion was a broader concept and also included the situation where a river changed its course, moving further into or away from an owner's land. The newly exposed river-bed acceded to the adjacent owner's land and the opposite owner lost the part of his or her land which acceded to the public river-bed, this being more an issue between opposite owners.[6] Where a river increased in size the river-bed was augmented and adjacent owners lost part of their land.[7] A further option suggested by the texts was

---

[2] D.41.1.7.1–2 (Gaius); Justinian's *Institutes* 2.1.20.

[3] D.18.6.7.pr. (Paul).

[4] See also A Watson, *The Law of Property in the Later Roman Republic* (1968) 75.

[5] See discussion of the institutional writers below, paras 4-08–4-25.

[6] A D E Lewis, 'Alluvio: The Meaning of Institutes II.1.20' in A D E Lewis and P G Stein (eds), *Studies in Justinian's Institutes: In Memory of J.A.C. Thomas* (1983) 87 (hereafter 'Lewis, "Alluvio"'); D.41.1.7.5 (Gaius); D.41.1.30.1–3 (Pomponius); D.41.1.38.pr. (Alfenus Varus).

[7] D.41.1.30.3 (Pomponius); D.43.12.1.5 (Ulpian). See also Lewis, 'Alluvio' 87–89.

a river abandoning its bed or drying up. In this event, the old river-bed was divided between opposite landowners to the mid-point.[8] These examples demonstrate that, although Gaius' description focuses on acquisition through addition, there must always be a corresponding diminution of other lands, and alluvion should refer to the whole process of loss and gain. The examples are also consistent with public (perennial) river-beds being either ownerless or state-owned because, if the *alveus* was owned by the adjacent landowners, the drying up or increase of a public river would not result in a change of ownership but merely a change in the status of land from *alveus* to dry land.[9]

4-04.   For alluvion to operate, the change was required to be gradual and imperceptible. Imperceptible here is likely to have meant unnoticeable in process but not necessarily in result.[10] The reason why the addition must be imperceptible was not explained or expanded upon in the Roman texts. Where changes were perceptible and an identifiable piece of land was torn away and carried downstream, this was avulsion and did not result in accession unless and until the piece of land became secured in its new location.[11] Although it was specified that sudden flooding did not change the ownership of land,[12] it is not clear whether this was also defined as avulsion.

4-05.   Alluvion was said not to be applicable to *ager limitatus*, this being land with strictly defined boundaries.[13] Lewis explains that this is consistent with the policy of the doctrine:

> 'The problem of alluvion is one created by the erratic behaviour of one of the more important natural boundaries, the river. The application of the principles of *alluvio* is designed to preserve the utility of the river as a boundary marker. But where the division of property has been executed on a scientific basis taking no explicit notice of natural features there is obviously no need to rely on them and so no application for a principle based upon that reliance.'[14]

Thus, where a river changed its course and moved away from land which had been defined, the newly exposed river-bed did not accede to the dry land but was open to *occupatio*.[15] However, it was not specified what happened to imperceptible particles which attached to lower lands which were *ager limitatus*.

---

[8] D.41.1.30.1 (Pomponius); D.41.1.56.1 (Proculus); D.43.12.1.7 (Ulpian); Justinian's *Institutes* 2.1.23.

[9] See also above, para 3-04.

[10] Lewis, 'Alluvio' 92–94. Lewis's suggestion that if the change is noticed, this would affect the good faith of the acquirer is a radical one.

[11] D.41.1.7.2 (Gaius); Justinian's *Institutes* 2.1.21. Avulsion is apparently not a Roman term. See J A C Thomas, *Textbook of Roman Law* (1976) 172 n 81.

[12] D.43.12.1.9 (Ulpian); Justinian's *Institutes* 2.1.24. See also the ambiguous D.41.1.30.3 (Pomponius).

[13] D.41.1.16 (Florentius); W W Buckland, *Textbook of Roman Law from Augustus to Justinian* (3rd edn, P Stein (ed), 1963) 211; F de Zulueta, *Digest 41, 1 & 2* (1950) 57–58; A Watson, *The Law of Property in the Later Roman Republic* (1968) 76.

[14] Lewis, 'Alluvio' 93.

[15] D.43.12.1.7 (Ulpian).

4-06. Alluvion was said not to be applicable to lakes or pools.[16] This may be because lakes were rarely boundary markers and they did not change course or result in the accumulation of soil in the same manner.[17] Interestingly, the application of alluvion to the sea was not detailed.[18] Lewis suggests this is due to the lack of dramatic tidal activity in the central Mediterranean.[19]

4-07. In addition to consideration of water transporting soil and of rivers changing course, there is discussion of the ownership of islands arising in rivers. This was also often considered as an aspect of accession.[20] Islands could be created in three ways: by the river carving out a section of the bank, by part of the river-bed becoming dry, or by an accumulation of soil on the *alveus*. Pomponius says that in the first case ownership did not change.[21] In the other cases, the island belonged to those whose land was closest when the island appeared.[22] Gaius states that if an island arose at the mid-point of a river, it was owned by the adjacent owners.[23] This was several ownership divided in straight lines parallel and perpendicular to the banks.[24] However, these rules would only make sense if the river-bed was owned by the adjacent owners to the mid-point. Indeed, Paul states:

> 'If an island should arise in a public river nearer to your land, it is yours. Let us consider whether this is not wrong in respect of an island which does not cohere to the actual riverbed, but which is held in the river by brushwood or some other light material in such a way that it does not touch the riverbed and can itself be moved; such an island would be virtually public and part of the river itself.'[25]

This suggests that it is the attachment of the island to the *alveus* which is the important factor in determining ownership, and if the river-bed was not owned by the adjacent owners, islands cannot be said to accede to their land.[26] It is difficult to see why islands belonged to the landowners and were not ownerless or owned by the state. Indeed Labeo argues that islands arising in a public river should be public too.[27] However, the predominant view is

---

[16] D.41.1.12 (Callistratus); D.18.1.69 (Proculus); D.39.3.24.3 (Alfenus). See also A Rodger, 'The Rise and Fall of Roman Lakes' (1987) 55 *TvR* 19; T Mayer-Maly, 'Rutilia's Lake' (1995) 29 *Israel Law Review* 151.

[17] For discussion see Lewis, 'Alluvio' 90–92; Rodger, 'The Rise and Fall of Roman Lakes' (n 16) at 27.

[18] D.41.2.3.17 (Paul), D.41.2.30.3 (Paul) and D.42.5.12.2 regarding possession.

[19] Lewis, 'Alluvio' 90.

[20] See Thomas, *Textbook of Roman Law* (n 11) 172–173; Buckland, *Roman Law* (n 13) 211.

[21] D.41.1.30.2 (Pomponius). See also D.41.1.7.4 (Gaius); Justinian's *Institutes* 2.1.22.

[22] D.41.1.30.2 (Pomponius). See also D.41.1.7.3 (Gaius); D.41.1.56.pr. (Proculus); D.41.1.65.2 (Labeo); D.43.12.1.6 (Ulpian); Justinian's *Institutes* 2.1.22. Although presumably when an island was carved out of a river bank, it was closest to the bank out of which it had been carved.

[23] D.41.1.7.2 (Gaius); See also D.42.12.1.6 (Ulpian); Justinian's *Institutes* 2.1.22.

[24] D.41.1.29 (Paul); D.41.1.30.pr. (Pomponius).

[25] D.41.1.65.2 (Paul).

[26] Buckland raises the same objection. See Buckland, *Roman Law* (n 13) 211–212.

[27] D.41.1.65.4 (Labeo). See also above, para 3-04.

that islands belonged to adjacent landowners.[28] In accordance with the rules of changing river-beds, islands arising next to *ager limitatus* were ownerless and open to *occupatio*.[29] Islands rising in the sea were also ownerless.[30] This would suggest that the sea-bed was similarly ownerless.

D. INSTITUTIONAL WRITERS

4-08. The institutional writers consider the effects of water on land in some detail. The length of their discussion of the topic and the authority cited for their statements reveal the strong influence of Roman law. Unfortunately, this means that some of the uncertainties of that law are imported into Scots law. However, from the institutional works, the general principles of alluvion and avulsion can be deduced.

(1) Craig

4-09. Craig mentions alluvion when discussing the extent of the vassal's estate. Any 'accession to the lands comprised in the feu by alluvion or other natural means becomes a part of them, and the relations of superior and vassal apply to such part in the same way as to the original estate'.[31] Article 1.4.6 of the Books of the Feus is cited for this. Craig characterises alluvion as natural accession but he does not explain what 'alluvion' is. Islands in the sea are considered separately, in the title on public things, and such islands belong to the 'prince of the neighbouring mainland'[32], suggesting the Crown owns the sea-bed.[33] Where no one owns the sea-bed, islands forming in the sea will not be owned by anyone. Therefore, Craig reports: 'Some think that, if an island is distant more than a hundred miles from any mainland, it should become the property of him who discovers it.'[34] This suggests the sea-bed outwith this limit is ownerless and islands arising there are open to occupation.

[28] That islands should be treated differently is also shown when Ulpian argues that usufruct of the land does not extend to islands: D.7.1.9.4 (Ulpian). But alluvial accretions will usually be covered by pledge, usufruct or legacy of the land: D.7.1.9.4 (Ulpian); D.13.7.18.1 (Paul); D.30.1.24.2 (Pomponius). However, D.32.1.16 (Pomponius); D.32.1.17.1 (Maecianus) suggest that islands are also covered by legacies.

[29] D.43.12.1.6 (Paul).

[30] D.41.1.73 (Gaius); Justinian's *Institutes* 2.1.22.

[31] Craig, *Jus Feudale* 2.8.1.

[32] Craig, *Jus Feudale* 1.15.14. He also says that islands belong to 'the people inhabiting the adjoining mainland' which may be synonymous to Crown ownership or relating to public rights.

[33] See also Craig, *Jus Feudale* 2.8.20 and above, para 2-20. It is not clear here, however, whether Craig is discussing *imperium* or *dominium*.

[34] Craig, *Jus Feudale* 1.15.14.

(2) Stair

4-10.   Stair also considers the doctrine of alluvion and the ownership of islands, and gives a detailed explanation of both. In contrast to Craig, Stair does not categorise alluvion as part of accession but rather as a separate method of acquiring ownership. Alluvion is 'the adjection of another's ground insensibly, and unperceivably, by the running of a river, [which] becomes a part of the ground to which it is adjected'.[35] Soil carried by the river becomes part of the land to which it is attached 'because it is uncertain from whose ground such small and unperceivable particles are carried by the water, and thereby also the frequent questions that would arise betwixt the proprietors upon the opposite banks of rivers are prevented; and though the adjection may be perceivable and considerable in a tract of time, it maketh no difference, if at no particular instant the adjection be considerable'.[36] Stair only mentions the adjection of land despite the fact that addition to one person's land will inevitably mean a loss to another's. The word 'alluvion' is better used to mean the doctrine which regulates the whole process of loss and gain.[37] Alluvion is also considered in the restricted way that Lewis highlights and Stair does not seem to be considering the possibility of a river moving its course because in that case it is obvious where the new land attached to one's land has come from. However, Stair also seems to think alluvion is an issue between opposite owners rather than consecutive owners. This is perhaps surprising as particles of soil are more likely to originate upstream. No Roman authority is cited for the doctrine despite the clear influence of both Justinian's *Institutes* and *Digest* on Stair's account.

4-11.   Stair discusses islands, separately from alluvion, as part of the doctrine of occupation. Precious stones are owned by those who appropriate them:

> 'And likewise lands not possest; or which do arise of new, as do some islands in the sea, or more frequently in public rivers, which by the civil law are accounted to accresce to these, whose ground lies nearest, proportionably according to that part of the ground that fronts them; but where such civil constitution is not, such islands are public as the rivers are in which they are bred.'[38]

Justinian's *Institutes* 2.1.22 is cited for these statements. This passage is confusing. Stair switches from discussing islands in the sea in Scots law – which seem to be ownerless and capable of acquisition through occupation – to islands arising in public rivers in Roman law – which belong to the adjacent landowners. He then continues to say that where the Roman rules have not been accepted, which may include Scotland, islands in public rivers are also classified as public. This could mean that such islands were also ownerless but it is by no means certain that these islands could then be privately owned: they could merely be subject to public rights.[39] If, in Stair's

[35] Stair, *Institutions* II.1.35.
[36] Stair, *Institutions* II.1.35.
[37] See also Scottish Law Commission see Report on Land Registration Vol 1 (Scot Law Com No 222, 2010) para 5.34 n 33.
[38] Stair, *Institutions* II.1.33.
[39] See discussion of Stair's concept of public things above, paras 2-43–2-45.

view, islands arising in the sea and public rivers are ownerless in Scots law, the implication is that the sea-bed and *alveus* of navigable rivers are similarly ownerless.[40]

(3) Forbes

4-12.   In contrast to Stair but like Craig, Forbes analyses alluvion as a species of accession.[41] Alluvion is 'the insensible[42] Accretion of Earth to Ground bordered on a River by the effect or Force of the Water; which belongs to the Master of the said Ground.'[43] Alluvion is to be distinguished from the case where the stream carries a piece of ground downstream, ownership of which is only lost when it becomes firmly attached in its new location.[44] Thus, Forbes adopts the Roman distinction between alluvion and avulsion, although without using the latter term, citing Justinian's *Institutes* 2.1.20–21.

4-13.   At this point Forbes seems only to be considering particles of soil being washed on to land. However, also included within the scope of natural accession, but not clearly as an aspect of alluvion is the movement of public (navigable) rivers: where 'a River forsaketh it's natural Channel, and gains a new one upon the Land of another, the old Channel falls to be divided betwixt the adjacent land (if not bounded and limited)'.[45] Thus, the adjacent owners' dry land is augmented by the newly exposed *alveus*. Sudden flooding, however, does not change ownership.[46] This analysis is consistent with Lewis' view of Roman law but the two instances, when analysed as accession, can be seen as quite different in character. In the event of particles being added to one's land, this is moveable-to-land alluvion.[47] Where there is an insensible or imperceptible addition to land in this way there is no method of establishing the origin of the particles which have been added,[48] and it is common sense that these moveable particles become owned by the owner of land to which they finally attach – it would be very difficult for the law to be otherwise. However, they have also satisfied all the other tests of moveable-to-land accession, of physical attachment, functional subordination and permanency.[49] These requirements are fulfilled through the natural operation

[40] This is consistent with Stair's limited consideration of the *regalia* see above, paras 2-43–2-45.

[41] Forbes, *Great Body* Vol 1, 495.

[42] Forbes gives a definition of insensible similar to Stair's definition of imperceptible, see at 496.

[43] Forbes, *Great Body* Vol 1, 495.

[44] Forbes, *Great Body* Vol 1, 495. The reason for the difference is said to be that imperceptible particles cannot be reclaimed by the owners: at 495–496

[45] Forbes, *Great Body* Vol 1, 496.

[46] Forbes, *Great Body* Vol 1, 496

[47] This is noted in Badenhorst et al para 8.3 n 56.

[48] Stair, *Institutions* II.1.35; Forbes, *Great Body* Vol 1, 495–496. See also Erskine, *Institute* II.1.14.

[49] Erskine notes that the particles 'cannot be distinguished from the ground itself': *Institutes* II.1.14. See Reid, *Property* paras 578–582 on moveable-to-land accession.

of the river and no further events need to occur for ownership of the particles to be lost, unlike avulsion which requires subsequent happenings such as the growing of tree roots into the displaced piece of earth.

4-14. By contrast, where a river shifts its course, the land is already physically attached to the land immediately adjoining and only the water boundaries are moving. This is land-to-land alluvion.[50] Classifying this process as accession may seem odd. Accession usually occurs when two things are joined together. However, all land is obviously already connected to all other land. This could be seen as stretching the principles of accession too far. Yet, despite the distinction between these types of alluvion being clear in theory, it will often be difficult to make in practice. Changes to a water boundary will often involve both types and defining land-to-land alluvion as a *sui generis* form of original acquisition would be artificial and unnecessarily complicated. Categorising land-to-land alluvion as accession is perhaps the lesser of two evils.

4-15. A requirement that the change is insensible or imperceptible here must be mainly to prevent the operation of accession on the occurrence of temporary or dramatic events such as flooding or a river suddenly creating a new course for itself. If these events were defined as alluvion, there might be many changes of ownership in a short period or the sudden and arbitrary addition (and corresponding subtraction) of significant areas of land. This analysis serves to demonstrate that the purpose of the doctrine is to give proprietary effect to the small inevitable changes in geography that occur when water flows in its natural and normal course.

4-16. In Forbes' analysis discussed above, it is implied that public river-beds are not owned by adjacent landowners. However, this is not consistent with his statements regarding islands. Islands are also treated within his section on accession. If an island arises in the middle of a river it is 'common to those whose Lands lie nearest to the Bank on each Side of the River according the Breadth of their respective Fronts, and if nearer to one Side than to the other accrues to Lands on that side to which it is nearest because such an upstart Isleland seems either to be pluck'd off the banks of the adjacent Lands, or to have risen out of the Channel of the River which is as it was a Part of these Lands, tho publick while covered with the River.'[51] Justinian's *Institutes* 2.1.22, D.41.1.7.3 (Gaius), D.41.1.29 (Paul) and D.43.12.1.6 (Paul) are cited in support. Thus, Forbes adopts the Roman analysis which categorises the emergence of islands as accession but this also imports the contradictory suggestion that public river-beds are not owned by adjacent landowners.

(4) Bankton

4-17. For Bankton, alluvion is also an aspect of natural accession occurring where a river adds to one's land but 'it takes place only in grounds bounded

---

[50] Although it is not clear that Forbes is classifying this process as alluvion, this is the approach adopted below, para 4-48.

[51] Forbes, *Great Body* Vol 1, 496.

by the river'.⁵² The doctrine is again viewed as dealing with natural boundaries which suggests that it will not apply when boundaries are determined by other methods such as, perhaps, by measurements.⁵³ This is a hint towards the Roman restriction of alluvion to *ager non limitatus* with D.41.1.16 (Florentinus) being cited. However, it is too much of a simplification to say that alluvion does not apply to limited grants. Alluvion will not operate to add land beyond boundaries made definite by measurements but it will not stop operating altogether.⁵⁴

4-18.   In a similar way to Forbes, Bankton explains alluvion is to be distinguished from avulsion, 'where part of one's grounds is, by the force of a river, at once sensibly carried to another's, which becomes the other's property, when it is incorporated with it by Coalition, but not till then'.⁵⁵ Cited for these statements are D.41.1.7.1 and 2 (Gaius) on the difference between alluvion and avulsion. *Digest* 39.2.19.2 is also cited but there is no such section and this may be a reference to D.39.2.9.2 (Ulpian) which states that, once a tree belonging to one person has coalesced with another's land, the original owner loses the right of *vindicatio*.⁵⁶ It is not specified whether avulsion also encompasses sudden flooding but as avulsion is not clearly defined as such in Roman law, the institutional writers did not consider it.

4-19.   Bankton discusses islands and deserted river-beds within accession but not clearly as part of alluvion. In Roman law, Bankton explains, when a public river deserted its course or where an island arose in such a river, the *alveus* or island was divided between the adjacent landowners. Conversely, an island rising in the sea or next to *ager limitatus* belonged to the first occupant.⁵⁷ However, in Holland, islands in the sea or public rivers, and channels of deserted public rivers, are public and *inter regalia*.⁵⁸ It is not said whether these changes happen suddenly or slowly. The categorisation as public here seems to mean subject to public rights and the reference to *regalia* suggests owned by the Crown. This would imply that the sea-bed and the *alveus* of navigable rivers belong to the Crown. Bankton does not decide which rule applies in Scotland but here seems to favour the Dutch analysis, citing Craig.⁵⁹ However, regarding river-beds, at a different point in the *Institute* it is said that when a river changes course, the newly exposed land becomes owned by the adjacent landowners and the new channel becomes public but

---

⁵² Bankton, *Institute* II.1.10.
⁵³ This is also referred to in the quote given from Forbes, *Great Body* Vol 1, 496.
⁵⁴ See discussion further below, para 4-59.
⁵⁵ Bankton, *Institute* II.1.10.
⁵⁶ See also J Voet, *The Selective Voet being the Commentary on the Pandects* (P Gane (trans), 1955) on D.41.1.16 (Florentinus).
⁵⁷ D.41.1.7.3 (Gaius); D.41.1.65.2 (Paul) and D.42.1.29 (Paul) concerning islands; D.41.1.7.5 (Gaius) concerning rivers abandoning their beds and Voet's commentary on D.41.1.17–18 (Ulpian) are cited in this passage.
⁵⁸ Bankton, *Institute* II.1.10.
⁵⁹ Presumably Craig, *Jus Feudale* 1.15.14, discussed above. D.5.1.9 (Ulpian) is also cited, which is not mentioned in the *Jus Feudale*.

sudden inundations do not change ownership.[60] Therefore, it is perhaps only when a river suddenly changes its course that ownership of the *alveus* remains with the Crown.

(5) Erskine

4-20.   Erskine joins Craig, Bankton and Forbes in categorising alluvion as accession. Erskine does not specify the issue as being one between opposite owners but merely that alluvion is the 'insensible addition which grounds lying on the banks of a river receive by what the water washes gradually from other grounds'.[61] Justinian's *Institutes* 2.1.20 is cited as authority. Erskine states that where a change is perceptible as in the case of avulsion there is no change in ownership even when the detached piece of land becomes joined to another piece of land. This view is contrary to Bankton, Forbes and Roman law.[62] Justinian's *Institutes* 2.1.21 is cited even though this does not support Erskine's position. Arguably, this is contrary to the general principles of accession, and accords the requirement of imperceptibility too much importance. Merely because the piece of land can still be identified does not mean it has not been permanently attached to the land.

4-21.   Elsewhere in the *Institute,* Erskine also deals with public (navigable) rivers deserting their beds. If a river 'deserting its first channel, shall form to itself a new one, the new channel, because it must necessarily follow the condition of the river, becomes public; and the old one, which for the same reason ceaseth to be public, becomes the property of those to whom the adjacent grounds on each side belong'.[63] Justinian's *Institutes* 2.1.23 is cited. Erskine does not consider deserted river-beds in the context of alluvion and, like Bankton, does not specify whether the change happens suddenly or gradually. An underlying assumption is that public river-beds belong to someone other than the adjacent owners, probably the Crown, otherwise there would be no change in ownership.

(6) Bell

4-22.   Finally, Bell also sees alluvion as a species of accession. Further, he makes clear that he is discussing the slow and imperceptible addition to land both by particles brought downstream and also the 'slow retiring of a river'.[64] Stair, *Institutions* II.1.35 and Erskine, *Institute* II.1.14 are cited despite the fact they only mention the first type of alluvion. Unlike any of his predecessors, Bell applies alluvion not only to rivers but to the sea as well.[65] Thus, the

---

[60] Bankton, *Institute* I.3.4. Justinian's *Institutes* II.1.23–24 and D.41.1.7.5–6 (Gaius) are cited for this.
[61] Erskine, *Institute* II.1.14.
[62] See Justinian's *Institutes* 2.1.21 and D.41.1.7.2 (Gaius).
[63] Erskine, *Institute* II.1.5.
[64] Bell, *Principles* para 934.
[65] See also Bell, *Principles* para 642.

doctrine is said to apply when the sea washes particles of sand on to the foreshore. It also applies when the sea recedes from dry land. What was sea-bed becomes foreshore and what was foreshore becomes dry land, often with the result that the Crown's ownership of the sea-bed is lost. This goes beyond the Roman texts and was no doubt influenced by developments in the case law.[66]

4-23.   Bell distinguishes alluvion from *alvei mutatio* which is 'the change frequently occasioned by a river, which bounds the property of conterminous heritors, deviating from its course'[67] and does not result in acquisition by accession. *Marquis of Tweeddale v Kerr*[68] is cited here. It must be assumed that this is only applicable to sudden and noticeable changes, which differentiates *alvei mutatio* from the gradual changes of alluvion. Although the term *alvei mutatio* makes clear that Bell is discussing changes to river-beds, the multiplication of terms seems undesirable. There is no reason why sudden and noticeable changes in the *alveus* cannot be classified as avulsion, if the latter is defined appropriately.

4-24.   Bell continues by explaining that alluvion is to be distinguished from avulsion, which is the 'violent tearing away of a part of the ground of one proprietor, and depositing it in a shape capable of identification, along the bank of another's land'.[69] Bell does not specify what happens when the piece of land becomes attached to the adjacent bank. Justinian's *Institutes* 2.1.21 is cited. Bell adds that, although *alvei mutatio* and avulsion do not result in acquisition through accession, there may be a change of ownership through acquiescence on the part of the owner who stands to lose his or her property.[70] At this time, it was still possible to argue that acquiescence could affect the acquisition of property rights. Reid and Blackie, however, have now demonstrated that acquiescence is merely an aspect of personal bar which does not affect property rights.[71]

(7) Summary

4-25.   Although there are differences between the institutional writers,[72] a general consensus on alluvion and avulsion can be seen. Primarily a response to problems which arise due to water boundaries, alluvion is a species of accession where the operation of a river increases one person's land and diminishes another's. This can be by the river changing course as well as where particles of soil are added from opposite or upstream properties. The change has to be gradual and imperceptible. The formation of islands can

---

[66] Discussed further below.

[67] Bell, *Principles* para 936.

[68] (1822) 1 S 373, discussed further below, para 4-39.

[69] Bell, *Principles* para 936.

[70] Bell, *Principles* para 936. See also paras 945–947.

[71] E C Reid and J W G Blackie, *Personal Bar* (2006) paras 3-04 and 5-03–5-04. Personal bar and the role of intention in alluvion are considered below, paras 4-53–4-54.

[72] Mackenzie, *Institutions* II.1 only mentions alluvion as a species of accession and Hume does not mention it in the *Lectures*.

also be considered in the context of alluvion, and the ownership of islands appears to follow the ownership of the sea-bed or *alveus* in which they are formed. The doctrine is not limited to rivers but can apply to the sea. There is, however, no mention of lochs, or of alluvion taking place through human intervention. Sudden and noticeable changes will not, at least initially, result in the operation of accession and are categorised as avulsion.

E. CASE LAW

(1) Lochs

4-26.   The first case concerning alluvion involved a loch, a subject not treated at all by the institutional writers. In *Dick v Earl of Abercorn*,[73] Dick sought declarator of exclusive ownership of the *alveus* of Duddingston loch[74] and wished to have its boundaries determined and staked off. The Sheriff of Edinburgh was sent by the court to establish the boundaries when not swollen by flood or made dry by drought. The Earl objected to having the boundaries so set on the basis that the principles of alluvion were applicable to lochs as 'there was not a single argument in support of this doctrine, with regard to rivers, which did not, with equal strength, militate, when applied to lakes'[75]. Thus, if the loch diminished in size, his lands were increased correspondingly and he could still access the loch to exercise his servitude of watering cattle. Justinian's *Institutes* 2.1.23 was cited for this view as well as works by Huber, Sande and Blackstone and reports from Brownlow.[76] To find otherwise, it was argued, would allow a claim of damages each time the loch encroached on the Earl's land.[77] Dick responded that Roman law had no application here. Rather, feudal law governed this case, 'according to which the *alveus derelictus* of a river, or an *insula in flumina nata*, belonged to the crown'.[78] Further, even if Roman law applied, it was of no help. The authority cited concerned the *alveus* of public rivers, which could not be privately owned, rather than the *alveus* of lochs which could. Citing D.41.1.12 (Callistratus) and

---

[73] (1769) Mor 12813.

[74] For discussion of other aspects of this case, see above, para 3-77.

[75] (1769) Mor 12813 at 12814.

[76] Whitty, 'Water' 466 n 441 suggests these citations are: U Huber, *Praelectiones Juris Civilis* (1690) Vol 3 *ad* D.41.1.10; J van den Sande, *Decisiones Frisicae* (4th edn, 1664) Book V, Title 2 (*De Flumine publico, ejusque exsiccatione*), Definitio 2 (*Ad lacum publicum excissandum omnes ejus accolas esse admittendos*). See also R Brownlow, *Reports of Divers Choice Cases* (1651) Vol 1 142. These citations could not be confirmed by the session papers available for the case. See Petition for the Earl of Abercorn 20 Jul 1768 (Robert McQueen), *Dick v Earl of Abercorn* Campbell Collection Vol 18, Paper 49; Answers for Dick 20 Sept 1768 (Henry Dundas), *Dick v Earl of Abercorn* WS 134:44a; Petition for Dick 3 Mar 1769 (Henry Dundas), *Dick v Earl of Abercorn* WS 346:20; Answers for the Earl of Abercorn 25 Apr 1769 (Robert McQueen), *Dick v Earl of Abercorn* WS 346:20.

[77] Although arguing on the basis of alluvion, the Earl seemed most concerned with seasonal variations. The extent of the *alveus*, however, would be determined by the land ordinarily covered by water and alluvion would not operate to change ownership on account of such variations.

[78] (1769) Mor 12813 at 12815.

16 (Florentinus), it was argued that there was authority that alluvion did not apply to lakes as the grant of a land bounded by a lake is a limited grant.[79] When the loch increased in size, the Earl was obliged to accept the water due to a natural servitude but did not lose any land.

4-27.   The court found for Dick and held that the boundaries set by the Sheriff were the true and permanent[80] boundaries of the loch but that in dry weather the Earl could follow the loch and in flood Dick could follow the loch. This rejects the application of land-to-land alluvion for lochs, a result consistent with Roman law as well as reflecting the fact that lochs are less likely to be boundaries between lands and also less liable to natural permanent movement. The right to follow the loch for watering was attributed to the Earl's servitude[81] whereas, although not specified in the case, the right to follow the loch for fishing could be attributed to common interest.[82]

4-28.   The question of the extent to which alluvion applied to lochs was revisited in *Cuninghame v Dunlop and Robertson*.[83] Here the sole owner of the *alveus* of a loch, Cuninghame, sought declarator to fix its boundaries. It was alleged that the tenant of an adjacent owner, Robertson, had drained the loch in order to extend a servitude of pasturage on the *alveus* of the loch when dry. The Lord Ordinary found that the extent of Cuninghame's property must vary with the rising and falling of the loch through natural or lawful artificial means and that he did not own the newly exposed dry land. It followed that Cuninghame was not entitled to have the boundary of the loch ascertained. However, the tenant was not entitled to carry out operations aimed at draining the loch. On appeal, and following *Dick v Earl of Abercorn*,[84] the court found that the natural boundaries of the loch could be marked off suggesting that alluvion does not operate. That Dunlop could follow the water to exercise his servitude was not disputed.

4-29.   The issue was considered once again in *Baird v Robertson*.[85] Artificial operations had been made on a loch, the *alveus* of which was solely owned by Baird, lowering the level of the water. The question was whether Robertson, an adjacent proprietor, was entitled to the newly exposed land.[86]

---

[79] Vinnius' commentary on D.39.3.24.3 (Alfenus) is also cited. This text states that when lakes rise or fall, the neighbouring owners cannot do anything to affect the fluctuations of the water.

[80] Although it could be argued that merely marking the boundaries of a loch does not mean that they could not subsequently change, Lord Gillies states the court in *Dick* established the permanent extent of the loch. See *Cuninghame v Dunlop and Robertson* (1838) 16 S 1080 at 1084. On this case see further below.

[81] This case is not dealt with in Cusine & Paisley but at para 3.83 it is said that a servitude of *aquaehaustus* implies a right of access to the water.

[82] See discussion below, para 7-75.

[83] (1836) 15 S 295 and (1838) 16 S 1080.

[84] (1769) Mor 12813.

[85] (1836) 14 S 396 and (1839) 1 D 1051.

[86] Embankments had been placed on this land but it is not mentioned in the interlocutor whether these had to be removed by Robertson.

The Lord Ordinary considered alluvion in detail. He quoted from an interlocutor granted by Lord Medwyn in the unreported case of *Graham of Kinross's Tr v Boswell*[87] concerning very similar facts which stated that:

'although the defender might have been entitled to appropriate the ground ex adverso of his lands, if the waters of the loch had, by some natural cause, receded, or by some act of his own not objected to, been excluded; it is quite different where the ground has been rendered dry and fit for use by artificial means employed by the proprietor of the loch, and at his expense, so that the solum of the loch, which was his property when covered by the water, still remains his property when the water is drained, nothing having been done by the parties to transfer the property from the one to the other.'[88]

4-30. The Lord Ordinary in *Baird* went further, however, and found alluvion applicable to lochs including changes caused by human acts after the passing of a period of time.[89] This decision was recalled on appeal. On the basis of *Dick v Earl of Abercorn*,[90] the natural and ordinary state of the loch was 'affected neither by floods nor by drought'[91] and its extent before the artificial operations[92] was held to be the boundary which Baird was entitled to have delineated. What was not mentioned was whether Robertson was entitled to follow the loch for the exercise of the servitude of watering.[93]

4-31. All these cases concerned non-tidal lochs, and the doctrine of alluvion was not held to operate to change the boundaries. There is no authority on tidal lochs. However, as tidal lochs may have a foreshore, to which alluvion does apply in this way, and are more susceptible to permanent fluctuations due to movement of the sea, it is suggested alluvion does apply to such lochs.

(2) The Foreshore and Human Acts

4-32. Cases involving the foreshore and human intervention were before the courts at an early stage. They tended to concern embankments on the shore which shut out the sea or caused the accumulation of soil resulting in

[87] Unreported 14 Nov 1835. The Lord Ordinary's discussion here is the only evidence I could find of this case.

[88] Quoted in *Baird v Robertson* (1839) 1 D 1051 at 1053. The application of alluvion to changes caused by human acts is considered further below.

[89] The Lord Ordinary specifies a period of 30 to 35 years which is less than immemorial possession. The reason for this requirement is unclear. See the highly inventive decision at (1839) 1 D 1051 at 1054–1060.

[90] (1769) Mor 12813.

[91] (1839) 1 D 1051 at 1058.

[92] The court did not seem to share the concerns of the Lord Ordinary that it was impossible to determine the natural extent of the loch.

[93] Recognised in the previous case *Baird v Robertson* (1836) 14 S 396 at 400. See also the odd case of *Glen v Bryden* (1830) 8 S 893 which decided that an owner with a limited grant of land was entitled to interdict interference of possession of the dry *alveus* of a loch but was not entitled to a possessory judgment. As this was a limited title, Glen could not acquire the *alveus* through prescription as it is outwith the boundaries of the grant. It is not revealed by the report who actually did own the *alveus*, as the owner could presumably have obtained interdict against Glen.

the gaining of land, and so involved both moveable-to-land as well as land-to-land alluvion. In *Smart v Magistrates of Dundee*,[94] Smart's land was described in the title deeds as 'that enclosed yard, lying within the burgh of Dundee, bounded by...the sea flood upon the south'. Smart argued that, as his property was bounded by the 'sea flood', all ground seaward, including the shore, belonged to him 'whether the same has been gained or occasioned by the gradual retiring of the tides, or whether the soil has been recovered from the sea by an *opus manufactum*'.[95] There was no discussion of whether this reclamation occurred rapidly or slowly. The Lord Ordinary (Monboddo) initially found that Smart had the right to the land seaward whether this was exposed through natural or human means. Smart's arguments in favour of this position were that, by Roman law, the banks of navigable rivers belonged to the adjacent landowners and each was entitled to alluvial increases. Further, the shore in Roman law was open to occupation. Therefore, whether the disputed land was seen as a bank or the shore, it was owned by Smart. The only authority given in the report is a passage in Erskine's *Institute* regarding the shore which states that adjacent owners 'inclose as their own property grounds far within the sea-mark'.[96] However, this statement does not suggest that owners are entitled to gain land from the sea. The Magistrates reclaimed, accepting the point that the owner of the shore was entitled to gain land from the sea but arguing that the grant of land was limited to an enclosed yard and therefore there was no entitlement to any land outwith the boundary. This leans towards the Roman restriction of alluvion to *ager non limitatus*.[97] The appeal court found for the Magistrates on the basis that this was a limited plot of land, a result confirmed by the House of Lords.[98] From this point onwards, however, it seems to have been accepted that alluvion operated even when the change was due to human intervention.

4-33.   In *Innes v Downie*[99] it was stated by Lord President Campbell, that Innes' 'property of the shore is subject to the risk of being impaired or destroyed by the sea; and, on the other hand, has the advantage of gaining on the sea *alluvione*, provided always he do not impede the uses of navigation, which is the single restraint of his right'. The Lord President did not limit this to acquisition by natural means. In *Magistrates of Culross v Geddes*,[100] the sea had receded naturally from the shore. It was argued for Geddes that it was a 'settled point in our law, that one whose charter gives him his lands

[94] (1797) 3 Pat 606 at 607. A fuller report is available in the English reports (1797) VIII Brown 119, 3 ER 481 where it is said the decision 'is only inserted here as of some importance on the general law of *alluvion*'.

[95] (1797) 3 Pat 606 at 607.

[96] Erskine, *Institute* II.6.17. Frustratingly the English report states 'The appellant then went into a discussion of some length as to the principles and maxims of the civil law on this subject, but with which it does not appear necessary to burden this report': (1797) 3 ER 481 at 490.

[97] See above, para 4-05.

[98] The reports reveal an impressive line-up of advocates. Smart had H Erskine, T Erskine, W Adam and H D Inglis acting for him. The Magistrates were represented by J Scott and W Tait. See also *Kerr v Dickson* (1840) 3 D 154 (aff'd 1842 1 Bell's App 499).

[99] (1807) Hume 552 at 553.

[100] (1809) Hume 554 at 555.

with the shore for boundary, not only has a right to all the space down to the high water-mark, but is entitled to embank and shut out the sea (provided he do not impede public uses of the strand), and still more to gain, as here, by natural alluvion and the recess of the sea-flood'. This argument implies that the shore is owned by the embanker, otherwise the embankment would be an unlawful encroachment. The court found Geddes entitled to build on the newly exposed dry land, and did not seek to challenge his assertion.[101] This case also shows that, where the sea recedes, part of the sea-bed becomes the foreshore and part of the shore becomes dry land, for it was argued by Geddes that the space in question was no longer part of the shore as it was not covered by the ordinary tides.[102] This case was cited with approval in *Boucher v Crawford*[103] and *Campbell v Brown*[104] where it was suggested that the owners of the shore were entitled to add to their lands through artificial means, with Lord Meadowbank in the latter case declaring that 'every proprietor has a right to gain ground from the shore'.[105] Again, there is no mention of whether this addition needs to happen slowly or can occur rapidly but if artificial means are used changes are bound to occur rapidly.

4-34. Despite this seemingly settled position, however, there is some contrary authority. In *Irvine v Robertson*,[106] Robertson was an owner of land adjacent to the shore and attempted to enclose land which had been gained from the sea through reclamation carried out by the inhabitants of Lerwick. Lord Cowan stated that ground 'gained from the sea must be viewed as belonging to the Crown, unless it has been conveyed to private parties'.[107] In this case, Lord Cowan interpreted Robertson's title to mean he had only a right of access to the shore rather than ownership. Thus, presumably the Crown owned the shore.[108] However, Robertson's land could still have been found to have been augmented by land which had been gained from the sea-bed and foreshore. The legality of the reclamation was not discussed but this may have been a factor in the prevention of alluvion.[109] Further, Robertson

---

[101] See also *Leven v Magistrates of Burntisland* (1812) Hume 555 but in this case is it not clear whether Leven owned the shore.

[102] This point was noticed in *Officers of State v Smith* (1846) 8 D 711. See also *Hunter v Lord Advocate* (1869) 7 M 899 where the adjacent landowner did not own the shore but his adjacent land was increased through alluvion. However, in *Boucher v Crawford* 30 Nov 1814 FC at 69 it is suggested that the land in question was still the shore.

[103] 30 Nov 1814 FC. However, Bell mentions that the case was appealed to the House of Lords and was to be reversed but on the death of one of the parties, the judgment was not signed: Bell, *Illustrations from Adjudged Cases of the Principles of the Law of Scotland* (1836–1838) Vol 2, 2. Thus, the case should not be relied upon as authority.

[104] 18 Nov 1813 FC.

[105] At 446–447. See also *Erskine of Dunn v Magistrates of Montrose* (1819) Hume 558 at 560; *Berry v Holden* (1840) 3 D 205 at 212 concerning artificial embankments; *Blyth's Trs v Shaw* (1883) 11 R 99; *Lockhart v Magistrates of North Berwick* (1902) 5 F 136 concerning natural recession.

[106] (1873) 11 M 298.

[107] At 301.

[108] Even though the case was in Shetland. See *Shetland Salmon Famers Association v Crown Estate Commissioners* 1991 SLT 166.

[109] See further below, para 4-55.

did seem to be claiming an area of land which included part of the shore beyond that which was immediately adjacent to his land, and in any event Lord Cowan made clear that this was merely a possessory judgment and so it might be 'within the power of the respondent by declaratory action to vindicate the right which he now asserts, as against the Crown and all other parties interested'.[110]

4-35.   In *Smith v Lerwick Harbour Trs*[111] Lord Kinnear also seemed to doubt that land could be gained from the sea through embankment. It was stated, in circumstances where the Crown owned the shore, that if 'the proprietor of the adjoining land encloses a part of the foreshore and converts it into dry ground that will no doubt be a very distinct assertion of a right, and it will go to establish a claim of property if he has possessed for a sufficient time upon an *ex facie* sufficient title. But apart from a valid title or prescriptive possession, I cannot see that it is a fact of much importance.'[112] However, where the Crown owns the shore any embankment on the shore will be an unlawful encroachment. Therefore, this may indicate that any embanking act must be lawful to result in alluvion. In any case, this was an *obiter* comment as the party in this case was found to own the foreshore.

4-36.   Allowing changes in ownership to occur when land is reclaimed from the sea or a tidal river is contrary to the general purpose of alluvion, which was identified from the discussions of the institutional writers as applying accession to the inevitable and natural changes which take place in water boundaries. If, as seems inevitable, changes by reclamation occur quickly and noticeably, classifying this as accession erodes the distinction between alluvion and avulsion.

4-37.   A potential explanation for the apparent willingness of the courts to extend alluvion to human acts of reclamation is that ownership of the sea-bed, foreshore and *alveus* of public rivers was uncertain at this time. The cases fail to consider in detail the interest of the Crown or other possible owners. The contrary authority comes at the end of the 19th and beginning of the 20th centuries, after the Crown had begun to assert its rights.[113] Reclaiming land may involve building on land under water. As ownership of such land is now established, this may amount to an encroachment which the owner – the Crown or its disponee – is entitled to have removed. A prerequisite of legality of the embankment or reclamation for the operation of alluvion may be implied by *Irvine v Robertson*[114] and *Smith v Lerwick Harbour Trs*.[115] However, even if the person reclaiming land owns the foreshore, building on the foreshore of a tidal river may materially affect the natural flow, in breach of common interest.[116] Thus, on the one hand, if a lawful act is a requirement of alluvion by human means, there will be few instances when the act will be

---

[110] (1873) 11 M 298 at 303.
[111] (1903) 5 F 680.
[112] At 691.
[113] See above, paras 3-30–3-39.
[114] (1873) 11 M 298.
[115] (1903) 5 F 680.
[116] See below, paras 7-63–7-68.

lawful. On the other hand, for the law to allow the adjacent landowner to increase his or her land by an act which is likely to be unlawful is incoherent. The foreshore cases in favour of alluvion applying to human acts also appear to conflict with some authority from cases involving rivers, which are considered in the next section.

(3) Rivers[117]

4-38. There is little authority on the operation of alluvion with regard to rivers. This is perhaps surprising because the Roman and the institutional jurists consider rivers to be the main subject of the doctrine.

4-39. In *Marquis of Tweeddale v Kerr*,[118] a private river which was the boundary between two properties had moved significantly into the Marquis' land. A civil jury had found the change to be slow, imperceptible and not caused by the operations of Kerr. The Marquis argued that because Kerr had never possessed the disputed land, the Marquis was still entitled to it. The Lord Ordinary found for Kerr. This interlocutor was upheld on appeal, but with a variety of opinions from the judges. While Lord Hermand and Lord President Hope did not seem to take issue with this being a case of alluvion, Lords Balgray, Gillies and Campbell thought otherwise. Lord Gillies, in his dissenting opinion, explained that 'Stair assigns, as his reason for allowing accession by alluvio, that the particles have been acquired imperceptibly from a property which is not known. But here it is evident that they were acquired from the pursuer; in which case the defender can have no claim.'[119] Lord Gillies saw moving river-beds, or *alvei mutatio* as he called it,[120] as different from the case of soil being transported from elsewhere. Thus, there had been no change of ownership. This is a plausible view, although as we have seen above, Bell (the *Principles* only being published subsequently) considered moving river-beds to be part of the doctrine of alluvion. Lords Balgray and Campbell also did not see the facts as coming within alluvion and defined it as *alvei mutatio*, but did not see this as a barrier to ownership changing, and mentioned the importance of acquiescence. As both owners could have chosen to embank their lands, they were deemed to have agreed to the change.[121] In fact, the ability of landowners to embank their lands was uncertain at the time.

---

[117] The distinction between cases concerning rivers and those concerning the foreshore is somewhat arbitrary as tidal rivers will usually have a foreshore. However, of the cases considered below only *Todd v Clyde Trs* (1840) 2 D 357 (aff'd by the House of Lords in (1841) 2 Rob 333) may concern a tidal river and the foreshore was not discussed.

[118] (1822) 1 S 373.

[119] At 375.

[120] Bell, strangely, takes the term *alvei mutatio*, citing *Marquis of Tweeddale v Kerr*, to be a term indicating where ownership does not change but it is suggested that here Bell, in order to be consistent with his own analysis, must be referring to sudden and noticeable changes. See Bell, *Principles* para 936 and discussion above, para 4-23.

[121] This was a time, as stated above, when it was still possible to argue that acquiescence could affect the acquisition of property rights rather than merely being an aspect of personal bar, see Reid and Blackie, *Personal Bar* (n 71) paras 3-04 and 5-03–5-04.

Certainly in modern law, if the embankment interfered with the natural flow of the water, this would breach common interest.[122]

4-40.   The issue of human acts and private rivers was raised in *Fisher v Duke of Atholl's Trs.*[123] It appears that the Duke and Fisher were opposite owners and each would therefore own the *alveus* to the *medium filum*. The Duke, and his trustees after his death, had deposited stones and rubbish on a part of the *alveus* belonging to Fisher as part of building a bridge – which had been authorised by statute – and which resulted in the extension of Fisher's bank. It was held that the embankment was owned by Fisher, even though it was not built by her. Presumably, the embankment had acceded to the *alveus* and this built-up piece of *alveus* had acceded to dry land although whether any aspect of this process is to be defined as alluvion is unclear.[124]

4-41.   That such acts could result in changes of ownership was questioned by the case of *Todd v Clyde Trs.*[125] Here the Clyde Trustees had been empowered by various Acts of Parliament to improve the navigation of the Clyde. At this time, public rivers were those which were navigable and so the *alveus* was owned by the Crown – although the point was not fully settled.[126] The Trustees had narrowed the channel through embankments on each side, allowing a considerable amount of land to be gained from the river. Todd, an adjacent proprietor, occupied and sold some of this land. The Trustees then decided to widen the channel once more. Todd objected and raised a declarator that he was owner of the newly exposed land. The Lord Ordinary's note favoured the Trustees and stated it is 'a long, and by no means an easy step, from the cause of gradual and imperceptible *accession*, by the action of natural causes, to great and sudden acquisition of additional land, by artificial operations of the acquirer himself: but it is a still greater and far more difficult step, from this last, to the allowance of such acquisitions to an inactive proprietor'.[127] The Inner House also found for the Trustees with Lord Justice-Clerk Boyle suggesting that the crucial factor was that Todd did not contribute or consent to the construction of the embankment and so could not gain by it. Lord Meadowbank did not seem to allow the application of alluvion to navigable rivers at all as the Crown or its disponees[128] were entitled to object to the embankment. Lord Medwyn did not think alluvion applied to artificial operations.

4-42.   The points made by the judges highlight the problems created by applying alluvion to human acts. If it is accepted that human acts may result in a change of ownership through alluvion, what is the justification for making

[122] See below, paras 7-63–7-68.
[123] (1836) 14 S 880.
[124] If it is to be defined as alluvion, it would follow that the line of the *medium filum* would also move and the opposite owner would lose a section of the *alveus*.
[125] (1840) 2 D 357 (aff'd by the House of Lords in (1841) 2 Rob 333).
[126] See above, paras 3-46–3-49.
[127] (1840) 2 D 357 at 363.
[128] Lord Meadowbank suggests that the Crown has alienated the *alveus* of the Clyde to the Trustees through the Acts of Parliament allowing them to improve navigation. However, the Acts do not expressly convey the *alveus*.

a difference between acts by the owner and acts by a third party? If the argument is that acts by the third party are likely to be unlawful, then the same must also be true of acts of the owner if the act interferes with the natural flow of a river. Further, what is the relevance of consent? Alluvion is part of the law of accession which is an objective doctrine and takes place regardless of the parties' intention.[129]

4-43.   The House of Lords dismissed the appeal against this decision and found the case regulated by *Smart v Magistrates of Dundee*[130] without a full explanation of why.[131] In truth, Todd's land was limited by precise measurements and thus alluvion would not have operated to add to his land beyond these measurements, with *Smart* being authority for this.[132]

4-44.   After *Todd* a period of 150 years elapsed until the next case on alluvion, *Stirling v Bartlett*.[133] In this case the boundary of two plots of land was a private river. The river was liable to flooding and in 1966 a large flood caused the river to be spread over a number of small channels. By agreement in 1967, the parties dug a new channel for the river which was mostly to the east of the old. The question was whether the *medium filum* of the new or old channel represented the boundary. Lord Coulsfield described alluvion as change effected 'by the gradual and imperceptible addition or subtraction of soil on one bank or the other'[134] which is a neat summary of both types of alluvion. Avulsion was defined as sudden or violent changes whether natural or brought about with human assistance (regard was not paid to the foreshore cases discussed above). Applying these principles, it might be thought that the boundary was the *medium filum* of the *alveus* before any artificial operations took place. It was not important to have regard to any agreement between the parties. Indeed Lord Coulsfield stated that 'without specific authority, there is, I think, no difficulty in reaching the conclusion that a mere agreement between proprietors to dig a wholly new channel for a river, without any agreement to a change in ownership, would not effect such a change: and in any event, a bare agreement, without appropriate formalities, would not transfer the title to heritage.'[135] This is a strong point: parties cannot change boundaries – and therefore transfer title – without writing and registration.

4-45.   However, Lord Coulsfield then decided that the *medium filum* of the artificial channel was the boundary between the parties. For it is:

[129] Reid, *Property* para 572.
[130] (1797) 3 Pat 606, VIII Brown 119, 3 ER 481.
[131] (1841) 2 Rob 333.
[132] In fact the Trustees and Todd came to a compromise that Todd would be paid half the value of the reclaimed land. The Crown, unsuccessfully, tried to claim this money: see *Lord Advocate v Clyde Trs* (1849) 11 D 391 (affirmed (1852) 15 D (HL) 1).
[133] 1992 SC 523. There is material available in the National Archives of Scotland in relation to this case under the reference *Roderick William Kenneth Stirling v William T Bartlett* CS258/1987/2704, CS258/1992/4400 and CS46/1993/721. My thanks go to Professor Paisley for providing the archive references which are noted throughout this book.
[134] 1992 SC 523 at 529.
[135] At 531.

'common sense to treat the channel dug out in 1967 as being the channel of the river for the purpose of fixing the boundary for the time being and subject to any further natural changes, and that there is nothing contrary to any established principle or authority in so holding. On the evidence available, this is not a case where there had been an *avulsio,* nor is it a case in which a wholly new artificial channel has been created, nor a case in which a change has been brought about by the actions of one proprietor alone. It is a case in which the proprietors agreed to restore a channel which had been effectively destroyed, and it is in my view entirely consistent with principle to regard the mid-line of that channel as the boundary between them for the time being.'[136]

4-46.   Lord Coulsfield contradicts his own reasoning in making this decision. He had, until this point, been of the opinion that sudden human acts were avulsion which did not result in a change of ownership and furthermore that agreement of the parties was of no importance to the issue. The effect of his decision is that when, in 1967, the parties dug a new channel and agreed this was the boundary, this transferred a piece of land from the defender's predecessor to the pursuer. Such informal transfer of property is not possible. Admittedly, to find otherwise would be challenging as the position of the original *alveus* would be difficult to establish, but that does not mean it is not the position that the law takes.

4-47.   How this case should have been decided is difficult to determine. The cases concerning human acts do not specify what the specific requirements are for alluvion to apply. If human acts are regarded as beyond the scope of alluvion – as suggested below – the situation would be as follows. When the flood occurred in 1966, this was avulsion and no land-to-land accession took place. The parties would have been entitled to restore the *alveus* to its natural condition as this would not breach common interest.[137] In digging a new channel that did not follow the original *alveus,* they materially interfered with the natural flow of the river. This was also avulsion because it was a sudden and artificial change which would not affect ownership. Ownership could then only be changed on the operation of prescription through a *habile* title in the Sasine Register.[138] On the Land Register, being plan-based, ownership of the ground between the old and new *medium filum* could not be acquired through prescription.

F. MODERN LAW

(1) General Principles

4-48.   The purpose of alluvion is to ensure that the inevitable geographical alterations to land caused by the natural movement of water are reflected in corresponding changes to the status or ownership of land. Alluvion is a

---

[136] At 532.

[137] See discussion below, para 7-62.

[138] Although we are not told in the case whether the titles were on the Sasine Register or the Land Register, the plots of land were in the County of Ross and Cromarty which was not operational for the Land Register until 1 April 2003.

species of accession.[139] The doctrine results in the addition, with corresponding subtraction, to land. The increase and diminution can be of particles of soil eroded through the movement of water (moveable-to-land alluvion) or caused by the moving of a water boundary (land-to-land alluvion).[140] Other legal systems such as Louisiana and England give these two processes different names but in this account both are included in the definition of alluvion and, as suggested above,[141] to do otherwise is unnecessarily complicated and artificial.[142] Any change has to be gradual and imperceptible.[143] Alluvion applies where a water boundary is the sea, a river or a public (tidal) loch.[144] Thus, for example, when particles of soil which are swept downstream attach to a lower bank, the upper owner loses ownership and the owner of the bank acquires ownership of the particles. When a private (non-tidal) river moves away from A's land, land which was formerly the *alveus* accedes to A's dry land; land which was formerly dry land on opposite owner B's land accedes to the *alveus*.[145] Where the sea encroaches on land, the land which was formerly dry accedes to the foreshore, and land which was the foreshore accedes to the sea-bed with the result that the Crown gains land.[146] As the sea can encroach, so it can also recede, with the result that the adjacent landowner can gain land and the Crown can lose.[147] Where a public river dries up, the Crown loses its ownership as the newly exposed land accedes to the adjacent dry land.[148] Louisiana has a novel, and perhaps odd, rule in this situation. Where a public (navigable) river, the bed of which is owned by the state,[149] abandons its course and forges a new

---

[139] Craig, *Jus Feudale* 2.8.1; Forbes, *Great Body* Vol 1, 495; Bankton, *Institute* II.1.10; Erskine, *Institutes* II.1.14; Bell, *Principles* para 934.

[140] Bell, *Principles* para 934.

[141] See above, paras 4-12–4-14.

[142] See Louisiana *Code civil* Art 499 for the distinction between alluvion and dereliction; C Marsh (ed) 'Water' in Halsbury's Law of England (Vol 49(2), 4th edn, 2004) (hereafter 'Halsbury, 'Water'') para 23 for the distinction between accretion, alluvion and dereliction. English law also makes a distinction between addition (alluvion) and subtraction (diluvion): see K Gray and S Gray, *Elements of Land Law* (5th edn, 2008) paras 1.2.6–1.2.8; Land Registration Act 2002 s 61(1). This latter distinction may originate from W Blackstone, *Commentaries on the Laws of England* (1765–1769) II.16.

[143] The change must only be imperceptible at the time rather than in the result. See the explanation of Forbes, *Great Body* Vol 1, 496; Stair, *Institutions* II.1.35 'as the motion of the palm of a horologe is insensible at any instant, though it be very perceivable when put together, in less than the quarter of the hour.'

[144] Bell, *Principles* para 934. See also cases discussed regarding the foreshore above, paras 4-32–4-37. Other legal systems have extended alluvion to the sea contrary to Roman law: see Halsbury, 'Water' para 23; Van der Merwe, 'Things' para 330. Alluvion will not operate to change the boundary of the sea in Louisiana: see Louisiana *Code civil* Art 500. For private lochs see below.

[145] *Marquis of Tweeddale v Kerr* (1822) 1 S 373.

[146] *Magistrates of Culross v Geddes* (1809) Hume 554.

[147] The need to emphasise symmetry in the law was identified by C T Reid and D J McGlashan, 'Erosion, Accretion and Intervention' 2005 *Jur Rev* 73.

[148] Forbes, *Great Body* Vol 1, 496; Erskine, *Institute* II.1.5.

[149] Louisiana *Code civil* Art 450.

one, the newly exposed land is divided between the owners of land who have lost part of their land to the state even though the exposed land is not contiguous to their lands.[150]

4-49.   The ownership of islands has been scarcely considered,[151] but it is suggested that the formation of islands can be brought within the scope of alluvion.[152] Islands may form through particles accumulating on the *alveus* and in this case the island will belong to the owner of the *alveus*.[153] This is moveable-to-land alluvion. In the event of a sea stack forming or an island being carved out of the bank of a river, the stack or island will accede to the *alveus*. This is land-to-land alluvion, and will result in a change of ownership if the bank or shore and the *alveus* or sea-bed are owned by different people. Islands can also form through land being forced upwards from underneath. This again would be land-to-land alluvion.[154] Here ownership does not change but the status of land does, from *alveus* or sea-bed to dry land.[155]

4-50.   If islands are formed on the boundary between properties – for example on the *medium filum* of a private river – ownership of the island will be determined by the extent of the ownership of the *alveus*.[156] The law in South Africa is the same.[157] If the island gradually migrates downstream, ownership will change according to which part of the *alveus* it is attached to[158] unlike in Louisiana where ownership is fixed from the time at which the island was formed.[159] As can be seen, alluvion will often operate to change ownership, but where one person owns all the land involved, accession will take place and the status of the land will be altered but ownership will not be affected.

4-51.   Any land added by alluvion becomes part of the principal land due to accession, so that the increase or decrease of land may affect the

---

[150] Art 504; A N Yiannopoulos, *Louisiana Civil Law Treatise: Property* (4th edn, 2001) para 76.

[151] Craig, *Jus Feudale* 1.15.14; Stair, *Institutions* II.1.33; Forbes, *Great Body* Vol 1, 496. See also the case of *Pool v Dirom* (1823) 2 S 466. However, this case seems to be primarily about salmon fishing and the result as to the island is unclear. There is material in the National Archives relating to this case under the reference *Magdalane Paisley (or Pasley) or Dirom and Spouse v James and Mathew Poole* (1805) CS271/55412 and *James Poole and Matthew v Mrs Dirom and Husband* (1805) CS234/P6/7. See also the related case of *Dirom v Dirom* (1885) 1 Sh Ct Rep 159. *Wedderburn v Paterson* (1864) 2 M 902; *Earl of Zetland v Glovers of Perth* (1870) 8 M (HL) 144 are often cited when discussing islands but these cases concerned the extent of salmon fishing rather than ownership of the islands. *Magistrates of Perth v Earl of Weymss* (1829) 8 S 82 shows after an island is formed, ownership can be acquired through express grant or positive prescription.

[152] See also Reid, *Property* para 594.

[153] Reid, *Property* para 594; Gordon & Wortley, *Land Law* para 3-22.

[154] See the discussion of different ways of island formation in Forbes, *Great Body* Vol 1, 496.

[155] For a case concerning the ownership of a newly emerged volcanic island in the Bismarck Archipelago where the island was analysed as ownerless and available for appropriation, see *Tolain, Tapalau, Tomaret, Towarunga and Other Villagers of Latlat Village v Administration of the Territory of Papua and New Guinea* [1965–66] PNGLR 232 (http://www.paclii.org/pg/cases/PNGLR/1965/232.html).

[156] Rankine, *Landownership* 114.

[157] Van der Merwe, 'Things' para 332; Badenhorst et al para 8.3.1.4.

[158] Rankine, *Landownership* 114–115.

[159] Yiannopoulos, *Louisiana: Property* (n 150) para 77; Louisiana *Code civil* Arts 503 and 505.

determination of other boundaries. For example, the carving of an island out of a river bank may result in a change of the position of the *medium filum*.[160]

4-52. Alluvion is to be distinguished from avulsion, which applies to sudden and noticeable change and does not automatically result in the operation of accession.[161] The balance of authority is that where a piece of land is torn from upstream lands and sent downstream, the original owner will lose ownership when the requirements of moveable-to-land accession are subsequently satisfied through, for example, tree roots growing into the piece of land.[162] This solution is also that of South Africa[163] but different from Louisiana where ownership is retained despite attachment to other lands until the owner of such lands takes possession, after which the original owner has a year to reclaim the lost land.[164] Where a river suddenly creates a new *alveus* for itself or temporarily increases in size through flooding, or where the sea overruns the foreshore after a storm, this does not change the status or ownership of the land and, where possible, the original water boundaries can be restored by the adjacent landowners. Treating these latter instances as avulsion avoids the undesirable multiplication of terms such as *alveus derelictus*[165] and *alvei mutatio*.[166]

(2) Intention

4-53. There is some support in academic literature for according weight to the role of intention in alluvion. It has been argued that parties who have a river as a boundary have consented to future gradual change.[167] However, this suggestion raises more questions than it answers. To apply this analysis to moveable-to-land alluvion would be contrary to the general principles of accession,[168] where intention is disregarded. As soon as particles washed

---

[160] See the determination of the *alveus* of a river in *Menzies v Breadalbane* (1901) 4 F 55. Compare with *Laird's Tr v Reid* (1871) 9 M 699.

[161] Bankton, *Institute* II.1.10; Erskine, *Institute* II.1.14; Bell, *Principles* para 934.

[162] Forbes, *Great Body* Vol 1, 496; Bankton, *Institute* II.1.10. Compare Erskine, *Institutes* II.1.14 and see discussion above, para 4-21.

[163] D L Carey Miller, *The Acquisition and Protection of Ownership* (1986) para 2.4.1; Van der Merwe, 'Things' para 331; Badenhorst et al para 8.3.1.3 citing H Grotius, *Inleidinge tot de Hollandsche Rechtsgeleerdheid* (1631) 2.9.13 and J Voet, *Commentarius ad Pandectus Comitum* (1707) 41.1.16.

[164] Louisiana *Code civil* Art 503. Compare with the less sophisticated solution of Erskine, *Institute* II.1.14.

[165] See the discussion of this term in South African jurisprudence: Carey Miller, *The Acquisition and Protection of Ownership* (n 163) para 2.6; Van der Merwe, 'Things' para 333.

[166] This latter term is used by Bell, *Principles* para 934; Rankine, *Landownership* 113–114; Reid, *Property* para 595; Gordon & Wortley, *Land Law* para 3-23 and in *Marquis of Tweeddale v Kerr* (1822) 1 S 373.

[167] D L Carey Miller, 'Alluvio, Avulsion and Fluvial Boundaries' 1994 SLT (News) 75; R Rennie, 'Alluvio in the Land Register' 1996 SLT (News) 41; Gordon & Wortley, *Land Law* para 3.23. The use of the word 'acquiescence' by these writers is unfortunate as it can lead to confusion with personal bar, for which see below.

[168] Reid, *Property* para 572.

downstream are fixed in place they become part of the new land regardless of intention. Or again, if parties with a river boundary do not in fact consent to the changes, would imperceptible and gradual change not still result in the operation of accession? What if one party consents to the loss of land but the opposite owner does not consent to the gain? Does this result in a sliver of land being ownerless and therefore belonging to the Crown? Focusing on the intention of the parties might suggest that alluvion can operate even when sudden and noticeable change takes place, as long as the parties consent.[169] This argument also ignores the formal requirements for the consensual transfer of property. Thus, it is suggested that the intention of the parties is irrelevant to the operation of alluvion.

(3) Personal Bar

4-54.   Personal bar may be relevant to avulsion but does not affect the status or ownership of land.[170] If parties have by agreement changed the position of a river, ownership will not change but the party who consented to allowing the river to flow further into his or her property may be personally barred from asserting ownership over the land between the new and old *medium filum*.[171] Successors in title will be unaffected. An upstream owner may be personally barred from reclaiming his or her discernible piece of land that has travelled downstream but as soon as it is fixed in its new location ownership is lost.[172]

(4) Human Acts

4-55.   The balance of authority is to the effect that alluvion can take place when changes result from human acts.[173] To be consistent with general principles, this would have to be change which occurred gradually and imperceptibly.[174] Yet human acts are overwhelmingly likely to result in rapid change and so this requirement greatly limits the operation of alluvion in

---

[169] See Bell, *Principles* para 934; *Stirling v Bartlett* 1992 SC 523.

[170] See a modern restatement of the law in Reid and Blackie, *Personal Bar* (n 71).

[171] Assuming that the requirements of personal bar are met: see Reid and Blackie, *Personal Bar* (n 71) lxv.

[172] Gordon raises the interesting point that if land travels downstream and the owner of land on which it lands does not want it to be there, there may be an action for nuisance against the owner of the deposited land: W M Gordon, 'Is Moving Land a Nuisance?' (1980) 25 *JLSS* 323 at 324–325.

[173] See *Smart v Magistrates of Dundee* (1797) 3 Pat 606, 8 Bro PC 119, 3 ER 481; *Innes v Downie* (1807) Hume 552; *Magistrates of Culross v Geddes* (1809) Hume 554; *Campbell v Brown* 18 Nov 1813 FC; *Erskine of Dunn v Magistrates of Montrose* (1819) Hume 558; *Fisher v Duke of Atholl's Trs* (1836) 14 S 880; *Berry v Holden* (1840) 3 D 205. See also Rankine, *Landownership* 115 (Rankine's statements are, however, qualified); Reid, *Property* para 593. Contrary authority is available in *Todd v Clyde Trs* (1840) 2 D 357; *Irvine v Robertson* (1873) 11 M 298 at 301; *Smith v Lerwick Harbour Trs* (1903) 5 F 680 at 691.

[174] See Rankine, *Landownership* 115.

such cases. It does not seem to matter whether the act was done by a third party[175] but there may be a requirement that the act is lawful.[176] Few acts will pass this test. The law of England appears similar to Scotland. Alluvion also takes place as the result of human acts so long as the act was lawful, not as a result of deliberate reclamation, and the change took place gradually.[177] These requirements almost eliminate the rule. The responses of other legal systems differ. In South Africa, alluvion only applies to natural events and not to those which have been 'induced or increased because of artificial walls or dykes'.[178] Louisiana's law on the other hand allows alluvion to operate where artificial works merely accelerated a natural process.[179]

4-56. The Scottish Law Commission has proposed that where the foreshore or sea-bed is altered through deliberate reclamation, this should not result in accession because it is contrary to the general policy of alluvion.[180] This recommendation is limited due to the scope of the Scottish Law Commission's remit but it would be desirable to have the same rule for all natural water boundaries. Moreover, it is suggested that not only deliberate reclamation should be taken out of the scope of alluvion but all artificial works – following the example of South Africa. Otherwise regard would have to be had to the intention of the person making the changes to the land, which is contrary to the concept of alluvion as an objective doctrine. Restricting the operation of alluvion to natural processes would not be a dramatic change to the law as the human acts to which alluvion applies at the moment appear to be rare.[181]

---

[175] *Fisher v Duke of Atholl's Trs* (1836) 14 S 880; *Hunter v Lord Advocate* (1869) 7 M 899; *Smith v Lerwick Harbour Trs* (1903) 5 F 680 (although see Lord Kinnear's view on Crown ownership above, para 4-35.); Reid, *Property* para 593. However, see *Todd v Clyde Trs* (1840) 2 D 357.

[176] See *Irvine v Robertson* (1873) 11 M 298; *Smith v Lerwick Harbour Trs* discussed above, paras 4-35–4-37. See also Rankine, *Landownership* 115. However, the only Scottish authority cited for this point is *Menzies v Breadalbane* (1828) 3 W & S 235 which concerned the right of a landowner to embank his property and *Morris v Bicket* (1864) 2 M 1982 on common interest. Compare with Reid, *Property* para 593.

[177] Halsbury, 'Water' paras 26–27. See also *Attorney-General of Southern Nigeria v Holt* [1915] AC 599; *Southern Centre of Theosophy Inc v State of South Australia* [1982] AC 706 at 720. Stair's definition of imperceptibility was cited in an earlier stage of this latter case at 721.

[178] Van der Merwe, 'Things' para 330. See also Carey Miller, *The Acquisition and Protection of Ownership* (n 163) para 2.3; P J Badenhorst, 'On Golden Pond: Meaning of Tailings, Mineral and Holder in Terms of the Minerals Act 50 of 1991' 1995 *Tydskrif vir die Suid-Afrikaanse Reg* 172 at 179–181 discussing the unreported case of *Elandsrand Gold Mining Company Ltd v JF Uys* TPD 19915/93; Badenhorst et al para 8.3.1.2 as well as *Colonial Government v Town Council of Cape Town* 1902 (19) SC 87.

[179] Yiannopoulos, *Louisiana: Property* (n 150) para 76.

[180] Report on the Law of the Foreshore and Seabed (Scot Law Com No 190, 2003) paras 6.1–6.5.

[181] See also Gordon & Wortley, *Land Law* para 3-24; C T Reid and D J McGlashan, 'Erosion, Accretion and Intervention' 2005 *Jur Rev* 73.

(5) Private Lochs

4-57.   The boundaries of a non-tidal loch determined by its natural condition are fixed and alluvion does not operate to change them.[182] This follows Roman law along with the law in Louisiana and South Africa but may be contrary to English law.[183] However, moveable-to-land alluvion can still take place, for example, where particles are eroded from the banks of an upstream river and become attached to the *alveus* of the loch. Rankine suggests that 'the state of the loch beyond the prescriptive period is accepted as its natural state'.[184] This would only be true if the adjacent landowners can be found to acquire the exposed *alveus* on a *habile* title by prescriptive possession.

4-58.   Tidal lochs have not been the subject of decision, but it is arguable that they are also subject to land-to-land alluvion.

(6) Limited Grants

4-59.   Alluvion was said not to apply to *ager limitatus* in Roman law.[185] This rule has been accepted into Scots law. Yet, this broad statement requires explanation. Where a grant of land is clearly delineated – for example by taxative measurements, written boundaries or plans – alluvion cannot operate to add to the land beyond these boundaries or (presumably) diminish the extent of the land within these boundaries.[186] The reason why alluvion does not operate in these ways is because the definite extent of land provided by the measurements or plan has been chosen as the boundary rather than, for example, the changeable *medium filum* of the river or low water mark of the ordinary spring tides on the shore. This aspect of alluvion has also been received into South African law.[187] The effect of the rule in Scotland is that land-to-land alluvion will operate to change ownership only where land is bounded by a description such as 'the river' or 'the shore'. Where a grant of land next to, for example, the foreshore is limited and defined by clear

---

[182] Rankine, *Landownership* 198; Ferguson, *Water* 149; Gordon & Wortley, *Land Law* para 3-32.

[183] Louisiana, *Code civil* Art 500; Van der Merwe, 'Things' para 330; Gray and Gray, *Land Law* (n 142) para 1.2.7. No English authority is cited by Gray and Gray, who mention only the Australian case *Southern Centre of Theosophy Inc v State of South Australia* [1982] AC 706 and the Hawaiian case of *State of Hawaii by Kobayashi v Zimring* (1977) 566 P2d 725.

[184] Rankine, *Landownership* 198.

[185] D.41.1.16 (Florentius); F de Zulueta, *Digest 41, 1 & 2* (1950) 57–58; Buckland, *Roman Law* (n 13) 211; A Watson, *The Law of Property in the Later Roman Republic* (1968) 76; Lewis, 'Alluvio' 93.

[186] Forbes, *Great Body* Vol 1, 496; Bankton, *Institute* II.1.10; *Smart v Magistrates of Dundee* (1797) 3 Pat 606, 8 Bro PC 119, 3 ER 481; *Kerr v Dickson* (1840) 3 D 154 (aff'd (1842) 1 Bell's App 499); *Secretary of State v Coombs* 1991 GWD 30-2404.

[187] See J E Scholtens, 'Ager Limitatus and Alluvio' (1957) 74 *SALJ* 272; Carey Miller, *The Acquisition and Protection of Ownership* (n 163) paras 2.3.1.1–2.3.1.2; Van der Merwe, 'Things' para 330; Badenhorst et al para 8.3.1.2 as well as *Van Nieker and Union Government (Minister of Lands) v Carter* 1917 AD 359; *Lange v Minister of Lands* 1957(1) AD 297 (A); *Durban City Council v Minister of Agriculture* 1982(2) AA 361 (D).

boundaries excluding the foreshore, it is the owner of the foreshore who will acquire any land emerging from the sea-bed and not the adjacent landowner.[188] Even in the above example, however, alluvion will operate to change the status of the foreshore to dry land and the sea-bed to foreshore. Further, in the case of moveable-to-land alluvion, the upstream owner will still lose ownership of the particles of soil washed from his or her land and ownership will be acquired by the owner of land to which they attach even though that land is limited by the titles. The provisions of the titles do not prevent the loss or acquisition of any particles of soil but merely specify the extent of the land to which they may become attached.

4-60. As land-to-land alluvion does not operate to add to or diminish land where such land is clearly delineated, the question arises as to how it applies to Land Register titles. Rennie has stated that there 'must be a good argument for saying that the red line on the original title sheet is immoveable and that if the water course changes then the red line will not move but will be in the same position, though not necessarily along the middle of the river as it now flows'.[189] However, through arguments based on the (now repealed) Land Registration (Scotland) Act 1979, Rennie goes on to conclude that alluvion does in fact change boundaries on the Land Register, for a variety of reasons.[190] The first is that the Land Register is 'essentially a matter of conveyancing and not pure property law and what is or is not included in heritable property remains a matter of property law'.[191] This may be true but as a matter of property law, alluvion does not change the boundaries of limited grants. Secondly, it is said that there 'is nothing in the Land Registration (Scotland) Act 1979 which states that a principle of property law which is inconsistent with the registration system is abrogated'.[192] Equally, however, there was nothing in the 1979 Act which stated that alluvion was applicable, unlike the corresponding English legislation.[193] Thirdly, land registration does not provide an absolute title guarantee especially with regard to boundaries because indemnity is not payable for loss arising from an inaccuracy which cannot be rectified by reference to the Ordnance Survey map.[194] However, if alluvion does not have the effect of changing the boundaries of ownership under land registration, the movement of a water boundary does not result in an 'inaccuracy' which requires rectification. Fourthly, Rennie states ownership is not constant, so that, for example, a flat may be demolished despite what is shown on the title sheet.[195] Yet, whilst the state of land may be subject to factual change, this does not affect legal ownership. In the

---

[188] *Kerr v Dickson* (1840) 3 D 154. The owner may be the granter who has not included the foreshore in the grant or the Crown. The position should not have changed after the abolition of feudal tenure. Compare Gordon & Wortley, *Land Law* para 3-21.

[189] R Rennie, 'Alluvio in the Land Register' 1996 SLT (News) 41.

[190] At 42–43.

[191] At 42.

[192] At 43.

[193] Land Registration Act 2002 s 61(1).

[194] Rennie, 'Alluvio in the Land Register' at 43; Land Registration (Scotland) Act 1979 s 12(3)(d).

[195] Rennie, 'Alluvio in the Land Register' at 43.

example given by Rennie, the owner of the demolished flat still owns the airspace that the flat once occupied.[196] Fifthly, parties 'who acquire property with a boundary adjacent to water must be held to accept that the boundary is not fixed'.[197] There is no justification given for why owners 'must' accept this, especially when their plots of land have definite boundaries on their title sheets. Sixthly, it is argued that the Keeper takes note of changes effected by the updating of the Ordnance Survey maps and sometimes recalls a certificate for alteration. This does not mean this practice was in accordance with law. Finally, Rennie states that ownership 'can be acquired on a wholly defective title after the period of positive prescription, even where indemnity has been totally excluded'.[198] In fact, ownership was, under the 1979 Act, acquired on a wholly defective title upon registration[199] but this situation is not comparable to the operation of alluvion where land is acquired beyond the boundaries of the registered title.

4-61.   Despite the flaws in these arguments, the Keeper of the Registers[200] and the Scottish Law Commission[201] also accept that alluvion applies to the Land Register. Provisions on alluvion were therefore included in the Land Registration etc (Scotland) Act 2012. However, as the Law Commission's report demonstrates, this leads to complex and technical problems the nature of which depends on whether the alluvion occurred before or after first registration.[202]

4-62.   Under the 2012 Act, once a title has been registered in the Land Register, the Keeper's warranty of title does not cover boundary changes due to alluvion. If title boundaries 'shift', the Register can be corrected through rectification.[203] Further, there is a provision for parties to agree to fix their boundaries by registered agreement which would prevent further alluvial change.[204]

4-63.   However, even though this legislation assumes that alluvion affects boundaries on the Land Register, it should be seriously doubted whether this is the case. The Land Register is a map-based system and it is an accepted rule that land-to-land alluvion does not operate to change ownership where land is clearly delineated. If this view is correct, current land registration

---

[196] *Barr v Bass Ltd* 1972 SLT (Lands Tribunal) 5; Reid, *Property* para 250; Tenements (Scotland) Act 2004 s 20(1).

[197] Rennie, 'Alluvio in the Land Register' at 43.

[198] Rennie, 'Alluvio in the Land Register' at 43.

[199] See K G C Reid, '*A Non Domino* Conveyances and the Land Register' 1991 *Jur Rev* 79.

[200] Registers of Scotland, General Guidance, *The Cadastral Map: The Land Register and Land Covered by Water* (2014; http://2012act.ros.gov.uk/guidance/General_Guidance_CM_water_boundaries.pdf).

[201] Discussion Paper on Land Registration: Miscellaneous Issues (Scot Law Com DP 130, 2005) para 3.7.

[202] See discussion of these issues in paras 3.10–3.16.

[203] Land Registration etc (Scotland) Act 2012 s 73(2)(i). See also Report on Land Registration Vol 1 (n 37) para 5.34; Registers of Scotland, Land Registration etc (Scotland) Act 2012 General Guidance, *The Cadastral Map: The Land Register and Land Covered by Water* (2014).

[204] Land Registration etc (Scotland) Act 2012 s 66.

practice is proceeding on a misunderstanding of alluvion and the 2012 Act provisions do not add anything to the existing law.

G. CONCLUSION

4-64.   The doctrines of alluvion and avulsion defy easy analysis. Despite their long history in Roman and Scots law, there are still many issues which remain unresolved. Sax has stated that the 'accretion/avulsion distinction embodies one of the baffling riddles of property law. Unfortunately, it cannot be dismissed as a mere artefact of antiquarian interest'.[205] As with many areas of law there is a balance which requires to be struck between competing policies. It is desirable that the law should reflect, to some extent, the geographical changes which take place due to the effect of water on land – especially when water features are the chosen boundaries of ownership. On the other hand, the stability and security of landownership would be affected if sudden events such as floods and storms resulted in frequent and dramatic changes in the status or ownership of land. Indeed, sudden topographical change is likely to be more frequent in the future.[206] Where the line is to be drawn between changes which are mirrored by alterations in the legal position and those which are not will always be difficult to determine but establishing clear rules, at least, seems essential.

---

[205] J Sax, 'The Accretion/Avulsion Puzzle: Its Past Revealed, Its Future Proposed' (2010) 23 *Tulane Environmental Law Journal* 305 at 306.

[206] See Intergovernmental Panel on Climate Change, 'Managing the Risks of Extreme Events and Disasters to Advance Climate Change Adaptation' (2011; http://ipcc-wg2.gov/ SREX/report/).

5 Common Interest: The Search for a Doctrine

A. INTRODUCTION

5-01. Common interest evolved in response to a number of factual and legal problems. As explained in Chapter 2, water in its natural state is a communal thing which is outwith private ownership except when captured and contained. Naturally, landowners have the best opportunity for capture in respect of the water on their land and it is, generally, a legitimate exercise of ownership rights to take the ownerless things present on one's land. Of course, to allow capture without restriction could result in those closest to a river or loch's source diverting or consuming all the water and leaving none to reach downstream properties. To prevent this situation and achieve equality amongst owners there needs to be a regime regulating the use of water.

5-02. Even without consuming or diverting water, otherwise normal and legitimate exercise of ownership rights may have an effect far beyond the boundaries of one's land. If an owner builds on the *alveus* of a loch or fortifies a river's banks against the water or changes a river's course, this can cause damage to down- or upstream lands and also affect the uses to which other owners can put, or are putting, the river or loch. Landowners' use of rivers and lochs is particularly vulnerable to neighbourly interference. It is therefore important to have legal rules which limit an owner's rights in the interests of other potentially affected parties. In the modern law these legal rules are known as 'common interest'.[1]

5-03. Scotland has never allowed owners unlimited rights to consume, divert, or to affect the flow of, water running in a definite channel through their lands. Limitations in the interests of neighbours were recognised at an early stage. However, without identification of the precise right which is infringed by interference with water, it was difficult to establish what activities could be prevented. It took many years for the doctrinal foundation of these limitations to be established. The struggle to determine this foundation of common interest is the focal point of this chapter, and this part of the history of the doctrine is a complex narrative which touches on broader themes of the development and composition of Scots private law.

5-04. Once its doctrinal underpinning was settled in 1768[2] common interest proved capable of further, swift development in response to the social, economic and legal changes ongoing in Scotland. This period culminated in the decision of *Morris v Bicket*[3] in 1864 which can be seen as marking the final settlement of the fundamental aspects of the doctrine. This later history of the doctrine is traced in the following chapter. The final instalment in this trio of chapters on common interest concerns the modern law. The nature of the doctrine, a detailed examination of the rights and obligations of common interest, remedies for breach and extinction, are all considered in order to provide a comprehensive analysis of the current law.

B. MILLS IN SCOTLAND

5-05. Most of the early case law concerning water involved mills and private (non-navigable) rivers. Mills had a catalytic role in the development of common interest. The use of water-powered mills has a long history. There are references to such mills in Scottish charters as early as the 12th century.[4] The technologically advanced, vertical water-wheel mills were being used by the late 16th century for the purpose of grinding grain and in other processes such as waulking[5] and coal mining.[6] The use of water power reached its peak between 1730 and 1830 in the textile, iron and other industries before

---

[1] Common interest also developed in relation to salmon fishing, tenements, boundary walls and, perhaps, gardens in common ownership: see Reid, *Property* para 359. The other situations listed by Reid are likely not to be governed by common interest: see D J Cusine 'Common Interest Revisited' (1998) 2 *Edin LR* 315.

[2] See below, paras 5-52–5-69.

[3] (1864) 2 M 1082.

[4] Shaw, *Water Power* 22. See also H MacQueen, *Common Law and Feudal Society in Medieval Scotland* (1993) 158–161.

[5] Waulking is a step in the process of making cloth where wool is cleaned and thickened. See Shaw, *Water Power* 44.

[6] Shaw, *Water Power* 44 and 62.

steam began to be used.[7] Mills required a water supply in order to function. The mill-owner often needed to cut an artificial mill-lade which channelled a river towards the water-wheel or into a mill-pond before being directed towards the mill.[8] It was essential to guarantee the force of the water powering the wheel. Due to the importance of water flow, and the need for works which might affect the flow of rivers, almost all of the cases concerning water rights throughout the 17th and 18th centuries involved mills and disputes regarding damming and diversions. In particular, in the early cases the pursuer was usually a downstream mill-owner who was objecting to an upstream diversion for a mill or some other purpose. The primary issue to determine was when a mill-owner had a right to prevent the permanent diversion of a river.

5-06.   A distinction is made in this chapter between 'permanent' and 'temporary' diversion. Permanent diversion is where an entire river is led away from its natural course and not returned.[9] Temporary diversion is where the river is conducted away from its bed but the water is then returned after being used, for example, to power a mill.

C. ROMAN LAW

5-07.   There was no comprehensive system of water rights in Roman law which provided a simple solution to the interference with the flow of rivers. Regarding 'casual waters', which included private rivers – these being defined as non-perennial rivers[10] – and water not in a defined channel, lower land had an obligation to receive water which flowed from upper land by virtue of a servitude which arose due to the nature of the land, otherwise called a natural servitude.[11] However, while the upper landowner had a right to send water on to the lower land there was no obligation to do so. Indeed, it was said that the owner of land could prevent the water flowing on to another's land entirely.[12] The *actio aquae pluviae arcendae*,[13] or the action to ward off rain water, was subject to much discussion but this action concerned the obligation not to carry out works on one's land which might throw water

---

[7] Shaw, *Water Power* 102.

[8] Shaw, *Water Power* 12.

[9] This was not unusual due to the small scale of the rivers being used to power mills. See the arguments for the pursuer and the defender in *Cunningham v Kennedy* (1713) Mor 8903 and 12778 discussed below, paras 5-30–5-35 and for the defender in Petition of Boyds 9 Dec 1767 (Robert MacQueen), *Kelso v Boyds* Pitfour Collection Vol 39, Paper 17 discussed further below, para 5-48; *Prestoun v Erskine* (1714) Mor 10919; *Kincaid v Stirling* (1752) Mor 12786; *Magistrates of Linlithgow v Elphinstone (No 2)* (1768) Mor 1280, Hailes 203.

[10] D.43.12.1.1–4 (Ulpian).

[11] D.39.3.2.pr. (Paul). This servitude has been received by Scots law.

[12] D.39.3.1.11–12 (Ulpian).

[13] Contained in D.39.3. This action was mainly applicable to the countryside due to its wording. In towns and cities, an owner could use the *actio negatoria* to ward off unwanted water: D.8.5.2.pr. (Ulpian). See A Rodger, *Owners and Neighbours in Roman Law* (1972) Ch 5.

on to a neighbour's land and cause damage.[14] Although one could acquire a right to a guaranteed water supply without interference by servitude or through ancient use,[15] there was no discussion of rights which arose by operation of law to receive, and prevent interference with, casual waters which flowed on to one's land.

5-08. Regarding public waters, which were perennial rivers and lakes and subject to public rights of use,[16] permission was required for a private conduit from a public aqueduct[17]. However, towns and cities normally had a water system which provided an open public supply.[18] Further, everyone was entitled to abstract water from public rivers unless the water was in public use[19] or the river was navigable,[20] and interdicts existed to prevent the interference with the flow of such rivers.[21] These rules, however, were not subject to the detailed academic discussion by jurists that was seen with the *actio aquae pluviae arcendae*. At one time, it could have been argued that the reason for this lack of scrutiny was the lack of widespread irrigation practice[22] and the slow acceptance of the water-mill[23] in the Roman Empire which would have meant that there was little demand for a consistent and guaranteed water supply. However, more recent studies have suggested that irrigation was used throughout the Roman Empire[24] and that the water-mill

---

[14] See, for example, E Schönbauer, 'Die Actio Aquae Pluviae Arcendae' 1934 *Zeitschrift der Savigny-Stiftung für Rechtsgeschichte (Romanistische Abteilung)* 233; A Rodger, 'Roman Rainwater' (1970) 38 *TvR* 417; A Rodger, *Owners and Neighbours in Roman Law* Ch 5; F Cairns, 'D.39.3.3.pr.-1 and the Actio Aquae Pluviae Arcendae' in J Napoli (ed), *Sodalitas: Scritti in Onore di Antonio Guarino* (1984); A Rodger, 'The Palingenesia of Paul's Commentary on the Actio Aquae Pluviae Arcaendae' 1988 *Zeitschrift der Savigny-Stiftung für Rechtsgeschichte (Romanistische Abteilung)* 726.

[15] See D.8.3.1.pr.-1 (Ulpian) concerning servitudes; D.43.20.3.4 (Pomponius) and C.3.34.7 concerning ancient use. The interdict regarding daily and summer water appeared to apply only to those who had already acquired rights of servitude, who believed a servitude existed or who were abstracting from water subject to public rights: D.43.20.1.39 (Ulpian). On servitudes see Cynthia Jordan Bannon, *Gardens and Neighbours: Private Water Rights in Roman Italy* (University of Michigan Press, 2009).

[16] See above, para 2-06.

[17] D.43.20.1.38 and 42 (Ulpian); C.11.43.11; C Bruun, 'Water Legislation in the Ancient World' in Ö Wikander (ed), *Handbook of Ancient Water Technology* (2000) 579 and 585–587.

[18] Bruun, 'Water Legislation in the Ancient World' (n 17) 585.

[19] It is unclear from the *Digest* what this particular public use is.

[20] D.43.12.2 (Pomponius). Taking water from public rivers did not require permission in the Classical period but this may have changed in the Post-Classical era. See Bruun, 'Water Legislation in the Ancient World' (n 17) 578–579.

[21] Contained in D.43.12–14. Whitty, considered in the following section, places great emphasis on one of these interdicts contained in D.43.13.

[22] R J Forbes, *Studies in Ancient Technology* Vol II (3rd edn, 1993) 43–46; J P Oleson, 'Irrigation' in Ö Wikander (ed), *Handbook of Ancient Water Technology* (2000).

[23] Forbes, *Studies in Ancient Technology* Vol II (n 22) 98–105.

[24] F B Lloris, 'An Irrigation Decree from Roman Spain: The Lex Rivi Hiberiensis' (2006) 96 *Journal of Roman Studies* 147; A I Wilson, 'Hydraulic Engineering and Water Supply' in J P Oelson (ed), *Oxford Handbook of Engineering and Technology in the Classical World* (2008) 309–311. Irrigation is mentioned at D.8.3.17 (Papirius Justus); D.39.3.3.2 (Ulpian); D.43.20.1.11 (Ulpian); D.43.20.1.13 (Ulpian); D.43.20.3.pr. (Pomponius); C.3.34.7.

was invented as early as the 3rd century BC and used to a significant degree in Roman times.[25] Watson puts forward the alternative argument that the lack of discussion of water rights is due to the Roman jurists' focus on private, as opposed to public, law without regard to the practical importance that the interdicts regarding public rivers would have had for society and the economy.[26] Or it may be that the social and economic conditions meant that the use of water was sufficiently regulated by servitudes together with formal or informal agreements.[27]

5-09.   Perhaps due to this lack of detailed treatment of a water rights regime in the *Digest*, the matter is little discussed in the early institutional writings in Scotland. When the proliferation of mills resulted in a substantial number of cases involving water coming before the courts, advocates and judges had to improvise on the basis of general principles. This is not to say that Roman law was insignificant in the development of common interest. Many *Digest* and *Codex* titles and Civilian authorities were cited to the courts in the early cases. But there was no detailed Roman water rights system available to be imported into Scotland. Thus, it is in the courts that our starting point lies.

D. WHITTY'S 'WATER LAW REGIMES'

5-10.   The history of common interest has been thoroughly researched by Professor Niall Whitty, the results being published as 'Water Law Regimes' in K G C Reid and R Zimmermann (eds), *A History of Private Law in Scotland* (2000). This important piece of work contributes significantly to our knowledge of common interest. However, the research for Whitty's work was confined to published sources, whereas in this book it has been possible to consult session papers held in the Advocates and Signet Libraries. These papers contain otherwise inaccessible information concerning the arguments made by the advocates to court in some of the earliest cases of common interest. In light of this information, Whitty's findings can be both supplemented and challenged, and a new history of common interest may be presented.

5-11.   It is helpful to begin by summarising Whitty's arguments.[28] Whitty acknowledges the lack of institutional authority on common interest despite disputes concerning private (non-navigable) rivers being commonplace in the courts at the time. He argues that common interest developed gradually beginning with the two foundational cases of *Bannatyne v Cranston*[29] and *Bairdie*

---

[25] Ö Wikander, 'The Water-Mill' in Ö Wikander (ed), *Handbook of Ancient Water Technology* (2000); A I Wilson, 'Machines, Power and the Ancient Economy' (2002) 92 *Journal of Roman Studies* 1. Indeed, water-mills are mentioned in C.11.43.10.3.

[26] A Watson, 'The Transformation of American Property Law: A Comparative Approach' (1990) 24 *Ga L Rev* 163 at 175–176.

[27] C Bruun, 'Water Legislation in the Ancient World' (n 17) 580–581; Jordan Bannon, *Gardens and Neighbours: Private Water Rights in Roman Italy* (n 15).

[28] See generally Whitty, 'Water' 446–448 and 452–465.

[29] (1624) Mor 12769.

v Scartsonse,[30] both decided in 1624. The most important Roman root of common interest, in Whitty's view, was the praetor's edict *uti priore aestate*, one of the public law interdicts mentioned above, which is the only authority cited in *Bannatyne*. The edict protects the natural flow of public (perennial) rivers and is contained in D.43.13.1.pr. (Ulpian) which states 'I forbid anything to be done in a public river or on its bank, or anything to be introduced into a public river or on its bank which might cause the water to flow otherwise than it did last summer.' It is said that this public law interdict was transformed into a private proprietary right to prevent interference with a river running through or adjoining one's land.

5-12. Whitty states that the next important step in the development of common interest was distinguishing between running water and the river itself, a distinction already mentioned in Chapter 2 concerning the Division of Things.[31] The distinction between the actual moving particles of water and the permanent entity of the river – which is treated almost like a separate tenement – is said to be 'essential to the modern doctrine of common interest in rivers because that doctrine predicates the concept of private proprietary rights attaching to the river itself, and its natural or accustomed flow, rather than to the particles of running water of which it is composed at any given time.'[32] Whitty comments that this distinction was raised in *Fairly v Earl of Eglinton*[33] and fully expounded in *Hamilton v Edington & Co*.[34]

5-13. Finally, Whitty claims that, from a Roman root, common interest developed into a 'largely indigenous concept'.[35] There was a period of modest experimentation with different rationalisations for the prohibition of diversion of rivers, such as natural servitude or common property, and *Magistrates of Linlithgow v Elphinstone (No 2)*[36] shows that the basis of the right to prevent interference with private rivers was unclear as late as 1768. However, *Hamilton v Edington & Co*,[37] decided in 1793, is said to mark the 'final establishment'[38] of the doctrine. The cases of common interest were then subject to 'institutional synthesis'[39] by Hume and Bell.[40] As a result of this process of indigenous development, the English doctrine of prior appropriation, which protects the first occupier of water regardless of need, position on the river or effect on other riparian proprietors,[41] was never received into Scots law. Only in the late 19th century did English cases begin to be cited in the Scottish courts on issues concerning common interest.

[30] (1624) Mor 14529; Hope, *Practicks* VI.40.6.
[31] See above, para 2-08.
[32] Whitty, 'Water' 454. This idea was considered in relation to lochs above, paras 3-77–3-82.
[33] (1744) Mor 12780.
[34] (1793) Mor 12824.
[35] Whitty, 'Water' 455.
[36] (1768) Mor 12805, Hailes 203.
[37] (1793) Mor 12824.
[38] Whitty, 'Water' 455.
[39] Whitty, 'Water' 453.
[40] Hume, *Lectures* III 216–225; Bell, *Principles* paras 1100–1111.
[41] See Getzler 154 for a summary.

5-14. Overall, the view of common interest given by Whitty is of the gradual development of a doctrine 'directly from the *jus commune*'[42] beginning in the early 17th century whereby a Roman public law interdict provided the foundation for the creation of a unique Scottish institution.

E. SURVIVAL OF THE FITTEST: COMPETING THEORIES IN THE COURTS

5-15. Some of Whitty's arguments can be challenged on the basis of the information contained in session papers.[43] His view that there was a gradual development from the foundational cases of *Bannatyne v Cranston*[44] and *Bairdie v Scartsonse*[45] in 1624 appears mistaken. Although these cases are evidence that there were some restrictions on the use of rivers, the extent of the restrictions and the rationale behind them were entirely uncertain. Instead, until the early 18th century, there were no clear rules about when, in the absence of immemorial possession, interference with water was prohibited or permitted, and the doctrinal foundation for such rules was only established in the late 18th century.

5-16. At first, there were attempts to create a system of water rights from the general principle that one may not use one's property in a way that prejudices another, but this did not result in rules which were certain. In 1713, the case of *Cunningham v Kennedy*[46] provided a compromise between up- and downstream owners by establishing the rule that owners may divert a river within their own land temporarily but must return the water to the channel. However, this rule did not seem based on any clear principle or doctrine and in the years following several different types of argument were used by advocates still seeking to establish a doctrinal foundation for the right to prevent the permanent diversion of rivers and lochs. There were also various rationales for court decisions. In the following sections, the main competing theories present in the courts in the 17th and 18th centuries will be outlined.

5-17. In 1768, a principled basis for common interest was finally accepted and expounded in *Magistrates of Linlithgow v Elphinstone (No 2)*.[47] Thus, rather than this case showing that the basis of common interest was still unclear, as Whitty suggests, it was in fact the foundational case for the doctrine, and the history of and circumstances surrounding this decision will be considered in detail.

[42] Whitty, 'Water' 451.

[43] See the useful table provided by A Stewart, 'The Session Papers in the Advocates Library' in *Miscellany IV* (H MacQueen (ed), Stair Society, Vol 49, 2002) as a guide for the years covered by the various collections in the Advocates Library. The Signet Library's collection covers the years 1713–1820.

[44] (1624) Mor 12769.

[45] (1624) Mor 14529; Hope, *Practicks* VI.40.6.

[46] (1713) Mor 8903 and 12778.

[47] (1768) Mor 12805, Hailes 203.

5-18.   Whitty's view that the main Roman root of common interest was the public law interdict *uti priore aestate* will also be contested. The text of this interdict was merely one of the many Civilian authorities cited to the courts in this formative period and these sources will be discussed in the following pages. The main Roman authority used in *Magistrates of Linlithgow v Elphinstone (No 2)* is a title we have already considered in detail: the Division of Things in Justinian's *Institutes*.[48]

(1) Immemorial Possession and Prescriptive Servitudes

5-19.   The first of the competing theories – an argument which was successful at an early stage in the courts – was that there had been acquisition of a right to use water flow, often to power a mill, through immemorial possession (of 40 years) of the water. Balfour's *Practicks* states, under the heading 'Anent milnis, multuris, and pertinentis belonging thairto':

> 'Gif ony man be in peciabill possessioun, past memorie of man, of ane burn or water cumand to his miln, he, be ressoun of his lang possessioun, quilk he and his predecessouris has had of lang time befoir, aucht and sould bruik and joise the samin burn or water, rinnand to his miln, like as he and his predecessouris did of befoir, swa that the samin may not be drawin away, stoppit or maid war be ony man, until the time that the said possessour be lauchfullie callit befoir ane Judge ordinar, and ordourlie put thairfra.'[49]

This account suggests that use of water for a mill for 40 years gave a right against interference with that use by permanent diversion by other owners. Balfour cites *Abbot of Scone v Johne Lord Drummond* (1500) as authority but unfortunately this case cannot be traced. Although Balfour cites other cases which protect water use without a requirement of immemorial possession, it is possible that these cases were decided on the basis of the brieve *de aqueductu* which was merely a possessory remedy to restore the *status quo* before the rights of the parties were adjudicated on their merits.[50] The argument based on immemorial possession was still succeeding up to the late 17th century. In *Beaton v Ogilvie*,[51] it was decided that immemorial possession of water for a mill and the use of a river by tenants for watering land were sufficient to establish the absolute privilege of diverting water which could not be prejudiced by upstream abstractions.

5-20.   From the late 17th century onwards, the precise source of rights acquired through immemorial possession began to become clearer. Usually the argument was that possession established a servitude of *aquaeductus*,[52] which burdened the upstream property and could not be prejudiced by

[48] Justinian's *Institutes* 2.1. See Ch 2.

[49] Balfour, *Practicks* 493–494.

[50] See Balfour, *Practicks* 493 and 496; H MacQueen, *Common Law and Feudal Society in Medieval Scotland* (1993) 158–161; Whitty, 'Water' 424. This may explain the last part of the quote above which suggests adjudication in court.

[51] (1670) Mor 10912. See also *Borthwick v Laird of Kirkland* (1677) Mor Supp (Stair) 66.

[52] This is the specific servitude that was plead: see *Cunningham v Kennedy* (1713) Mor 8903 and 12778; *Pringle v Duke of Roxburgh* (1767) 2 Pat 134.

operations of the burdened proprietor.[53] This argument presupposed that, in the absence of a servitude, there was a right to divert.[54] In *Prestoun v Erskine*,[55] a case concerning the use of water running from two lochs, the authorities used for this argument were D.8.5.10 (Ulpian), which states that an owner can obtain a servitude right to channel water by long use, D.39.3.26 (Scaevola), which says that 'those who are responsible for giving judgment normally uphold aqueducts to which antiquity of use gives some authority' even where their legal right has not been established, and the, perhaps peripheral, case of *Laird of Gairlton v Laird of Stevenson*,[56] concerning a servitude of dam-head established through prescription. In *Cunningham v Kennedy*, D.43.20.3.4 (Pomponius) on ancient use was cited which simply states that: 'Drawing off water which goes back beyond anyone's memory is held as if constituted by right', and the 'recent' unreported and now untraceable case of *Thomas Aitkenhead of Jaw v Russell of Elrig* was also mentioned as authority.[57] Indeed, some institutional writers also consider water rights in the context of servitudes,[58] perhaps influenced by Roman law which may have used servitude rights extensively as a way of adjudicating water disputes in the absence of a system which arose by operation of law.

5-21.   Cusine and Paisley say in the 'wider sense, it entitles the dominant proprietor to enjoy the use of the water on the servient tenement...[and t]he more strict sense [entitles] taking water from the servient tenement, by means of pipes, canals or aqueducts, or similar means, for the use of the dominant tenement'.[59] Generally speaking, only positive servitudes[60] could be acquired by prescription[61] and the activity on the (to be) burdened property for the prescriptive period, such as digging or maintaining an aqueduct, satisfies the requirement of publicity for the creation of the real right. However, the main issue in early water rights cases was establishing a negative right against diversion of a river or loch rather than a positive right either to lead water through or enjoy water on another's land. Thus, typically there had been no positive acts by the purported benefited proprietors on the upstream property[62] and any acts which had been carried out were by the purported burdened proprietors for their own benefit.[63] The pursuers had merely used

---

[53] See *Borthwick v Laird of Kirkland* (where both immemorial possession and prescriptive servitude are argued); *Cunningham v Kennedy*; *Prestoun v Erskine* (1714) Mor 10919; *Pringle v Duke of Roxburgh*. See also *Wallace v Morrison* (1761) Mor 14511.

[54] Indeed, see the case of *Lady Bass v Laird of Balgowan* (1616) in Hope, *Practicks* III.16.28.

[55] (1714) Mor 10919.

[56] (1677) Mor 14535.

[57] This reference in *Cunningham* was the only evidence of this case I could find. A text from the *actio aquae pluviae arcendae* was also cited but cannot be located.

[58] Stair, *Institutions* II.7.1; Bankton, *Institute* II.7.29; Erskine, *Institute* II.9.13.

[59] Cusine & Paisley para 3.80.

[60] Negative servitudes have now been converted into real burdens by the Title Conditions (Scotland) Act 2003 ss 79–80.

[61] See discussion of negative servitudes and prescription in Cusine & Paisley para 10.02; Gordon, *Land Law* para 24-42.

[62] See *Cunningham v Kennedy* (1713) Mor 8903 and 12778; *Pringle v Duke of Roxburgh* (1767) 2 Pat 134.

[63] See *Borthwick v Laird of Kirkland* (1677) Mor Supp (Stair) 66; *Pringle v Duke of Roxburgh*.

the water wholly within their own land and sought to impose an obligation not to interfere with this use on upstream owners. As a result, the argument that a servitude had been created was frequently unfounded[64] and it is suggested that landowners cannot establish a servitude by prescription on upstream or downstream lands through using the natural flow of a river or loch wholly within their own land. This has implications for the modern law.[65]

5-22. There were further objections to the prescriptive servitude argument. Servitudes generally deal with the relationship between two pieces of adjacent land and the adjudication between the interests of two landowners. However, as a river or loch may flow through several pieces of land, the effects of operations may extend far beyond the directly adjacent properties and therefore a system of water rights should take the interests of all potentially affected parties into account. There was also economic inefficiency in a system which required at least 40 years to establish rights and then blocked future, potentially more productive, users.[66] Thus, although immemorial possession provided a workable solution to some conflicts for a time, increasing competition for water in the 18th century resulted in the need for a more developed and coherent system.

(2) Prejudicial Use of Property

5-23. In the absence of prescription, it was unclear during the 17th and early 18th centuries whether lower owners had any right to prevent the permanent diversion of rivers or lochs. In support of such a right, arguments and decisions based on the familiar principle that property could not be used in a way that prejudiced others were made. These debates took place long before the influence of nuisance from England.[67] Although Whitty has written that originally 'Scots law imposed no general restraint on the use of property, except *aemulatio vicini* and the prohibition of direct damage',[68] it appears that

---

[64] See the argument for Kennedy in *Cunningham v Kennedy* and Information for Kennedy 13 Jul 1713 (Hugh Dalrymple), *Cunningham v Kennedy* Arniston Collection Vol 4, Paper 35. See also the argument for the Magistrates of Linlithgow in Memorial for Linlithgow 27 Sept 1766 (Henry Dundas), *Magistrates of Linlithgow v Elphinstone (No 1)* Campbell Collection Vol 17, Paper 62 and the decision of the *Magistrates of Linlithgow v Elphinstone (No 1)* (1767) 5 Brown's Supp 935 at 936, discussed below, paras 5-57–5-62. This decision was later affirmed in *Magistates of Linlithgow v Elphinstone (No 2)* (1768) Mor 1280, Hailes 203. An exception was *Prestoun v Erskine* (1714) Mor 10919 where the pursuers had tended to dams and aqueducts on the upstream property.

[65] See below, paras 7-101–7-105.

[66] See discussion of the economic inefficiency of the immemorial possession rules in Getzler 331 and 334. Such rights could, of course, be purchased from neighbours to bypass the requirement of 40 years prescriptive use.

[67] See G D L Cameron, 'Neighbourhood Liability in Scotland 1850–2000' in J Gordley (ed), *The Development of Liability Between Neighbours* (2010) 132-133; Whitty, 'Nuisance' para 16.

[68] Whitty, 'Nuisance' para 17.

arguing on the basis of a general restraint on prejudicial use of property was seen as fruitful by advocates and judges until the end of the 18th century.

5-24.   The problem was identifying exactly what was prohibited or, in other words, what was the identifiable interest protected against neighbourly interference. Craig states that building a mill on a private river is 'unlawful if the result is to cause any prejudice to another mill, older but still extant, lower down stream. Prejudice occurs whenever the new structure diminishes the force of the water at the lower mill.'[69] This identifies the lower mill-owner's use of the water as a protected interest, and Bartolus – the 14th-century Italian jurist – is cited as authority despite the fact that the latter considers mills in the context of public rivers.[70] Further, it is unclear how this standard applied to cases not involving mills.

5-25.   In 1624, a broader definition of prejudice was offered by *Bannatyne v Cranston*[71] which decided that a landowner was not entitled to divert a river which separates two properties if a potential future use of the opposite owner would be affected. The report reads 'the Lords found it enough of a prejudice, that he wanted his pleasure, seeing he had the use thereof *ad amoenitatem et voluptatem*, and also had sometimes fishing therein of trouts, whereof he alleged he was prejudiced, and which could not be altered without his consent'.[72] Erskine comments that the only prejudice was 'depriving him of the pleasure of trouting and, the chance that he may have occasion for the water at some future time'.[73] This is the most open-ended definition of prejudice in all the cases concerning the diversion of rivers and suggests an owner has a multifarious interest which is subject to protection by restriction on neighbouring lands. That this river was a boundary may have prompted such a strong restriction. Although, as Whitty has highlighted, the interdict *uti priori aestate* is mentioned in *Bannatyne*, the case does not seem to be decided on this Roman interdict but on a general principle of Scots private law.

5-26.   It is difficult to reach clear conclusions concerning *Bairdie v Scartsonse*,[74] a case decided in the same year, due to the brevity of the report but it may be that this case required a higher level of prejudice than *Bannatyne*. Erskine states that *Bairdie* decided that no one can alter a river 'if the alteration should bring real prejudice to the owner of that tenement'[75] which suggests that tangible damage or loss must be proved. Whether this difference in prejudice required is due to the dispute being between successive owners rather than opposite owners is not certain as the facts of *Bairdie* are not given in the report.[76]

---

[69] Craig, *Jus Feudale* 2.8.5.

[70] It is assumed Craig is citing Bartolus de Saxoferrato, *Commentaria Corpus Iuris Civilis* (1615) on D.43.12. See J Gordley, *Foundations of Private Law* (2006) 104 where Bartolus is translated and summarised.

[71] (1624) Mor 12769.

[72] At 12770.

[73] Erskine, *Institute* II.9.13.

[74] (1624) Mor 14529; Hope, *Practicks* VI.40.6.

[75] Erskine, *Institute* II.9.13.

[76] Erskine assumes the case is between successive owners.

5-27.   *Mayor of Berwick v Laird of Haining*[77] confirms that Scots law was in a state of flux at the end of the 17th century. In this case the Laird drained his loch into the River Tweed, in the process colouring the water red and allegedly prejudicing salmon fishings. Although strictly this case does not fit into the category of private water rights, as it concerns the owners of salmon fishings objecting to the pollution of a public (navigable) river, the arguments regarding ownership are of interest. It was argued for the Laird that 'freedom of *dominium* was universally true in law, *dummodo non fecerit ut alteri noceat,* and that it be not done *ex animo malitioso* to the prejudice of his neighbour'.[78] This view suggests an owner is only restrained from exercising rights when damage or loss is caused or where acting with malicious or spiteful intent – a reference to the doctrine of *aemulatio vicini.*[79] To this it was responded that an owner 'may build upon his own ground, albeit to the detriment of his neighbour's light or prospect, or may dig a well in his own ground, albeit thereby cut off the veins of his neighbour's well,[80] yet he can not otherwise prejudice his neighbours; as if he had a loch on a hill, he might not cut it if it drowned his neighbour's ground below, nor may he build a mill upon his own ground, so as to take the water from his neighbour's mill, nor may he turn the water out of the old channel, or make it run otherways upon his neighbours than was accustomed'.[81] The authority for this was reported merely as being 'many interdicts in the civil law'.[82] Thus, up to the end of the 17th century, it appears that the principle prohibiting prejudicial use of property was broad enough to prevent diversion of rivers although of the definition of prejudice was uncertain.

5-28.   Later, through case law and institutional writings restrictions on the prejudicial use of ownership became clearer as the definition of prohibited prejudice became more precise. Stair analysed the prohibition against diversion of water as stemming from general principles:

'though it may appear from the common rule, *Cujus est solum, ejus est usque ad coelum,* that thereby the owner may build upon any part of his own ground what he will, even though it be to the detriment of his neighbours' prospect and light; yet no man may dispose so upon his ground, as to put any positive prejudice, hurt or damage upon his neighbour's; as if he should alter the course of any river or water running within his ground, so that it cause an alteration in his neighbour's ground: and therefore he may not so build upon his own ground, as

---

[77] (1661) Mor 12772, 2 Brown's Supp 292. The pleadings to this case can be found in the National Archives under the reference *Heritors of Fishings of River Tweed v John Riddall, of Haining: Unstated* (1661) CS149/268.

[78] 2 Brown's Supp 292 at 292.

[79] See D Johnston, 'Owners and Neighbours: From Rome to Scotland' in *The Civil Law Tradition in Scotland* (R Evans-Jones (ed), Stair Society, Supp Vol 2, 1995); E Reid, 'The Doctrine of Abuse of Rights: Perspective from a Mixed Jurisdiction' (2004) *EJCL* Vol 8.3.

[80] The exceptions which allow blocking light and cutting off underground water are based in Roman law. See D.39.3.24.12 (Ulpian) for water; D.8.2.9 (Ulpian) for light.

[81] (1661) Mor 12772 at 12773.

[82] The case was decided in favour of the Laird on the archaic view that it was 'the proper use of rivers to carry away the corruption and filth of the earth' (at 12773).

by gathering the water from its natural way, he should make it fall together upon his neighbour's ground.'[83]

'Positive prejudice' seems to have the specific meaning of direct physical damage,[84] which limits an owner's interest to the physical integrity of land and sets a relatively high standard to meet to restrict the use of neighbouring land.

5-29.   The movement towards a narrow definition of prohibited prejudice continued in subsequent cases and writings. In *Magistrates and Town of Dumfries v Heritors of the Water of Nith*[85] it was argued for the Magistrates, who were seeking to build a dam to serve their mill, that 'accidental' prejudice is permissible. A similar argument was made in *Brodie v Cadel*,[86] a case regarding the disruption of fishing in a public river, to the effect that accidental prejudice is not prohibited if owners act not out of spite but for their own benefit.[87] A distinction between direct physical damage to land, which is a prohibited form of prejudice, and indirect or consequential damage – such as the deprivation of light or prospect – which is not prohibited in the absence of spite or malice, was then outlined by Kames and accepted by Hume.[88] Kames' likely authority is Ulpian's distinction between *damnum* and deprivation of a benefit.[89] These developments limited the usefulness of arguments based on the prejudicial use of property as often there was no direct physical damage caused by the diversion of a river, only loss of profits due to a slow-working mill. The early broader definition of prejudice was, however, to have a future role in the development of other aspects of common interest.[90]

(3) The Compromise of *Cunningham v Kennedy*

5-30.   If the decisions concerning prejudicial use of property did little to ease the uncertainty concerning whether water could be diverted, a more certain, but perhaps more arbitrary, rule was established by *Cunningham v Kennedy*[91] in 1713. The full circumstances of this case are only revealed in the session papers. Kennedy had begun to repair a dam which had become ruinous. Cunningham, a downstream mill-owner, objected to these works as interfering with the flow of water to his mill.

---

[83] Stair, *Institutions* II.7.7. These statements will also be considered below in regard to the *immissio* principle. Stair acknowledges both *Bannatyne* and *Bairdie* but merely states that one cannot divert a watercourse from its course without a servitude (the reverse form of the argument that was considered above) but does not provide any justification for this: see II.7.12.

[84] Johnston, 'Owners and Neighbours' (n 79) 185.

[85] (1705) Mor 12776. This case concerned damage to fishings.

[86] (1707) 4 Brown's Supp 660. See further Johnston, 'Owners and Neighbours' (n 79) 188.

[87] Remarkably in this case, *aemulatio vicini* was proven.

[88] Kames, *Principles* 46–47; Hume, *Lectures* III 209–210; Whitty, 'Nuisance' para 10. This distinction was lost when nuisance began to take precedence.

[89] D.39.2.26 (Ulpian). See also discussion below, para 5-38 and Whitty, 'Nuisance' para 10

[90] See below, paras 6-23–6-24.

[91] (1713) Mor 8903 and 12778.

5-31. It was argued for Kennedy that he was entitled to use his property, though it caused prejudice to Cunningham, where there was no malice or intention to harm.[92] A text from the *Digest* concerning new works, or *operis novi nuntiatione*, was cited in support of the argument that operations wholly *in suo* could not be prevented.[93] It was also argued that, although there is a natural servitude on the downstream property to receive water, there is no obligation on the upstream property to send water downstream.[94] A text of Roman law to the effect that an owner can intercept a neighbour's water supply was cited in support of this argument.[95] Further, highlighting the inadequacies of the immemorial possession argument, it was stated that the right of the downstream property to receive water unimpeded could not have been acquired by Cunningham because Kennedy had merely allowed the water to run its natural course through his land, which was not sufficient to establish a servitude of *aquaeductus* on his property.[96]

5-32. For Cunningham it was argued that he had acquired a servitude of *aquaeductus* through immemorial possession and a *Digest* text supporting ancient use was cited.[97] This argument, as shown above, has its flaws. More persuasively, Cunningham stated that if Kennedy were to succeed in this action, Cunningham could turn this victory to his own advantage, for he also owned land above Kennedy's land and could dam the water before it reached Kennedy's mill.[98] Such a factual situation shows the delicate balancing of the interests of multiple parties which must take place when deciding water rights cases.

5-33. The judges, in light of this dilemma, came to the compromise view that an owner may divert a river temporarily but must return the water to its former channel before it leaves his or her land. The court cited the freedom of an owner to dispose of the river at pleasure as the overriding principle as it is 'considered as part of the lands it runs through'.[99] No authority was given for this point which seems unsupported by other decisions or institutional authority and may just be a badly-worded assertion of the freedom of owners to do as they wish within their own land. Further, this assertion does not explain the obligation to return the water. Why is a landowner not entitled to divert the river permanently and prevent any water reaching downstream lands? How does this rule operate between opposite owners where both could claim freedom to divert?

---

[92] The Italian humanist Alciatus is cited in support of the argument that if an act is done with benefit to the owner, it is presumed there is no malice. This may be a reference to Andreas Alciatus, *Tractabus de Praesumptionibus* (1551) Presumption 23.

[93] D.39.1.2 (Julianus) was cited but the relevance of this particular text is questionable.

[94] This argument is considered further below, paras 5-47–5-50.

[95] D.39.3.1.12 (Ulpian).

[96] (1713) Mor 8903; Information for Kennedy 13 Jul 1713 (Hugh Dalrymple), *Cunningham v Kennedy* Arniston Collection Vol 4, Paper 35.

[97] D.43.30.3.4 (Pomponius).

[98] Information for Cunningham 13 Jul 1713 (RO Alexander), *Cunningham v Kennedy* Arniston Collection Vol 4, Paper 35.

[99] (1713) Mor 8903 at 8904.

5-34.   In discussing what was then a new decision, Forbes in his *Great Body* focuses on the *operis novi nuntiatione*, or the prohibition of new works, as a partial explanation for *Cunningham*.[100] The Roman law against new works applied where an owner (i) physically encroached on another's land, (ii) infringed public law regulations, or (iii) breached a servitude right.[101] This implies that a new work diverting a river within one's own land would be allowed. Forbes then suggests that the river had to be returned in *Cunningham* because 'the water had always before the memory of man run free without interruption to that inferior mill'.[102] This carries the idea that immemorial possession constituted the right against permanent diversion although there was no suggestion in *Cunningham* that this was the actual ground of the judgment. Further, Forbes contradicts himself and replicates, without acknowledgment, a large tract of the elaboration of new works in William Strahan's translation[103] of Jean Domat's *Les Lois Civiles Dans Leur Ordre Naturel* (1689) when he later states:

> 'If rain Water or other Waters have their Course regulated from one Ground to another, whither it be by the Nature of the Place, or by some Regulations, or by a Title, or by an ancient Possession, the Proprietors of the said Grounds cannot innovate any Thing as to the ancient Course of the Water. Thus he who has the upper Grounds cannot change the Course of the Water, either by turning it some other Way, or rendering it more rapid, or making any other Change in it to the prejudice of the Owner of the lower Grounds.'[104]

This suggests a far stricter limitation on an owner's operations *in suo* than was previously outlined when Forbes was discussing *Cunningham v Kennedy* and was most probably the result of the large-scale importation of Strahan's translation.

5-35.   The decision in *Cunningham v Kennedy* was a compromise which provided a rule against permanent diversion while still allowing successive landowners to use rivers to power mills. The decision was followed by subsequent case law.[105] The rule is welcome in light of previous uncertainty, but the lack of principle underpinning it left the doctrinal basis for the right to prevent interference with rivers still open.

(4) The *Immissio* Principle

5-36.   Linked to the issue of the prejudicial use of property is the *immissio* principle. This was another basis of arguments, made both before and after the decision of *Cunningham v Kennedy*,[106] against interference with water. The principle derives from D.8.5.8.5 (Ulpian) which reads 'it is not permissible to

---

[100] Forbes, *Great Body* Vol 1, 606–607.
[101] See D.39.1.5.9 (Ulpian).
[102] Forbes, *Great Body* Vol 1, 605.
[103] J Domat, *The Civil Law in its Natural Order* (W Strahan (trans), 1722) II.8.3.11.
[104] Forbes, *Great Body* Vol 1, 607.
[105] See *Kelso v Boyds* (1768) Mor 12807, Hailes 224; *Hamilton v Edington & Co* (1793) Mor 12824.
[106] (1713) Mor 8903 and 12778.

discharge water or any other substance on to the lower property, as a man is only permitted to carry out operations on his own premises to this extent, that he discharge nothing onto those of another'. Affected owners could raise the *actio negatoria* to declare their property free of a servitude to receive such substances.[107] However, a second text stated that a moderate amount of smoke from a hearth was not objectionable.[108] These two Roman texts were subject to much discussion during the *jus commune* principally to clarify which emissions were allowed.[109] Bartolus saw the difference as based on the degree of the emission and whether the use of land creating the emission was normal.[110] A similar solution was developed and adopted in many Civilian jurisdictions to create a general limitation on the use of property.[111]

5-37. In Scotland the *immissio* principle was cited in water rights cases[112] and referred to by institutional writers. Stair's statement, in the section concerning the diversion of water quoted above,[113] that one cannot throw water on to another's land contains echoes of the *immissio* principle. Yet, the principle originally concerned the obligation *not* to throw water on to another's land by one's operations rather than the right to receive such water. Thus, it was mainly applicable to situations where owners objected to water being diverted on to, rather than away from, their lands and so it was generally not a particularly useful basis of argument.

5-38. However, the *immissio* principle did prove useful in a case concerning regorgement. In *Fairly v Earl of Eglinton*,[114] decided in 1744, after *Cunningham v Kennedy*,[115] the Earl had erected a mill downstream of Fairly's mill, the dam of which had caused the water to regorge and affect the working of the upstream mill. The Earl offered to alter Fairly's mill-wheel at his own expense. Fairly refused and raised an action requiring the Earl to lower the dam. Unusually, therefore, it was the upstream owner who was objecting to interference with the flow of water. The counsel for Fairly, Henry Home

---

[107] D.8.5.2.pr. (Ulpian). An alternative action regarding water causing damage due to artificial works, mainly applicable to the countryside due to its wording, was the *actio aquae pluviae arcendae* contained in D.39.3.

[108] D.8.5.8.6 (Ulpian). There was no natural servitude to receive the water as such servitudes applied only to casual water which naturally flowed between lands whereas the *immissio* principle applied to operations on land causing the emission of water.

[109] See J Gordley, 'Immissionsschutz, Nuisance and Troubles de Voisinage in Comparative and Historical Perspective' 1998 ZEuP13.

[110] Gordley (n 109) at 14–15.

[111] Gordley (n 109) at 15; N Whitty, 'Nuisance' para 9. See also R von Jhering, 'Zur Lehre von den Beschränkungen des Grundeigenthümers im Interesse der Nachbarn' (1863) *Jahrbücher für die Dogmatik des Heutigen Römischen und Deutschen Privatrechts* 6; J Gordley (ed), *The Development of Liability Between Neighbours* (2010).

[112] *Mayor of Berwick v Laird of Haining* (1661) 2 Brown's Supp 292; *Hall v Corbet* (1698) Mor 12775; *Brodie v Cadel* (1707) 4 Brown's Supp 660 although the relevance of this argument in the latter case is unclear. See also Johnston, 'Owners and Neighbours' (n 79) 187–194.

[113] See above, para 5-28.

[114] (1744) Mor 12780.

[115] (1713) Mor 8903 and 12778.

(later Lord Kames), began by quoting the *immissio* principle from the *Digest*[116] which he rendered broadly as 'no person's property can be subject to the will of another'.[117] The principle was said to have three effects. Firstly, in the absence of a positive servitude, no one may use another's land. As such one cannot throw water on to another's land. This reflects the *actio negatoria* of Roman law.[118] Secondly, owners cannot be restrained from using their own property even if this causes consequential damage to another – for there is a difference between the withdrawal of a benefit (which is enjoyed by owners but not protected against interference by neighbours) and direct physical damage (which is prohibited).[119] Thirdly, owners cannot use their property *in aemulationem vicini*.[120] Home successfully argued that the Earl could not throw water back upstream or forcibly alter Fairly's mill as this would be subjecting Fairly's property to the Earl's will.

5-39.   Twenty years later, in the second edition of his *Principles of Equity*, Kames returned to the subject of the *immissio* principle and developed it further.[121] Building on the translation of the principle as 'no person's property can be subject to the will of another', Kames states with regard to the interference with the flow of rivers that, where 'a river is interjected between my property and that of my neighbour, it is not lawful for me to alter its natural course, whether by throwing it upon my neighbour's ground, or by depriving him of it; because these acts, both of them, are direct encroachments upon his property'.[122] In the situation where the definition of prohibited prejudice was becoming narrower, Kames shows that, with broad creative interpretation, the *immissio* principle had the potential to explain the rights of landowners and provide a doctrinal formulation for the restrictions on interference with rivers by opposite owners as well as downstream owners (although the restrictions on upstream owners, which was the primary issue of contention, were later to be given a different justification[123]). Yet, despite Kames' attempt to utilise the *immissio* principle both as an advocate and jurist, his novel explanation of the concept was not accepted by other writers or in court decisions. Bankton and Erskine both summarise the principle merely to mean that one cannot throw water on to another's land, which limited the potential role of D.8.5.8.5 (Ulpian) in the foundation of common interest.[124]

---

[116] '*In suo hactenus facere licet quatenus nihil in alienum immittat*': D.8.5.8.5 (Ulpian).

[117] (1744) Mor 12780 at 12781.

[118] D.8.5.2.pr. (Ulpian).

[119] Home cites Ulpian's distinction between *lucrum cessans et damnum datum* here D.39.2.26. See further, Kames, *Principles* 46–47; Hume, *Lectures* III 209–210; Whitty, 'Nuisance' para 10 and above, para 5-29.

[120] Ulpian's statement in D.39.3.1.12 which formed the basis of the creation of the doctrine of *aemulatio vicini* is cited here: (1744) Mor 12780 at 12781–12786. Related to this point is the citation of D.39.3.1.10 (Ulpian). Home also cites the German jurist Johannes Heringius' work on mills *Tractatus Singularis de Molendinis* (1625) as cited in J Nisbet, Lord Dirleton, *Some Doubts and Questions in the Law of Scotland* (1698) 128.

[121] Kames, *Principles of Equity* (2nd edn, 1767) 58–59.

[122] Kames, *Equity* 58.

[123] See below, paras 6-07–6-10.

[124] Bankton, *Institute* IV.45.111; Erskine, *Institute* II.9.9. Only Bankton explicitly cites D.8.5.8.5 (Ulpian).

(5) Common Property

5-40.   The argument that the *alveus* of a river, or the river itself as a separate entity, was the common property of adjacent landowners was also made before the courts.[125] The theory received a mixed response. Assessing its merits is not straightforward as it is often unclear to what extent the advocates were arguing for common property as we understand this concept now,[126] and judges were equally unclear as to the basis of their decisions.

5-41.   Bankton may analyse *Bannatyne v Cranston*,[127] discussed above, from the point of view of common property. He states that water running on the boundary between two properties cannot be diverted by one owner without the consent of the other because the water-course is 'common to both, and each has an equal right to the pleasure and conveniency of it'.[128] He then quotes the maxim *in re communi potior est conditio prohibentis*[129] associated with common property. By 'water-course' it is unclear whether Bankton means the body of water constituting the river or merely the *alveus*.

5-42.   Arguments of common property were also seen to be relevant with respect to successive owners. In *Gibson v Earl of Weems*[130] from 1723, Gibson sought declarator of his right to divert a river. It was argued that the Earl, as a downstream owner, could only stop Gibson if it was shown that there was an express or implied contract, a servitude or a 'joynt Interest of Property, which he, who pretends to hinder the Water from being diverted, hath in the Rivulet, which is the Case of Burns running through betwixt the Properties of different Proprietors'.[131] The last of these was referred to, dismissively, as 'a supposed Right of common Property, that Heritors lying upon the same Rivulet pretend to have in it'.[132] Again it is unclear whether this argument refers to the *alveus* or river. The result of this case is unknown.

5-43.   The Earl in *Fairly v Earl of Eglinton*[133] argued that 'the channel of a river, from head to foot, is a common property, so far at least as to be subservient to the receiving the water which naturally composes that river'.[134] No authority was offered for this statement. To this Home responded 'Tis but shuffling, to call the Channel of a private River, a common Property. The Channel, joined to the Defender's Lands, is his Property, and he has used it as such, by building a Damm-Dyke from Side to Side; and, in like Manner, the

---

[125] Common property was also used for a time to explain the rights owners have to sail and fish over the whole surface of a loch which are now attributed to common interest but this is explored separately above, paras 3-77–3-82.

[126] See Reid, *Property* paras 17–40.

[127] (1624) Mor 12769.

[128] Bankton, *Institute* II.7.29.

[129] Reid, *Property* para 23.

[130] (Unreported), Information for Gibson 27 Nov 1723 (Robert Dundas), *Gibson v Weems* WS 8:32.

[131] At 3.

[132] At 5.

[133] (1744) Mor 12780.

[134] At 12784. Unusually, the Earl is using this argument to support his damming of the river.

Channel, adjoining to the Pursuer's Lands, is his Property.'[135] The Lords did not accept the Earl's common property argument.

5-44.   Indeed, it appears the courts were not receptive to arguments that the *alveus* was common property but there was a slight indication in *Lyon and Gray v Bakers of Glasgow*[136] that they might be open to the concept of common property in the river itself. It was observed that 'the *alveus* was the property of the conterminous heritors, and the river might be considered as common; but the water flowing therein was not their property, but subject to occupation.'[137] Yet again no authority was cited and whether the judges were referring to the concept of common property here is open to debate.

5-45.   In *Magistrates of Linlithgow v Elphinstone (No 2)*[138] the court took a strong stance against the argument. As it was becoming established that the *alveus* was owned by the conterminous owners, the idea that the river itself was common property of the adjacent owners was rejected with the statement that a river cannot be appropriated and subject to ownership. Instead, inspired by the Division of Things, the court said that 'a river may be considered as the common property of the whole nation, but the law declares against separate property of the whole or part'.[139]

5-46.   Despite this apparently conclusive statement, the common property argument was resurrected in *Hamilton v Edington & Co.*[140] This case was decided after the doctrinal establishment of common interest and will be considered in detail in Chapter 6.

(6) Natural Servitudes

5-47.   Most of the arguments considered in the preceding pages were made by those seeking to prevent diversion,[141] and in attempting to rebut them, advocates would claim that owners were free to do as they wished with their property. It was often asserted that, though there was a natural servitude upon the lower property to receive water from the upper, there was no obligation to send the water down in the first place. Therefore, the upper owner could stop a river running on to the lower land altogether.

5-48.   This argument was made for Kennedy in *Cunningham v Kennedy*[142] discussed above.[143] Counsel for Boyds in *Kelso v Boyds*[144] made a similar

---

[135] Replies for Fairly 3 Jan 1744 3 (Henry Home), *Fairly v Earl of Eglinton* WS 4:117. See also (1744) Mor 12780 at 12786.

[136] (1749) Mor 12789.

[137] At 12790.

[138] (1768) Mor 12805, Hailes 203.

[139] (1768) Mor 12805 at 12806.

[140] (1793) Mor 12824.

[141] The notable exception is *Fairly v Earl of Eglinton* (1744) Mor 12780.

[142] (1713) Mor 8903 and 12778; Information for Kennedy 13 Jul 1713 (Hugh Dalrymple), *Cunningham v Kennedy* Arniston Collection Vol 4, Paper 35.

[143] See above, paras 5-30–5-35.

[144] (1768) Mor 12807, Hailes 224.

argument to the effect that 'although every inferior Tenement is subjected to a natural Servitude in favour of the Superior, whereby the former is obliged to receive the Water that naturally falls from the superior Grounds, yet there is no natural Servitude upon the superior Grounds in favour of the inferior'.[145] For Kennedy in *Cunningham*, there was cited D.39.3.1.12 (Ulpian) on the *actio aquae pluviae arcendae*, which states that no action can be taken against those who divert their neighbour's water supply whilst digging on their land, as well as the French jurist Hugo Donellus' comments on natural servitudes.[146] Counsel for Boyds in *Kelso* cited D.39.3.1.21–23 (Ulpian), where the interaction between the *actio aquae pluviae arcendae* and natural servitudes is discussed and it is clarified that the *actio* cannot be brought for preventing water flowing on to lower land.[147] Bankton was also cited by counsel in *Kelso* where it is stated, using the authority of D.39.3.1.21 (Ulpian), that 'the owner of the higher ground may wholly intercept the water within his own grounds, and hinder it from running into the lower, unless the heritor has a servitude against him'.[148] In both cases, the argument was unsuccessful and it was decided that the river could not be permanently diverted.

5-49. If these arguments of the advocates had been accepted by the courts this would not only be contrary to the general position of Scots law, which had always seemed to recognise at least some restrictions on the use of rivers and lochs even if the extent of, and rationale behind, these restrictions were unclear, but would also have a significant effect on industries using water-powered mills.

5-50. In *Magistrates of Linlithgow v Elphinstone (No 1)*[149] the exact application of natural servitudes was clarified. In the first decision in this case,[150] which was later affirmed,[151] it was said that perennial rivers were subject to particular rules which prevented permanent diversion[152] but that '*stagnum* or *torrens* which has not a perpetual course, is entirely *privati juris*, and therefore the heritor upon whose ground it is may make what use of it he pleases...And if such a collection of water should in its natural course, and without any *opus manufactum*, fall down upon the inferior tenement, it would still be more absurd to say that thereby any servitude could be acquired to the inferior tenement; for upon that tenement there is a servitude imposed by nature, of receiving that water from the superior, but it never can acquire any upon the superior.'[153] The natural servitude doctrine only applies to casual waters, not to perennial rivers in a definite channel. Comments of the institutional writers should be read in this light.[154] This, in fact, was the position in Roman

---

[145] Petition of Boyds 9 Dec 1767 12 (Robert MacQueen), *Kelso v Boyds* Pitfour Collection Vol 39, Paper 17. This advocate was later to be raised to the bench as Lord Braxfield.

[146] It is unclear which of Donellus' works is being referred to.

[147] D.39.3.2.9 (Paul) and C.3.34.10 are also cited.

[148] Bankton, *Institute* II.7.29.

[149] (1767) 5 Brown's Supp 935.

[150] The exact procedure of this case will be outlined below.

[151] (1768) Mor 12805, Hailes 203.

[152] This aspect of the judgment is explained further below.

[153] (1767) 5 Brown's Supp 935 at 936.

[154] See Bankton, *Institute* II.7.29 and Erskine, *Institute* II.6.17 and II.9.35.

law[155] and given the economic conditions, it is not surprising that the natural servitude argument, which would have allowed permanent diversion of rivers, was not found to be generally applicable.

(7) Summary

5-51.   From the foregoing analysis, it can be seen that, by the mid-18th century, the doctrinal foundation for the right to prevent permanent diversion of rivers and lochs was still unclear. A compromise had been established by *Cunningham v Kennedy*,[156] allowing the temporary diversion of private rivers provided the water was returned to the natural channel before it left the owner's land. There was also a vague impression that the rules for diversion as between opposite owners were stricter than as between successive owners.[157] Yet, these rules were not justified by any accepted theory.

F. THE FOUNDATION OF COMMON INTEREST: NATURAL RIGHTS

5-52.   The last argument to be considered in this chapter, which I entitle the 'natural rights' theory,[158] came to be accepted by the courts and provided the doctrinal foundation of what is today known as common interest. Many of the theories outlined above focused only on (negative) rights to prevent interference with water – understandably, as this was the main concern at the time – but perhaps the more logically anterior issue to be considered was, what were the rights of landowners in respect of the water running through their lands? If this issue could be settled, the accompanying restrictions would be easily analysed. Considering the issue from this perspective focuses less on how to solve individual instances of interference as they come before the courts and makes progress towards providing a general theory of water rights. The natural rights theory broached this topic. The person who appears to have invented this theory, and who had significant influence on its development, was the advocate, judge and jurist whose role in this area of law has already been shown to be important: Henry Home, elevated to the bench in 1752 as Lord Kames.[159]

---

[155] A Rodger, *Owners and Neighbours in Roman Law* (1972) Ch 5; Whitty, 'Water' 457–458. In South Africa, the natural servitude doctrine has been expanded to cover other water bodies. See A J van der Walt, *The Law of Neighbours* (2010) para 5.1.1.

[156] (1713) Mor 8903 and 12778.

[157] Stair, *Institutions* II.7.12; Bankton, *Institute* II.7.29; Erskine, *Institute* II.9.13 using the authority of *Bannatyne v Cranstoun* (1624) Mor 12769.

[158] Getzler 204 names Kames' theory as 'Romanist Natural Rights'. 'Natural' here refers to the fact that the rights arise by operation of law.

[159] See I S Ross, *Lord Kames and the Scotland of his Day* (1972) 115.

(1) Initial Rejection

5-53.   First elaborated by Henry Home as an advocate, the natural rights theory of water rights was initially rejected by the courts. In *Kincaid v Stirling*,[160] Stirling had diverted a burn which had flowed into a river above Kincaid's downstream mill. Home, acting for Kincaid, objected to the diversion by making use of a novel argument:

'For though it may be true, that Waters which are not navigable are in some Sense the Property of the neighbouring Heritors; yet as every adjacent Heritor has an equal Interest, it is inconsistent even with this supposed Property, to give any one a Power to divert the Course of the Water, so as to prevent its running, as formerly, through the Grounds of the Heritors below. And this was found in a pointed Case, observed by Durie, 25th June 1624, *Bannatyne contra Cranston*...And your Petitioner apprehends, that the Case must be the same with the Rivulets which compose a Water or River. For if one Man can divert the Course of a Burn which runs through his Lands, another has the same Privilege; whereby the Channel of the greatest Rivers may be left dry. And, in the *Roman* Law, it is a Rule, That whatever holds of a navigable River, holds of the smaller Rivers which compose it: *Si aut navigabile est, aut ex eo aliad navigabile fit.* And here all Authors make a Distinction betwixt *flumen* & *aqua profluens*...*Vinn In Institut. I.2.t.1.* Hence it is, that though every Heritor, and indeed every Person may have Use of the Water for drinking, washing, and perhaps for improving their Land; yet he has no Power to divert the Course of the Water, or to deprive his Neighbours of the Benefit thereof. Superiority in Place gives no Privilege in this Case. But all the neighbouring Heritors, high and low, have an equal Interest.

In the *second* place, This Doctrine holds *à fortiori*, where a Mill is erected upon a River or Water. For here is a substantial Interest far beyond *amœnitas & voluptas*. And it must be extremely plain, that if either a Water or its Feeders could be diverted by the superior Heritors, no Man could be in Safety to build a Mill; which, next to drinking, is the most general and necessary Use that Water can be applied to. This must hold, had *Kincaid's* two Mills been erected Yesterday.'[161]

5-54.   The only authorities cited by Home are the case of *Bannatyne v Cranston*,[162] discussed above, and a commentary on title 2.1 of Justinian's *Institutes*[163] concerning the Division of Things by the Dutch jurist Arnoldus Vinnius.[164] The Latin text of this commentary is translated by Whitty as follows: 'that there is a distinction between a river and flowing water, whence from the use of each a difference emerges. The river is the whole entity, one and the same body, which has existed for a thousand years. Finally it is under the control of those within whose boundaries it is confined.'[165] The distinction Vinnius makes here stems from the classification of perennial rivers as *res*

[160] (1752) Mor 12786.

[161] Petition of Kincaid 4 Dec 1749 7–8 (Henry Home), *Kincaid v Stirling* Arniston Collection Vol 23, Paper 27.

[162] (1624) Mor 12769.

[163] Justinian's *Institutes* 2.1.

[164] A Vinnius, *Institutionum Imperialium Commentarius* (1642) II.1.2. See also R Feenstra, *Seventeenth-century Leyden Law Professors* (1975) 24–35 and 83–88.

[165] Whitty, 'Water' 455. In *Mason v Hill* (1833) 110 ER 692 at 700 a similar translation is provided.

publicae and running water as *res communes* in Justinian's *Institutes*.[166] These categories were the topic of Chapter 2 where it was discussed how running water and rivers could be subject to different classifications. It was argued that defining running water as *res communes* means that it is generally outwith ownership while in its natural state but that portions of water can be appropriated through *occupatio*. The focus of the *res publicae* category is public use and means rivers can be used for activities such as navigation and fishing. Here, Vinnius is explaining the distinction between the classifications and seems to take the view, also taken by some institutional writers, that defining rivers as public limits the use of them to the citizens of the state within which they run.

5-55.   Home does not use Vinnius' distinction and the classifications of the Division of Things to argue that the river as a distinct object is subject to private property rights despite the water being outwith ownership.[167] Instead, he argues that everyone has a natural public right to take the water of rivers for basic needs, and also for irrigation or powering machinery where possible, but this does not mean that one can subject the whole river to *occupatio*. Diverting a river entirely is prohibited as this would be depriving others of their natural rights to occupy the water. This is the practical application and adaptation of the abstract classification of Roman law which has as its starting point the rights of people to take water and uses this as the basis for the prohibition on permanent diversion. This emphasises the interests of all parties – not even merely landowners – in using water.

5-56.   The judges did not accept this novel argument. Home was unsuccessful and Stirling was found entitled to divert the river on the basis that the burn had originally flowed into the river below Kincaid's mill and Stirling was merely restoring its natural course.

(2) Magistrates of Linlithgow v Elphinstone (No 1)

5-57.   Less than twenty years later, the case of *Magistrates of Linlithgow v Elphinstone (No 1)* came before the courts. Elphinstone owned a large tract of land comprising two lochs, the water from which powered his mill before running into the River Avon. Elphinstone proposed to divert the water from the lochs into the River Carron to serve the Carron Company. The owners of mills served by the River Avon objected to the diversion.

5-58.   The action came before the Lord Ordinary who granted proof before the whole Court.[168] A proof was led and memorials were lodged by both

---

[166] These classifications are considered in Chapter 2 of this book.

[167] Whitty suggests this is how Vinnius is later used in *Hamilton v Edington & Co* (1793) Mor 12824. See Whitty, 'Water' 455 and below, para 6-34.

[168] The Court of Session was not split formally into the modern Inner and Outer Houses until 1808. See T Cooper, Lord Cooper of Culross, 'The Central Courts after 1532' in *An Introduction to Scottish Legal History* (G C H Paton (ed), Stair Society, Vol 20, 1958) 341 and 343.

parties.[169] The arguments by the parties at this stage were unremarkable and based on immemorial possession and servitudes. Counsel for the pursuers argued that rights had been acquired to use the water for the mills through immemorial possession of the water which could not be prejudiced by diversion by an upstream owner.[170] Counsel for the defender argued that there was no perennial flow from the lochs to the River Avon and thus there was no perpetual cause sufficient to create a servitude.[171] In addition, the pursuers had not carried out any positive acts on the burdened property.[172]

5-59. Due to the continued dispute as to whether there was a perennial flow from the lochs into the river, the Lords appointed a surveyor to report on the lochs, and the sluices controlling the flow from the lochs to the river were ordered to be closed for a month. This experiment seemed to suggest that there was no perennial run from the lochs.[173]

5-60. Following this report, the parties submitted further memorials on the evidence. Counsel for the pursuers developed the concept of immemorial possession and sought to rely less on the need to prove the formal requirements of a servitude:

> 'Other servitudes, such as *via, iter,* &c. must either depend on an express grant from some proprietor or another, or at least from an implied grant presumed from immemorial usage; but this is not the case with regard to immemorial usage which conterminous proprietors have to water running through their grounds. Such rights are the original gifts of Heaven. They are improperly termed servitudes; they are burdens upon no particular property, but common benefits bestowed, which every proprietor is entitled to make use of in the manner more beneficial, and in the course Heaven itself had prescribed: But no one proprietor is entitled at his own hand, and without the consent of all interested in those common benefits, to divert the course which nature has prescribed for them.'[174]

This is coming closer to the argument which was submitted to the court by Home in *Kincaid v Stirling*.[175] However, it is still firmly grounded in the doctrine of immemorial possession and prescription.

5-61. The pursuers were unsuccessful and the defenders were assoilzied on 13 November 1767. The decision of the court is documented in *Brown's Supplement* to *Morison's Dictionary*.[176] Henry Home, now Lord Kames, was a

---

[169] The facts and procedure of the case are outlined in Memorial for Linlithgow 25 Sept 1767 (Henry Dundas), *Magistrates of Linlithgow v Elphinstone (No 1)* Arniston Collection Vol 86, Paper 1.

[170] Memorial for Linlithgow 27 Sept 1766 (Henry Dundas), *Magistrates of Linlithgow v Elphinstone (No1)* Campbell Collection Vol 17, Paper 62.

[171] On the importance of perpetual cause see Cusine & Paisley para 2.93.

[172] Memorial for Elphinstone 27 Sept 1766 (Robert MacQueen), *Magistrates of Linlithgow v Elphinstone (No 1)* Campbell Collection Vol 17, Paper 62.

[173] See the comment following the decision, *Magistrates of Linlithgow v Elphinstone (No 1)* (1767) 5 Brown's Supp 935 at 936.

[174] Memorial for Linlithgow 25 Sept 1767 19–20 (Henry Dundas), *Magistrates of Linlithgow v Elphinstone (No 1)* Arniston Collection Vol 86, Paper 1.

[175] (1752) Mor 12786 and see above, para 5-53.

[176] *Magistrates of Linlithgow v Elphinstone (No 1)* (1767) 5 Brown's Supp 935.

judge of the Court of Session, and although the report does not specify the opinions of the individual judges, the main thrust of the decision has a striking similarity to the argument constructed by Home when an advocate. It was decided that:

> 'the true answer is, that the inferior mill upon a burn has not that right [against diversion] by prescription, but upon this principle, that a burn is a *flumen* in the sense of Roman law, being perennial and having an established channel or course; it is therefore, according to the doctrine of the Roman law, *publici juris*[177], so that no man through whose ground it passes can stop or alter the course of it.'[178]

5-62. A total breach has been made with the concept of immemorial possession and prescription and it is stated that perennial rivers cannot be diverted due to being subject to the public rights to water. This decision is the first judicial recognition of the natural rights theory and finally provided a doctrinal justification for the compromise established in *Cunningham v Kennedy*[179] that successive owners may divert water temporarily within their lands but must return it. The theory also explains why there may be stricter rules between opposite owners as even temporary diversion would deprive opposite owners of their rights.[180] These rules, however, did not apply to non-perennial water and, as the 'lochs' in question were not perennial, Elphinstone was free to divert them.[181]

(3) *Magistrates of Linlithgow v Elphinstone (No 2)*

5-63. The pursuers, however, were not satisfied with this decision and submitted a reclaiming petition on 25 November 1767.[182] By now the pursuers had natural rights of use as an independent ground of argument. They wished to 'in the *first* place, show, that they have a natural right to the water running from these lochs; and 2*do*, That, independent of this right, they have also acquired a right to it by prescription.'[183] Counsel submitted:

> 'With regard to the *first* point therefore, the petitioners will lay it down as an established principle of law, that inferior heritors cannot be deprived of the benefit of water that has immemorially run through their grounds, by the superior heritors, from whatever source that water rises, as they do, by the water having naturally and immemorially run through their grounds, acquire such a natural right to it, that it cannot be diverted by the superior heritor, without their own

---

[177] Meaning subject to public rights.
[178] (1767) 5 Brown's Supp 935 at 936.
[179] (1713) Mor 8903 and 12778.
[180] Although Kames' analysis of opposite owners was supplemented by the *immissio* principle: see para 5-39 above. It was still not clear, however, whether opposite owners could divert a portion, rather than the whole of, a river. In *Lyon and Gray v Bakers of Glasgow* (1749) Mor 12789 it was decided that they could but the doctrinal basis of this decision is questionable; see below para 6-62.
[181] Non-perennial water is unlikely to be running and therefore could be capable of ownership.
[182] Petition for Linlithgow 25 Nov 1767 (C Brown), *Magistrates of Linlithgow v Elphinstone (No 2)* Arniston Collection Vol 86, Paper 1.
[183] At 16.

consent. This principle is established not only by various texts of the civil law, but also by the practice of this Court...Nay, the Roman law carried this natural right so high that they did not even allow the superior heritor to divert the course of a water, although the inferior heritor made no sort of use of it, but used it only *amœnitatis causa*.'[184]

This argument makes reference to an immemorial running of water but not of immemorial usage (for this is not an argument based on prescription). Thus, owners of land through which established rivers run have natural rights to the river.

5-64.   As it turned out, this was a common assumption between the parties, counsel for Elphinstone submitting:

'He may admit, that a person through whose grounds a river runs, cannot alter the course of that river, so as to debar those through whose property it afterwards flows from enjoying that natural use of it while it passes through their grounds, whether they have been in the custom of applying it to profitable and beneficial purposes, such as mills or other machines, of have used it only *amœnitatis causa*...But even when this is admitted, it will not aid the petitioners: for here the question does not relate to either a *rivus* or a *flumen*, which has a continued progress, and a *perpetual causa*; but to a loch arising within the respondent's property.'[185]

Thus, the argument which Kames had invented as an advocate and which influenced the advocates in this formative case was now a matter of agreement between the parties. The decision which followed was itself based firmly on a theory of natural rights. However, as can be seen, the arguments seem to assume that it is not everyone who has these natural rights but only the owners of land next to water. Rights which were seen by Kames as public were being analysed as an aspect of ownership. Kames' original argument did not contain that assumption and neither, in the event, did the final decision in *Magistrates of Linlithgow v Elphinstone (No 2)*.[186]

5-65.   The court, in which Kames was among the judges, gave as its final decision that a river cannot be subject to *occupatio* because a 'river, which is in perpetual motion, is not naturally susceptible to appropriation; and were it susceptible, it would be greatly against the public interest that it should be suffered to be brought under private property'.[187] Instead:

'A river may be considered as the common property of the whole nation, but the law declares against separate property of the whole or part. 'Et quide, naturali jure communia sunt haec; aer, aqua profluens, et mare.' § I. *Instit. De rerum divisione*. A river is one subject composed of a trunk and branches. No individual can appropriate a river or any branch of it; but every individual of the nation, those especially who have land adjoining, are entitled to use the water for their private purposes. Hence it follows, that no man is entitled to divert the course of

[184] At 16–18.
[185] Answers for Elphinstone 17 Dec 1767 12–13 (Alex Wight), *Magistrates of Linlithgow v Elphinstone (No 2)* Arniston Collection Vol 86, Paper 1.
[186] (1768) Mor 12805, Hailes 203.
[187] (1768) Mor 12805 at 12805.

a river or of any of its branches; which would be depriving others of their right, viz. the use of the water.'[188]

5-66.   Lochs which have a perennial outflow are said to be branches of a river and subject to the same rules. If a river is diverted completely, such diversion would require 40 years' use to be beyond challenge through *negative* prescription. But, it is said, these rules cannot apply to all water and thus an 'excellent practical rule is laid down in the Roman law, which is, that we cannot divert from a river any rill or runner that has a perennial course, but that we may use freedom with all other water within our bounds.'[189] As it was proved there was no perennial flow from the 'lochs', Elphinstone was assoilzied.

5-67.   The main points of the natural rights theory, and its interaction with the rules which had been established by case law by this stage, can be summarised as follows:

- In title 2.1 of Justinian's *Institutes* running water is among the *res communes* and perennial rivers are *res publicae*.
- Thus, everyone, not just those with land next to water, has a public right to appropriate water for basic needs.
- However, permanent diversion of a perennial river or loch is prohibited as this would be depriving others of their public rights.
- Temporary diversion is allowed between successive owners as long as water is returned within one's own land.
- Temporary diversion is not allowed between opposite owners.
- Diversion can only be legitimised by negative prescription of 40 years.
- Water which is not perennial can be diverted.

5-68.   The main principle of this decision, that the flow of perennial rivers and lochs cannot be diverted owing to the rights of use of others, was accepted by later cases[190] and the natural rights theory, created by Lord Kames, became established as the foundation for the doctrine of common interest.

5-69.   The acceptance of Kames' theory of natural rights was not, however, as unequivocal as it seems. Although it was fully entrenched in the final decision reported in *Morison's Dictionary* – which is derived from the *Select Decisions*[191] compiled by Kames himself – this may have been the result of selective editing, as both decisions were controversial. Hailes' report reveals that three judges had dissented from the first decision and four from the second.[192] Even the concurring judges in the second case show a variety of

---

[188] At 12806.

[189] At 12806–12807.

[190] See *Kelso v Boyds* (1768) Mor 12807, Hailes 224; *Miller v Stein* (1791) Mor 12823, Bell's Octavo Cases 334; *Russell v Haig* (1791) Mor 12823, Bell's Octavo Cases 338; *Ogilvy v Kincaid* (1791) Mor 12824, Hume 508; *Hamilton v Edington & Co* (1793) Mor 12824; *Lord Glenlee v Gordon* (1804) Mor 12834.

[191] Kames, *Select Decisions of the Court of Session 1752–1768* (1780) 331–333.

[192] (1768) Hailes 203 at 206.

opinion as to the basis of the petitioner's failure with some judges still discussing prescription and servitude rights.[193]

(4) The Influences on Kames

5-70.   Determining the influences on Kames in the development of his theory is difficult. The only authorities he cited, whether as advocate or judge, were *Bannatyne v Cranston*,[194] Vinnius' commentary,[195] and title 2.1 concerning the Division of Things in Justinian's *Institutes*. But these sources do not contain anything like the analysis provided by Kames.

5-71.   A possible source of inspiration is Stair's discussion of the real right of commonty in the first edition of the *Institutions*,[196] although there is no evidence that Kames was familiar with the passage in question. Here, Stair transforms the Roman category of *res communes* into a right to appropriate running water with limitations on such appropriation in the interests of the community. This is the only institutional work which seems relevant to Kames' account, as Bankton's and Erskine's works contain little to inspire the natural rights doctrine. Further, the previous case law concerning water comprised a mixture of different and barely satisfactory rationalisations.

5-72.   Another source of inspiration for Kames could have been developments in England. The English history of private water rights has been extensively researched by Professor Joshua Getzler. He states that, like Scotland, although at an earlier stage, English courts used the concept of immemorial possession as the basis for the prescriptive acquisition of rights to protect water use especially by mills.[197] However, over the course of the 17th century, this theory gradually gave way to a natural rights theory. Getzler places the beginning of this development in 1601 with *Luttrel's case*[198] where, in addition to a prescriptive rights theory, there was a suggestion that it was a natural incident of ownership to use water flowing past one's land. This theory was extended beyond water to other natural resources in *Aldred's case*[199] with the aid of the maxim *sic utere tuo ut alienum non laedas*.[200] It was found in this case that an owner has a right to light and air which should not be interfered with.

5-73.   The triumph of natural rights, as Getzler described it, occurred in *Sury v Pigot*.[201] In this case, downstream owner Sury brought an action against Pigot for diverting a stream. There had been a recent unity of ownership of the two pieces of land and so the nature of the water rights was a point of

---

[193] See the opinions of Lords Monboddo, Pitfour and Auchinleck.
[194] (1624) Mor 12769.
[195] A Vinnius, *Institutionum Imperialium Commentarius* (1642) II.1.2.
[196] See above paras 2-31–2-33.
[197] English courts used this concept during the 15th and 16th centuries: Getzler 117.
[198] *Cottel v Luttrel* (1601) 4 Co Rep 84b, 76 ER 1063.
[199] (1610) 9 Co Rep 57b, 77 ER 816.
[200] This maxim has similarities to the *immissio* principle and doctrine of *aemulatio vicini*.
[201] (1625) Poph 166, 79 ER 1263, 3 Bulst 339, 81 ER 280; Getzler 129–140.

issue. It was decided by the King's Bench that the right to prevent diversion of water was not a prescriptive right or servitude but a natural right. A *res communes* argument was sometimes employed by advocates or judges to support this natural rights theory.[202]

5-74.   This reasoning and the sources used sound similar to Kames' theory of natural rights. However, there is one important difference. In England it was clear from the beginning that what was being established was a right appurtenant to ownership.[203] In Scotland, the right to prevent diversion was not initially dependent on the ownership of land. This was because in Kames' view everyone had a public right to use water. No doubt it was the accident of owning land with water flowing over it which made that public right able to be realised in full but it was not a precondition of the right.

5-75.   Despite the growing importance of the natural rights doctrine in England during the 17th century, for a substantial period of time and in a manner similar to Scotland, it was unclear upon what basis decisions of courts were being made and there were many conflicting theories in use by counsel and judges.[204]

5-76.   In the 18th century, the theory of water rights in England was significantly affected by Blackstone's *Commentaries*,[205] published between 1765 and 1769,[206] which put forward what has become known as the prior appropriation theory.[207] According to this theory, which also adapts Roman law concepts, water is *res nullius* or ownerless and thus open to occupation. As the first person to occupy acquires ownership, so the first to divert the water of a river acquires the right to do so, which cannot be prejudiced by later diversions,[208] This theory was adopted by the English courts in the early 19th century with the case of *Bealey v Shaw*.[209] This theory is rejected in *Magistrates of Linlithgow v Elphinstone (No 2)*,[210] with the statement that a river cannot be appropriated like a field or horse. It is said 'by the laws of all polished nations, appropriation is authorised with respect to every subject that is best enjoyed separately; but barred with respect to every subject that is best enjoyed in common'.

5-77.   To state conclusively that Kames was influenced by English law is not possible. It is true that there are some similarities between the natural rights theory which he constructed in Scotland and the theory present in the courts in England. But there are also important differences. Further, it is clear that Kames was not a blind follower of developments in England as his

---

[202] See discussion by Getzler 123 and 133

[203] Getzler 127.

[204] Getzler 140.

[205] W Blackstone, *Commentaries on the Law of England* (1765–1769).

[206] The property book containing the prior appropriation theory – Book II – was published in 1766, just before Kames' decisions in *Magistrates of Linlithgow v Elphinstone*.

[207] Getzler Ch 5.

[208] See a summary of this theory in Getzler 191.

[209] (1805) 6 East 208, 102 ER 1266; Getzler 207.

[210] (1768) Mor 12805 at 12805–12806.

fervent rejection of the prior appropriation theory shows. Perhaps, then, the natural rights doctrine was the invention of this highly original and thoughtful intellectual who saw the need for a doctrinal foundation for water rights in Scotland and persevered until he achieved its implementation.

G. CONCLUSION

5-78.   Rankine begins his chapter on water rights with the statement: 'No part of the law of the neighbourhood has given rise to so many difficult and delicate questions as the law which relates to right in water. The shifting and inconstant nature of the element itself, while doubtless the chief cause of the difficulties which pervade this department of jurisprudence in all systems of law, is a fair symbol of the vagueness which has too often characterised the body of legal doctrine that forms the subject of this chapter.'[211] The unpredictable effects that the use of water within one area of land can have on the many up- and downstream pieces of land over the course of a river make water rights an interesting topic for a study of the limitations on ownership. Further, as Rankine points out, the nature of water results in difficult questions. For a significant period of time, these difficulties were represented in Scots law by the fact that, despite the evident importance of the issue, it was unclear when landowners had the right to prevent the diversion of a river or loch flowing through their lands or why. Although the rule that successive owners may temporarily divert, but must return, a river was established in *Cunningham v Kennedy* in 1713,[212] it lacked clear doctrinal justification.

5-79.   In the end, the need for principle was satisfied by Kames' invention of the natural rights theory which formed the basis of the doctrine of common interest in *Magistrates of Linlithgow v Elphinstone (No 2)*.[213] Kames used the categories of Justinian's Division of Things[214] as inspiration for the theory that, as everyone is entitled to take running water, so no one is entitled to deprive others of their rights by permanent diversion of a river or loch. In its original form, this theory not only balanced the rights of owners, but acknowledged that the public at large were entitled to use water. This case, however, marks only the beginning of common interest. The doctrine was to be subject to substantial adaptation in response to the changing social, economic and legal circumstances in Scotland during the Industrial Revolution. This later development of common interest is the topic of the next chapter.

---

[211] Rankine, *Landownership* 511.
[212] (1713) Mor 8903 and 12778.
[213] (1768) Mor 12805, Hailes 203.
[214] Justinian's *Institutes* 2.1.

6 Common Interest: The Establishment of a Special Regime

A. INTRODUCTION

6-01. In the previous chapter it was shown that *Magistrates of Linlithgow v Elphinstone (No 2)*,[1] finally, provided a doctrinal foundation for common interest. However, this can be seen as only the beginning of the doctrine. The main aspects which comprise the modern law were established in the subsequent 100 years. Up to the 1760s, there had been attempts to regulate the use of water by applying general principles of property law. Spurred by changing social, economic and legal conditions, from the late 18th century onwards, common interest was established as a special regime and the precise nature and extent of the *sui generis* rights and obligations comprising the doctrine gradually crystallised over time. To begin with, a distinction between primary and secondary uses of water was recognised with the former given preference. This was accompanied by the transformation of

---

[1] (1768) Mor 12805, Hailes 203.

common interest rights from public to private rights. Finally, the right to natural flow was developed which entitled owners to object not only to permanent diversion but also to changes in the quantity, quality, natural force and direction of water in a river or loch. This chapter will trace these developments.

B. SOCIAL AND ECONOMIC CHANGES

6-02. In the previous chapter, it was shown how mills had an important role in the establishment of common interest. In this early period – up to the mid-18th century – water power was mainly used for grinding grain in relatively small-scale mills[2] and the primary issue was establishing when lower mill-owners could object to upstream permanent diversions of a river or loch. The compromise was reached that a river might be diverted temporarily as long as it was returned within the owner's land. By the end of the 18th century, however, many new industries developed and large-scale mills came into use which competed with existing users. Increasingly, cases began to involve iron works,[3] cotton mills[4] and coal works.[5] As well as using water to power mills, many industries, such as bleaching, brewing and distilling, consumed water.[6] The result was that the main issue in the case law shifted from lower mill-owners objecting to diversions, to complaints about consumption of water[7] and the creation of reservoirs designed to provide regular, guaranteed flow to large mills.[8] The arguments on behalf of pursuers reflected a wish for certainty, security and stability in the rights of established users and sought to prevent any interference with the flow of a river. On the other hand, the defenders sought to establish rights to consume and detain water for industrial purposes.

---

[2] Between 1550 and 1730 there were about 4,000 grain mills in active use: Shaw, *Water Power* Ch 2.

[3] See *Magistrates of Linlithgow v Elphinstone (No 2)* (1768) Mor 12805, Hailes 203 (concerning the Carron Iron Company); *Hamilton v Edington & Co* (1793) Mor 12824 (concerning the Clyde Iron Works). The iron industry was beginning its trajectory at the end of the 18th century: see Shaw, *Water Power* Ch 25.

[4] See *Lord Glenlee v Gordon* (1804) Mor 12834; *Lanark Twist Co v Edmonstone* (1810) Hume 520. The cotton industry started to grow rapidly in the second half of the 18th century: see Shaw, *Water Power* Ch 20.

[5] See *Hope v Wauchope* (1779) Mor 14538; *Marquis of Abercorn v Jamieson* (1791) Hume 510. Water was, perhaps surprisingly, used in the coal industry until steam took over: see Shaw, *Water Power* Ch 23.

[6] Brewing and distilling became industrialised in the late 18th century: see Shaw, *Water Power* Ch 13. Bleaching, similarly, began to grow as an industry in the mid-18th century: see Shaw, *Water Power* Ch 16. See *Braid v Douglas* (1800) Mor App 2; *Aytoun v Douglas* (1800) Mor App 7 for cases concerning a bleachfield.

[7] Such as *Ogilvy v Kincaid* (1791) Mor 12824, Hume 508; *Cruikshanks and Bell v Henderson* (1791) Hume 506.

[8] Such as *Lord Glenlee v Gordon* (1804) Mor 12834.

6-03.   In addition to the Industrial Revolution, the Agricultural Revolution[9] was in progress. Furthermore, as Shaw notes, for the 'improving landowner the extension and beautification of his house and parks was as necessary a measure as enclosing fields or rebuilding steadings'.[10] Such beautification was also reflected in the case law through objection to pollution impinging on newly created pleasure grounds[11] or complaints from lower mill-owners of interference with flow due to the creation of ponds and artificial lakes.[12]

6-04.   The social impact of the Industrial Revolution should also be taken into account. Particularly after 1750, Scotland's population began to move from the country into the cities.[13] This resulted in a sudden and unprecedented demand for a centralised water supply. Most towns and cities had public wells but water was often insufficient or polluted.[14] Although there were private companies supplying water, a substantial proportion of the population did not have enough money to benefit from such supplies; even when water was provided there were complaints of corruption and profiteering.[15] In Edwin Chadwick's *Report on the Sanitary Condition of the Labouring Population of Great Britain* of 1842, lack of clean water was identified as a chief cause of diseases such as cholera, typhus and tuberculosis which were rampant across Britain.[16] Chadwick's report, and various typhus and cholera epidemics, spurred sanitary reform.[17] This eventually led to the Public Health (Scotland) Act 1867 which imposed responsibilities on local authorities to provide wholesome water.[18] This was the beginning of the provision of piped clean water in houses being seen as a public service.[19] This

---

[9] See generally T M Devine, 'The Transformation of Agriculture: Cultivation and Clearance' in T M Devine, C Howard Lee and G C Peden (eds), *The Transformation of Scotland: The Economy Since 1700* (2005).

[10] Shaw, *Water Power* 119.

[11] Such as *Miller v Stein* (1791) Mor 12823, Bell's Octavo Cases 334.

[12] Such as *Marquis of Abercorn v Jamieson* (1791) Hume 510.

[13] Devine, 'Industrialisation' in Devine et al, *The Transformation of Scotland* (n 9) 39–41. For example, Glasgow's population grew by 37% between 1831 and 1841. See E Chadwick, *Report on the Sanitary Condition of the Labouring Population of Great Britain* (1842; reprinted M W Flinn (ed), 1965) 4 (hereafter 'Chadwick').

[14] Chadwick 138–140; A A Templeton, 'Water' in M R McLarty and G C H Paton (eds), *A Source Book and History of Administrative Law in Scotland* (1956) 220–221. In J H F Brotherston, *Observations on the Early Public Health Movement in Scotland* (1952) 81 it is said that 'if the Scottish people were not famed for their cleanliness they had at least the excuse that water was often difficult to procure'. The story of Edinburgh's water supply is a case in point: see D Lewis, *Edinburgh Water Supply* (1908).

[15] For complaints against the water companies generally, see Chadwick 142–145.

[16] 'The subsequent extracts from the sanitary reports from different places will show that the impurity and its evil consequences are greater or less in different places, according as there is more or less sufficient drainage of houses, streets, roads, and land, combined with more or less sufficient means of cleansing and moving solid refuse and impurities, by available supplies of water for the purpose': Chadwick 79.

[17] Brotherston, *Early Public Health Movement in Scotland* 82–88.

[18] See Public Health (Scotland) Act 1867 ss 88–89; Templeton, 'Water' in McLarty and Paton (n 14) 222.

[19] See generally Whitty, 'Water' 472–473; Templeton, 'Water' in McLarty and Paton (n 14).

evident need for clean water seems likely to have had an important impact on the way in which private water rights developed.

6-05.   These socio-economic changes indicated a need for common interest to develop beyond the simple rule that one may take water but must return it. What was needed were detailed solutions to new conflicts which involved the balancing of many different interests.

C. PRIMARY AND SECONDARY USES

(1) The Consumption of Water

 6-06.   The natural rights theory, established as the doctrinal foundation for common interest in *Magistrates of Linlithgow v Elphinstone (No 2)*,[20] was based on the classification of water as a communal thing. As everyone had a right to take water, to deprive someone else of it through diversion of a river or loch was prohibited. However, *Magistrates of Linlithgow v Elphinstone (No 2)* only dealt with permanent diversion. Consumption was another matter: there were no rules about how much water could be consumed from a river or loch or for what purposes. When restating the natural rights theory in *Principles of Equity*,[21] Kames, a pioneer as ever, tried to fill the gap by providing a hierarchy of uses. In doing so he focused on rights between landowners despite the basis for his theory being that everyone was entitled to water.

(2) *Principles of Equity*

6-07.   The natural rights theory first appeared in juristic writing in the third edition of Kames' *Principles of Equity* published in 1778.[22] It was stated that a 'river or any running stream directs its course through the land of many proprietors; who are thereby connected by common interest, being equally intitled to the water for useful purposes. Whence it follows, that the course of the river or running stream cannot be diverted by any one of the proprietors, so as to deprive others of it.'[23] This is the first time the expression which has become the title of this doctrine – 'common interest' – appears to have been used.

6-08.   Not content with merely reiterating this doctrine, Kames went on produce a hierarchy of uses which outlined how much water landowners could consume and for what purposes. This hierarchy could already be seen in embryonic form in the argument which Kames submitted in *Kincaid v Stirling*[24] almost 30 years before. In *Principles of Equity*, he wrote:

---

[20] (1768) Mor 12803, Hailes 203.

[21] Kames, *Principles of Equity* 50–52.

[22] But not in the previous two editions of 1760 and 1767. Both these editions would have been written before the decisions of *Magistrates of Linlithgow v Elphinstone*.

[23] Kames, *Principles* 50–51.

[24] (1752) Mor 12786. See below, para 5-53.

'Where there is plenty for all, there can be no interference: but many streams are so scanty, as to be exhausted by using the water too freely, leaving little or none to others. In such a case, there ought to be a rule for using it with discretion; though hitherto no rule has been laid down. To supply the defect in some measure, I venture to suggest the following particulars, which practice may in time ripen to a precise rule. It will be granted me, that if there be not a sufficiency of water for every purpose, those purposes ought to be preferred that are the most essential to the well-being of the adjacent proprietors. The most essential use is drink for man and beast; because they can not subsist without it. What is next essential, is water for washing; because cleanness contributes greatly to health. The third is water for a cornmill, which saves labour, and cheapens bread. The fourth is watering land for enriching it. The fifth is water for a bleachfield. And the lowest I shall mention, is water for machinery, necessary for cheapening the productions of several arts.'[25]

At first sight, the inclusion of the cornmill is curious, as all the other uses listed involve the consumption of water. It is suggested, however, that taking water for a mill here means diverting a portion of a river without the requirement to return the water; for the temporary diversion of water, sanctioned by *Cunningham v Kennedy*,[26] would not deprive lower owners of their natural rights.

6-09.   The hierarchy is a highly detailed account of the uses to which a river can be put. Inevitably, it is also entirely coloured by the circumstances of the time. As a result, Kames' hierarchy could never have become a fully entrenched part of common interest. Nevertheless, there are aspects which are of universal value. Kames states that the amount of water which can be consumed should be dependent on the circumstances. The consumption of water for basic needs is seen as paramount – the provision of clean water would, by this time, have been becoming a serious issue. One may use the water for essential uses such as drinking even if this exhausts the stream. Conversely, owners may not consume water for mechanical or industrial purposes if that deprives other owners of essential uses. Kames' analysis marked the beginning of a distinction between 'primary' and 'secondary' uses which is still a fundamental part of the modern law of common interest.[27]

6-10.   Such a discussion of water rights was a novelty in a Scots text. However, in contrast to his arguments and decisions as advocate and judge, Kames focuses on landowners rather than the public at large. This is perhaps because he is discussing the topic within the context of property law.[28] Focusing on landowners also provides context to the levels of consumption as well as acknowledging that third parties would not usually be able to access water in a private river without trespassing. However, in its original

[25] Kames, *Principles* 50–51.

[26] (1713) Mor 8903 and 12778.

[27] See below, paras 7-32–7-47. Again, it is not known what sources – if any – inspired Kames to create this hierarchy. English law developed a similar distinction between 'ordinary' and 'extraordinary' uses but at a later stage; see Getzler 294.

[28] Common interest is considered under the heading 'Harm done by a man in exercising a right or privilege': Kames, *Principles* 45–59.

version Kames' theory highlighted the categorisation of running water as a thing which is generally outwith ownership and in principle open to general use of all, and this emphasis is lost in his account in *Principles of Equity*.

(3) *Miller v Stein* and *Russell v Haig*

6-11. The first cases concerning water to be decided after the publication of the third edition of *Principles of Equity* were *Miller v Stein*[29] and *Russell v Haig*.[30] Although normally viewed in the context of nuisance,[31] these cases are milestones in the development of common interest. They were decided at the very time when the focus was shifting from diversion to detention and consumption. Counsel and judges seemed open to addressing difficult problems with new arguments, and aspects of the judgments were to have significant influence on the subsequent development of common interest. Both cases involved lower owners objecting to water being returned to a river after being used by a distillery on the basis that it was polluting the river.

6-12. Alex Wright, the advocate for the defender in *Magistrates of Linlithgow v Elphinstone (No 2)*,[32] acted for the pursuer in both *Miller v Stein* and *Russell v Haig* in the Court of Session.[33] He argued that owners are entitled to use the water running through their lands:

'No person whose property lies on the banks of a perennial stream, can appropriate such stream to himself. It is destined by nature for the general use of all those who reside upon its banks. He has indeed a twofold right in it. The first is of a usufructuary nature, intitleing him to make use of it for all domestic purposes; and this with great propriety is said to be the primary use of water: The second is a right to apply it, while it passes through his own ground, to artificial purposes, such as driving wheels and other machinery employed either in grinding corn or in other manufactories.'[34]

As the pollution from the distilleries was rendering the rivers unfit for primary purposes, such use was unlawful.

6-13. The argument is an interesting one. A division is made between primary or domestic uses such as drinking, washing and watering animals, and secondary or industrial uses such as powering machinery. No authority is cited but the similarity to Kames' hierarchy of uses in *Principles of Equity* is striking and unlikely to be a coincidence. There are, however, some important differences. Counsel's argument is far more conservative than Kames'

---

[29] (1791) Mor 12823, Bell's Octavo Cases 334.

[30] (1791) Mor 12823, Bell's Octavo Cases 338.

[31] See Whitty, 'Nuisance' para 79.

[32] See Answers for Elphinstone 17 Dec 1767 (Alex Wright), *Magistrates of Linlithgow v Elphinstone (No 2)* Arniston Collection Vol 86, Paper 1.

[33] *Russell v Haig* was appealed to the House of Lords on the issue of whether the river was liable to the service of a common sewer. The case was remitted back to the Court of Session but no further steps were taken under the remit: (1792) 3 Pat 403.

[34] Answers for Russell 18 Sept 1791 2 (Alex Wright), *Russell v Haig* Campbell Collection Vol 63, Paper 19.

account. Upon close reading, it becomes apparent that the secondary purposes which are said to be legitimate are merely powering machinery such as a mill. Such use – as long as involving only temporary diversion – had been found to be lawful between successive owners as early as 1713 with *Cunningham v Kennedy*.[35] There is no mention of consumption which would necessarily diminish the amount of water in a river.

6-14.   Both cases were decided in favour of the pursuers. Lord Justice-Clerk Braxfield stated:

> 'I think that a proprietor is entitled to every use to which water may be applied, where there is enough for all purposes; but if he cannot have all the uses of it without hurting others, there is a certain order of uses: the natural and primary uses, are preferable to all others; these are drink for man and beast. If, by this distillery, the water is destroyed and unfitted for use, the manufactory must yield and the inferior proprietor must have the natural and primary uses of the water.'[36]

6-15.   In this decision, it can be seen that a distinction, influenced by Kames, between primary and secondary uses is adopted. Further, a hierarchy of uses is created, as primary purposes are seen as fundamental and not to be compromised by other purposes. However, this is the limit of Kames' influence and, crucially, the consumption of water for industrial purposes is not explicitly condoned as a legitimate use. No doubt this is because the cases were not primarily concerned with consumption of water, and the lower owners were not mill-owners complaining of diminished flow but merely landowners objecting to pollution. However, what may with hindsight be seen as a missed opportunity to develop a more general theory is of considerable importance as in later cases the dogma of protection of natural flow hindered any development which would generally entitle landowners to consume water running through their lands for secondary purposes.

D. COMMON INTEREST RIGHTS ATTACH TO LANDOWNERSHIP

6-16.   A by-product of the influence of Kames' hierarchy of uses is that the arguments of counsel in *Miller v Stein*[37] and *Russell v Haig*[38] focus solely on the rights of owners. A river is said to be common only to those who have legitimate access to it.[39] The nature of rights to use water is entitled 'usufructuary', ownership presumably being rejected as an explanation because, whilst it is running, water is a communal thing.[40] Instead, an analogy is made with usufruct or liferent where there is a right to use property

---

[35] (1713) Mor 8903 and 12778.

[36] *Russell v Haig* (1791) Bell's Octavo Cases 338 at 347.

[37] (1791) Mor 12823, Bell's Octavo Cases 334.

[38] (1791) Mor 12823, Bell's Octavo Cases 338.

[39] Answers for Russell 18 Sept 1791 2–4 (Alex Wright), *Russell v Haig* Campbell Collection Vol 63, Paper 19.

[40] See Ch 2.

without exhausting the whole.[41] This was one of the first times the analogy of usufruct was used and the term is adopted in future case law.[42] The analogy is interesting but imperfect. Usufruct gives a real right in an object; in contrast, a landowner does not have a real right in the water or over the river. Running water is incapable of being owned or subject to subordinate real rights, and it has not been accepted (although it has been suggested) that a river is an object distinct from the land. Further, water may be consumed for basic needs and Kames argued that a landowner could exhaust a small stream through consumption for primary purposes.[43] Counsel may have been influenced by Blackstone's *Commentaries* where water is said only to be capable of 'usufructuary property'.[44] Indeed, Blackstone on nuisance is cited by the pursuer,[45] this new source being evidence of a burgeoning English influence. But it appears that only the term, rather than the substance, influenced counsel as they are far from putting forward the theory of prior appropriation which Blackstone inspired in England.[46]

6-17. The rights which owners have to use the water running through their lands, as analysed by counsel, are restricted in important ways. It is said:

> 'But these rights he enjoys only under two conditions; 1st, That he shall not cause the water to regorge upon the ground of a superior heritor; and 2dly, That he shall send it down to the inferior heritors in such a state, as to intitle them to make every lawful use of it their situation will permit; and cannot divert to their prejudice what is common to all who have it in their power to derive benefit from it...In short, it is an established point, as well as any can possibly be, that an inferior heritor is equally entitled with a superior, both to primary or natural uses, and to the secondary or artificial uses of the water that runs through his grounds.'[47]

The first restriction recalls the *immissio* argument of Home accepted in *Fairly v Earl of Eglinton*,[48] and the second prevents permanent diversion. For landowners to have equal enjoyment of water running through their land, there must be limitations imposed on each in favour of each. This gives owners a real right over other land to protect the uses of water within their own. This real right derives from common interest. The judgment of Lord Justice-Clerk Braxfield in *Russell v Haig*[49] confirms this analysis by focusing on the rights of proprietors and not on public rights.[50] This was the first judicial

---

[41] As defined by Erskine, *Institute* II.9.39.

[42] See, for example, *Lord Glenlee v Gordon* (1804) Mor 12834; *Morris v Bicket* (1864) 2 M 1082 at 1092; *Duke of Buccleuch v Cowan* (1866) 5 M 214 at 238.

[43] Kames, *Principles* 51 and below, para 7-39.

[44] W Blackstone, *Commentaries on the Law of England* (1765–1769) 2.1.1.

[45] Blackstone, *Commentaries* 3.13.1.

[46] See a summary of this theory in Getzler 191.

[47] Answers for Russell 18 Sept 1791 2–4 (Alex Wright), *Russell v Haig* Campbell Collection Vol 63, Paper 19.

[48] (1744) Mor 12780.

[49] (1791) Mor 12823, Bell's Octavo Cases 338.

[50] After *Magistrates of Linlithgow v Elphinstone (No 2)* (1768) Mor 12805, Hailes 203 judges, for a short time, viewed water rights as public rights, as shown in *Kelso v Boyds* (1768) Hailes

indication that the rights of common interest are real rights attached to landownership. It was to be developed in future cases.[51]

6-18.   In this way, the adoption of a hierarchy of uses and the attachment of common interest rights to landownership can be seen as linked. It is suggested that, not least because of the absence of other authority on water rights, counsel for the pursuer and Lord Justice-Clerk Braxfield in *Russell v Haig*[52] were influenced by Kames' account in *Principles of Equity*.[53] As Kames' hierarchy focused on the rights of landowners, the neighbourly restrictions which arose in order to allow fulfilment of these rights were seen as real rights.

6-19.   These developments provided a helpful context for water rights, promoting certainty and focusing on the use of a specific class of people. The legally preferential primary use could be defined as the amount of water required to serve the occupiers of the adjacent land. This was a quantifiable and relatively small amount which was unlikely to involve material operations to the stream or to interfere with downstream users. However, in order to ensure consistency with the concept of water as a communal thing, the only right which landowners could have *to* water itself should be the public right to appropriate it. The common interest rights which attached to landownership, therefore, were rights, not of use but to prevent interference with the water by upstream (or downstream) owners.

E. NATURAL FLOW

6-20.   The adoption of a primary/secondary distinction and the attachment of common interest rights to landownership provide a background for the beginning of natural flow protection. By this point in the history of common interest, it was settled both that landowners could consume water for primary purposes, and that successive owners could power a mill if the water was returned within their own lands. Opposite owners were more restricted not, it seems, being entitled to divert the river even temporarily. Insofar as landowners were restrained in their use of rivers or lochs, this was attributable to a real right held by other landowners along the river or loch. Kames' analysis in *Principles of Equity*[54] offered the opportunity to develop the law to allow the consumption of water for secondary purposes, but although this account was influential, case law did not explicitly condone consumption for industrial purposes. In due course cases involving consumption and detention of water began to come before the courts. These cases particularly demonstrated the opposing concerns of water users at the time. The court

---

224. The judgments of Lords Monboddo and Alemore are particularly focused on rights to use water being public and these judges were both present in *Magistrates of Linlithgow*.
    [51] See further below.
    [52] (1791) Mor 12823.
    [53] See paras 6-07–6-10 above.
    [54] Kames, *Principles* 50–51.

was presented with a difficult choice between facilitating new industries or protecting established users. Favouring the latter, a right to natural flow developed which prevented interference with aspects such as quantity, quality, natural force and direction of water. This development was influenced both by past case law, which had recently become more accessible, and by the broader context of social change.

(1) Early Cases

(a) Consumption as Diversion

6-21. As most of the past case law had concerned diversions – for the issue was diverting water to power mills – pursuers in subsequent cases initially argued that consuming water for *any* secondary purpose was a form of diversion. As the water was not returned, this was then prohibited due to the established rule from *Cunningham v Kennedy*.[55] In two cases decided in 1791, *Ogilvy v Kincaid*[56] and *Marquis of Abercorn v Jamieson*,[57] lower mill-owners objected to the consumption of water for a distillery and coal and salt works respectively. In *Ogilvy* it was argued that, although adjacent landowners may consume water for primary purposes, they were not allowed to divert the river in whole or in part[58] and thus water could not be consumed in a distillery. In both cases consumption for industrial purposes which had not been put beyond challenge by prescription was prohibited. In *Marquis of Abercorn* the river was said to be a matter of 'common interest',[59] the first time this expression appears in a judgment: while owners can use the river for natural (primary) purposes, it is 'not at the disposal of any of them by turning it, or any portion of it, aside, or otherwise to the prejudice of the others'.[60] Analysing consumption as permanent diversion was the sign of increasing influence of past cases, a topic which will be explained further below.[61] However, the rule against permanent diversion concerned the whole river not a portion of it. Further, to consume water for a specified purpose would always involve taking water and not returning it. To prohibit all consumption, other than that serving primary purposes would greatly limit the use of water in industry. It reflected an attempt to apply an old rule to a new economic environment.

(b) Detention

6-22. In *Marquis of Abercorn*, the Marquis not only consumed water but also detained it in artificial ponds which were controlled by sluices. It was alleged

[55] (1713) Mor 8903 and 12778.
[56] (1791) Mor 12824, Hume 508.
[57] (1791) Hume 510.
[58] See Memorial for Ogilvy 7 Jul 1791 (Adam Rolland), *Ogilvy v Kincaid* Hume Collection Vol 42, Paper 4.
[59] (1791) Hume 510 at 511.
[60] At 511.
[61] See below, paras 6-44–6-50.

in argument for Jamieson that damage had been done when, 'by the sudden opening of these sluices, the water was poured down in a torrent, to the injury of [his] lands, and the disturbance of the work at the mills'.[62] Such physical injury to land was rare in water rights cases, although it was well established that causing direct physical damage was a prohibited use of property.[63] In *Marquis of Abercorn*,[64] the court sought to re-express this rule in terms of natural flow:

> 'it is none of the natural uses of a stream, to stop the water and gather it into pools on its passage. It is, then a usurpation on the part of Lord Abercorn, if the effect of his pools be to lessen the supply of water to the stream; and even if the supply is not lessened, he still does wrong if he restrains and withholds, or discharges the water in an arbitrary or irregular way, to the prejudice of Mr Jamieson...'

This is a significant statement which suggests that even if there was no permanent diversion, and no decrease in the amount of water, merely changing the natural flow was prohibited.

(c) The Requirement of Prejudice

6-23.   In both *Ogilvy* and *Marquis of Abercorn* the concept of prohibition of prejudicial operations was used. In *Ogilvy*, counsel argued that diversion was prohibited without need to prove prejudice and that, if this was not accepted, there was sufficient prejudice in this particular case to prevent the operations. The prejudice was merely that the working of the mill had been affected due to less water. *Bannatyne v Cranstoun*,[65] Stair[66] and Erskine[67] were cited for these points,[68] authorities which were a relic of a past (unsuccessful) struggle in case law to create a doctrinal basis for a prohibition on diversion on the basis of a broad definition of the prejudicial use of property.[69]

6-24.   In the passages from *Marquis of Abercorn* quoted above, it was stated that the Marquis was not entitled to discharge water in a prejudicial way. In this case, there had been actual physical injury to lands of a kind which would have been prohibited by coming within the category of direct damage as defined by Kames and Hume.[70] Thus, as can be seen, 'prejudice' was used both in the strict sense of direct damage and in the earlier formulation of causing inconvenience and economic loss.

---

[62] (1791) Hume 510 at 510.

[63] See Kames, *Principles* 46–47; Hume, *Lectures* III 209–210 and discussion above, paras 5-23–5-29.

[64] (1791) Hume 510 at 511.

[65] (1624) Mor 12793.

[66] Stair, *Institutions* II.7.12.

[67] Erskine, *Institute* II.9.13.

[68] See Memorial for Ogilvy 7 Jul 1791 (Adam Rolland), *Ogilvy v Kincaid* Hume Collection Vol 42, Paper 4. Bankton was also mentioned but the precise section is unclear.

[69] See the discussion above, paras 5-23–5-29.

[70] See Kames, *Principles* 46–47; Hume, *Lectures* III 209–210.

(2) Lord Glenlee v Gordon

6-25.   The arguments in the next major case, *Lord Glenlee v Gordon*,[71] fully demonstrate the conflicting concerns of water users and the decision confirms that landowners are not merely prevented from diverting the river but are also prohibited from affecting its natural flow in a prejudicial way which includes aspects such as quantity and force. In this case, upstream owners had created a large reservoir to ensure adequate water supply to power the machinery for their cotton works. Lord Glenlee, the lower owner, had been deprived of water supply to his mills during the period when water was accumulating in the reservoir.

6-26.   The basic proposition put forward for the pursuer was that every landowner has a 'joint usufructuary right to the stream in its natural condition'.[72] The familiar analogy of usufruct was now tied to the natural condition of the stream. This right prevents any operations which affect the flow of the river because: 'Every heritor is entitled to the use and enjoyment of a river in its natural condition, as it passes through his property, From the nature of a stream, any material innovation in its condition affects not only the portion of it where the alteration is made, but the whole course of the river; and consequently, the interest of all the inferior proprietors.'[73] Adjacent landowners are linked by a common vulnerability to being affected by a change in the river's flow. The material innovation on the river's condition was prejudicial in preventing Lord Glenlee's mill from working. In addition, his fishings had deteriorated and his amenity was affected. The 'material' requirement was a new one,[74] perhaps to mitigate in part an otherwise stringent restriction and to allow some small-scale operations.

6-27.   It was further argued that if:

> 'the natural limits of an heritor's right to the usufructuary use of a stream be transgressed, it is impossible to ascertain the mischief that might consequently ensue. The right which an heritor has to the use and enjoyment of a river, instead of being a valid and substantial right, would be fluctuating, ambulatory, and defeasible, possessed at the mercy of every other heritor, whose property happened to be nearer to its source. It would not deserve the name of a right of property at all, the very essence of which is security and stability.'[75]

Thus, Lord Glenlee argued, there might not only be economic loss but also damage to the concept of property itself.

6-28.   Finally, it was argued that, despite the importance of manufacture, the rights of individuals could not be sacrificed. Of course, as many forms of consumption or detention of a river to serve an industrial process would involve a material innovation on a river's natural condition, the effect of these arguments might prevent the use of water for many secondary purposes.

[71] (1804) Mor 12834.
[72] At 12835.
[73] At 12835.
[74] Although it had been used with regard to opposite owners, see paras 6-34–6-38 below.
[75] (1804) Mor 12834 at 12836. For the problems with this usufruct analogy see discussion above, para 6-16.

6-29.   The pursuer's arguments in *Lord Glenlee* can be seen as a ready extrapolation from the decision of *Marquis of Abercorn v Jamieson*.[76] However, in *Lord Glenlee* no direct physical damage to land had taken place, and prejudice was being used in the broader sense as had been argued by counsel in *Ogilvy v Kincaid*.[77]

6-30.   Various sources were cited in support of these arguments. As in *Ogilvy v Kincaid*, Stair and Erskine[78] were mentioned. Reference was made to D.39.3.1.1 (Ulpian) on the *actio aquae pluviae arcendae*, which prohibits causing 'water to flow elsewhere than in its normal or natural course, for example, if by letting it in he makes the flow greater or faster or stronger'. Further, the praetor's edict *uti priore aestate* was mentioned.[79] Whitty sees these texts as the origin of the protection of natural flow,[80] whilst acknowledging the problems of using texts on the *actio aquae pluviae arcendae*, which deal with casual waters, to regulate perennial rivers. They may indeed have had a bearing on the final decision of the court. The English case of *Brown v Best*[81] was also cited when discussing the interest of manufacturers. While again showing evidence of English influence, this confusing case did little to aid Lord Glenlee's argument. It concerned the prohibition on diversion, which was an established point in Scots law, and did not relate to mills or secondary uses. Much more important than any of these, however, were the many Scottish cases, old and recent, cited to the court. Their influence will be explored below.[82]

6-31.   In response to this onslaught, the defenders made an argument in favour of flexibility and minimal restraints on ownership. All cases should be considered on their merits and here there was no real prejudice to the pursuer. The defenders disputed the applicability and authority of Roman law and stated that owners were entitled to use the water running through their land provided they avoided restagnation, flooding of the lower land, or permanent diversion. There was also the obvious argument on grounds of legal policy: 'if any alteration on the natural condition of a stream be sufficient to entitle an inferior heritor to object, there would be an effectual bar to all those uses of a river, by which it is made subservient to the purposes of machinery'.[83] Such restriction would 'prevent the extension of useful manufactures'.[84] These pleas in favour of manufactures fell on deaf ears. Lord

---

[76] (1791) Hume 510.

[77] (1791) Mor 12824, Hume 508.

[78] Bankton is also mentioned but the precise section is, again, unclear.

[79] D.43.13.1 (Ulpian). D.43.12.1.12 (Ulpian), which states that 'no force should be used to prevent the removal and demolition of work done in a river channel or bank to impair its course, and the cleaning and restoration of the channel at the discretion of an upright man' is also cited.

[80] Whitty, 'Water' 458.

[81] (1747) 1 Wils KB 174, 95 ER 557.

[82] See below, paras 6-44–6-50.

[83] (1804) Mor 12834 at 12836.

[84] At 12837.

Glenlee was successful[85] and, finding that the operations were attended with prejudice, the court granted an interdict which prevented the use of the reservoir or any other operation which would divert the river, detain or arrest the water or would prevent the river running continuously through the pursuer's property.[86]

6-32.   Earlier *Ogilvy v Kincaid*[87] and *Marquis of Abercorn v Jamieson*[88] represented a movement towards restricting the use of a river for secondary purposes by viewing consumption as diversion and by preventing interference with the flow when direct damage resulted. *Lord Glenlee v Gordon*[89] then secured the protection of natural flow and suggested that an owner had a right to the natural condition of the river which prohibited any operation which was both a material innovation to flow and prejudicial. Prejudice, however, did not require direct damage but was a broader concept which included economic loss and loss of amenity. This protection of natural flow restricted the consumption and detention of water and protected lower (and upper) mill-owners without the need to resort to grounds such as the *immissio* principle or the contrived argument that consumption was a diversion. It was to be followed by future cases.[90]

6-33.   It was not explained in *Lord Glenlee v Gordon* how the right to natural flow interacted with the permitted temporary diversion of rivers for mill-lades which had been authorised a century before by *Cunningham v Kennedy*.[91] However, diverting water for a mill-lade on condition of returning it would still be legitimate as long as it did not have a material effect on the natural flow. Further, where a mill-lade did breach the right to natural flow, *Marquis of Abercorn v Jamieson*[92] suggests, the default rules of common interest could be varied through prescription.[93] However, requiring 40 years to put a use beyond challenge was a position which would favour established users and

---

[85] In reaching this crucial (and uncommercial) decision is it possible that the judges were influenced by the fact the Lord Glenlee was one of their number. Lord Glenlee is shown on the front cover of this book, fifth from the right. This decision is uncommercial because in order to use the river for secondary purposes, one would either have to buy all the land along a river, extinguish the rights of all the affected owners along a river (who will often request payment), wait for the period of prescription to pass (then 40 years) or enter into a contractual agreement with the affected owners. Any of these options could be prohibitively expensive, time-consuming or impossible. In the event, the last option seems to have been the one favoured by industrialists. See below, para 6-55.

[86] (1804) Mor 12834 at 12838.

[87] (1791) Mor 12824, Hume 508.

[88] (1791) Hume 510.

[89] (1804) Mor 12834.

[90] See, for example, *Lanark Twist Co v Edmonstone* (1810) Hume 520 at 521; *Lord Blantyre v Dunn* (1848) 10 D 509 at 543 and below, paras 6-39–6-43.

[91] (1713) Mor 8903 and 12778.

[92] (1791) Hume 510.

[93] Whether this is negative or positive prescription seemed open to question at this time. In *Magistrates of Linlithgow v Elphinstone (No 2)* (1768) Mor 12805, Hailes 203 it was fervently argued that it must be negative prescription, but in *Marquis of Abercorn v Jamieson* (1791) Hume 510 it appears that positive prescription was being argued.

discriminate against the new industries. Thus for this reason, among others, the evolution of the right to natural flow was a conservative move which favoured existing uses and did not develop the law to facilitate the changing economy.

(3) Opposite Owners

6-34.   Thus far, the discussion has focused on consecutive owners along a river. For a period, it seemed that the application of the right to natural flow as between opposite owners – in cases where the river marked the boundary between two estates – was more stringent. This can be seen in *Hamilton v Edington & Co*,[94] decided in 1793. Edington, who had iron-works on the opposite bank of the River Clyde from Hamilton, wanted to enlarge an existing mill-race. Hamilton objected, arguing that, although water was ownerless, the stream was the object of permanent rights[95] which could not be interfered with by an upper owner diverting a river and not returning it within his or her property. Furthermore:

> 'a common property arises where a stream forms a march between two tenements, and each is entitled to all the ordinary uses of the subject; but neither can make any material alterations on it, without the concurrence of the other; for, in re communi melior est conditio prohibentis...Nor is either party under the necessity of assigning a reason to justify his refusal.'[96]

On this view a river was a separate entity which was common property when it ran between two properties. The application of the strict common property regime – if that is indeed what was being argued[97] – would then prevent any alterations without consent. Prejudice was not required, in contrast to the position developing between successive owners as suggested in *Marquis of Abercorn v Jamieson*[98] and *Ogilvy v Kincaid*.[99]

6-35.   In support of this argument many authorities were cited but there is little support for the common property argument. Inspiration is likely to have come from Bankton, cited by the pursuer, where it is stated that a river running between two properties cannot be diverted by either owner without the consent of the other due to it being common to both, and the maxim of common property, *re communi potior est conditio prohibentis*, is used.[100] Bankton's statement was based on *Bannatyne v Cranstoun*[101] which was also cited by the pursuer. However, Bankton's comments should perhaps not be interpreted in a rigid doctrinal fashion. It is questionable whether he meant that the

---

[94] (1793) Mor 12824.

[95] The advocate for the pursuer uses the same passage of Vinnius as Henry Home did in *Kincaid v Stirling* (1752) Mor 12796, see above, para 5-54.

[96] (1793) Mor 12824 at 12825.

[97] It has been mentioned before that caution must be exercised when analysing references to common property.

[98] (1791) Hume 510.

[99] (1791) Mor 12824, Hume 508.

[100] Bankton, *Institute* II.7.29.

[101] (1624) Mor 12769.

stream was common property in the modern sense as such strict categories were not then fully established. Therefore, the argument as to common property was based on slender authority.

6-36. In response, the defender argued that water was ownerless but that adjoining landowners could use it for all lawful purposes. Every purpose, primary and secondary, could be served by this large river whether or not water was returned and thus there was no harm in diverting a portion for a useful purpose. If a river was seen to be common property between opposite owners, consent would be required 'even with regard to the largest river in the world, which surely cannot be maintained'.[102]

6-37. The view of the majority of the court was that: 'Whatever may be said (it was observed) of the water of which it is composed, the stream itself is the object of property, or at least of a right equally entitled to protection. The water may be used for all ordinary purposes, but the stream cannot be diverted.'[103] The court was not fully committing to the argument of common property or a complex delineation between the river and the water as separate entities capable of being subject to different ownership regimes, as suggested by Whitty,[104] but merely confirming that rights which landowners have to prevent interference with a river running through their lands are property – presumably real – rights. Such real rights entitled opposite owners to object to operations as 'in the case of a private river, of whatever extent, running between the lands of opposite proprietors, the mere possibility of damage, (and as some expressed themselves) even in point of amenity, gave either a title to object to any material alteration upon its course'.[105]

6-38. The substantive decision, that a stream could not be diverted, was in application of an established rule, but the decision in *Hamilton* goes further by suggesting there is no requirement of proof of prejudice in order to object to material alterations to the river. This, a stricter application of natural flow protection than was developing between successive owners, was expounded and established by later cases such as *Braid v Douglas*,[106] *Lanark Twist Co v Edmonstone*[107] and *Duke of Roxburghe v Waldie*.[108]

(4) The Right to Natural Flow

6-39. Although Whitty describes *Hamilton v Edington & Co*[109] as marking the 'final establishment'[110] of common interest, aspects of the doctrine

---

[102] (1793) Mor 12824 at 12826.

[103] At 12826.

[104] Whitty, 'Water' 455.

[105] (1793) Mor 12824 at 12826.

[106] (1800) Mor App 2. See also *Aytoun v Douglas* (1800) Mor App 7; *Aytoun v Melville* (1801) Mor App 8.

[107] (1810) Hume 520.

[108] (1821) Hume 524.

[109] (1793) Mor 12824.

[110] Whitty, 'Water' 455.

remained unclear. Much later, in *Morris v Bicket*,[111] the law of common interest was revisited and the right to natural flow was considered in detail. There is little indication of a complex distinction between the river – which could be subject to ownership – and the water – which could not – as a legal construct. Only Lord Benholme, with unfortunate inconsistency of terminology, at one point states that there is common property in the stream. He later, more accurately, uses the term common interest.[112] To say there is common interest 'in the stream' does not necessarily mean that the river as a body of water is being analysed separately from the water which comprises it but merely that the natural flow of the river is protected through the doctrine of common interest. This is to be welcomed. To develop the concept of the river as a body of water, which could then be the subject of ownership and other subordinate rights, would result in an artificial and unnecessarily complicated legal construct.[113] The main reason for attempting to create this construct is to circumvent the classification of running water as a communal thing in order to explain the rights of landowners regarding water. This classification, however, is of worth and importance,[114] and the rights of owners can be explained in a different way.

6-40.   The judgments of the Inner House, later confirmed by the House of Lords, are a significant restatement of the law.[115] Whitty's comment that in this case the expression 'riparian proprietors' was used by all of the judges of the House of Lords but none of the Court of Session is incorrect: Lord Neaves referred to adjacent owners as 'riparian proprietors'[116] as did the pursuer.[117] This was the first time this phrase had been used in a Scottish case and, although undoubtedly a result of English influence,[118] the case as a whole can be seen as the culmination of the development of a distinctively Scottish doctrine.

6-41.   The court in *Morris v Bicket*[119] said that every landowner who has a river on his or her property can use the water for domestic purposes, and for other purposes too subject to the obligation not to interfere with the natural

---

[111] (1864) 2 M 1082.

[112] At 1090–1091. Again, it should be remembered that the difference between these concepts was, at this point, not fully settled. Interestingly, this case comes at the mid-point between *Menzies v Macdonald* (1854) 16 D 927 (aff'd by the House of Lords (1856) 2 MacQ 463) where common property was applied to lochs and *Mackenzie v Bankes* (1878) LR 3 App Cas 1324 where the application of common property was not accepted. See above, paras 3-77–3-86.

[113] See also comment in *Magistrates of Linlithgow v Elphinstone (No 2)* (1768) Mor 12805 at 12805–12806 that a river cannot be appropriated like a field or a horse.

[114] See Ch 2.

[115] (1866) 4 M (HL) 44.

[116] (1864) 2 M 1082 at 1093.

[117] At 1086.

[118] See Whitty, 'Water' 457. The phrase rapidly became commonplace which suggests that it was already common currency although not in the case reports: see, for example, *Anderson v Anderson* (1867) 5 Irvine 499. See also the use of the phrase in Anon, 'On the Law of Flowing Water' (1859) 1 Scottish Law Magazine and Sheriff Court Reporter 106–111 and 113–117.

[119] (1864) 2 M 1082.

flow.[120] Generally, when discussing water rights, it is easy to make the mistake that common interest gives landowners positive rights *to* the water. However, this is inconsistent with the fact, identified by Lord Neaves, that running water is incapable of ownership in its natural state.[121] Instead, a lower owner has the right to have the water 'transmitted to him undiminished in quantity, unpolluted in quality, and unaffected in force and natural direction and current, except in so far as the primary uses of it may legitimately operate upon it within the lands of the upper heritor'.[122] Each landowner has a real right in upstream (and downstream) lands which entitles him or her to object to an operation which materially interferes with the flow of the river. The requirement that it must be material means that not every 'trifling interference'[123] can be prevented, only that which 'palpably affects the water'.[124]

6-42.   It was made clear that, as between opposite owners, no prejudice is required to be proved. This was because if one owner materially interferes with the natural flow this will inevitably affect the opposite owner and so 'the idea of compelling a party to define how it will operate on him, of what damage or injury it will produce, is out of the question'.[125] However, whether there was still a requirement that successive owners must prove prejudice is unclear from reading the opinions of the judges. Lord Neaves mentioned that the 'rights of parties in private streams of water, depend upon their relative situations'[126] which seems to suggest some difference in treatment.

6-43.   In due course Lord Blackburn in *Colquhoun's Trs v Orr Ewing*[127] clarified this point. Where there is an operation which is a 'sensible injury to the proprietary rights of an individual',[128] by which Lord Blackburn meant a material interference with the natural flow of the river,[129] the affected party may claim nominal damages. However, 'the Court of Session in Scotland, in the exercise of its equitable jurisdiction, would not order the removal of the erection if convinced that the damage was only nominal, but where there is an injury to the proprietary rights in running streams, the present injury, now producing no damage, may hereafter produce as much'.[130] Thus, a court may not exercise its discretionary jurisdiction and grant a decree *ad factum praestandum* if little or no damage is caused by the breach of the right to natural flow. This is application of the principle *de minimus non curat praetor*.[131] However, if the interference is material, it is likely to cause damage. This reasoning

---

[120] At 1092. The analogy of usufruct is used, for which see above, para 6-16.
[121] At 1092.
[122] At 1092. (Lord Neaves)
[123] At 1093.
[124] At 1093.
[125] At 1093 (Lord Neaves)
[126] At 1092.
[127] (1877) 4 R (HL) 116.
[128] At 126.
[129] See also at 130.
[130] At 126.
[131] See discussion of remedies in below, paras 7-76–7-96.

applies equally to interdict. Thus, prejudice in any form is not required for a breach of natural flow to take place. Damage or potential damage is only important with regard to remedies.

(5) Reasons for Natural Flow Protection

6-44.   Why the judges decided in favour of protecting natural flow to the detriment of new economic uses is an intriguing question. Whitty has suggested that water rights as property rights were seen as sacred and that manufacturers could always buy the rights. This approach is said to have been strengthened due to debates on property influenced by the French Revolution.[132] But while these factors may have influenced the judges' decisions after it became settled that common interest rights were attached to landownership – as the judges' decisions could be interpreted as protecting established property rights – they do not explain why the content of the real right extended from preventing permanent diversions to preventing any material interference with the quality, quantity, natural direction and force of the water.

6-45.   Another factor which potentially influenced the courts was the increase in law reporting. Once again, Lord Kames is an important figure. During the 16th and 17th centuries, the concept of judicial precedent was vague.[133] A line of consistent cases was required for evidence of binding judicial custom. Over the course of the 18th century, this began to change as the view that custom was a dominant form of law declined and case law was increasingly seen as the declaration of the sovereign's will and therefore binding. Accompanying this changing view of authority was the fact that cases were becoming more accessible. Before 1750 there were only nine printed collections available covering, in a patchy way, the period 1621–1746. Twelve more were published before the end of the 18th century.[134] Particularly important in this period was the publication of collections of decisions which brought together cases from different series of reports, both printed and manuscript. *Kames' Dictionary of Decisions,* the first two volumes of which covered the period 1540–1728, were published in 1741,[135] and *Morison's Dictionary* which covered the period 1540–1801 was published between 1801 and 1804. These collections meant that older case law was more accessible and useful. The result was for a greater number of cases to be cited to the courts in argument. Gardner observes with regard to the *Faculty*

---

[132] Whitty, 'Water' 464.

[133] See J C Gardner, *Judicial Precedent in Scots Law* (1936) 23–28; G Maher, 'The Nature of Judicial Precedent' in SME (Vol 22, 1987) para 251 and generally T B Smith, *Doctrines of Judicial Precedent in Scots Law* (1952) 1–17. See also Stair, *Institutions* I.1.16; Mackenzie, *Institutions* I.1.10. Evidence of this can also be seen in the various rationales for decisions on water rights in the 17th and 18th centuries, see Ch 5.

[134] For a full list see J S Leadbetter, 'The Printed Law Reports' in *An Introductory Survey of the Sources and Literature of Scots Law* (H McKechnie (ed), Stair Society, Vol 1, 1936) 42.

[135] Volumes 1 and 2 were by Lord Kames. Volumes 3 and 4 were published in 1797 by Lord Woodhouselee and the final volume in 1804 by Thomas McGrugar.

Decisions, covering the end of the 18th century, that: 'The citation of previous cases becomes more frequent, and the impression is conveyed that Counsel had by that time come to regard previous decisions as affording a much more important, if not the main, criterion for the judgment.'[136]

6-46. It is noticeable from the mid-18th century onward, that counsel in cases involving water begin citing past decisions far more than previously. In *Magistrates of Linlithgow v Elphinstone (No 2)*,[137] the cases of *Cunningham v Kennedy*[138] and *Beaton v Ogilvie*[139] were cited.[140] In *Kelso v Boyds*,[141] *Bannatyne v Cranston*[142] and *Magistrates of Aberdeen v Menzies*[143] were discussed. In *Brown v Burgess*[144] of 1790 regarding regorgement, *Fairly v Earl of Eglinton*[145] was mentioned. By the end of the century, even more authorities were being used. In *Hamilton v Edington & Co*[146] and *Lord Glenlee v Gordon*,[147] the cases cited to the court included *Bannatyne, Bairdie v Scarstone*,[148] *Cunningham* and *Fairly*, as well as more recent cases such as *Magistrates of Linlithgow v Elphinstone (No 2)*, *Kelso v Boyds*, *Ogilvy v Kincaid*[149] and *Marquis of Abercorn v Jamieson*,[150] *Fairly* had been published in Kames' *Remarkable Decisions of the Court of Session* in 1766. Three of the earliest cases on this list, *Bannatyne, Beaton* and *Cunningham*, were published in *Kames' Dictionary of Decisions* in 1741 and thereafter became standard authorities. Previously their citation in cases had been rare.[151] This suggests that the rising influence of precedent and increased accessibility placed a new significance on these cases. Relevant cases which had not been collected at this time, such as *Kincaid v Stirling*,[152] were not later cited.

[136] Gardner, *Judicial Precedent* (n 133) at 35.
[137] (1768) Mor 12805, Hailes 203.
[138] (1713) Mor 8903 and 12778.
[139] (1670) Mor 10912.
[140] Memorial for Elphinstone 27 Sept 1766 (Robert MacQueen), *Magistrates of Linlithgow v Elphinstone* Campbell Collection Vol 17, Paper 62.
[141] (1768) Mor 12807, Hailes 224
[142] (1624) Mor 12769.
[143] (1748) Mor 12787.
[144] (1790) Hume 504.
[145] (1744) Mor 12780.
[146] (1793) Mor 12824.
[147] (1804) Mor 12834.
[148] (1624) Mor 14529.
[149] (1791) Mor 12824, Hume 508.
[150] (1791) Hume 510.
[151] I have only found one case, Information for Gibson 27 Nov 1723 (Robert Dundas), *Gibson v Weems* WS 8:32 in which *Bannatyne* was cited but the case was not reported and the outcome is unknown.
[152] (1752) Mor 12796. It is interesting to note that Kames omitted to publish this decision in which he acted for the unsuccessful pursuer. However, Kames was 'attentive to admit no case but what, being resolvable into some principle, may serve as a rule for cases of the same kind. To pester the world with circumstantiate cases that admit not any precise or single *ratio decidendi* is a heavy tax': Preface to the second volume of *Remarkable Decisions of the Court of Session* (1766).

6-47.   The early cases which were now consistently being cited are likely to have influenced the development in the law towards the protection of natural flow. *Cunningham,* the compromise case discussed in the previous chapter,[153] stated that diversion of a river was allowed only if the water was returned. This may have led later judges to the view that returning water was the only legitimate manner of use for secondary purposes, and explains why early cases of natural flow prohibited consumptive use as diversion.[154]

6-48.   The influence of *Bannatyne* – a decision which by now was almost two hundred years old – appears two-fold and indeed even contradictory. The decision was based on the general principle that one may not use one's property in a manner prejudicial to others: it was held that a stream running between two properties could not be diverted without consent as it was sufficient prejudice that amenity would be affected. In the natural flow cases between successive landowners, *Bannatyne* was cited in *Lord Glenlee v Gordon*[155] to support the argument in favour of restricting uses which affect the natural condition of a river to the prejudice of the downstream owner – with prejudice being defined in a broad way which included more than direct physical damage. Conversely, in *Hamilton v Edington & Co,*[156] *Bannatyne* was used to support the argument that *no prejudice* was required in operations between opposite owners, which is the practical effect of interpreting prejudice to include affecting mere amenity. *Hamilton v Edington & Co* can perhaps indeed be seen as the turning point in the influence of past cases as the decision was a close one with a minority of judges submitting that heritors could use the river for every lawful purpose, and that the question of whether the erection of machinery was lawful depended on the circumstances of each case.[157] The conflicting use of *Bannatyne* may be the source of the difficulty which existed until the late 19th century of deciding whether, and between whom, prejudice is required to be proved for a breach of the right to natural flow.

6-49.   *Beaton v Ogilvie,*[158] a decision of 1670, concerned the acquisition of a right to divert water for agricultural purposes through immemorial possession. A century later this may have led courts to the view that the restrictive rules of natural flow could be varied through prescription and, that, in order to acquire rights beyond primary uses, use for 40 years was required.[159]

6-50.   Finally, the emphasis on precedent meant that more recent cases were also cited to the court. *Marquis of Abercorn v Jamieson*[160] was cited in *Hamilton v Edington & Co*. Both of these cases along with *Ogilvy v Kincaid*[161] were cited in

---

[153] See above, paras 5-30–5-35.
[154] See above, para 6-21.
[155] (1804) Mor 12834.
[156] (1793) Mor 12824.
[157] At 12827.
[158] (1670) Mor 10912.
[159] See *Marquis of Abercorn v Jamieson* (1791) Hume 510.
[160] (1791) Hume 510.
[161] (1791) Mor 12824, Hume 508.

Lord Glenlee v Gordon.[162] This allowed a line of authority to develop quickly and a doctrine to become swiftly settled. This tendency is shown by Lord President Blair's comments in *Lanark Twist Co v Edmonstone*[163] that 'the general point of law, which was finally settled in Edington's case, and carried still farther in Lord Glenlee's case…is not now to be touched'.

6-51. A second possible reason that the judges developed the right to natural flow may be the changing social circumstances. At the turn of the 19th century, due to population increases and urbanisation, water for domestic purposes was often in short supply.[164] Use of water for domestic purposes and industrial purposes often clashed. In Chadwick's report there are instances of domestic supplies of water in Scotland being affected by the demand for water to cool steam engines and it is said in many colliery and manufacturing districts people suffered from a want of water.[165] *Russell v Haig*,[166] *Miller v Stein*[167] and *Dunn v Hamilton*[168] are all examples of the use of water for primary and secondary purposes coming into conflict when a distillery, brewery or dye-works polluted the water of rivers used for drinking, cooking and washing. Further, when large-scale supplies to cities were being created, lower owners (often using water for secondary purposes) needed to be compensated. For example, when water was led from springs in the Pentlands to supply Edinburgh, compensation reservoirs[169] were required to meet the claims of lower mill-owners.[170]

6-52. Some judgments show that the importance of preserving water for domestic purposes in light of increasing industrial demands may have been an active principle in the judges' minds. In *Russell v Haig*,[171] Lord Monboddo stated: 'The use of water is necessary. The primary use is not for carrying off impurities, but for drinking.' In the same case, Lord Justice-Clerk Braxfield states that primary purposes were seen as preferential and not to be affected by secondary purposes.[172] That preserving the use of water for domestic purposes might be at the expense of industry seemed acceptable. Lord Swinton in *Russell v Haig*[173] said that 'since there are evils, we should admit those only which are necessary: dwelling houses cannot be avoided, but manufactures may'. Lord Monboddo and Lord President Campbell in this

---

[162] (1804) Mor 12834.
[163] (1810) Hume 520 at 521.
[164] See discussion above, paras 6-02–6-05.
[165] Chadwick 140
[166] (1791) Mor 12823, Bell's Octavo Cases 338.
[167] (1791) Mor 12823, Bell's Octavo Cases 334.
[168] (1837) 15 S 853.
[169] This is where water is stored and allowed to flow to downstream mill-owners when required.
[170] D Lewis, *Edinburgh Water Supply* (1908) 12–13. See also *Peterhead Granite Polishing Co v Peterhead Parochial Board* (1880) 7 R 536 overruled by *Peterhead Commissioners v Forbes* (1895) 22 R 852.
[171] (1791) Bell's Octavo Cases 338 at 345.
[172] At 347.
[173] At 347.

case showed particular disrespect for distilleries.[174] The argument that manufacturing would be significantly affected if the pursuer succeeded fell on deaf ears in *Lord Glenlee v Gordon*.[175] In *Hamilton v Edington & Co*[176] it was said that manufactures 'will not be injured by this doctrine, because there is little danger that consent will be refused where an adequate consideration is offered'. Thus, if any person wished to use water for secondary purposes and breach common interest, the right would have to be purchased from a neighbour.

6-53.   In light of water shortages and the strong emphasis placed by judges on use for domestic purposes, it seems clear that the social circumstances of the time had an influence on the development of the right to natural flow. Landowners were not to be free to appropriate large quantities of water or store water in reservoirs but had to transmit the river downstream so that each owner could benefit equally from the water.

6-54.   In summary, the doctrine of natural flow was the result of the coming together of many different social, economic and legal factors. One of these factors appears to be that the pursuers began to put forward strong arguments aimed to protect their use of rivers against the new economic purposes for which water was being used. Judges will have noticed the water shortages in cities and might have considered that the right to natural flow was consistent with the need to preserve water for domestic purposes. Faced with these disputes, judges seemed to have preferred the recently published, but in some cases elderly, decisions to the forward-looking hierarchy of uses in Kames' *Principles of Equity*. However, the old cases were decided before a doctrinal rationale for common interest had been established and in any event concerned a different economic environment. Ironically, it was Kames, the father of common interest, who caused many of these decisions to be published.

(6) A Way Around the Common Law

6-55.   One reason why the majority in *Hamilton v Edington & Co*[177] felt justified in its view was because it was open to manufacturers to buy the appropriate rights. To some extent, this premonition of consensual resolution was realised. The protection of natural flow and the restrictive rules between opposite owners practically barred the consumption of water for secondary purposes. One result was the establishment, in the 1820s and 1830s, of voluntary management schemes to regulate the water flow on whole rivers so as to provide for industrial purposes.[178] Shaw has identified a number of factors leading to these schemes including a smaller number of larger mills for which a guaranteed water supply was essential, and steam-powered

---

[174] At 346 and 348.
[175] (1804) Mor 12834.
[176] (1793) Mor 12824 at 12826–12827.
[177] (1793) Mor 12824.
[178] See Shaw, *Water Power* Ch 24. Such schemes would not bind singular successors.

factories being seen as a common enemy to unite against.[179] When such
arrangements were made, limitations on the use of water were relatively
unimportant. However, they also removed some of the pressure to change
what was still a highly restrictive rule as to consumption. In any event, steam
power quickly replaced water power as the fight with the common enemy
was lost.

F. LOCHS

6-56.   There are few cases on the development of common interest
concerning lochs. Some institutional writers mention that if a loch is wholly
contained within one piece of land and does not discharge into a river, the
landowner is free to consume all the water or drain the loch without
restriction.[180] *Magistrates of Linlithgow v Elphinstone (No 2)*[181] stated that lochs
with a perennial outflow are regarded as branches of a river and are subject
to the same rules. In any event, the possibility of interference with the natural
flow of a loch is perhaps reduced as such bodies of water are usually slower
moving.[182]

6-57.   However, common interest has been enrolled to serve another
purpose with regard to lochs. Unlike rivers, where ownership of the river as
a body of water never became established, at one point there was the
possibility that where a loch was surrounded by many landowners, the loch
– as a body of water separate from the *alveus* – was common property.[183] This
resulted in each landowner having the right to fish and sail over the whole
surface of the loch. In modern times these rights, instead of being attributed
to common property, have come to be regarded as arising from common
interest.[184]

6-58.   As has been seen from the preceding analysis, common interest
regarding rivers and lochs usually acts as a restriction on the ownership of
lands. Thus, the adaptation of the doctrine to grant positive rights to use
neighbouring properties is anomalous. It is perhaps merely an indication of
the nature of a doctrine which has, during the course of its development,
provided solutions to problems when other doctrines have failed.

G. INSTITUTIONAL INFLUENCE

6-59.   From the foregoing analysis, it can be seen that common interest
developed primarily through case law, against a background of socio-

[179] At 490.
[180] Stair, *Institutions* II.3.73; Bankton, *Institute* II.3.165. See also Hume, *Lectures* III 225; Bell,
Principles para 648.
[181] (1768) Mor 12805 at 12807. See also Hume, *Lectures* III 225; Bell, *Principles* para 1110.
[182] See further below, para 7-33.
[183] See above, paras 3-77–3-82.
[184] See *Kilsyth Fish Protection Association v McFarlane* 1937 SC 757 at 769; Reid, *Property* para
306; Whitty, 'Water' 467.

economic and legal change. Unlike many other areas of private law, the institutional writers had little influence. However, after the creation of the special regime of common interest, the institutional writers sought to relocate the doctrine within the general principles of property law. Common interest is analysed by the later institutional writers as neighbourhood law.[185]

(I) Hume

6-60.   Hume discusses water in a chapter on 'The Right of Property'. Property, it is said, entitles an owner to use and enjoy the thing, recover it and dispose of it at pleasure. The right to use includes the power to prevent others from using.[186] These rights, however, are not absolute: 'With all this attention to the interest of the proprietor, it is however still remembered that…every notion of separate property is founded, at least in some measure, on considerations of the common interest of society.'[187] Society means not only the country in general but also the neighbourhood. In a neighbourhood there arises 'a certain limitation of a proprietor's right of enjoyment, in certain reciprocal concessions, by each heritor to another, for the sake of peace and general convenience and accommodation'.[188] Such restrictions include the doctrine of *aemulatio vicini*, the *immissio* principle and nuisance.

6-61.   Restrictions based in common interest, in Hume's view, are more prominent in types of property in which 'no material changes can be made upon any one portion of them, without affecting, less or more, the interest of others who are concerned in the other parts and portions of the same subjects'.[189] One of these subjects is a stream of water, another a tenement building. This account sees the rules regulating rivers (and lochs[190]) as an application of general principles on the restrictions on ownership. Overall, this is a welcome contextualisation but there are problems with Hume's account of water rights. To understand fully Hume's treatment of common interest, I have consulted the original manuscript from which the Stair Society published the *Lectures*[191] as well as students' notes from lectures Hume gave at various points between 1789 and 1820.[192] In the early years of his lectures, Hume talks of the rights of an adjacent landowner in robust language. The 'doctrine of property in water'[193] is mentioned and it is said

---

[185] Whitty calls this 'institutional synthesis', Whitty, 'Water' 453.

[186] Hume, *Lectures* III 201.

[187] Hume, *Lectures* III 205.

[188] Hume, *Lectures* III. The term 'common interest' had not yet acquired the technical meaning ascribed to it in the modern law.

[189] Hume, *Lectures* III 216.

[190] See Hume, *Lectures* III 225.

[191] Available in the National Library of Scotland: ADV.MS.86.6.10.

[192] Available in the Special Collections of the University of Edinburgh Library: (1788) Dc.5.37-38; (1790) Dc.6.122–124; (1795) Dc.4.18–19; (1808–1809) Gen.860–861; (1810–1811) Gen.862 and Gen.1391–1397; (1810–1812) Dc.10.42/1–3; (1815–1816) MSS 2673–2677 and Dc.3.8–10; (1817–1818) Dc.4.61–64; (1820–1821) Dc.5.2–4, and in the National Library of Scotland: (1822) ADV.25.6.10 and 26.2.14

[193] (1788) Dc.5.37 at 42. These are Bell's student notes.

that an owner has the 'exclusive use of the stream within his own property'.[194] Over time, however, influenced by case law, his view of the nature of water rights changes. By 1810 he states: 'The Interest which a heritor has in a stream of water passing *through* (or along)[195] his property is different from his Right to his Lands. No Heritor can be said to be a *Proprietor* of a stream, but he has a species of joint usufructuary Interest with the other heritors.'[196] This characterisation adopts the language used in *Miller v Stein*,[197] *Russell v Haig*[198] and *Lord Glenlee v Gordon*.[199]

6-62. Although Hume adapts his characterisation of water rights, the basic rules of use set out in his earliest lectures do not change. These rules of use appear to be largely Hume's creation and the modifications he makes to take case law into account create contradictions. For successive owners Hume's rules are that each can use water for the primary purposes[200] but also that 'it is always in his power to take the higher & more extraordinary uses by erecting more factories of any kind (as Tanworks, Bleachfields etc.) tho' they consume more water'.[201] This is 'notwithstanding of the injury the inferior proprietors might suffer'.[202] The upstream owner is said to have a preferable right to downstream owners in this regard.[203] Such statements from Hume's early lectures are almost identical to those made in 1822.[204] Hume cites *Lyon and Gray v Bakers of Glasgow*[205] from 1749 as authority. In this case, bakers had built more mills and increased the capacity of their mill-lade to the prejudice of the opposite mill-owner. It was decided that this increase could not be objected to as water was ownerless and open to *occupatio*.[206] This case does not concern consumption for secondary purposes but temporary diversion. Further, the case was decided before the doctrinal foundation of common interest was ascertained and seemingly ignores the growing sense that opposite owners are restricted with regard to temporary diversion. The principle in *Lyon and Gray v Bakers of Glasgow*, although mentioned by the

---

[194] (1790) Dc.6.123 at 24.
[195] Added in pencil.
[196] (1810–1811) Gen.1393 at 80–81.
[197] (1791) Mor 12823, Bell's Octavo Cases 334.
[198] (1791) Mor 12823, Bell's Octavo Cases 338.
[199] (1804) Mor 12834. Indeed, this case is cited by Hume and in the manuscript of Hume's lectures the initials 'W M' appear in the margin next to the statement that a new use which requires variation of the channel and which wastes water can be objected to by a lower owner. The editor G C H Paton suggests in the biography of Hume in Vol VI of *Lectures* that W M refers to William Miller, otherwise known as Lord Glenlee, who was of course the pursuer in the famous case and with whom Hume discussed issues.
[200] (1788) Dc.5.37 at 38–39.
[201] (1790) Dc.6.123 at 24–25.
[202] (1810–1811) Gen.862 at 6 of Real Rights (no pagination).
[203] (1788) Dc.5.37–38 at 38–39.
[204] See Hume *Lectures* III 217.
[205] (1749) Mor 12789.
[206] This is similar to the prior appropriation theory but this case was decided before the publication of W Blackstone, *Commentaries on the Law of England* (1765–1769).

defenders in *Hamilton v Edington & Co*[207] and *Lord Glenlee v Gordon*,[208] was not adopted by these cases, which instead established the right to natural flow.[209] Hume, however, does indicate that there are limitations on the use of water. In his early lectures these restrictions are that superior owners must use their rights *comiter* and not change the course of the river so that the water is consumed at a distance from the natural bed.[210] Both of these requirements resemble those applicable to servitudes and indicate Hume may have regarded common interest as akin to a servitude.[211] Hume's scheme, in short, is that one can consume water for secondary purposes to the prejudice of the lower owners as long as any operation can be established right next to the river.[212]

6-63. Later additions restricted use further. By 1810, Hume had added that the lower owner cannot be deprived of the river,[213] that the channel of the river cannot be materially altered to change the flow to the injury of the lower owners,[214] and that the river cannot be locked up in ponds or reservoirs,[215] with *Marquis of Abercorn v Jamieson*[216] and *Lord Glenlee v Gordon*[217] being cited for the latter two propositions. Such additions were attempts to include the recently established right to natural flow, but they had the effect of undermining Hume's still asserted basic rule that one may consume water for secondary purposes to the prejudice of lower owners. Hume states further with regard to these restrictions: 'What is true of the whole Stream is true of any part of it; provided the Abstraction thereof inflicts a substantial Injury to the inferior heritor.'[218] This confuses the issue further as it suggests consumption can be viewed as a permanent diversion and therefore prohibited – which was also an argument in the early natural flow cases[219] – despite it seemingly being Hume's belief that consumption for secondary purposes is legitimate regardless of prejudice.

[207] (1793) Mor 12824.
[208] (1804) Mor 12834.
[209] The case was, briefly, used and discussed in the case of *J & M White v J White & Sons* (1905) 12 SLT 663 but this was reversed on appeal to the House of Lords (1906) 8 F (HL) 41.
[210] (1790) Dc.6.123 at 25.
[211] The word 'comiter' is used here as a synonym for *civiliter*. See Hume, *Lectures* III 272; *Borthwick v Strang* (1799) Hume 513 at 514.
[212] Hume's view is shown in his commentary to *Ogilvy v Kincaid* (1791) Hume 508 at 509 where he states that a lower owner cannot object if the amount of water consumed for primary purposes on upstream lands increases and further that: 'It may even be maintained (though this may sometimes be nicer) that the like rule applies, though more water came to be consumed in machinery and manufacture recently established in the upper lands, if established on the natural bed and course of the stream, which happens to afford the natural condition for such works.'
[213] (1810) Gen.862 at 6 of Real Rights.
[214] (1810) Gen.1393 at 82.
[215] (1810) Gen.862 at 7 of Real Rights.
[216] (1791) Hume 510.
[217] (1804) Mor 12834.
[218] (1810) Gen.1393 at 82.
[219] See above, para 6-21.

6-64.   Hume's partiality towards allowing the use of water for industrial processes is further shown by his early analysis of opposite owners. Here there is no priority of situation. Hume says in 1790: 'It is a nicer question whether any of them can draw a canal from the principal stream to supply any useful worth or manufactory – It is thought that each proprietor has this in his power provided the other can qualify no damage from the operation; but there is no decision on the point.'[220] Of course, this statement had to be changed following the decision of *Hamilton v Edington & Co*[221] after which Hume states that no water can be conducted from a river without the opposite owner's consent.[222]

6-65.   It is fascinating to see the development of Hume's views at a time when the law was changing rapidly. His starting point was to allow the use of water for secondary purposes to an extensive degree. When this economically sympathetic stance was not adopted by the courts, Hume attempted to maintain his theory with adaptations. The result was an inconsistent and misleading account of the law.

(2) Bell

6-66.   The other institutional writer of the period, Bell, in his *Principles of the Law of Scotland,* similarly considers common interest in the context of restrictions on ownership, along with servitudes and nuisance. However, while Bell distinguishes between common property, common interest and commonty (which suggests that common interest is becoming a technical term), his definition of common interest – that it 'takes place among owners of subjects possessed in separate portions, but still united by their common interest'[223] – is unhelpfully circular. Further, in his discussion of water rights it is unclear whether this is an instance of common interest or merely an issue related to rights in common.[224] The heading of the discussion of water rights in his second edition is 'Property in Water'.[225] In the fourth edition of 1839, the heading becomes 'Common Right in Water'. 'Property in Water', however, remains in the table of contents.[226]

6-67.   Despite these terminological difficulties, Bell creates a summary of the law of water rights which is a fairly uncontroversial restatement of the

[220] (1790) Dc.6.123 at 27.
[221] (1793) Mor 12824.
[222] See (1810) Gen.862 at 7–8 of Real Rights; Hume, *Lectures* III 222–223. This is perhaps a little strongly put as it appears that opposite owners may still at least withdraw water for domestic purposes without consent.
[223] Bell, *Principles* para 1086.
[224] Bell, *Principles* paras 1097 and 1100.
[225] Bell, *Principles of the Law of Scotland* (2nd edn, 1830) para 1100.
[226] Bell, *Principles of the Law of Scotland* (4th edn, 1839) para 1100. Bell's table of contents is often wrong.

case law.[227] In general, therefore, it can be seen that the later institutional writers were helpful in locating common interest within the general context of property law but the fundamentals of the doctrine were established elsewhere.

H. CONCLUSION

6-68.   This account of the development of common interest is an intriguing mixture of individual influence, socio-economic change and chance. Undoubtedly, the central figure is Lord Kames. Yet, like operations affecting the flow of a river, the smallest interference with legal development may produce effects that no one could have foreseen. Kames was strongly influential in the establishment of the doctrinal foundation of common interest. Seeking to facilitate industry he produced a hierarchy of consumptive uses. However, despite aspects of this hierarchy being influential in the courts – shown by the distinction made between primary and secondary uses, and the preferential status of the former – general consumption for secondary purposes was not to be allowed. Instead, the right to natural flow was developed. This was the final step in the establishment of the special regime of common interest as a *sui generis* collection of rights and obligations regarding rivers and lochs. That rights to prevent interference with the flow of rivers and lochs were established as proprietary rights and that secondary uses were significantly restricted would perhaps not have been welcomed by Lord Kames, but he indirectly contributed to these developments.

6-69.   Knowledge of the history and reasons behind the development of the doctrine allows greater insight into the way that common interest fits into the modern law – which is considered in detail in the next chapter. The past debates around water were centred on benefiting industry whilst ensuring that the population had sufficient supplies of water for drinking, cooking and washing. With recent concerns as to climate change, interest in water power to produce energy is increasing once again. Scotland's abundance of water places the country in a good position in terms of access to the natural resource, which makes it a prime candidate for testing this form of green energy. However, as such operations would certainly affect the flow of a river, it remains to be seen how the law of common interest will adapt to changing social and economic pressures in the future.

---

[227] See Bell, *Principles* paras 1100–1111, although at para 1107 Bell does make a slightly contradictory comment regarding secondary uses – citing *Lyon and Gray v Bakers of Glasgow* (1749) Mor 12789 – which is likely to have been influenced by Hume.

7 Common Interest: Modern Law

A. INTRODUCTION

7-01.   The previous two chapters have traced the history of the doctrine of common interest. This chapter will consider the modern law. An awareness of how and why common interest developed is of great value if the modern doctrine is to be consistent, coherent and capable of adapting to new demands and developments. Since the seminal case of *Morris v Bicket*,[1] which authoritatively restated the doctrine of common interest, there have been refinements through case law and much academic debate as well as legislative activity within the broader field of property law. Further, the uses to which water is now being put are different in comparison to the 18th and 19th centuries due to socio-economic change. This needs to be taken into account when considering the current law.

7-02. This chapter provides a comprehensive treatment of common interest regarding rivers and lochs beginning with a discussion of the nature of the doctrine and of its relationship with its English counterpart. This is followed by a detailed consideration of the rights and obligations of common interest and an examination of the remedies for breach. Finally, the ways in which common interest is extinguished are analysed.

B. NATURE OF COMMON INTEREST

(1) Historical Justifications

7-03. The reasons for development of common interest with regard to rivers and lochs can be seen from the preceding two chapters. Landowners' use of rivers and lochs running through their lands is unusually vulnerable to neighbourly interference. Initially, it was the important economic activities of mill-owners which were at stake but there were no specific rights or obligations being breached when, for example, a river was diverted, detained or consumed upstream. Many doctrines were appealed to such as the general principle prohibiting the prejudicial use of property, natural and prescriptive servitudes, the *immissio* principle and common property but none proved sufficient.[2] Without a specific doctrine, the water or flow of a river could potentially be monopolised by those closest to its source. A special regime was needed to give parity among proprietors. An evident need by landowners and industrialists for certainty and stability required that the regime defined clearly the rights and obligations with regard to rivers and lochs, and was not dependent on a lengthy period of prescription or a potentially expensive and time-consuming individual agreement. Further, the regime needed to provide more than just a restriction on damage to neighbouring land because the interests at risk were economic as well as physical. Common interest was the doctrine which filled this gap. The initial rule was a prohibition on the permanent diversion of a river in the interest of public rights to take water. The restriction on diversion then became established as a property right held by the owners along the course of a river. Later, this right became one to protect natural flow which prevented any material interference with the quality, quantity, natural direction and force of water. This development was influenced by a changing concept of precedent and by the social conditions of the time. Although some of the

---

[1] (1864) 2 M 1082 (aff'd (1866) 4 M (HL) 44).

content of common interest is attributable to the historical uses to which rivers were being put, the regime is equally applicable to lochs.

7-04. For the most part, common interest comprises restrictions on use. Such positive rights as exist arose for a slightly different historical reason. As outlined in Chapter 3, it was once thought that a loch – as a body of water distinct from the water itself and the *alveus* – was the common property of the surrounding owners. This analysis allowed each owner to sail and fish over the whole loch despite only owning a section of the *alveus*. Today, these rights are attributed to common interest. An extension of these rights has recently been established as proprietors on rivers now have similar rights with regard to fishing.[3] It can be seen that both the negative obligations and positive rights of common interest have as their object maximising the enjoyment of property. The balancing of rights in a neighbourhood to maximise enjoyment usually results in negative obligations but lochs and, to a certain extent rivers, are of a different nature than land in the sense that the uses to which lochs can be put are only fully realised when rights can be exercised over the whole surface rather than limited to the individually owned sections of the *alveus* beneath.

(2) Juridical Nature

7-05. As this book concerns water rights, a comprehensive explanation of the juridical nature of common interest in all its manifestations is outwith its scope. However, it is necessary to consider aspects of the general juridical character of common interest and how they apply to rivers and lochs.

7-06. Common interest is an aspect of the law of the neighbourhood.[4] As such, it is part of the contextual category of doctrines which have arisen to mitigate the particular problems caused by the physical proximity of different pieces of land. In particular, common interest can be aligned with doctrines which concern inherent limitations on the exercise of ownership in favour of neighbours such as nuisance, *aemulatio vicini* and the obligation of support. Indeed, before the establishment of common interest as a technical term, Hume used 'common interest' to refer to neighbourly limitations on ownership.[5] Like other doctrines in this group, common interest is a restriction on the exercise of ownership which arises by operation of law rather than through agreement or prescription.[6]

---

[2] See above, Ch 5.

[3] See discussion further below, paras 7-72–7-75.

[4] For reference to this category see Bell, *Principles* paras 962–972; Rankine, *Landownership* 367; T B Smith, *A Short Commentary on the Law of Scotland* (1962) 527 and 530; G L Gretton and A J M Steven, *Property, Trusts and Succession* (2009) Ch 17. Compare with South Africa; A J van der Walt, *The Law of Neighbours* (2010). The neighbourhood regulated by common interest is an unusual one shaped by the topography of land with some neighbours miles down- or upstream.

[5] Hume, *Lectures* III 207 and discussion above, paras 6-60–6-61.

[6] It is impossible to create a right of common interest: Title Conditions (Scotland) Act 2003 s 118.

7-07. In a manner similar to nuisance and *aemulatio vicini*, common interest creates a generally balanced reciprocal network of rights and obligations.[7] Each property is, for the most part, both subject to the obligations and granted the right to enforce these obligations against every other property. This contrasts with the unbalanced position of servitudes and real burdens where often one property is benefited, and another is burdened without any corresponding benefit.[8]

7-08. However, common interest does not impose a universal and flexible reasonableness standard such as nuisance, where one is not entitled to exercise rights of ownership intentionally in a way which is a *plus quam tolerabile* invasion of a neighbour's interest,[9] or *aemulatio vicini*, where one is not entitled to carry out the (otherwise legitimate) exercise of one's rights of ownership if motivated by spite or malice for a neighbour.[10] Instead, common interest imposes particular and strictly defined rules about the rights and obligations of owners. This aspect of common interest can be seen to be similar to real burdens and servitudes.

7-09. In a further parallel with servitudes and real burdens, common interest does not merely restrict the exercise of rights of ownership (like nuisance, *aemulatio vicini* and the obligation of support) but also, to a limited extent, grants rights to use other property. It can even impose positive obligations, although not it seems in the case of rivers and lochs. Both the right to enforce negative obligations and the right to use other property are real rights, held by the owner of land, and can be enforced against third parties.[11] Although nuisance can be enforced against third parties, it is analysed as a branch of delict and does not give a real right in neighbouring property.

7-10. Due to the similarities with servitudes and real burdens, the useful terms 'benefited' and 'burdened' property will be used in this account of common interest. This is the terminology of title conditions. Yet, although common interest was defined as a 'real condition' by Reid,[12] it has been omitted from the definition of 'title condition' in s 122(1) of the Title Conditions (Scotland) Act 2003.

7-11. Distinct from other doctrines, common interest is applicable only to certain types of property, the enjoyment of which are particularly susceptible to neighbourly interference.[13] In the case of rivers and lochs, the

---

[7] See Reid, *Property* para 360.

[8] However, real burdens can be created in a manner which mimics this aspect of common interest. See the 'Community Burdens' regulated by Title Conditions (Scotland) Act 2003 Part 2 and the discussion in A Brand, A J M Steven and S Wortley, *Professor McDonald's Conveyancing Manual* (7th edn, 2004) para 15.6.

[9] Whitty, 'Nusiance' para 105.

[10] Whitty, 'Nusiance' para 34.

[11] See below, para 7-78. For parallels with servitudes see Cusine & Paisley para 1.62.

[12] K G C Reid, 'Defining Real Conditions' 1989 *Jur Rev* 69; K G C Reid, 'Common Interest: A Reassessment' (1983) 28 *JLSS* 428; Reid, *Property* paras 344–374.

[13] Reid, 'Common Interest: A Reassessment' at 430.

property in question is the channel or hollow of the body of water which includes the *alveus* and banks. Common interest seeks to protect the use of water – for consumption, recreation or any other purpose – by the owners of this property.

7-12. In summary, it can be seen that, although common interest shares characteristics with title conditions and inherent limitations on ownership in favour of neighbours, it does not fit neatly into either category. In this sense, the rights and obligations which are created by common interest are *sui generis*.

(3) Conclusions

7-13. Common interest with respect to rivers and lochs was the product of judicial creativity in the light of economic and social demands. Its haphazard development was driven by a number of diverse factors which helps to explain the difficulty of analysing the doctrine in the modern law. However, it can be said that the establishment of common interest was beneficial due to its providing a solution not offered by other doctrines and that the doctrine still serves a valid purpose.[14] Common interest with respect to rivers and lochs can be summarised as a special regime which comprises a *sui generis* set of generally reciprocal rights and obligations attached to the *alveus* and banks of rivers and lochs.

C. RELATIONSHIP TO ENGLISH LAW

7-14. It is sometimes claimed that there is little difference between the Scottish and English law regarding water rights.[15] As has been demonstrated in the previous two chapters, however, the Scottish law of common interest has a history which is particular to Scotland. As a result, the free borrowing of authority from English law, which has its own distinct history, is a dangerous exercise.[16]

7-15. The main difference between the jurisdictions in the modern law is England's criterion of reasonableness. English law has been summarised in a standard work in the following terms:

---

[14] See the promotion of reform of common interest in Land Reform Review Group, *The Land of Scotland and the Common Good* (2014; http://www.scotland.gov.uk/Resource/0045/00451597.pdf) paras 30.1–30.13.

[15] For example, Lord Shand stated 'I know of no distinction between the law of Scotland and the law of England in the class of questions relating to the common interest and rights of upper and lower proprietors on the banks of a running stream' in *Young & Co v Bankier Distillery Co* (1893) 20 R (HL) 76 at 80, and Whitty states 'the Scottish doctrine of common interest is very similar if not identical to the English doctrine of riparian rights' (Whitty, 'Water' at 451).

[16] For an example of the dangers see Anon, 'On the Law of Flowing Water' (1859) 1 *Scottish Law Magazine and Sheriff Court Reporter* 106–111 and 113–117.

'The flow of a natural watercourse creates riparian rights and duties between all the riparian owners along the whole of its course, and subject to exercising reasonable use, each proprietor is bound to allow the water to flow on without altering its quality or quantity. Correspondingly, apart from a use authorised by statute, grant or prescription, any unreasonable and unauthorised interference with the use of the water to the prejudice of other riparian owners may become the subject of an action from damages, and may be restrained by an injunction, even though there is no actual damage to the claimant.'[17]

This reasonableness criterion allows scope for the use of water for secondary purposes.[18] In contrast, a general test of reasonableness is not present in most of the Scottish authorities. The three instances where reasonableness had a significant presence are *Marquis of Abercorn v Jamieson*,[19] *Lady Willoughby de Eresby v Wood*[20] and *Young & Co v Bankier Distillery Co*.[21] In *Marquis of Abercorn v Jamieson* it was said that an owner has to reconcile his or her water use with a 'neighbour's reasonable rights'.[22] However, this comment does not seem to import a reasonableness standard into common interest but is rather a loosely-framed statement confirming that the ownership of land containing water is burdened by obligations in favour of neighbours. Further, this decision was given before the authoritative restatement of the right of natural flow in *Morris v Bicket*[23] where reasonableness is not mentioned.

7-16.   In *Lady Willoughby de Eresby v Wood*,[24] it was stated by Lord Fraser that the right of an owner to use a river is 'liable to be modified and abrogated by the reasonable use of the stream by others'. It was said that an upstream owner is entitled to divert, detain a river and also consume water for not only domestic but also agricultural and manufacturing purposes if reasonable. This decision is utterly contrary to Scottish authorities both before and since[25] and was influenced by American and English law.[26] It should certainly not be regarded as representing Scots law.[27]

---

[17] W Howarth, *Wisdom's Law of Watercourses* (6th edn, 2011) at 58.

[18] Howarth, *Law of Watercourses* at 60–63; S R Hobday, *Coulson & Forbes on the Law of Waters* (6th edn, 1952) 145–151.

[19] (1791) Hume 510.

[20] (1884) 22 SLR 471.

[21] (1893) 20 R (HL) 76.

[22] At 511.

[23] (1864) 2 M 1082.

[24] (1884) 22 SLR 471 at 473.

[25] See above, paras 6-20–6-54 and discussion below. Lord Fraser cites *Lord Glenlee v Gordon* (1804) Mor 12834 and *Marquis of Abercorn v Jamieson* (1791) Hume 510 but attempts to explain the former case as an example of the unreasonable detention of water when the requirement of reasonableness is not mentioned in the judgment, and the latter as being a case not between two millers and so not a valid precedent when there had been little previous suggestion as to a separate law of mills regarding water.

[26] The American works J K Angell, *Treatise on Watercourses* (edition not given); E Washburn, *Washburn on Easements* (edition not given); the English case of *Wright v Howard* (1823) 1 Sim & St 192, 57 ER 76 and the American cases of *Hetrich v Deacler* (1847) 6 Barr (Penn) R 32; *Dumont v Kellog* (1874) 18 Am Rep 102 are cited.

[27] The judgment also makes the far-fetched claims that when an owner has prescriptively acquired the right to dam water, the dam may be relocated or increased in capacity at any time

7-17.   In a more restrained Anglicisation, in *Young & Co v Bankier Distillery Co*[28] Lord MacNaughten in the House of Lords declared that a:

'riparian proprietor is entitled to have the water of the stream on the banks of which his property lies flow down as it has been accustomed to flow down to his property, subject to the ordinary use of the flowing water by upper proprietors, and such further use, if any, on their part in connection with their property as may be reasonable under the circumstances.'

This summary by Lord McNaughten is relied upon by Gordon and Whitty as reflecting modern Scots law.[29] However, apart from these isolated statements, the Scottish case law demonstrates that the solution which has been adopted in regard to rivers and lochs is to define strictly the rights and obligations of landowners rather than imposing a flexible reasonableness standard which is dependent on all the circumstances. This makes the Scottish doctrine potentially more restrictive than its English equivalent.

D. WHAT PROPERTY?

7-18.   Common interest is a doctrine which creates a network of reciprocal rights and obligations, which places limitations on the ownership of the *alveus* or banks of a river or loch and also grants rights over other parts of the *alveus*.[30] There are no rights in the water itself whilst flowing although it is sometimes said that there is a 'common right' or 'common interest' in the water.[31] As running water is a communal thing and incapable of ownership,[32] it is similarly incapable of other subordinate property rights. Owners merely have a greater opportunity than others to use running water whilst it is on their lands because they have legitimate access to it.[33] The only right which one can have to running water is the only right which can exist with regard to ownerless property – the public right to acquire ownership by *occupatio* by acquiring sufficient control over it. As was stated by Lord Neaves in *Morris v Bicket*:[34] 'When you get it into your pitcher or pipe it becomes your property,

---

and that an action for damages is the only remedy for the breach of common interest. See (1884) 22 SLR 471 at 474 and 475. On remedies and prescription see paras 7-76–7-96 and 7-101–7-105 below.

[28] (1893) 20 R (HL) 76 at 78.

[29] Whitty, 'Water' 450; Gordon & Wortley, *Land Law* paras 6-24 and 6-31.

[30] Common interest is also applicable to salmon fishings but consideration of this topic is outwith the scope of this book. The most modern treatment is contained in Gordon &Wortley, *Land Law* paras 8-40-8–128 but see also Reid, *Property* paras 320–330; J H Tait, *A Treatise on the Law of Scotland: As Applied to Game Laws, Trout and Salmon Fishing* (1901) Ch XIV.

[31] See, for example, Bell, *Principles* para 1100 and Lord Justice-Clerk Inglis states in 'water alone, as such, there can be no property either sole or conjunct; but there is a common interest in the water': *Morris v Bicket* (1864) 2 M 1082 at 1087. See also discussion above at para 6-39 in relation to the expression 'common interest in the stream'.

[32] See *Patrick v Napier* (1867) 5 M 683 at 698–699 and for discussion of the classification of running water in Ch 2.

[33] For a summary of the rights which the public have to access water see above, paras 2-92–2-102.

[34] (1864) 2 M 1082 at 1092.

just as game and fish when they are caught become the property of the person who catches them; but while it is flowing and in its channel, no portion of the water, either on one side of the *alveus* or the other, belongs to one party or the other.' Common interest, however, operates as a restraint on *occupatio*, as will be considered below.[35]

(1) Private Rivers

7-19. Most of the early case law on common interest concerns private rivers. The limitations imposed by common interest apply only where a river runs through two or more pieces of land. If a river is wholly contained within the land of one person, the ownership of the *alveus* and banks is not bound by the restrictions of common interest, as there is no neighbouring property at risk of damage or interference.[36]

7-20. In the modern law, a private river is a non-tidal body of water beyond the highest point reached by the flow of ordinary spring tides[37] and which runs perennially in a definite channel. A perennial river is one which contains a constant flow of water and not merely after a period of wet weather.[38] In *Magistrates of Ardrossan v Dickie*,[39] the Lord Ordinary stated that a flow does not need to be absolutely perennial but merely 'substantially perennial', and this was not challenged by the judges of the Inner House on appeal.[40] Thus, if a river is temporarily dry during a drought it will still be considered perennial[41] but each case will, of course, depend on its circumstances.[42] A decision of the Sheriff in the unreported case of *Macgregor v Moncreiffe's Trs*[43]

[35] See below, para 7-43.

[36] See *Lord Blantyre v Dunn* (1848) 10 D 509 at 529; *Fergusson v Shirreff* (1844) 6 D 1363 at 1374. See also Rankine, *Landownership* 532; Ferguson 198. A landowner may still be liable in nuisance, however, if the course of a river was changed and damage to adjacent land was caused. See *Macfarlane v Lowis* (1857) 19 D 1038.

[37] *Bowie v Marquis of Ailsa* (1853) 15 D 853. See Ferguson 107; Reid, *Property* para 276; Gordon & Wortley, *Land Law* para 6-05; proposals in Report on the Law of the Foreshore and Seabed (Scot Law Com No 190, 2003) para 2.22 and discussion above, para 3-52.

[38] See *Magistrates of Linlithgow v Elphinstone (No 2)* (1768) Mor 12805, Hailes 203; *Magistrates of Ardrossan v Dickie* (1906) 14 SLT 349; Rankine, *Landownership* 518–519; Whitty, 'Water' 446–448.

[39] (1906) 14 SLT 349 at 353.

[40] At 356. Although the interlocutor of the Lord Ordinary was recalled on the basis that the 'loch' was not perennial.

[41] See *Cruikshanks and Bell v Henderson* (1791) Hume 506 at 507 where the stream was said to be 'not quite constant'; *Cowan v Lord Kinnaird* (1865) 4 M 236 at 240; Ferguson 302–303, who comments that this accords with the Roman definition of perennial in D.43.12.1.2 (Ulpian).

[42] Despite the comments in *Murdoch v Wallace* (1881) 8 R 855 at 861, size does not matter. See also Reid, *Property* para 286 n 2.

[43] Unreported 7 Sept 1936 at 40. The various Sheriff Court decisions of this case are available in the National Archives of Scotland: NAS02024 SC49-7-1933-6-00001. The appeal of this decision to the Court of Session on 21 September 1936 was dismissed on 24 November 1936. See *Robert MacGregor (Appellant) v Dame Evelyn V Hay or Moncreiffe and Another (Sir Robert D Moncreiffe's Trs)* (1937) CS258/2049, and also related material under CS258/2048, in

held that, if water can only form a perennial flow through the upkeep of artificial operations, the land will not be subject to common interest. This suggests that a river requires a natural source; but common interest can apply to the flow of a river which has been increased through artificial operations.[44]

7-21. What constitutes a definite channel has not been the subject of much discussion.[45] Rankine and Ferguson[46] consider the issue using American authority which, while instructive, is not authoritative.[47] It is clear that a distinction should be drawn between water in a distinct channel and that 'squandered over the soil'.[48] 'Separate and unconnected pools' or a 'myriad of channels'[49] will not suffice. Artificial channels are included in this definition if the channel does not require extensive maintenance in order to exist.[50] As long as the channel is definite, which implies knowledge of its existence,[51] there appears to be no obstacle to applying common interest to underground rivers, although the point is undecided.[52]

7-22. What land is subject to – and has the corresponding benefit of – common interest? A piece of land adjoining a river may extend only to the banks and exclude the *alveus*, or much more commonly it may include both the bank and part of the *alveus*. One of the main functions of common interest, as explained above, is to reduce the unusually high risk of neighbourly interference with the use of water running through land. As a result, common interest should apply only where this risk is present.

7-23. It is sometimes argued that only ownership of the banks is required to allow use of the water of a river. These arguments derive from English authority[53] or the etymology of the word 'riparian'.[54] However, without

---

the National Archives. I would like to thank Professor Paisley for bringing this case to my attention. See also *Gordons v Suttie* (1826) Mur 86 at 92–93.

[44] See below, paras 7-51–7-53.

[45] In *McNab v Robertson* (1896) 24 R (HL) 34 the interpretation of the word 'stream' was considered in a lease but this cannot be taken as authoritative in determining the scope of common interest. See Gordon & Wortley, *Land Law* para 6-25 n 80.

[46] See Rankine, *Landownership* 532–533; Ferguson 167–168.

[47] Whitty, 'Water' 473–477 comments on the use of English and American authority which is not common in modern authorities.

[48] Rankine, *Landownership* 532.

[49] *Magistrates of Ardrossan v Dickie* (1906) 14 SLT 349 at 356–357.

[50] See the comments in *Lord Blantyre v Dunn* (1848) 10 D 509 at 525 and 541.

[51] *Buchanan v Coubrough* (1869) 7 SLR 88 at 95–96.

[52] Reid, *Property* para 301; Ferguson 332–334. This may be rare in Scotland due to the scarcity of limestone. English and Irish authority on this point mention the difficulty of establishing whether an underground channel is definite without excavation but perhaps advances in technology can assist this process.

[53] Rankine, *Landownership* 533; Ferguson 206; Murray et al, 'Water' paras 1162–1163; F Lyall, 'Water and Water Rights' in SME (Vol 25, 1989) para 303.

[54] Rankine, *Landownership* 533; Whitty, 'Water' 448. The term 'riparian rights' seems to be used in a way which encompasses both the ability to use water while it is on one's land and to prevent operations on other lands. This is confusing and the term has been mostly avoided in these chapters. As the word 'riparian' did not come to be used in Scots law until after the establishment of the doctrine of common interest, it is suggested relying on the etymology

ownership of a part of the *alveus*, an owner of the bank who wished to use the water of a river for any purpose might, depending on the circumstances, be trespassing on the property of the person who owns the *alveus* of the river *ad coelum et ad inferos*.[55] Only public rights of use are available.[56] This is supported by case law, where it is implied that, in order to have the greatest opportunity to use water, ownership of the *alveus* is required.[57] It is even suggested that an insignificant part of the *alveus* is insufficient for this purpose.[58] Although owners of just the banks are exposed to the risk of damage to their property through operations on the river, they are not entitled to use the water beyond their public rights. Therefore, there is no unusually high risk of interference by neighbours with the use of water which requires to be controlled by common interest. As a result, it is suggested that the owner of the banks is not a benefited proprietor in common interest. There is, however, no authority on this point.

7-24.   By contrast, operations on the banks can significantly affect the flow of a river. Ownership of the banks is therefore subject to common interest obligations.[59] It follows that the owner of the banks is a burdened, but probably not a benefited, proprietor.[60] This is an exception to the generally reciprocal nature of common interest.[61] The possibility of mineral owners also being burdened, but not benefited proprietors, is discussed separately below.[62]

7-25.   Ownership just of the banks and not the *alveus* will, however, be a rare occurrence as, where a river separates two properties, it is presumed

---

of the word could be misleading. Further, 'riparian' could derive from the Latin for break or cut, such as that which is cut by the river, which would imply the *alveus*. On the assumptions we can draw from the word riparian, see S C Wiel, 'Origin and Comparative Development of the Law of Watercourses in the Common Law and in the Civil Law' (1918) 6 *Cal L Rev* 245; S C Wiel, 'Waters: American Law and French Authority' (1919–20) 33 *Harv L Rev* 133. But see also W A Hutchins, *Water Rights Laws in the Nineteen Western States* (2004) 181–183.

[55] See *Fergusson v Shirreff* (1844) 6 D 1363; *Grant v Henry* (1894) 21 R 358 where it was held that acquiring legitimate access to a non-tidal river did not allow fishing for trout as this would be trespassing on ownership of the *alveus*.

[56] These being common law and statutory public rights. See above, paras 2-92–2-102.

[57] I have not found one case where the rights of common interest were found to be held by the owner of only the banks. In *Lord Blantyre v Waterworks Commissioners of Dumbarton* (1886) 15 R (HL) 56 at 66 it is stated one 'cannot acquire an interest in the water of the reservoir without also acquiring an interest in the basin with contains it'. See *Dicksons v Hawick* (1885) 13 R 163 and *Hilson v Scott* (1895) 23 R 241 where the method employed to secure water rights was the disposition of the *alveus* of mill-lades and *Marquis of Breadalbane v West Highland Railway Co* (1895) 22 R 307 where it was attempted to become fully entitled to use water by buying a small piece of the *alveus*. See also Reid, *Property* para 278; Gordon & Wortley, *Land Law* para 8-131.

[58] *Marquis of Breadalbane v West Highland Railway Co* (1895) 22 R 307.

[59] See discussion below, paras 7-63–7-68.

[60] See also Reid, *Property* para 283.

[61] See above, para 7-07.

[62] See below, para 7-82.

that land extends to the *medium filum* of the river.[63] Where a non-tidal river runs consecutively through or between several properties, each property normally extends to include a section of the *alveus*. Each section of the channel – both the banks and *alveus* – of the river is a benefited and burdened property.

7-26. Where the *alveus* is owned alone its owner can use the water in a river and the property is both benefited and burdened. However, the extent of use would depend on legitimate access to the *alveus*. This situation is most likely to occur in tidal rivers which are considered further below.

(2) Private Lochs

7-27. Many of the elements in the definition of private rivers are similar to those of private lochs. Private lochs are those which are non-tidal.[64] A loch requires a perennial outflow and to exist in a definite hollow.[65] So long as the hollow is definite, which implies knowledge of its existence, there is no obstacle to applying common interest to underground lochs.[66] Land which wholly contains a loch is not bound by the obligations of common interest if the perennial outflow of the loch is not discharged into the definite channel of a river.[67] Where a loch is contained within the lands of several proprietors but does not feed perennially into a river, the rights and obligations of common interest only apply to the properties containing the loch. Where, however, the loch also has a perennial outflow into a river, it is treated as a branch of the river and as a result the land containing the loch is additionally subject to the rights and obligations of common interest in regard to the proprietors of the channel of the river which the loch feeds, and presumably, if applicable, which the loch receives.[68]

7-28. For the reasons explained above in regard to non-tidal rivers, it is suggested that a person who owns the banks of a loch, but not the *alveus*, would only be a burdened, not a benefited, proprietor.[69]

7-29. As the owners of land containing lochs have specific rights over the whole *alveus* which are not available to the owners of the channel of private rivers, it is necessary but not easy to elaborate a distinction between the

[63] See above, para 3-67.

[64] See the definition of tidality above, para 3-52.

[65] *Magistrates of Linlithgow v Elphinstone (No 2)* (1768) Mor 12805, Hailes 203. See discussion regarding rivers above. Without these characteristics, the water is merely *stagnum* and is not subject to common interest.

[66] Reid, *Property* para 301; Ferguson 332–334. Scottish Water specifically mention underground lakes as a source of water supply: see http://www.scottishwater.co.uk/clearer-fresher-learning/all-about-water/all-about-water/water-treatment.

[67] Stair, *Institutions* II.3.73; Bankton, *Institute* II.3.165; Bell, *Principles* para 648.

[68] *Magistrates of Linlithgow v Elphinstone (No 2)*; *Magistrates of Ardrossan v Dickie* (1906) 14 SLT 349; Hume, *Lectures* III 225; Bell, *Principles* para 1110; Rankine, *Landownership* 195; Whitty, 'Water' 467–468; Gordon & Wortley, *Land Law* para 6-14 and further justification below, para 7-33.

[69] See above. See also *Montgomery v Watson* (1861) 23 D 635 which applies the decision of *Fergusson v Shirreff* (1844) 6 D 1363 to non-tidal lochs.

two.[70] In *Magistrates of Ardrossan v Dickie*[71] a loch was defined as a 'sheet of water'. A more precise definition is that a loch is a large collected body of water formed within a hollow[72] (as opposed to a channel) which contains slow-running water.[73]

(3) Public Rivers and Lochs

7-30. The Crown originally owns the *alveus* of tidal rivers and lochs,[74] which are those perennial stretches of water in a definite channel or hollow below the highest mark of the ordinary spring tides.[75] Such ownership is patrimonial and the Crown can exercise rights such as preventing trespass and encroachment.[76] Although there is no authority on the point, it is suggested that the *alveus* is both a benefited and burdened property for the purposes of common interest. The other burdened and benefited land in this instance will be, in the usual case, the *alveus* and banks of the upstream non-tidal, private stretch of the river.

7-31. There is conflicting authority on whether common interest rights are attached to land – the foreshore or banks – next to tidal waters.[77] As the owners do not have the full opportunity to use the water because they are not owners of the *alveus*,[78] the potential for neighbourly interference with the use of water is reduced. As a result, it is suggested that this land, as with private rivers, is not benefited property but will be burdened property for the purposes of common interest.[79] The adjoining landowners have public rights to use the water but, as settled by *Colquhoun's Trs v Orr Ewing*,[80] public rights are not of the nature of common interest and do not give the holders

---

[70] See Lord Adam's attempt that 'a loch is not...anything else but a loch': *Magistrates of Ardrossan v Dickie* at 357. However, the editor of the Scots Law Times does mention that the judgments of Lord Adam and Lord Kinnear are taken from shorthand notes and were not revised by their Lordships.

[71] (1906) 14 SLT 349 at 357. See also *Mackenzie v Bankes* (1878) LR 3 App Cas 1324; Ferguson 137.

[72] The word 'hollow' is used by Lord Auchinleck in *Magistrates of Linlithgow v Elphinstone (No 2)* at 205; Lord Hatherley in *Mackenzie v Bankes* (1878) LR 3 App Cas 1324 at 1335. I have preferred this word to 'basin' which is also used in *Mackenzie v Bankes* to avoid confusion with 'river-basin' as defined in the European Water Framework Directive.

[73] Otherwise the loch would not be perennial.

[74] See above, para 3-51.

[75] See authority above at n 37 and discussion of tidality above, para 3-52.

[76] *Lord Advocate v Clyde Navigation Trs* (1891) 19 R 174 at 182.

[77] Doubt whether common interest can be enforced by the owners of land next to tidal rivers was expressed in *Macbraire v Mather* (1873) 9 M 913; *Moncreiffe v Perth Police Commissioners* (1886) 13 R 921. See also H Burn-Murdoch, *Interdict in the Law of Scotland* (1933) para 46; Reid, *Property* para 312. In *Ross v Powrie and Pitcaithley* (1891) 18 R 314 there are *obiter* comments to the contrary and in *Gay v Malloch* 1959 SC 110 the issue was not disputed by the defenders. See also Murray et al, 'Water' para 1134; Whitty, 'Water' 448.

[78] See analysis above regarding private rivers.

[79] See *Macbraire v Mather*; *Moncreiffe v Perth Police Commissioners*; Reid, *Property* para 312.

[80] (1877) 4 R (HL) 166. The contrary position was held by the Inner House of the Court of Session (1877) 4 R 344 but overturned by the House of Lords on appeal.

title to prevent operations unless they interfere with the exercise of public rights.[81] Instead, where an owner of the banks of a river wishes to object to operations on the Crown-owned *alveus*, an action of nuisance would be more appropriate.[82] The issue is clouded by the fact that all of the cases considering this point concern damage to salmon fishings, the owners of which have independent rights against interference with the free passage of salmon which, it has been held, are applicable to tidal rivers.[83] Of course, with the *alveus* of tidal waters now settled as *regalia minora*,[84] if the owner of the banks or foreshore did become owner of the *alveus*, the land would then also be benefited property. This may in practice, however, be rare.[85]

E. RIGHTS AND OBLIGATIONS OF COMMON INTEREST

7-32.   At first common interest was no more than a prohibition against permanent diversion and successive owners were entitled to change the course of a river within their own property on condition that they returned the water to its channel before the boundary with downstream property.[86] When, later, a right to natural flow developed, owners were considerably more restricted with respect to the use of water, and to operations on the *alveus* and banks.

(1) Natural Flow

(a) The Protection of Natural Flow

7-33.   Each owner of a section of *alveus* has the right to be protected against interference with the natural flow of water. This results in a corresponding obligation on everyone – but in particular every other owner of the *alveus* or banks – not to interfere with this right. The importance of this rule is clear. The natural flow of a river may be essential for its use and small changes could affect this use and also cause damage to the banks and *alveus*. The application of the rule to lochs is less clear. At first sight, the significance of the flow to lochs may not seem as great. Indeed, as lochs are slower-flowing bodies of water, the natural flow will be less easily affected. However, it is still possible that the natural flow of a loch will be of value for activities such

---

[81] Consider also the similar position of frontagers who, as members of the public entitled to a public right of highway, enjoy a right of light over a public street. See *Donald & Sons v Esslemont & Macintosh* 1923 SC 122.

[82] For the basis of liability in nuisance see Whitty, 'Nuisance' para 105.

[83] Reid, *Property* para 330. See also Burn-Murdoch, *Interdict* (n 77) para 46.

[84] Gordon, *Land Law* para 27-07; Reid, *Property* para 311.

[85] The Crown Estate Commissioners state that the Crown owns 50% of the foreshore and beds of tidal rivers but it is not clear how these figures have been established: see Crown Estate, *Building Strong Partnerships: Scotland Report* (2011; http://www.thecrownestate.co.uk/media/160000/scotland_report_2011.pdf) 2. See also discussion above at para 3-41 with respect to the foreshore.

[86] Opposite owners were not entitled to temporarily divert the river at all, see Ch 5.

as sailing and fishing and for the protection of banks. Certainly, the flow into and from a loch will be important. For example, owners may want to prevent changes to the outflow into a river for fear of raising the level of the loch, covering existing moorings for boats, and flooding part of the land,[87] while the owners along the river will wish to maintain the flow from the loch. Thus, it is suggested that the owners of the banks and *alveus* of lochs are bound by the obligation not to interfere with both the natural flow of the loch and also the in- or out-flowing rivers.[88]

7-34. Lord Neaves in *Morris v Bicket*[89] gave the seminal statement of the right to natural flow. He said that a 'lower heritor has this interest in the stream, that in passing through the lands of others it shall be transmitted to him undiminished in quantity, unpolluted in quality, and unaffected in force and natural direction, except in so far as the primary uses of it may legitimately operate upon it within the lands of the upper heritor'.[90] This comment was made in the context of successive owners but it is clear that the obligation not to interfere with natural flow applies equally between opposite owners.[91] Indeed, operations on a river are more likely to interfere with the opposite owner's right to natural flow rather than that of a distant downstream owner. Similarly, an upstream owner has the same right against a downstream owner, although the opportunity for interference is relatively slight.[92] The natural flow includes seasonal variations such as ordinary floods but not extraordinary or accidental floods.[93]

7-35. The obligation is not absolute. Reid comments: 'Every act performed by a riparian proprietor on a river or stream interferes to some extent with the flow of the water. But not every act is a breach of common interest, for otherwise riparian ownership could never be exercised.'[94] Instead, the interference with the natural flow of water must be material.[95] What 'material' entails has not been subject to much discussion. Lord Neaves states it is not every 'trifling interference'[96] but must be something that 'palpably affects the water'.[97] Reid summarises, echoing the little noticed statement of

[87] A lease where the rising of the level of a loch was anticipated was considered in *Stirling v Dunn* (1827) 6 S 272.
[88] See authority cited at n 68.
[89] (1864) 2 M 1082.
[90] At 1092.
[91] *Colquhoun's Trs v Orr Ewing* (1877) 4 R (HL) 166 at 126.
[92] Rankine, *Landownership* 546–547; Ferguson 222–226.
[93] *Menzies v Breadalbane* (1828) 3 W & S 235; *McLean v Hamilton* (1857) 19 D 1006; *Jackson v Marshall* (1872) 10 M 913.
[94] Reid, *Property* para 289.
[95] Lord Cockburn in *Colquhoun's Trs v Orr Ewing* (1877) 4 R (HL) 116 at 130 uses the alterative definition of a 'sensible alteration'. See also *Young & Co v Bankier Distillery Co* (1893) 20 R (HL) 76 at 78.
[96] (1864) 2 M 1082 at 1093.
[97] At 1093. Reid adds a requirement that there is an 'act of violent alteration' for breach in Reid, *Property* para 289. However, this quote is taken from Hume, *Lectures* III 217 whose view of common interest cannot be relied upon to any great extent. See discussion above, paras 6-60–6-65.

Kames:[98] 'Whether or not the disturbance caused by a particular act is material will depend to a considerable extent on the size of the river or stream in question.'[99] Each case must be considered upon its individual circumstances but the standard 'is an objective one and does not depend on achieving a balance between the subjective, personal interests of the parties who are riparian proprietors for the time being'.[100] This has application to specific activities which owners can carry out which will be considered further below.

(b) Primary Purposes

7-36. The right to natural flow does not apply to water which is consumed for primary purposes by landowners. Thus in *Magistrates of Linlithgow v Elphinstone (No 2)*[101] the court stated that: 'No individual can appropriate a river or any branch of it; but every individual of the nation, those especially who have land adjoining, are entitled to use the water for their private purposes.' In taking water for primary purposes, landowners are exercising their public right to appropriate water. In the seminal cases of *Miller v Stein*[102] and *Russell v Haig*,[103] it was confirmed that primary purposes are hierarchically superior to other purposes, Lord Justice-Clerk Braxfield explaining that 'if [a landowner] cannot have all the uses of it without hurting others, there is a certain order of uses: the natural and primary uses are preferable to all others'.[104] The preferential status of primary uses means that landowners can take water for such purposes even if this materially interferes with the natural flow. Even today, around 150,000 people still rely on private water supply in Scotland.[105]

(i) WHAT ARE PRIMARY PURPOSES?

7-37. The definition of primary purposes given by Bell is coloured by the circumstances of his time. Water, he states, may be used for 'drink for man or

---

[98] Kames, *Principles* 50.

[99] Reid, *Property* para 289.

[100] Reid, *Property* para 289. See also Lord Cockburn's explanation in *Colquhoun's Trs v Orr Ewing* (1877) 4 R (HL) 116 at 131 that the 'Amazon is many miles wide, and, assuming the law of Brazil to be the same as that of this country, I think a proprietor of land on the one bank of a stream of that width would not be in a position to require one on the opposite shore to remove an encroachment of one or two feet into the river, for it would do him no sensible injury, though in the narrow Kilmarnock Water such an encroachment did do the opposite proprietor sensible *injuria*, which, especially seeing it was in a town and was or might be building land, was very likely to produce substantial damage, though he might not as yet be able to shew present damage.'

[101] (1768) Mor 12805 at 12806.

[102] (1791) Mor 12823, Bell's Octavo Cases 334.

[103] (1791) Mor 12823, Bell's Octavo Cases 338.

[104] *Russell v Haig* (1791) Bell's Octavo Cases 338 at 346.

[105] That is roughly equivalent to the population of Dundee: see http://www.scotland.gov.uk/Topics/Environment/Water/17670/pws. It is unclear to what extent these figures include water supplied from private boreholes.

beast, and for the family purposes of cooking, washing, bleaching, brewing for domestic use'.[106] Ferguson provides the more era-neutral definition of 'all ordinary domestic purposes, such as cooking, baking, and washing of all sorts, the term being regarded as embracing the ordinary service of a farmsteading as well as a dwelling-house'.[107] Water can be consumed for all the requirements of a self-sufficient piece of land. Of course, these requirements must be flexible enough to adapt to different social conditions. In *Bonthrone v Downie*[108] it was suggested that using water for flushing toilets was not a primary purpose but as Reid states 'it may be doubted whether this is the modern law'.[109]

7-38.   The privileged position of consumption for primary purposes by landowners in common interest only applies to supplying the needs of the adjacent land and not for the needs of another piece of land which does not include part of the *alveus*.[110] There is no indication in the case law of any limit on the extent of the adjacent dry land. It may be that water could legitimately be taken from a small stream to serve the adjoining 100 acres.[111] Further, the needs of the occupiers of the land next to a river or loch may increase over time. If the number of occupants increases, it is suggested that their increased consumption cannot be objected to. In relation to the consumption of water from a well by the inhabitants of a village for primary purposes Lord Gillies stated:

'I conceive there is one thing perfectly clear, that the primary use of water is for domestic purposes, and that all other uses must yield to that. How much water is or ought to be consumed for these purposes may give rise to various opinions, but it is generally to be wished that a great quantity should be consumed.[112] Although one family may use ten times more than another, it does not follow that quantity may not be legitimately, laudably, and properly required. I am far from saying that there should be any distinction between rich and poor, but all should be placed on the same level.'[113]

---

[106] Bell, *Principles* para 1105. For the use of water for brewing see *Johnstone v Ritchie* (1822) 1 S 327.

[107] Ferguson 238–239.

[108] (1878) 6 R 324. Although the consumption was also prohibited on the basis that it was carried out by the owner of land distant from the stream in a way that infringed a downstream proprietor's right to natural flow.

[109] Reid, *Property* para 287. See also Gordon & Wortley, *Land Law* para 6-31.

[110] *Lord Melville v Denniston* (1842) 4 D 1231 at 1241; *Marquis of Breadalbane v West Highland Railway Co* (1895) 22 R 307 at 313. See also *Donaldson v Earl of Strathmore* (1877) 14 SLR 587; *Bonthrone v Downie* (1878) 6 R 324. Ownership of an insignificant part of the *alveus*, however, does not entitle the landowner to the full opportunities to use the water: see *Marquis of Breadalbane v West Highland Railway Co.*

[111] This presumes that the land is in single ownership. Whether there would be a limitation on appropriation here based on the concept of water as a communal thing is open to question, see above, paras 2-34–2-36.

[112] This comment must be taken in the context of the time when the public health movement was encouraging the use of water. See discussion above, paras 6-02–6-05 and 6-51–6-64. This view is obviously changing now in light of environmental concerns.

[113] *Lord Melville v Denniston* (1842) 4 D 1231 at 1238. See also Hume's commentary to *Ogilvy v Kincaid* (1791) Hume 508 at 509. However, aspects of this commentary must be read with reservation; see the discussion of consumption below.

Although this quote is not about common interest, it does show the extent of the favoured position of use of water for primary purposes in general.

7-39. If the use for primary purposes by an upstream owner results in exhaustion of the river, there is authority that this does not breach common interest. Kames states that a proprietor may take water for primary purposes, 'however little be left to the inferior heritors'.[114] In this very limited sense, the upstream proprietors are in a better position due to their natural situation on the river.[115]

7-40. Rankine suggests that, in the event of a stream being exhausted, a court could intervene to regulate the proportionate use of water.[116] That the court can regulate the use of water is a claim often made. However, this possibility has also been questioned.[117] In *Hood v Williamsons*,[118] the Lord Ordinary's opinion was that in the event that if:

> 'there be not enough water for both the upper and lower heritor, the Lord Ordinary conceives it cannot be held that the lower heritor is entitled to demand from the upper that the rations, so to speak, of both should be reduced so as to give a participation to each, either equal, or according to some other defined proportion. Such a division of the water has, so far as the Lord Ordinary knows, never been sanctioned; and, practically, any attempt at apportionment would lead to disputes of daily occurrence, and disputes probably interminable, as the proportion between the respective lands could not be defined by any satisfactory ratio, or any which would not be liable to incessant fluctuation. In the view of the Lord Ordinary, the upper heritor has a preference over the lower, arising from the nature of his position – but a preference which is limited to the use of water for primary purposes.'

The interlocutor of the Lord Ordinary in this case was recalled[119] but the Inner House did not express an opinion on the issue of regulation. It appears, therefore, that the ability of the court to regulate such matters has been left open.

7-41. An owner is not confined to taking water through pitchers and buckets but can construct pipes or channels to lead water away,[120] even though this may involve operations on the banks or *alveus*. This rule is the

---

[114] Kames, *Principles* 51. See also 53–54.

[115] Again, it is possible that there would be a limitation on appropriation in this situation, see above, paras 7-34–7-36.

[116] Rankine, *Landownership* 555. See also Ferguson 240.

[117] See below, paras 7-89–7-92.

[118] (1861) 23 D 496 at 499.

[119] At 505. The interlocutor was recalled in so far as it found *inter alia* that the downstream owner's rights were subject to the upstream owner's prior use. However, the upstream owner's use seemed to be objectionable with regard to the method of abstraction (diverting water for primary purposes by an artificial channel and not ensuring the surplus was returned) rather than the use itself.

[120] *Ogilvy v Kincaid* (1791) Mor 12824, Hume 508; *Johnstone v Ritchie* (1822) 1 S 327; *Hood v Williamsons* (1861) 23 D 496.

same between opposite proprietors as between successive proprietors.[121] Any works constructed, however, will probably have to be carried out with as little waste as possible[122] and any surplus must be returned.[123] This latter rule shows the continuing influence of the compromise reached in the case of *Cunningham v Kennedy*.[124] The onus is on the consuming party to show this requirement has been met.[125]

(II) POLLUTION AS A PRIMARY PURPOSE

7-42.   So far, the discussion of the limits within which an owner can use water for primary purposes has been confined to consumption. At one time, it seemed that the polluting of water with material such as sewage would not be seen as a breach of common interest if it was an incident of the occupation of land. In the case of *Dunn v Hamilton*,[126] Lord Jeffrey charged the jury that 'for all the necessary purposes of occupation of land and of ordinary life, not only was the abstraction of the water of a running stream permitted to the proprietors on the banks of that stream as it passed their property, but also such deterioration of the water, as might be ultimately fatal to its use by inferior heritors'. On appeal, Lord Gillies in the Inner House expressed doubts as to this statement, commenting that it was 'too broadly laid down to be supported'.[127] It was thereafter quickly established that it was not part of the preferential primary purposes to pollute a river.[128] In *Duke of Buccleuch v Cowan*[129] it was stated that an 'upper heritor is entitled to the free use of the water as it flows through his ground, but he is not entitled to pollute it to the injury of the under heritors by destroying its use for primary purposes. He cannot pollute it with filth, or otherwise adulterate it so as to render it noxious and unwholesome to the rest.' Pollution as a breach of common interest will be further considered below.[130]

[121] See *Johnstone v Ritchie* (1822) 1 S 327 and *Morris v Bicket* (1864) 2 M 1086 at 1093 concerning opposite proprietors; *Ogilvy v Kincaid* (1791) Mor 12824, Hume 508 and *Hood v Williamsons* (1861) 23 D 496 concerning successive proprietors.
[122] *Johnstone v Ritchie* (1822) 1 S 327.
[123] *Ogilvy v Kincaid* (1791) Mor 12824; *Hood v Williamsons* (1861) 23 D 496.
[124] (1713) Mor 8903 and 12778. Explained below, paras 7-69–7-71.
[125] *Hood v Williamsons* (1861) 23 D 496.
[126] (1837) 15 S 853 at 858.
[127] At 860. The decision of the Inner House that the judge had erred in directing the jury was upheld on appeal to the House of Lords (1838) 3 S & McL 356.
[128] *Montgomerie v Buchanan's Trs* (1853) 15 D 853; *Duke of Buccleuch v Cowan* (1866) 5 M 214; *Caledonian Railway Co v Baird & Co* (1876) 3 R 839. In the latter case where pollution resulted from the building of a mining village, Lord Gifford stated at 848: 'If he cannot erect a village without polluting this stream, and, it may be, depriving his neighbours of their only supply of pure water, then he can let the village alone.' See also *Dumfries Waterworks Commissioners v McCulloch* (1874) 1 R 975 at 978 where, although not being an action solely between the owners of land containing a loch, it is said that the right to pollute a loch to the detriment of primary purposes was not included in the rights of an owner. See also J C C Broun, *Law of Nuisance in Scotland* (1891) 12–15.
[129] (1866) 5 M 214 at 226. See also 232.
[130] See below paras 7-54–7-59.

(c) Operations Interfering with the Natural Flow

(I) CONSUMPTION AND DETENTION

7-43. The freedom to consume water for primary purposes is accompanied by restrictions on consumption for other purposes. The first aspect of natural flow considered by Lord Neaves in *Morris v Bicket*[131] is the right to have water transmitted undiminished in quantity. This means that owners are subject to common interest obligations regarding the amount of water that can be consumed for secondary purposes.[132] 'Secondary' purposes are all the remaining uses of water such as agricultural[133] or commercial uses.[134] Kames gives the examples of use of water for irrigation, to power a grain-mill or for a bleachfield.[135]

7-44. The extent to which owners can consume water for secondary purposes has been subject to conflicting authority. Rankine suggests that water may be consumed for irrigation which 'is a secondary use, to which the same considerations of necessity do not apply. On the other hand, agriculture has always been a favourite with the law; and the rule which prohibits any artificial diminution of the natural flow will not be enforced with the same strictness as in the case of manufactures properly so called.'[136] To back up this proposition, the French *Code civil* Art 644 and French writer Jean-Marie Pardessus' *Traité des Servitudes*[137] are cited. This authority, although of interest, is of little help in determining Scots law. The other authorities mentioned by Rankine are *Beaton v Ogilvie*[138] and *Kelso v Boyds*.[139] In the first of these cases irrigation, not being put beyond challenge by prescription, was prohibited, and in the second an upstream owner was held entitled to divert a river within his own lands and let it overflow his meadows as long as the river was returned to its course.[140] *Kelso v Boyds* is a precarious foundation for the proposition that consumption of water through irrigation is allowed. This case was decided before a rationale for common interest was

---

[131] (1864) 2 M 1082.

[132] At 1092–1093. See also Reid, *Property* para 288; Gordon & Wortley, *Land Law* para 6-31.

[133] Although, presumably, allowing the use of water to grow fruit and vegetables for consumption on the adjacent land would be defined as a primary purpose. See Ferguson's definition quoted above.

[134] See Kames, *Principles* 51. See further *Cruikshanks and Bell v Henderson* (1791) Mor 506; *Ogilvy v Kincaid* (1791) Mor 12824, Hume 508 concerning consumption for a distillery; *Marquis of Abercorn v Jamieson* (1791) Hume 510 concerning a colliery and salt-works. It must be remembered, however, that these cases were decided before the settlement of the right to natural flow.

[135] Kames, *Principles* 50–51, although Kames does not use the term 'secondary' uses.

[136] Rankine, *Landownership* 555. French authority is cited in some pivotal English cases in the 19th century, see Getzler 272.

[137] (6th edn, 1823) Art 105.

[138] (1670) Mor 10912.

[139] (1768) Mor 12807, Hailes 224.

[140] This is not clear from reading the report, but see Petition of Boyds 9 Dec 1767 (Robert MacQueen), *Kelso v Boyds* Pitfour Collection Vol 39, Paper 17.

established,[141] before any attempt had been made to distinguish primary and secondary uses,[142] and before the development of the right to natural flow.[143]

7-45.   In the absence of any relevant authority to the effect that use for irrigation or agriculture is given special preference,[144] it is suggested that all types of consumption for secondary purposes can be viewed together. Hume's view is that an upstream owner can take water for secondary purposes, with little regard to the interests of downstream owners, provided the river is not diverted from its natural channel.[145] A full explanation of why Hume takes this view is given in Chapter 6. Here, it is sufficient to say that Hume seems to be relying primarily on *Lyon and Gray v Bakers of Glasgow*[146] as authority for these statements.[147] Again, this case was decided before the doctrinal foundation of common interest was ascertained and the right to natural flow established.

7-46.   That the position of consumption for secondary purposes was still a vexed question at the end of the 19th century is seen in the judgment of the Lord Ordinary in *Milton v Glen-Moray Glenlivet Distillery Co Ltd*:[148]

> 'It is said to be the law of Scotland that no water can be taken from a running stream, except for primary purposes. It is said, on the other hand, that the law of Scotland, while not perhaps going so far as the law of America, permits, like the law of England, abstraction for manufacturing uses to a reasonable extent – the question of reasonableness being one of degree, and the test being whether the domestic or other primary uses are materially abridged. I reserve my opinion on that question until it arises, as it some day must.'

It is surprising that, although this statement was made over one hundred years ago, the issue is still not settled. Further, in *Morris v Bicket*,[149] the right to natural flow seems to apply to all water apart from that used for primary purposes. Therefore, consumption for secondary purposes must not interfere materially with natural flow, which includes the quantity of water. Rankine gives a good summary when he states in regard to commercial purposes that the 'true question for the jury'[150] will be, whether, taking all the circumstances

---

[141] By *Magistrates of Linlithgow v Elphinstone (No 2)* (1768) Mor 12805, Hailes 203.

[142] In *Miller v Stein* (1791) Mor 12823, Bell's Octavo Cases 334; *Russell v Haig* (1791) Mor 12823, Bell's Octavo Cases 338.

[143] For which see above, paras 6-20–6-54.

[144] A more recent case which touches on the issue of irrigation is *Mackenzie v Woddrop* (1854) 16 D 381. However, the report merely concerns whether there is a relevant issue to be determined and the pursuer had used the water of a river from time immemorial so any right to use water for irrigation may have been based on prescription.

[145] Hume, *Lectures* III 217. See also Hume's commentary to *Ogilvy v Kincaid* (1791) Hume 508 at 509.

[146] (1749) Mor 12789.

[147] Bell, who makes a similar, though less radical, statement to Hume also cites this case: Bell, *Principles* para 1107.

[148] (1898) 1 F 135 at 142–143. The reference to reasonableness in this quote cannot be relied upon. See discussion at paras 7-14–7-17 above.

[149] (1864) 2 M 1082 at 1092–1093 (Lord Neaves).

[150] On the use of civil juries during this period see J W Cairns, ''The Dearest Birth Right of the People of England': The Civil Jury in Modern Scottish Legal History' in J W Cairns and G McLeod (eds), *The Jury in the History of the Common Law* (2002); A M Hajducki, *Civil Jury Trials* (2006) 15–25.

into consideration – the size of the stream, the amount of water consumed, the times of diverting it – there is a material injury to the lower heritor's right to have the stream flowing down to him undiminished in quantity'.[151] Landowners are not entitled to evade their obligation by taking water and replacing it from another source.[152] In summary, a proprietor can consume water for secondary purposes but there are many restrictions in favour of other owners to observe and so any legitimate use may be minimal.[153] This is the result of the development of the right to natural flow within a period when the availability of water for primary purposes was being threatened.[154] Restricting the consumption of water for secondary purposes can be seen as compatible with the categorisation of water as a communal thing, the use of which is principally reserved for basic needs.

7-47. Although without actual consumption, the quantity of water might be reduced by detention, either temporary or permanent. This is also subject to restriction if it causes a material alteration of the flow.[155] Rankine's view that 'every case will turn on its special circumstances, and on the determination of the question "whether under all the circumstances of the case the use is reasonable and consistent with a corresponding enjoyment of right by the other party"'[156] is, as Reid has pointed out,[157] too widely stated and again relies on the erroneous idea that rights regarding water are regulated by a reasonableness principle.[158]

(II) ADDITION?

7-48. In *Morris v Bicket*,[159] Lord Neaves only mentions diminishing the quantity of water and does not consider the opposite situation of owners augmenting the flow of a river or loch. What obligations are placed on owners in this regard? If the addition materially affects the force or natural direction of the flow, this would be prohibited under Lord Neaves' description of the

---

[151] Rankine, *Landownership* 558. See also Ferguson 242, although Rankine's reference (at 557) to 'ordinary' and 'extraordinary' uses is an unfortunate Anglicism at Rankine. Ferguson copies Rankine's reference.

[152] *Cowan v Lord Kinnaird* (1865) 4 M 236; *Stevenson v Hogganfield Bleaching Co* (1892) 30 SLR 86; Gordon & Wortley, *Land Law* para 6-31. In *Cowan*, the amount of water diverted was not greater than that thrown into the river by the artificial draining of *stagnum*. In *Stevenson*, water abstracted for use in bleaching was replaced by a supply from Loch Katrine.

[153] See Reid, *Property* para 288. Compare with Whitty, 'Water' 450; Gordon & Wortley, *Land Law* para 6-32 and see discussion below.

[154] See above, paras 6-02–6-05 and 6-51–6-54.

[155] *Marquis of Abercorn v Jamieson* (1791) Hume 510; *Lord Glenlee v Gordon* (1804) Mor 12834; *Hunter and Aitkenhead v Aitken* (1880) 7 R 510. See also Ferguson 233–237; Reid, *Property* para 293.

[156] Rankine, *Landownership* 550.

[157] Reid, *Property* para 293 n 4.

[158] The statement in *Marquis of Abercorn v Jamieson* at 511 that a proprietor has to reconcile his/her use with a 'neighbour's reasonable rights' is relied upon by Rankine. See discussion of this comment at paras 7-14–7-17 above.

[159] (1864) 2 M 1082.

right of natural flow.[160] How to analyse an increase which affects other aspects of the flow is not specified.

7-49. However, there are statements elsewhere which suggest that the protection of the right of natural flow includes a prohibition on material increases. Lord Macnaghten in *Young & Co v Bankier Distillery Co*[161] said that every owner is 'entitled to the water of his stream in its natural flow without sensible diminution or increase'. Yet, caution should be exercised in relying on a summary of the law which is obviously influenced by English authority.[162] Lord Moncreiff in *Lord Blantyre v Dunn*[163] when referring to a proprietor stated, 'I take it to be beyond question, that, if he chose, he would be entitled to object to any thing, beyond his neighbour's primary uses of the stream, that altered its nature. I am not aware of any ground on which the owner of a stream is bound to let its character be changed by artificial augmentation.' Similar comments were made in *Irving v Leadhills Mining Co*,[164] these being followed by the Lord Ordinary in *Blair v Hunter Finlay & Co*[165] and not challenged on appeal. Lord Young in *Filshill v Campbell*[166] equated increasing the flow of water with an erection on the *alveus*,[167] the latter undoubtedly being an aspect of natural flow protection. Some writers also take the same view. Ross Stewart states in the context of mining that an upper owner on a river 'must send down the same quantity of water as he receives. He must neither add to it nor diminish it'.[168] Rankine and Gordon make similar comments.[169] Thus, although not included in the seminal definition of Lord Neaves, it is suggested that each owner along a river or loch has a right to the natural flow unaugmented in quantity and there is a corresponding obligation on every owner.

7-50. This right, however, is subject to the qualification that owners cannot object to a change in the flow caused by the more efficient drainage of upstream lands unless there was a material alteration in the force or direction.[170] Such operations are within the rights of a landowner due to the natural servitude on the lower land to receive surface water.[171] Therefore, the operations which will breach common interest will be those such as pumping up water from underground and discharging it into a river or diverting a stream's course so that it joins and augments another river.

---

[160] At 1092.

[161] (1893) 20 R (HL) 76 at 78.

[162] See discussion above, paras 7-14–7-17.

[163] (1848) 10 D 509 at 547.

[164] (1856) 18 D 833 at 841–842.

[165] (1870) 9 M 204 at 206–207.

[166] (1887) 14 R 592. See also *Colquhoun's Trs v Orr Ewing* (1877) 4 R (HL) 116 at 126–127

[167] (1887) 14 R 592 at 595.

[168] D Ross Stewart, *A Treatise on the Law Relating to Mines, Quarries and Mines in Scotland* (1894) at 226.

[169] Rankine, *Landownership* 553; Gordon & Wortley, *Land Law* para 6-30. See also Ferguson 320–321.

[170] Rankine, *Landownership* 553; Gordon & Wortley, *Land Law* para 6-30.

[171] See generally Reid, *Property* para 340; Gordon &Wortley, *Land Law* para 6-62.

7-51. In certain circumstances, it seems the augmented flow can become part of the natural flow and be protected by common interest.[172] The case of *Macgregor v Moncreiffe's Trs*[173] was mentioned above in regard to the point that, if water will only form a perennial flow through the upkeep of artificial operations, the land through which the water flows will not be subject to common interest. A similar rule seems to be applied to artificial additions. It appears that in order to constitute part of a natural flow, the addition needs to have a 'permanent origin or character'.[174] This suggests that water introduced through artificial operations does not qualify if it requires the continuation of such operations to exist and, also, probably that the augmented flow should have a natural source.[175]

7-52. In any event, the augmented flow must persist for some period of time before it becomes protected by common interest. In *Lord Blantyre v Dunn*[176] there were differing views as to whether this was the prescriptive period or less. Lord Justice-Clerk Hope stated that, once the augmented flow is formed and fairly established, it is protected by common interest.[177] Lords Medwyn and Moncreiff required the full prescriptive period which, at the time, was 40 years. This latter view is preferable, as once the period of negative prescription passes,[178] the augmenting water is no longer in breach of common interest and this would accord with when the downstream owners acquire the right to the augmented flow. The basis of this right, however, is unfortunately unclear. Rankine, Ferguson and Reid view the acquisition of a right to the continuation of a supply as being the acquisition of a servitude.[179] However, there will often not be any positive acts carried out by the purported benefited proprietor on the purported burdened property, and in *Lord Blantyre v Dunn*[180] it was said the issue was less one of servitude and more one of property.

7-53. In *Heggie v Nairn*[181] opinion was reserved as to whether use of the additional water for the prescriptive period by a downstream owner (rather than mere existence of the enhanced flow) could result in a right to a water supply which requires the upkeep of artificial operations. However, it was

---

[172] See *Lord Blantyre v Dunn* (1848) 10 D 509; *Mackenzie v Woddrop* (1854) 16 D 381.

[173] Unreported 7 Sept 1936 at 40. The various decisions of this case are available in the National Archives of Scotland: NAS02024 SC49-7-1933-6-00001, CS258/2048 and CS258/2049.

[174] *Irving v Leadhills Mining Co* (1856) 18 D 833 at 838.

[175] The natural flow will therefore generally not include water produced through mining. See *Irving v Leadhills Mining Co*; *Blair v Hunter Finlay & Co* (1870) 9 M 204; *Heggie v Nairn* (1882) 9 R 704. See also the comments in *Munro v Ross* (1846) 8 D 1029 at 1036; Rankine, *Landownership* 529.

[176] (1848) 10 D 509 followed by *Mackenzie v Woddrop* (1854) 16 D 381.

[177] At 525.

[178] For the explanation of why this is negative prescription, see discussion below, paras 7-101–7-105.

[179] Rankine, *Landownership* 576–577; Ferguson 277–581; Reid, *Property* para 286.

[180] (1848) 10 D 509 at 534. Compare with the discussion of prescription below, paras 7-101–7-105.

[181] (1882) 9 R 704 at 709.

not clear what right could be acquired through such use. It could not be a servitude as the downstream owner was not exercising any rights over the upstream lands. It would be highly unlikely for the right acquired to be based on common interest as positive obligations are extremely rare, or even non-existent, in the case of rivers and lochs. The Sheriff in *Macgregor v Moncreiffe's Trs* held that use for the prescriptive period does not constitute a right to the continuation of operations creating a perennial flow[182] and it is suggested that the same rule be adopted for augmented supply. This finding makes sense as the contrary would mean that a landowner may have to carry on activities such as mining merely to protect the use of water by a downstream owner.

(iii) POLLUTION

7-54.   Linked to the preceding discussion concerning addition of water is consideration of pollution. The previous discussion was based on the premise that the water augmenting the flow was pure and unpolluted. Different considerations apply if it is not. Pollution is regulated by both private and public law.[183] Within private law, there is a possibility that an action could be raised in either common interest or nuisance. However, the literature on the subject makes for confusing reading. The modern tendency is to consider pollution of water in the context of nuisance.[184] Broun in his late-Victorian treatise on nuisance mentions common interest as giving title to object to pollution by upstream owners,[185] although it is not clear whether he thinks this is a ground of objection separate from nuisance. Hume, Bell and Rankine all consider pollution as part of water rights rather than nuisance.[186] Whitty states that one reason behind this is that Hume thought that nuisance was applicable only in the burgh which justified separate consideration of pollution under common interest.[187] This separate consideration may just have been copied by Bell. Rankine treats rights of landowners relating to rivers and lochs within a chapter on water which is separate from his chapter on nuisance but states: 'Such being the natural rights incident to riparian ownership, with respect to natural flow and volume of a stream, any infringement of them is a nuisance.'[188] Similar claims are made with regard to pollution which suggests that Rankine saw breach of common interest as nuisance.[189]

[182] Unreported 7 Sept 1936 at 42.

[183] For a summary of public law regulation see Gordon & Wortley, *Land Law* paras 6-41–6-51.

[184] J C C Broun, *Law of Nuisance in Scotland* (1891) Ch 2; Ferguson Part VI, Ch 1 (although Ferguson deals with pollution in a separate chapter wherein it is suggested that he is primarily considering pollution under nuisance, pollution is also briefly mentioned in a chapter on riparian rights and obligations at 242–243); Whitty, 'Water' 460–461; Whitty, 'Nuisance' para 79; Gordon & Wortley, *Land Law* para 6-34.

[185] Broun, *Nuisance* (n 184) at 11.

[186] Hume, *Lectures* III 220–221; Bell, *Principles* para 1106; Rankine, *Landownership* 561–571.

[187] Whitty, 'Water' 460; Hume, *Lectures* III 213–214.

[188] Rankine, *Landownership* 560.

[189] Rankine, *Landownership* 567. Rankine's approach indicates a retreat from regarding common interest as a servitude and shows influence of a 'soft' or English concept of real rights.

7-55. A potential source of the confusion is that the history of common interest and nuisance are intertwined. Most pollution cases concern the destruction of water for primary purposes. The distinction between primary and secondary uses was developed by Kames in the context of common interest,[190] separate from nuisance,[191] but under consideration of the same principle that one should not use one's rights in a manner that directly harms another.[192] In the cases of *Miller v Stein*[193] and *Russell v Haig*,[194] the distinction between primary and secondary uses was accepted, and it was said that polluting a river was analogous to diverting it as it prevented the use of the water for primary purposes further downstream. The primary/secondary distinction was carried forward and used in subsequent cases concerning diversion or consumption in common interest and pollution in nuisance. Thus, these cases are pivotal for both doctrines as, though being based on nuisance, they had obvious implications for common interest.

7-56. At the time of *Miller* and *Russell*, rules on water use had been developing incrementally for over a century and yet the doctrinal basis of common interest had only just been established, whereas nuisance, although having some basis in Roman law, was at the beginning of a quickening period of development, fed by English law influence and the socio-economic changes of the Industrial Revolution.[195] Hume and Bell wrote shortly after this transitional period. In the modern law, nuisance is still a topic of academic dispute and a common action in the courts, whereas common interest has been marginalised and is hardly litigated. This may explain why there is more emphasis on nuisance being the ground of action for pollution.

7-57. However, there is authority in case law that common interest provides a distinct ground of action. In *Duke of Buccleuch v Cowan*,[196] which was an action founded on nuisance, Lord Neaves stated:

'when a party pollutes running water, of which each proprietor has only what has been called a usufruct,[197] he is not operating *in suo*, – he is operating *in alieno*.[198] The water running in a stream having a definite channel, is destined to go to the lower heritor by its physical position; the water that is passing the upper heritor's door is ticketed and kept sacred for the primary purposes of life to that lower heritor; and any use of it which goes beyond that is an encroachment on the rights of our neighbour. Therefore the wrong-doer is not operating *in suo*, for he is trespassing on rights which belong to one who has a common interest in the whole stream; and when you come to encroach upon that, your position is very different from that of a person who merely makes additional noise, or who has a chimney which gives forth a little more smoke than others, and where all

---

[190] Kames, *Principles* 50–51.
[191] Kames, *Principles* 49. Kames may have also believed that nuisance was confined to the burgh.
[192] Kames, *Principles* 45–49.
[193] (1791) Mor 12823, Bell's Octavo Cases 334.
[194] (1791) Mor 12823, Bell's Octavo Cases 338.
[195] Whitty, 'Nuisance' paras 7–16.
[196] (1866) 5 M 214 at 238.
[197] For discussion of the use of this term, see above, para 6-16.
[198] This is an allusion to the *immissio* principle, see above, paras 5-36–5-39.

circumstances must be taken into view, because it depends on rights of a totally different kind.'

This interesting quotation suggests that where pollution affects primary purposes, common interest provides a ground of objection to pollution and also that the obligations of common interest will impose a higher standard than nuisance. Lord Neaves also mentions the right to have water 'unpolluted in quality'[199] as part of natural flow in *Morris v Bicket*. Further, in *Young & Co v Bankier Distillery Co*[200] the House of Lords decided that owners could prevent pollution even though the water would still be suitable for primary purposes. This latter decision appears to be based on common interest and it was said that every 'riparian proprietor is thus entitled to the water of his stream, in its natural flow...without sensible alteration in its character or quality'.[201] Although aspects of the judgment in this case should not be relied upon,[202] the suggestion that any material alteration in the natural quality of the water can be prevented seems well founded.[203]

7-58. The balance of authority is that there is an independent ground of objection to pollution in common interest.[204] Whitty explains that it 'is thought that under Scots law, in principle, common interest and nuisance relate as overlapping rather than mutually exclusive categories'.[205] The issue becomes important if the requirements of each area of law are different. As Reid comments, the 'significance of a common interest remedy supplementary to the established remedy in nuisance is that with common interest the standard imposed on the defender may be higher; for, on analogy with other common interest obligations, any material deterioration in the quality of the water is an infringement of common interest.'[206] Whitty also comments that riparian rights should be higher than non-riparian rights and that in 'common interest, the test of infringement is interference with natural flow otherwise than for legally protected "primary" purposes. In nuisance the "*plus quam tolerabile*" test of liability depends much more on a balancing of interests and is more elastic and uncertain.'[207]

7-59. It appears, therefore, that the obligations placed on owners under common interest are stricter than those under nuisance. It is important to distinguish between pollution which destroys primary uses and pollution which does not or where a river or loch is already unfit for primary uses and is subject to additional pollution.[208] Affecting the use of water for primary

---

[199] (1864) 2 M 1082 at 1092.

[200] (1893) 20 R (HL) 76.

[201] At 78.

[202] See discussion above, paras 7-14–7-17.

[203] See Reid, *Property* para 299.

[204] See discussion in Reid, *Property* paras 298–299.

[205] Whitty, 'Water' 461 n 389. See also Whitty, 'Nuisance' para 31.

[206] Reid, *Property* para 299.

[207] Whitty, 'Water' 461 n 389. See also Whitty, 'Nuisance' para 31.

[208] Under nuisance, although the cases involving a destruction of primary uses have not referred to the balancing of different interests, it seems this is the modern law: Whitty, *Nuisance* para 31, although compare with para 79.

purposes would automatically be deemed a material interference with natural flow:[209] this is the import of the passage from Lord Neaves from *Duke of Buccleuch v Cowan*[210] cited above. If, on the other hand, a river or loch is polluted in such a way as does not affect primary uses, such as by changing the natural qualities of the water by heating it[211] or rendering soft water hard,[212] this is an issue of natural flow: to breach common interest any pollution will need to be a material alteration in the quality of the water. Where a river or loch has already been polluted and is no longer suitable for primary purposes, it is suggested that any material addition to the pollution is also actionable under common interest although, again, most of the cases dealing with this issue have been decided on the basis of nuisance.[213]

(IV) OPERATIONS ON THE *ALVEUS*

7-60. Each owner has a right to the natural flow unaffected in force, direction and current. One of the most obvious ways to interfere with these aspects of flow is through operations on the *alveus*.[214] That there are obligations on owners with respect to operations on the *alveus* was established at an early stage, and those which materially affect the flow of the river or loch are prohibited.[215] This prohibition does not prevent operations to provide land with water for primary purposes.[216] If, in performing operations on the *alveus*, an owner uses another owner's section of *alveus*, this is prohibited on the separate ground of encroachment even if there is no material interference with the natural flow.[217]

[209] A good factual example of this, although not a common interest case, is *Dumfries Waterworks Commissioners v McCulloch* (1874) 1 R 975 where a farmer was prohibited from washing his sheep in a loch when they had been dipped in arsenic even though it was not actually proven to have an effect on the water. In relation to this water supply see also the earlier case of *McCulloch v Dumfries and Maxwelltown Waterworks Commissioners* (1863) 1 M 334.

[210] (1866) 5 M 214.

[211] Rankine, *Landownership* 562 n 53; *Russell v Haig* (1791) Mor 12823, Bell's Octavo Cases 338

[212] *Young & Co v Bankier Distillery Co* (1893) 20 R (HL) 76.

[213] See Whitty, 'Nuisance' para 79. Whitty also comments 'that "primary use" should in principle give a riparian owner a defence to a nuisance action because a non-riparian suing in nuisance should not in principle have a higher right than a riparian suing under common interest:' Whitty, 'Water' 461 n 389. However, it is difficult to think of a situation when this would result for, as explained above, use for primary purposes does not justify pollution.

[214] Discussion of this topic as separate from diversion, consumption or detention is to a certain extent artificial as all will probably include operations on the *alveus*. However, common interest obligations cover operations which do less than divert the water of a river and those which are not for the purpose of consuming or detaining water.

[215] Bell, *Principles* paras 1102 and 1108; Hume, *Lectures* III 221 and 224; Rankine, *Landownership* 538–540; Ferguson 227–228; Reid, *Property* para 296; Gordon & Wortley, *Land Law* paras 6-52–6-60.

[216] *Ogilvy v Kincaid* (1791) Mor 12824, Hume 508; *Johnstone v Ritchie* (1822) 1 S 327; *Hood v Williamsons* (1861) 23 D 496.

[217] See the opinion of the Lord Ordinary in *McGavin v McIntyre* (1890) 17 R 818 at 824. This analysis was not challenged on appeal to the Inner House or House of Lords (1893) 20 R (HL) 49. See also Reid, *Property* para 175.

7-61.   An operation on the *alveus* on one side of a river was the situation at issue in *Morris v Bicket*.[218] The owner opposite objected. The court said that owners have:

'an interest in the whole of the *alveus*, and for this obvious reason, that no operation can, by the nature of things, be performed upon one half of the *alveus*, that shall not affect the flow of the water in the whole...If it will operate prejudicially; nay, if it will materially operate at all; if it will bring water to one side of the stream, or take it from it, either deepening the channel or making it more shallow, the interests of the other proprietor are thereby affected, and he is entitled to interpose and say that he will not consent. We all know what an empirical affair this operation of water is.'

This prohibition is broad and covers building operations,[219] taking away parts of the *alveus*[220] or merely affecting the natural condition of the bed of the river or loch.[221]

7-62.   Hume states that proprietors are entitled to perform operations to restore a river to its original *alveus* after its course has been altered by extraordinary floods[222] and this view has been accepted by some modern commentators.[223] Although, there is very little authority directly on this point,[224] it would seem to be an acceptable and common-sense rule. It appears that any restoration must take place within a reasonable space of time from the change.[225] In *Magistrates of Aberdeen v Menzies*,[226] a case decided before the establishment of the right of natural flow, restoration was not allowed as the period of time which had elapsed since the river last changed course was deemed too long.[227] But the period suggested is less than the period of prescription and it is said that the length of time within which operations

[218] (1864) 2 M 1082 at 1093 (Lord Neaves).

[219] See for example *Earl of Kinnoull v Keir* 18 Jan 1814 FC; *Duke of Roxburghe v Waldie* (1821) Hume 524; *Menzies v Breadalbane* (1828) 2 W & S 235; *Jackson v Marshall* (1872) 10 M 913; *Duke of Roxburghe v Waldie's Trs* (1879) 6 R 663; *McGavin v McIntyre Brothers* (1893) 20 R (HL) 49.

[220] See *Robertson v Foote* (1879) 6 R 1290 (concerning salmon fishing but much was said about landowners' rights).

[221] See *Lanark Twist Co v Edmonstone* (1810) Hume 520; *Morris v Bicket* (1864) 2 M 1082 at 1093. See also Rankine, *Landownership* 538–540; Ferguson 227; Gordon & Wortley, *Land Law* para 6-60.

[222] Hume, *Lectures* III 224.

[223] See Reid, *Property* para 285; Gordon & Wortley, *Land Law* para 6-56.

[224] The cases cited in this context include *Town of Nairn v Brodie* (1738) Mor 12779 and *Mather v Macbraire* (1873) 11 M 522 which concern operations by owners of the banks on the *alveus* of the (then public) navigable rivers; *Duke of Gordon v Duff* (1735) Mor 12778 where a bulwark was allowed to be constructed to prevent the gradual encroachment of a river upon giving a bond of caution to indemnify potential damage; *Menzies v Breadalbane* (1828) 3 W & S 235 at 244 where it was stated that an owner may protect his or her land from extraordinary floods but not that he or she can restore the *alveus* after a flood; *Magistrates of Aberdeen v Menzies* (1748) Mor 12787 where alteration was not allowed.

[225] Hume, *Lectures* III 225; Gordon & Wortley, *Land Law* para 6-56.

[226] (1748) Mor 12787.

[227] The period which had elapsed varies in the different reports between 17 and 20 years: see (1748) Mor 12787 at 12787.

must be carried out 'must in the nature of the thing be *arbitrii*'.[228] This uncertainty is regrettable and perhaps a better view would be that the *alveus* may be restored within the 20-year period of negative prescription after which common interest obligations will apply to the new natural flow.[229] Although there may be a right to carry out restoration, there is certainly no obligation to do so. Further, there is no obligation on proprietors to clear silt or other debris which naturally accumulates and interferes with flow.[230] This is consistent with the notion that common interest with regard to rivers and lochs does not impose positive obligations.[231]

(v) Operations On The Banks

7-63.   Operations on the banks – or foreshore of a tidal river or loch – are much less likely to interfere with the natural flow, but there is still a possibility for interference with a neighbour's rights through, for example, building bulwarks to protect one's land against floods which throw water on to the opposite land. For this reason the banks – and by extension of the principle the foreshore – are subject to common interest obligations.[232]

7-64.   The content of the obligations has been subject to conflicting authority.[233] The case of *Farquharson v Farquharson*[234] decided that an owner was entitled to build a bulwark against floods even if the opposite land was damaged as a result. Kames[235] and Hume[236] make similar comments. Erskine, however, states that an owner is not entitled to build on the banks to the prejudice of opposite land.[237] The issue was reconsidered in *Menzies v Breadalbane*,[238] a decision confirmed and explained by *Morris v Bicket*.[239] A distinction was made between fortifying a bank and raising an embankment. The former comprises 'converting a bank which is friable – of mud or of gravel – into a solid mass, which is the proper meaning of *munire ripam*; to convert

---

[228] (1748) Mor 12787 at 12787.

[229] However, the basis of this would be unclear. Compare with the discussion of prescription below, paras 7-101–7-105.

[230] *Hope v Govenors of Heriot's Hospital* (1878) 15 SLR 400.

[231] Gordon & Wortley, *Land Law* para 6-53. The deficiencies of common interest led Parliament to enact various statutes such as Land Drainage (Scotland) Act 1930, see Gordon & Wortley, *Land Law* paras 6-64–6-82. However, at least as regards the 1930 Act, these provisions appear to have been little better at imposing a positive obligation to maintain: see *Armstrong v Sproat* (1988) in R R M Paisley and D J Cusine, *Unreported Property Cases from the Sheriff Courts* (2000) at 482.

[232] *Menzies v Breadalbane* (1828) 3 W & S 235 at 243; *Morris v Bicket* (1864) 2 M 1082 at 1087; Reid, *Property* para 297.

[233] The confusion on this issue may stem from Roman law. Compare D.39.3.1.2 (Ulpian) regarding surface water with D.43.15.1 (Ulpian) and D.43.13.6–7 (Ulpian) regarding rivers. See also *Duke of Gordon v Duff* (1735) Mor 12778.

[234] (1741) Mor 12779.

[235] Kames, *Principles* 48.

[236] Hume, *Lectures* III 210 and 224.

[237] Erskine, *Institute* II.1.5.

[238] (1828) 3 W & S 235.

[239] (1864) 2 M 1082.

into solid stone that which is friable, and thus to prevent the river from making a change upon the bank by its flow'.[240] This method is 'within the power of a riparian proprietor. He is there making no change; he is keeping things as they are; he is not preventing the river from flowing in its ordinary course; he is only securing that it shall flow in time to come, as it has in times past, in that course'.[241] Thus, fortifying a bank in this way is permitted.[242]

7-65. The other method, of raising an embankment, is in a different position.[243] Lord Benholme summarises: if an embankment is constructed 'so close to the river as that when a flood occurs it alters the course of the river, and does not allow the flood water to escape in the natural way, partly by overflowing one bank, and partly by overflowing another, but secures the one at the expense of the other, then you derive, from the principle that one is not allowed to use his property to injure his neighbour, the conclusion that that is an illegal operation'.[244] Owners are thus not entitled to raise embankments even if the aim is purely to protect their own land.

7-66. It can be seen that Lord Benholme uses the principle prohibiting prejudicial use of property. A preferable analysis is to say that owners are not entitled to execute works on the banks which materially interfere with the force, natural direction or current of the water including ordinary seasonal variations. Raising an embankment will be likely to interfere with the natural flow but fortifying a bank will not.

7-67. If operations on the banks or foreshore are analysed in terms of the right to natural flow, this has implications for whether damage needs to be proved. There is some authority from Lord Benholme himself that an objecting party must prove that damage has been caused or is anticipated.[245] However, this is inconsistent with the general position that common interest is breached whenever there is a material interference with the natural flow. It will then be open to the court, if it wishes, to refuse to grant interdict if it is proved there is little or no likelihood of damage.[246] Reflecting the natural flow analysis, Rankine states that 'the *onus* will lie on the builder, similar to that which is imposed on the erector of a structure *in alveo*, of showing that

---

[240] At 1090–1091. This distinction is based on the report by James Jardine submitted to the court in *Menzies v Breadalbane*. Jardine was an engineer who was heavily involved in matters concerning water in Scotland in the early 19th century and he was consulted in many water rights cases. See also *Aitchison v Magistrates of Glasgow* (1823) 2 S 377; *Lord Melville v Denniston* (1842) 4 D 1231.

[241] (1864) 2 M 1082 at 1091.

[242] Bell, *Principles* para 971; Rankine, *Landownership* 540–541; Ferguson 213–214 and 228; Reid, *Property* para 297.

[243] *Morris v Bicket* (1864) 2 M 1082 at 1091. See Bell, *Principles* para 297 (see also para 1102 which mentions bulwarks but seems to be actually concerned with operations on the *alveus*); Rankine, *Landownership* 542; Ferguson 213–214 and 228; Reid, *Property* para 297.

[244] (1864) 2 M 1082 at 1091.

[245] See *Morris v Bicket* at 1090 (see also Lord Justice-Clerk Inglis at 1089); *Jackson v Marshall* (1872) 10 M 913 at 919. See also Reid, *Property* para 297 n 1. Although *Johnstone v Scott* (1834) 12 S 492 suggests that injury must be incurred before objection can be made, this statement is made too widely.

[246] See below, paras 7-85–7-86.

there was no possibility of material damage to the land *ex adverso*, at least in ordinary floods'.[247]

7-68. Once again, as with operations on the *alveus*, although there may be a right to fortify one's banks, there is no positive obligation to do so under common interest.[248]

(d) Temporary Diversion: Using the Water as Power

7-69. As can be seen, owners are under strict obligations in relation to the natural flow of a river but common interest is not completely prohibitory. A traditionally important practice was using the flow of a river to power a mill. Temporary diversion of a river was found to be legitimate between successive owners, so long as the water was returned within the boundaries of their land.[249] Opposite owners were not entitled to divert rivers in this way, as it would be depriving their neighbours of the water.[250] Many of the cases on this point, however, were decided before the development of the right of natural flow. Is this still a legitimate use in the modern law?

7-70. Lord Blackburn in *Colquhoun's Trs v Orr Ewing*[251] stated each owner along a river:

'has an interest in having the water above him flow down to him, and in having the water below him flow away from him as it has been wont to do; yet I apprehend that a proprietor may, without any illegality, build a mill-dam across the stream within his own property and divert the water into a mill-lade without asking the leave of the proprietors above him, provided he builds it at a place so much below the lands of those proprietors as not to obstruct the water from flowing away as freely as it was wont, and without asking the leave of the proprietors below him, if he takes care to restore the water to its natural course before it enters their lands.

It would require strong authorities to lead me to believe that the law of Scotland does give the proprietors on the banks of the stream a right to act the part of the dog in the manger to such an extent to hinder this.'

7-71. Thus, it appears that successive owners may in principle divert a river, or a portion of it, as long as the natural flow of the river is not materially affected but this qualification may significantly reduce potential use.[252] It is possible that opposite owners may also divert a portion of water from a river but as diversion is more likely to materially interfere with the right of natural flow held by an opposite owner than with the rights held by any successive

---

[247] Rankine, *Landownership* 542.

[248] See generally Gordon & Wortley, *Land Law* para 6-53.

[249] *Cunningham v Kennedy* (1713) Mor 8903 and 12778; *Magistrates of Linlithgow v Elphinstone (No 2)* 1768 Mor 12805 at 12806; *Kelso v Boyds* (1768) Mor 12807, Hailes 224.

[250] See *Bannatyne v Cranstoun* (1624) Mor 12769; Stair, *Institutions* II.7.12; Bankton, *Institute* II.7.29; Erskine, *Institute* II.9.13; *Magistrates of Linlithgow v Elphinstone (No 2)* 1768 Mor 12805.

[251] (1877) 4 R (HL) 166 at 127–128. See also *Cowan v Lord Kinnaird* (1865) 4 M 236 at 241; *Earl of Kintore v Alex Pirie & Sons Ltd* (1903) 5 F 818 at 845 and 851.

[252] See also Reid, *Property* para 292.

owners, potential use is likely to be even more restricted. This issue is of continuing relevance today as water-mills have given way to hydro-schemes for electricity generation but the issues remain the same.[253] In addition to the various public law consents which need to be obtained for a hydro-scheme – in particular those required under the Water Environment (Controlled Activities) (Scotland) Regulations 2011[254] – common interest also needs to be considered. The relationship between public law and private law regulation of water can be seen as similar to that between planning permission and title conditions. Despite acquiring the former, the consent of neighbours with legal rights to object also needs to be obtained. As the Scottish rules on natural flow are quite restrictive, and as hydro-schemes often change the current or force of the water, it is probable that such schemes will be a breach of common interest and will require the consent of all affected proprietors. This aspect of the scheme is rarely considered in detail in the guidance literature.[255]

(2) Rights of Owners over Other Parts of the *Alveus*

7-72.   In addition to the rights and obligations centred on natural flow, common interest also, in limited circumstances, grants positive rights over other property. It is these rights which most closely resemble servitudes. The positive rights which owners have over rivers are different in scope from those over lochs.

7-73.   The proprietors of land containing rivers are not generally entitled to use the *alveus* of a river belonging to opposite or adjacent proprietors or the water flowing above it. The only exception appears to be a right to fish over the *medium filum* where the *alveus* is owned to the mid-point by opposite owners.[256] This right may be applicable only to small rivers – defined as those, by rod-fishing, 'which, with or without wading, can be commanded from bank to bank'.[257] However, in *Fothringham v Passmore*,[258] the House of Lords decided that with regard to salmon fishing by rod and line, the rights of owners were not limited to small or narrow rivers due to the uncertainty of determining when the *medium filum* could be passed.[259] Instead, proprietors could fish over the *medium filum* as long as they themselves remained within

---

[253] See the Scottish Government, *Policy Statement: Balancing the Benefits of Renewables Generation and Protection of the Water Environment* (2010; http://www.scotland.gov.uk/Topics/ Business-Industry/Energy/Energy-sources/19185/17851-1/HydroPolicy).

[254] Issued under the Water Environment and Water Services (Scotland) Act 2003 which implements the European Water Framework Directive 2000/60/EC (23 Oct 2000). The Scottish Environment Protection Agency provides much guidance on how to comply with these regulations: see http://www.sepa.org.uk/water/hydropower.aspx.

[255] A Scott, 'Mini Hydro-Schemes' (2010) 108 *Prop LB* 6. An exception is the article by N MacKay, 'Power Flows' (2008) 53(1) *JLSS* 22.

[256] *Arthur v Aird* 1907 SC 1170. See also Rankine, *Landownership* 583.

[257] *Arthur v Aird* at 1174.

[258] 1984 SC (HL) 96.

[259] See also Reid, *Property* para 329.

their portion of the *alveus*.[260] This decision has been criticised[261] and it is questionable whether it has a broader application than salmon fishing, or even just salmon fishing by rod and line. In the interests of consistency, it would be preferable that the extent to which owners can cast their line should be the same regardless of what type of fish they wish to catch or which method of fishing they use.[262] It was also suggested in *Fothringham* that where owners cannot agree as to the exercise of their rights, the court can regulate the matter.[263] This, however, may be open to question.[264]

7-74. There is no indication that use of water above another owner's *alveus* extends to other rights such as swimming or sailing.[265]

7-75. Lochs are in a different position. Although the *alveus* of a loch which is contained within the lands of many proprietors is separately owned in sections from the bank to the centre of the loch, landowners are entitled to use the water which covers the whole area for activities such as fishing and sailing.[266] These rights only apply to use of the water, and it has been suggested that if the boundaries of the loch moves, the right follows the water.[267] An owner is not allowed to use the opposite banks for activities such as drying nets.[268] Again, it has been said that the use of the loch can be subject to regulation by the court. This issue is discussed further below.

F. REMEDIES FOR BREACH

7-76. Much of the law of common interest has arisen through *ad hoc* decision-making in cases which reflect the socio-economic changes and challenges of their time. The rules as to remedies for breach of common interest are no exception and to understand the law fully it is necessary to preface some of the remedies with historical context.

(1) Enforcement of Common Interest

7-77. When there has been a breach of common interest, there are several remedies available but first it must be established who is entitled to raise an

---

[260] At 129.

[261] Anon 'Regulation' 1984 SLT (News) 336; K G C Reid, 'Salmon Fishing in Troubled Waters' 1985 SLT (News) 217; C F Forder, 'Tales from the River Bank' 1986 *Jur Rev* 25.

[262] S Scott Robinson, *The Law of Game, Salmon & Freshwater Fishing in Scotland* (1990) 229.

[263] At 130.

[264] See below, paras 7-89–7-92.

[265] Indeed, it is suggested in *Fothringham v Passmore* 1984 SC (HL) 96 at 129 that the owner of one half of the *alveus* cannot cross the *medium filum* by boat.

[266] *Mackenzie v Bankes* (1878) LR 3 App Cas 1324; *Leny v Linlithgow Magistrates* (1894) 2 SLT 294; *Meacher v Blair-Oliphant* 1913 SC 417; *Kilsyth Fish Protection Association v McFarlane* 1937 SC 757; *Menzies v Wentworth* (1901) 3 F 941. See also Reid, *Property* para 306; Whitty, 'Water' 467; Gordon & Wortley, *Land Law* para 6-13.

[267] *Dick v Earl of Abercorn* (1769) Mor 12813.

[268] *Menzies v Macdonald* (1854) 16 D 827 (aff'd by the House of Lords (1856) 2 MacQ 463); Gordon & Wortley, *Land Law* para 6-13.

action in common interest against whom. It is clear that owners have title to sue for breach of common interest. Further, despite Reid's assertion to the contrary based on the then rules for real burdens[269] and although throughout these chapters owners have been the subject of discussion, it has not been questioned that tenants are equally entitled to raise actions for breach of common interest.[270] An analogy can be made with nuisance where it is said that tenants are protecting their interest in using and possessing the leased property and landlords are protecting their ownership of the land.[271] Indeed, it may be that any person with lawful possession of land containing a river or loch can sue for breach of common interest.[272]

7-78.   Although common interest is typically enforced against owners, it appears that the rights of common interest in relation to rivers and lochs are real rights[273] and can be enforced against anyone who interferes with them such as tenants[274] or even third parties.[275] People who have legitimate access to the water, however, cannot be prevented from exercising public rights. This allows the public to consume water for basic needs but further appropriation may be prohibited[276] and the public are not entitled to construct pipes or other structures, as owners are, or otherwise interfere with natural flow in order to exercise this right.[277]

7-79.   To what extent are landlords responsible for the actions of their tenants? To have an action against the landlord, analogies can again be made with nuisance, where liability will lie only if the landlord authorises the activity in the lease, has consented to it or was negligent as to the acts of the tenant.[278] Mere authorisation in the lease of an operation which is not itself a

---

[269] Reid, *Property* paras 363 and 406.

[270] *Tassie v Miller and Wright* (1826) 4 S 578 (tenant raised an action for damages against upstream tenants but see discussion below of some of these cases); *Graham v Loch* (1829) 5 Mur 75 (tenant raised an action for damages caused by the erection of a dam); *Hood v Williamsons* (1861) 23 D 496 (a joint action was raised by the landlord and tenants); *Gardner v Walker and Donald* (1862) 24 D 1430 (an action was brought by a tenant against an upstream tenant and landlord); *McGavin v McIntyre* (1890) 17 R 818 especially statement of the Lord Ordinary at 825 (an action was brought by downstream owners and tenants, not challenged on appeal by Inner House or House of Lords (1893) 20 R (HL) 49).

[271] Whitty, 'Nuisance' para 133. See also the comments of Lord President Murray in *Fleming v Gemmill* 1908 SC 340 at 348 concerning nuisance which can have analogous application to common interest explained in Whitty, 'Nuisance' para 134.

[272] See with regard to nuisance, Whitty, 'Nuisance' para 134.

[273] This is not the case for positive obligations of common interest, which can be enforced only against the owner: see Reid, *Property* para 347. But such obligations do not seem to be part of the common interest regarding rivers and lochs.

[274] See *Miller v Stein* (1791) Mor 12823, Bell's Octavo Cases 334; *Hood v Williamsons* (1861) 23 D 496; *Hunter and Aitkenhead v Aitken* (1880) 7 R 510.

[275] *Bonthrone v Downie* (1878) 6 R 324; *Marquis of Breadalbane v West Highland Railway Co* (1895) 22 R 307 at 312–313 (ownership of an insignificant part of the *alveus* in this case did not entitle the owner to the full opportunities to use the water). For parallels with servitudes see Cusine & Paisley para 1.62.

[276] See above, paras 2-34–2-36.

[277] See cases cited in n 275.

[278] See Whitty, 'Nuisance' para 140; *Dunn v Hamilton* (1837) 15 S 853 affirmed by the House of Lords (1838) 3 S & McL 356.

breach of common interest is not sufficient.[279] A related issue is whether landlords can raise an action against tenants to fulfil their common interest obligations. The answer would depend on the terms, express or implied, of the lease.[280]

7-80.   Where two adjacent sections of channel owned by the same person are leased to separate tenants, it is uncertain whether one tenant can raise an action against the other tenant for breach of common interest. As a matter of general principle, for common interest to arise, there would need to be two pieces of land in separate ownership.[281] However, this rule creates practical problems and there are cases which have allowed an action to be raised by a tenant against another tenant of the same landlord. In *Tassie v Miller and Wright*,[282] the issue was put to the jury as to whether an upper tenant was liable in damages to a lower tenant for interference with the flow.[283] Further, in *Gardner v Walker and Donald*,[284] the Inner House found it was a relevant issue for a tenant to raise an action in damages against a tenant of upstream lands, holding from the same landlord. In *Tassie* there was an obligation in the upper tenant's lease to open the sluices of his mill for at least three hours a day for the benefit of lower mills, and in *Gardner* the upper tenant was prohibited from damming the water of the river to the prejudice of lower mills. Thus, these decisions may perhaps be better explained as cases of third parties having rights in leases[285] rather than actions of common interest. Alternatively, they can more convincingly be regarded as instances in which third parties (who, by coincidence were tenants sometimes holding of the same landlord as the party seeking to enforce a right) had leasehold rights enforced against them – thus suggesting that these leasehold rights, albeit not servitudes, were indeed real rights.

7-81.   A related issue arises when an action is raised by a tenant against his or her landlord in respect of the landlord's ownership of the adjacent land.

---

[279] See also *Henderson and Thomson v Stewart* (1818) 15 S 868, Hume 522.

[280] See the analogous case of liferent, in *Dickson v Douglas Dickson* (1823) 2 S 152 where an action was raised by a fiar against a liferenter but it was found that the latter had no positive obligation to embank the property against encroachments by the River Clyde.

[281] See Reid, *Property* para 371. See also the discussion of the *res sua nemini servit* rule in relation to servitudes in Cusine & Paisley paras 2.04–2.12 and in relation to leasehold conditions in Discussion Paper on the Conversion of Long Leases (Scot Law Com DP 112, 2001) paras 3.28–3.58; Report on the Conversion of Long Leases (Scot Law Com No 204, 2006) paras 3.34–4.77; Long Leases (Scotland) Act 2012 Parts 1 and 2. The rule that *confusio* extinguishes real burdens has now been disapplied by the Title Conditions (Scotland) Act 2003 s 19.

[282] (1826) 4 S 578. This case is merely one aspect of a lengthy dispute. See *Tassie v Magistrates of Glasgow* (1822) 1 S 467; *Tassie v Miller* (1822) 1 S 468; *Magistrates of Glasgow v Aitchison* (1822) 1 S 469; *Aitchison v Magistrates of Glasgow* (1823) 2 S 377; *Henderson v Magistrates of Glasgow* (1824) 3 S 133; *Aitchison v Magistrates of Glasgow* (1825) 1 W & S 153.

[283] The pursuers claimed for £1,500 which The National Archives Currency Converter suggests would be approximately £62,880 today.

[284] (1862) 24 D 1430.

[285] Which are themselves rare occurrences: K Gerber et al 'Landlord and Tenant' in SME (Reissue, 2011) para 202.

In *Gordon v Suttie*[286] an action was raised against the landlord for the actions of the tenant of the adjacent ground in diminishing the flow of water. The issue was sent to the jury. In *Gardner v Walker and Donald*,[287] an action against the landlord was not allowed as there was no relevant case stated against him. In both cases there is a suggestion that the only ground of action against the landlord would be based on implied grant and thus founded on the lease rather than common interest.

7-82.   Issues of a similar kind arise when landowners lease both the surface and, separately, the minerals. It is suggested that the surface tenant would not be able to raise an action against either the landowner or the mineral tenant in common interest as there are no pieces of land in separate ownership. When minerals are held separately, however, different considerations apply.[288] Where the minerals are below land through which a river or loch runs, the acts of the mineral-owner could interfere with the use of down- and upstream owners. In these circumstances, it is suggested that the mine-owner is a burdened proprietor for the purposes of common interest. But he or she would generally not be a benefited proprietor due to the absence of an ability to use the water beyond public rights.[289] That mineral-owners may require special consideration was noticed by Lord McLaren in *Young & Co v Bankier Distillery Co*[290] but not pursued by their Lordships on appeal.[291]

(2) Declarator

7-83.   By far the most popular remedy during the early development of common interest was declarator of the pursuer's rights usually in combination with suspension, interdict or a decree *ad factum praestandum*.[292] This made sense when the extent of the rights of owners to use water running through their lands was unclear. The remedy is, of course, still available in the modern law where the pursuer is seeking to establish authoritatively the extent of his or her rights and may be useful where there are issues of variation of rights on the basis of, for example, prescription.[293] In practice, standard applications for interdict are often accompanied by a declarator.

[286] (1826) 4 Mur 86.

[287] (1862) 24 D 1430.

[288] See in general D Ross Stewart, *A Treatise on the Law Relating to Mines, Quarries and Mines in Scotland* (1894).

[289] On this analysis the comment by Lord McLaren is too generally stated in *Young & Co v Bankier Distillery Co* (1892) 19 R 1083 at 1089 that 'in the present case we are not engaged in determining or adjusting the relative rights of riparian owners, nor is there any relation of common interest in the water that I can discover between the mineowner and the proprietors of the bed of the stream'.

[290] (1892) 19 R 1083 at 1089–1090

[291] (1893) 20 R (HL) 76.

[292] A glance through the cases on water rights contained under 'Property' in *Morison's Dictionary* will confirm this.

[293] See D Walker, *Civil Remedies* (1974) 126–127 and also the analogous position of nuisance, Whitty, 'Nuisance' para 149.

(3) Interdict

7-84. Interdict was another popular remedy sought in early cases, as the main concern of a downstream owner was usually to have a functioning mill again, free from interference by another proprietor.[294] Early cases often involve suspension and interdict.[295] This reflects a practice where suspension was brought to put a stop to a wrong in progress and interdict to prevent its repetition. This usage is now unnecessary as it is competent to use interdict for wrongs in progress.[296]

7-85. In order for interdict to be granted, there must be proof of a continuing wrong or reasonable grounds to anticipate such a wrong.[297] Interdict is not available for wrongs which have occurred in the past.[298] The wrong in the case of common interest is breaching the obligation not to interfere materially with natural flow. Thus, where it is reasonably anticipated that this obligation will be breached, interdict can be granted. There is no need to prove damage or that damage is reasonably anticipated.[299]

7-86. The court's jurisdiction in deciding whether to grant or refuse interdict is, however, discretionary.[300] As such, even if it is proved that the flow may be materially interfered with, it is open to the court to refuse interdict. This may happen if interference with the flow will result in no or very little damage or loss – in application of the principle *de minimis non curat praetor*.[301] Yet, if the interference is material, it is likely to cause damage.

7-87. Although interdict cannot be used to enforce a positive obligation, it seems competent to grant interdict where some remedial measures require to be carried out.[302] Where specific remedial measures are required, however, it is perhaps preferable to request a decree *ad factum praestandum*.

[294] For the general context of early disputes on water see above, paras 5-05–5-06.

[295] Or merely one of these remedies. See, for example, *Magistrates of Dumfries v Heritors on the Water of Nith* (1705) Mor 12776; *Magistrates of Aberdeen v Menzies* (1748) Mor 12787 which refer to suspension. *Burgess v Brown* (1790) Hume 504; *Russell v Haig* (1791) Mor 12823, Bell's Octavo Cases 338; *Braid v Douglas* (1800) Mor App 2 refer to interdict. In *Miller v Stein* (1791) Mor 12823, Bell's Octavo Cases 334; *Cruikshanks and Bell v Henderson* (1791) Hume 506; *Lanark Twist Co v Edmonstone* (1810) Hume 520 both suspension and interdict are referred to. These cases accord with Burn-Murdoch's claim in *Interdict* (n 77) 6 that the modern law of interdict evolved from the process of suspension.

[296] Walker, *Civil Remedies* 214.

[297] See *King v Hamilton* (1844) 6 D 399.

[298] Walker, *Civil Remedies* 215; Burn-Murdoch, *Interdict* (n 77) 1.

[299] *Morris v Bicket* (1864) 2 M 1082 at 1093; *Jackson v Marshall* (1872) 10 M 913. See also Rankine, *Landownership* 539; Murray et al, 'Water' para 1144; Reid, *Property* para 290. The comments of Lord Justice-Clerk Moncreiff in *Murdoch v Wallace* (1881) 8 R 855 at 861 of a requirement of a 'very substantial amount of damage' cannot be relied upon. This case is better thought of as one of personal bar.

[300] Walker, *Civil Remedies* 222–223. But see Burn-Murdoch, *Interdict* (n 77) at 2–4; Whitty, 'Nuisance' para 146.

[301] *Morris v Bicket* at 1093; Rankine, *Landownership* 539 and 545; Murray et al, 'Water' para 1145; Burn-Murdoch, *Interdict* (n 77) at 82–83; Walker, *Civil Remedies* 224.

[302] See discussion in Whitty, 'Nuisance' para 148; N R Whitty, 'Positive and Negative Interdicts' (1990) 35 *JLSS* 453 and 510.

(4) Decree *ad factum praestandum*

7-88.   Early cases involving decrees *ad factum praestandum* seek removal of a *novum opus*, or the lowering of a dam and restoration of the natural course of the river,[303] and this remains a useful function of the remedy today.[304] Again, this remedy is discretionary and the court may choose not to interfere where there is little or no damage caused by the breach.[305]

(5) Regulation

7-89.   It is sometimes suggested that the court can intervene to regulate rights in relation to rivers and lochs in the event of disagreement[306] such as regarding the exercise of fishing rights over the *medium filum* of a river,[307] the exercise of fishing and sailing rights in a loch,[308] or when an owner would exhaust the stream by using the water for primary purposes.[309] This, however, has been questioned. It has been commented that:

> 'one is entitled to query the need for any regulatory power let alone its basis in jurisprudence...Since it is difficult to think of any other situation in which common law rights are subject to alteration by the court, no assistance can be derived from cognate areas of the law...With the greatest respect to the most recent dicta in the House of Lords, it is possible that it will be found to be not just elusive but, in truth, illusory?'[310]

7-90.   The point is that owners are either exercising their rights legitimately or not. There is no indication that judicial regulation is available for the comparable institutions of servitudes or real burdens.[311] The instances subject to common interest differ from common property, where regulation is

[303] See for example *Fairly v Earl of Eglinton* (1744) Mor 12780; *Bugress v Brown* (1790) Hume 504; *Ogilvy v Kincaid* (1791) Mor 12824, Hume 508; *Aytoun v Meville* (1801) Mor App 8.

[304] Walker, *Civil Remedies* 275; Reid, *Property* para 290.

[305] *Jackson v Marshall* (1872) 10 M 913; *Colquhoun's Trs v Orr Ewing* (1877) 4 R (HL) 116 at 126; Murray et al, 'Water' para 1144; Reid, *Property* para 290. In *Duke of Roxburghe v Waldie's Trs* (1879) 6 R 663 at 671, Lord Gifford goes as far as to say that 'even if such an operation did the pursuer good instead of hurting him I think he would be entitled to object'. However, in this situation the court may decide not to intervene.

[306] In *Marquis of Abercorn v Jamieson* (1791) Hume 510 at 512 it was said that the Marquis 'must be subjected to proper regulations, to prevent damage to Mr Jamieson by shutting or opening the sluices of the said ponds at improper times, or in an improper manner, or in an improper manner, and remit to the Lord Ordinary to proceed accordingly, and to do further as he shall see cause'. However, this may merely have resulted in an interdict or decree *ad factum praestandum*.

[307] *Fothringham v Passmore* 1984 SC (HL) 96 at 130. See also *Gay v Malloch* 1959 SC 110 concerning the regulation of salmon fishing in a tidal river.

[308] *Menzies v Wentworth* (1901) 3 F 941.

[309] Rankine, *Landownership* 555; Ferguson 240. See also *Earl of Kintore v Alex Pirie & Sons Ltd* (1903) 5 F 818.

[310] Anon, 'Regulation' 1984 SLT (News) 336 at 337.

[311] Although these title conditions can be varied by application to the Lands Tribunal under Part 9 of the Title Conditions (Scotland) Act 2003.

undoubtedly available. In common property, several parties have potentially competing and equally valid rights over the entire management and disposal of a single subject. A 'managerial deadlock'[312] is possible and one of the few solutions available is judicial regulation. Regarding common interest, however, each piece of land is owned separately but subject to clear obligations in relation to certain activities or with the benefit of certain rights to use other lands. Owners cannot go beyond the limits of their rights and are also limited in the exercise of these rights through other neighbourhood doctrines such as nuisance and *aemulatio vicini*. It may be questioned whether any further potential restraint is required. Indeed, the only case where an application for regulation was made – *Menzies v Wentworth*[313] – appears to have proceeded on the now outdated view that a loch, as a body of water separate from the *alveus*, was the common property of the surrounding owners.[314] It may be that no power of regulation exists outside common property.

7-91. Even if regulation is an option, there are practical difficulties with the remedy. In *Menzies v Macdonald*,[315] again decided at a time when a loch was regarded as common property, Lord Deas expressed the view that:

'No permanent regulation could be laid down which would not become inapplicable on every change of circumstances, – such as an increase or diminution in the number of joint proprietors. A regulation which was to be varied from time to time, at the instance of any party interested according to the varying views of the judges, would be arbitrary, if not intolerable. Besides what would this be but to make the Court permanent managers for the proprietors.'

The practical fulfilment of such regulation seems difficult to imagine.

7-92. Further, it appears there is a level of abuse of right to be reached before the power to regulate will be exercised. In *Menzies v Wentworth*,[316] one owner brought an action against the others for declarator that trout fishing in a loch was being injured and should be regulated by the court. The pursuer was unsuccessful and it was stated that:

'regulation is a restriction of the enjoyment of a legal right, and where there can be no encroachment by one party enjoying such a right against the adverse or separate right of another party, it seems to me that the only excess which can afford ground for regulation or restriction of legal right must be such a use as amounts to abuse, either by destroying or materially diminishing the subject-matter of the right, or by destroying or materially diminishing the sporting enjoyment of the right.'[317]

This is a high standard which was not satisfied in the case.[318] In light of the difficulties of imposing regulation and the high standard to be reached before

[312] Reid, *Property* para 30.
[313] (1901) 3 F 941.
[314] See above, paras 3-77–3-82.
[315] (1854) 16 D 827 at 857. See also the opinion of the Lord Ordinary in *Hood v Williamson* (1861) 23 D 496 at 499 cited above and Reid, *Property* para 30.
[316] (1901) 3 F 941.
[317] At 959 (Lord Kinnear).
[318] Lord McLaren was of a different opinion, and did not think the pursuer need prove injury to his/her rights, see at 958.

an action can be contemplated, even if regulation is a possible remedy, its potential usefulness can be doubted.

(6) Damages

7-93.   An action for damages was a rare occurrence in the early case law, perhaps because in the context of these disputes mill-owners merely tended to want to have a working mill again. Most loss would be of profits due to the mill-wheel not turning. Before the Industrial Revolution, actions for loss of profits may have been barely thought of or the loss was not substantial enough to justify a court case. Or it could be that water issues were resolved quickly through interdict or decree *ad factum praestandum*, before any loss was suffered. However, there was always the potential for damages claims when tangible damage was caused to land through flooding[319] and indeed this seems to be the most contentious issue in the modern law.

7-94.   In *Thomson v St Cuthbert's Co-operative Association Ltd*[320] it was found that liability for breaching the common interest obligation of support in the context of the tenement was not strict. Despite common interest in tenements now being largely abolished,[321] this decision may be of general application and fault may have to be proved before damages can be claimed in respect of rivers and lochs. It may be questioned, however, whether the effect of this case is to assimilate liability for common interest with the general law of negligence or whether a high standard of care is imposed due to common interest being a special regime.[322]

7-95.   Cases concerning damage caused by interference with the flow of a river are, however, usually considered from a different viewpoint: that of nuisance.[323] It is possible that liability for damage caused by the interference with the natural flow of a river is strict – an exception to liability for nuisance being (generally) fault-based.[324] The paradoxical result is that liability under

---

[319] See, for example, *Henderson and Thomson v Stewart* (1818) 15 S 868, Hume 522 regarding liability of a landowner for operations by his tenant; *Graham v Loch* (1829) 5 Mur 75 an unsuccessful action for damages.

[320] 1958 SC 380. Followed by *Kerr v McGreevy* 1970 SLT (Sh Ct) 7; *Doran v Smith* 1971 SLT (Sh Ct) 46. See also Reid, *Property* para 366.

[321] Tenements (Scotland) Act 2004 s 7.

[322] See K G C Reid, 'Common Interest: A Reassessment' (1983) 28 *JLSS* 428 at 434–435.

[323] Ferguson 234 goes as far as to say that liability for interference with the flow of a river is not deducible from the law of riparian proprietors. This issue has become entangled with whether the rule in *Rylands v Fletcher* (1868) 3 H & C 774 is part of Scots law: see Thirteenth Report of the Law Reform Committee for Scotland, The Law Relating to Civil Liability for Loss, Injury and Damage Cause by Dangerous Agencies Escaping from Land (Cmnd 2348, 1964); E Clive, 'Case and Comment Note on the Thirteenth Report of the Law Reform Committee for Scotland' 1964 *Jur Rev* 250.

[324] See discussion in Whitty, 'Nuisance' paras 93 and 108; *RHM Bakeries (Scotland) Ltd v Strathclyde Regional Council* 1985 SC (HL) 17 at 42–44. That interference with the natural flow is an exception is disputed by G D L Cameron, 'Strict Liability and the Rule in *Caledonian Railway Co v Greenock Corporation*' (2000) 5 *SLPQ* 356; G D L Cameron, 'Interference with Natural Watercourses: Nuisance, Negligence and Strict Liability' (2008) 12 *Edin LR* 105. See also F McManus, 'Liability for *Opera Manufacta* (New Works) in Scots Law' 1998 *Jur Rev* 281.

common interest may be fault-based and under nuisance may be strict with
respect to this exceptional rule. Detailed discussion of this difficult topic is
outwith the scope of the book. However, it is to be regretted that it is not
sufficiently highlighted in the case law or commentary that interfering with
the natural flow of a river is a wrong in itself (albeit under common
interest).[325]

(7) Self-help

7-96.   Breach of common interest by one owner does not justify breach by
another.[326] However, a breach by one owner may justify entering another's
land to remedy the breach.[327] Further, it has been suggested that when an
aqueduct becomes silted or obstructed on one piece of land (although this
would not breach common interest) adjacent proprietors may clean the
channel as long as no damage is caused.[328] It is unclear, however, whether
this suggestion was made on the basis of principles applicable to the
obstruction of a servitude right of *aquaeductus* rather than common interest.[329]
Indeed, in *Hope v Governors of Heriot's Hospital and Methven*[330] it was suggested
that an upper owner was not acting lawfully when he entered lower
property to clean the channel of a river.[331]

G. EXTINCTION

7-97.   The final issue to consider is the ways in which common interest is
extinguished. Rights of common interest can be relinquished through consent
or varied through prescription. At one time it was thought that application
might be made to the Lands Tribunal to extinguish common interest[332] but
this is no longer possible: under Part 9 of the Title Conditions (Scotland) Act
2003, the Tribunal has jurisdiction only over 'title conditions' which does
not extend to common interest.[333]

---

[325] See, for example, Cameron, 'Strict Liability and the Rule in *Caledonian Railway Co v
Greenock Corporation*' (n 324) at 373–374.

[326] *Brand v Charters* (1842) 4 D 345; Gordon & Wortley, *Land Law* para 6-58.

[327] See *Newton v Godfrey* (2000) in R R M Paisley and D J Cusine, *Unreported Property Cases
from the Sheriff Courts* (2000) 86. Compare with Reid, *Property* paras 225–226; Gordon &
Wortley, *Land Law* para 6-58 and the analogous case of *Geils v Thompson* (1872) 10 M 327
which concerned a diversion of water to a public well.

[328] *Carlile v Douglas* (1731) Mor 14524; *Gray v Maxwell* (1762) Mor 12800. See also *Pringle
v Duke of Roxburgh* (1767) 2 Pat 134.

[329] For discussion in the context of servitudes see Cusine & Paisley paras 2.85, 3.81 and
16.13.

[330] (1878) 15 SLR 400.

[331] See also *Weir v Glenny* (1834) 7 W & S 244 where it was said that common interest does
not give a general right to inspect the river.

[332] Reid, *Property* para 374.

[333] Title Conditions (Scotland) Act 2003 s 122(1).

(1) Consent

7-98.   The Land Registration (Scotland) Act 1979, section 18 (now repealed) allowed the registration of a deed of discharge of 'land obligations', a term which on one view included common interest.[334] Despite the repeal, it seems likely that registering a deed of discharge, granted by the owners entitled to enforce the obligation,[335] would be effective to extinguish common interest obligations. In the absence of registration, it is undecided whether mere consent in writing would be effective to extinguish an obligation under common interest.[336]

7-99.   Like real burdens, common interest potentially involves multiple parties,[337] and obtaining consent from them all may be unduly costly and time-consuming as each benefited property would have to be identified (some of which may be miles down- or upstream), consent would have to be sought and a deed of discharge granted in respect of each property. Rights of common interest may require to be varied where a new servitude of water abstraction is granted. The usual method is to have the parties entitled to common interest rights consent *in gremio* in the deed of servitude. However, this has the potential that the consent would not appear in their titles as they are not burdened proprietors in relation to the servitude. This may lead to a lack of publicity of the variation and, again, it is not at all clear if this has any effect on the validity of the variation in an issue with singular successors of the party so consenting. Further, the identity of the parties who should so consent remains to be addressed.

(2) Acquiescence

7-100.   At one time, implied consent by acquiescence may have been considered a method of extinguishing common interest.[338] However, despite the willingness of defenders to plead it,[339] there was reluctance by judges to accept the idea.[340] Reid and Blackie have now demonstrated that acquiescence is merely an aspect of personal bar which does not bind singular successors.[341]

---

[334] See Reid, *Property* para 368.

[335] Although other people such as tenants are entitled to enforce common interest, it is suggested that their authority ultimately derives from the owner. As such, the owner would be the only person entitled to consent to extinction of his or her rights. See a similar rule for servitudes in Cusine & Paisley para 17.05.

[336] For discussion in relation to real burdens, see Reid, *Property* para 426. In contrast to real burdens, however, common interest is not created through registration.

[337] As can be seen in *Cowan v Lord Kinnaird* (1865) 4 M 236 where consent was obtained from two owners but then an action was raised by others.

[338] See, for example, *McIntyre v Orr* (1868) 41 Sc Jur 112 at 115.

[339] See the cases involving acquiescence of *Aytoun v Douglas* (1800) Mor App 7; *Aytoun v Melville* (1801) Mor App 8; *Stirling v Haldane* (1829) 8 S 131; *Lord Forbes, Leys, Masson and Co* (1830) 5 Mur 287; *Johnstone v Scott* (1834) 12 S 492; *Cowan v Lord Kinnaird* (1865) 4 M 236; *McIntyre v Orr* (1868) 41 Sc Jur 112.

[340] See the comments of Lord President Inglis in *McIntyre v Orr* at 115.

[341] E C Reid and J W G Blackie, *Personal Bar* (2006) paras 3-04 and 5-03–5-04. For the defence of personal bar to succeed, the requirements outlined by Reid and Blackie at lxy

(3) Prescription

7-101. As with nuisance, there is a difference between extinction by prescription of the right to object to a breach of common interest and the extinction of the right to damages for loss.[342] In another parallel with nuisance, the law developed at a time when the period for positive and negative prescription was 40 years and therefore it was not necessary to decide what type of prescription was taking place.[343] For a time, prescription and immemorial possession were used in an attempt to create a rationale for water rights. This approach, however, had its flaws, which were explored earlier.[344] Although using prescription as the basis of the doctrine fell away, the idea persists that to vary common interest through prescription is to acquire a servitude right.[345] This is problematic. When breaching common interest through, for example, consuming water from a river in a manner which materially affects the natural flow, an owner is not using another's land, which is an essential mark of a servitude. This was one of the main reasons why a servitude analysis was not accepted by the courts in the early stages of the development of common interest.

7-102. The father of common interest, Lord Kames, was adamant that the doctrine was varied through negative, and not positive, prescription.[346] On this analysis the operation of prescription results in the affected proprietors losing their right to object rather than the proprietor in breach acquiring a servitude right. This approach also has problems. In the context of nuisance, Johnston has explained that where there is a continuing breach of an obligation, there is an argument that the right to object can never prescribe because there is a fresh breach every day.[347] However, Johnston states that it is also possible that as soon as the obligation first is breached, the right to object arises and the prescriptive period begins to run. This latter analysis is perhaps preferable. The measure of the extinction of common interest would only be the extent of the breach for the prescriptive period. This issue has not been noticed in the case law on common interest due to the servitude analysis employed. The only remaining option is that the right to object to a breach in common interest never prescribes.[348]

---

would have to be met. See also paras 6-65–6-67 on water rights. *Murdoch v Wallace* (1881) 8 R 855 is perhaps best thought of as a case of personal bar.

[342] Whitty, 'Nuisance' para 123.

[343] Whitty, 'Nuisance' para 123.

[344] See above, paras 5-19–5-22.

[345] See, for example, *Bridges v Lord Saltoun* (1873) 11 M 588; *Hunter and Aitkenhead v Aitken* (1880) 7 R 510; *J & M White v J White & Sons* (1906) 8 F (HL) 41; Reid, *Property* para 295. See also *Robert Craig & Sons Ltd v Glen* 1927 SN 35.

[346] *Magistrates of Linlithgow v Elphinstone (No 2)* (1768) Mor 12805 at 12806.

[347] Johnston, *Prescription* at para 7.14 using the authority of *Stevenson v Pontifex and Wood* (1887) 15 R 125. See also Whitty, 'Nuisance' para 123. The obligation of reparation in relation to a continuous act would begin to prescribe when the act ceased: Prescription and Limitation (Scotland) Act 1973 s 11(2).

[348] See with regard to nuisance Johnston, *Prescription* para 7.14; Whitty, 'Nuisance' para 123.

7-103. Another difficulty is encountered in the following situation: if an operation has been put beyond challenge through negative prescription and the owner then ceases that operation, it is uncertain if and when other owners 're-acquire' their right to object. In *Bridges v Lord Saltoun*,[349] an owner who had diverted water from a stream for 40 years was found able to restore the river in a manner which would not cause injury to lower owners. Whether the lower owners then had the right to the restored natural flow is unclear. In *Hunter and Aitkenhead v Aitken*,[350] it was held that the right to store up the water of a river by a dam every night was lost through negative prescription and so lower owners could object to subsequent instances of damming but this was based on a servitude analysis.

7-104. If it is correct to favour negative prescription, the relevant time period for losing the right to object is 20 years. However, it is unclear whether the extinction of the right to object would be determined by section 7 of the Prescription and Limitation (Scotland) Act 1973 concerning obligations and correlative rights or section 8 concerning rights relating to property. Reid assumes that section 7 is the relevant provision[351] and this would be consistent with the foregoing analysis of common interest as a set of reciprocal rights and obligations.[352] A relevant claim or relevant acknowledgment interrupts the time period.[353] The right to object accrues when the wrong occurs – when the natural flow is materially interfered with – whether or not this is accompanied by damage. This will be when prescription begins to run.[354]

7-105. Any obligation to make reparation will, generally, begin to prescribe when the loss occurs[355] and it may be that the period of short negative prescription of 5 years applies.[356] However, Schedule 1 to the 1973 Act exempts obligations relating to land from this period.[357] As such, it is possible that the period of 20 years is applicable.[358]

H. CONCLUSION

7-106. Reid has commented that common interest is 'part of that oral tradition by which the law of conveyancing is passed on from one generation

[349] (1873) 11 M 588.

[350] (1880) 7 R 510.

[351] Reid, *Property* para 370. See also Whitty, 'Nuisance' para 123; Johnston, *Prescription* para 7.14.

[352] See the contrary analysis of servitudes in Cusine & Paisley para 17.34.

[353] Prescription and Limitation (Scotland) Act 1973 s 7(1).

[354] The comments in *Johnstone v Scott* (1834) 12 S 492 that damage is required to found an action should not be relied upon. This is another difference between nuisance and common interest actions in pollution. See Whitty, 'Nuisance' para 123 and the comments in *Duke of Buccleuch v Cowan* (1866) 5 M 214 at 217.

[355] Prescription and Limitation (Scotland) Act 1973 s 11(1). See also above n 347.

[356] Prescription and Limitation (Scotland) Act 1973 s 6.

[357] Prescription and Limitation (Scotland) Act 1973 Sch 1, para 2(e).

[358] See discussion in Johnston, *Prescription* paras 6.54–6.62.

to the next by word of mouth, as a series of irrational and magical incantations never entrusted to paper for fear, perhaps, that the magic escape'.[359] As the common law of common interest has largely been abolished with respect to tenements,[360] common interest regarding rivers and lochs is arguably the most important remaining instance of this magical doctrine. Although often seen as anomalous and difficult to analyse, the *sui generis* collection of rights and obligations created by common interest filled an important doctrinal gap when other legal structures failed to provide a solution. Today, the doctrine continues to fulfil a useful purpose by allowing owners to use water but not to the detriment of other owners. The classification of water as a communal thing is also respected as water is principally reserved for use for basic needs. In the future, with the increasing interest in green energy and particular focus on hydro-power schemes, common interest may once again become a doctrine of great practical significance and the subject of attention for jurists and judges.

---

[359] K G C Reid, 'Common Interest: A Reassessment' (1983) 28 *JLSS* 428 at 428.
[360] Although common interest still operates between tenements and other lands or buildings: Tenements (Scotland) Act 2004 s 7.

Index

Writers are indexed if they are named in the body of the text. Location references are to paragraph numbers, with 'n' denoting a footnote to the paragraph.

rivers
see also alveus; *private rivers*; *public rivers*
alluvion, 4-38–4-47
banks, works on, 7-24, 7-63–7-68
definite channel, 7-21
diversion, *see diversion of water*
embankments, 7-65
flooding, effect, 4-15
fortification of banks, 7-64
perennial, 1-18, 2-06, 7-20
property classification, 1-18, 5-54
public rights over, 2-93 – 2-95
Roman law, 1-18, 2-06, 2-24
tidal, 7-30
Roman law
alluvion, 3-04, 4-03–4-07
avulsion, 4-04
diversion of river, 5-07–5-08
flooding, effect, 4-04
foreshore, 3-14
immissio principle, 5-36
islands, ownership, 3-04, 3-05
land beneath water, 3-03–3-06
natural servitude, 5-07
new works, 5-34
private river, 3-06
property classification, 1-05, 2-04–2-13
public waters, 5-08
rivers, 1-18, 5-07–5-08
running water, 5-07–5-08
sea, 3-05
water rights, 5-07–5-09
Ross Stewart, D, 7-49
running water
see also rivers
landowner's rights, 6-17
ownership, 2-06, 2-70–2-72, 2-88
property classification, 2-06–2-07
rights to, 7-18
Roman law, 5-07–5-08

S

sailing rights
lochs, 3-71, 3-73, 3-81, 3-83, 7-75
private rivers, 7-74
salmon fishing rights, 2-26, 2-45, 3-07, 7-17n, 7-31, 7-73
sanitary reforms, 6-04

Sax, J, accretion/avulsion, 4-64
Scottish Law Commission proposals
alluvion, 4-56, 4-61
foreshore, 3-42n, 3-52, 4-56
public rights, 2-102
sea
alluvion, 4-22, 4-25
appropriation, 2-37–2-40, 2-71
commonty and, 2-37–2-40
ownership, 2-06, 2-17, 2-20–2-21, 2-37, 2-86–2-87
public rights over, 2-92
Roman law, 3-05
sea-bed
case law, 3-09
exploitation, 3-13
institutional writers, 3-08–3-10
registration of ownership, 3-11–3-12
sea-greens, 3-21n
sea-weed, right to, 3-17–3-19
secondary uses of water
consumption of water for, 7-43–7-46
detention of water, 7-47
meaning, 7-33, 7-43
natural flow, 6-55, 7-43
primary uses distinguished, 6-12–6-15, 6-20, 6-52, 7-36–7-46
servitudes and common interest, 5-19–5-22, 7-07–7-10
session papers, 1-09, 1-12
Shaw, J P
social developments, 6-03
voluntary management schemes, 6-55
shipwrecks, 3-17n
shore, *see foreshore*
sic utere tuo ut alienum non laedes, 5-72
Smith Commission, 3-13
South Africa
alluvion, 4-50, 4-52, 4-55, 4-57
lakes, 2-28
ownership of water, 2-104n
public rivers, 2-24
res communes, 2-60
spring tides, 3-15n
Sri Lanka
lakes, 2-28
public rivers, 2-24
Stair, James Dalrymple, Viscount
alluvion, 4-10
commonty, right of, 2-32–2-33, 5-71
Craig compared, 2-47–2-49
Division of Things, 2-29–2-30, 2-48–2-49